MINDWORLDS

By the same author

**LIFEBALL
GODBLOGS
www.andyross.net**

MINDWORLDS

A Decade of Consciousness Studies

J. Andrew Ross

Imprint Academic

Exeter, UK

J. Andrew Ross
www.andyross.net

Second revised edition 2009
First published online by the author 2004
World copyright © J. Andrew Ross 2004, 2009

The moral rights of the author have been asserted
No part of this publication may be reproduced in any form
without permission, except for the quotation of brief passages
in criticism and discussion.

Published in the UK by Imprint Academic
PO Box 200, Exeter EX5 5YX, UK

Published in the USA by Imprint Academic
Philosophy Documentation Center
PO Box 7147, Charlottesville, VA 22906-7147, USA

ISBN 978 184540 185 6

A CIP catalogue record for this book is available from the
British Library and US Library of Congress

Preface

Consciousness is hard to understand. The ongoing attempt to understand it is one of the central scientific challenges of our time.

This book is a portrait of consciousness with two sides. The introvert side presents my own recent work, while the extrovert side discusses a range of other perspectives on the issues. The chapters are based on essays written for a variety of occasions and audiences. Reading them in serial order, one senses a growing clarity in the articulation of the new ideas, some of which are deep and rather subtle, and this adds movement to the introvert side of the picture. As for other perspectives, many ideas in this field are still provisional, and it is interesting to see how they have evolved over the decade during which the essays accumulated.

I have taken pains to unify the two sides of the portrait and make the main thread clearly visible. It seems to me that my new ideas are of fundamental importance, and I hope that readers who grapple with them will gain enough insight to feel their effort has been rewarded.

In this public and printed edition of the collection, five years after a pilot online edition, I have deleted four earlier essays of lesser scientific interest and replaced them with four more recent works. The result, with a fresh application of editorial polish, is an anthology that should be of real value to serious researchers.

Europe, 2009

A Handy Guide

	Chapter	Pages	Written	Grade
1	Introduction	12	2009	Easy
2	Portrait of a Philosopher	17	2009	Easy
3	Fundamentals of Consciousness	13	1997	Hard
4	Consciousness: A Logical Model	19	2000	Hard
5	Mindworlds	46	2002	Middle
6	First-Person Consciousness	33	2002	Middle
7	The Self: From Soul to Brain	22	2002	Middle
8	A Photonic Theory of Consciousness	26	2003	Hard
9	Toward a Theory of Consciousness	14	2003	Hard
10	Consciousness as a Physical Process	12	2004	Middle
11	Purpose in Life and Science	9	2004	Easy
12	Roads to Reality	17	2004	Hard
13	About Time	26	2006	Hard
14	Blinded by the Light	2	2006	Easy
15	Will Robots See Humans as Dinosaurs?	8	2006	Middle
16	Hitting on Consciousness	21	2008	Easy

Acknowledgments

The person whose kick in the head finally moved me to start the work that led to this volume was David Chalmers with his book *The Conscious Mind* (1996) – thanks, Dave.

Chapter 3 is based on a paper I wrote in early 1997. Shorter versions were published in the proceedings of the conference Cognitive Science 1997, held at Stanford University in August, and the Brain and Self Workshop, Elsinore, Denmark, also in August.

Chapter 4 is based on my presentation at the Toward a Science of Consciousness conference held in Tucson, Arizona, in 2000. I congratulate the organizers for their achievement in creating a great conference.

Chapter 5 is based on slides presented at two conferences in the Toward a Science of Consciousness series, held in Skövde, Sweden, in 2001, and in Tucson, Arizona, in 2002. At Skövde the slides accompanied a 20-minute lecture and at Tucson they appeared as printouts on a poster panel.

Chapter 6 presents an extended book review that was first published in the *Journal of Consciousness Studies*, 9(7), 2002. I am happy to record that the reviewed authors Ted Honderich and Colin McGinn reacted with great magnanimity to my words.

Chapter 7 presents a conference report that was first published in the *Journal of Consciousness Studies*, 10(2), 2003. I thank Joseph LeDoux and Daniel Dennett for reacting well to a preprint version. The proceedings of the conference were published by the New York Academy of Sciences as volume 1001 in their *Annals* series in 2003.

Chapter 8 is an improved version of a paper stating in a satisfactory form my own photonic theory of consciousness. I am grateful to two anonymous reviewers, who read the paper carefully but found it hard going. I presented the main ideas (with slides) as an invited lecture at the conference *Towards a Science of Consciousness: Between Phenomenology and Neuroscience*, held in Prague, Czech Republic, in July 2003.

Chapter 9 is a simplified presentation of the ideas laid out in chapter 8, but with a more realistic appreciation of the amount of technical detail the reader can be expected to tolerate. I thank Susan Blackmore and Johnjoe McFadden for their gentle criticism and support.

Chapter 10 is based on a paper I drafted with the thought of publishing it in *Scientific American*. After several revisions, I hope it is good enough in editorial quality, if not in orthodoxy of content, for such readers.

Chapter 11 is an essay conceived and submitted for the Power of Purpose Awards, a worldwide essay competition sponsored by the John Templeton Foundation. I am grateful to the foundation for thus prompting me to write up my views on purpose in this way.

Chapter 12 is an extended review of a pair of big books, respectively by Roger Penrose and Stephen Wolfram. A shortened version was published in the *Journal of Consciousness Studies*, 12(2), 2005.

Chapter 13 is a sketch for a unified account of time that can work for both physics and psychology. I thank Springer editor Angela Lahee for our discussions of its basic ideas. In 2006 I submitted the essay to the journal *Mind and Matter* and received two gracious anonymous reviews, which left me happy with the essay.

Chapter 14 is a brief response to a target article by Christian de Quincey, published together with the target in the *Journal of Consciousness Studies*, 13(4), 2006.

Chapter 15 is my reply to a conference report by Claude Pasquini on the tenth annual meeting of the Association for the Scientific Study of Consciousness (ASSC10) at St. Anne's College, Oxford, held in June 2006. The report was published in the *Journal of Consciousness Studies* 13(6), 2006, and my reply was published in the 13(12) issue.

Chapter 16 is my report on a blazing row that suddenly erupted in 2007 between my old friends Ted Honderich and Colin McGinn, whose work I had analyzed in detail in the review reprinted here as chapter 6. My report on the new row was published in the *Journal of Consciousness Studies*, 15(1), 2008.

I thank Imprint Academic and its managing editor Anthony Freeman for their gracious cooperation in the publication of this volume.

Contents

1	Introduction	1
2	Portrait of a Philosopher	13
3	Fundamentals of Consciousness	30
4	Consciousness: A Logical Model	43
5	Mindworlds	62
6	First-Person Consciousness	108
7	The Self: From Soul to Brain	141
8	A Photonic Theory of Consciousness	163
9	Toward a Theory of Consciousness	189
10	Consciousness as a Physical Process	203
11	Purpose in Life and Science	215
12	Roads to Reality	224
13	About Time	241
14	Blinded by the Light	267
15	Will Robots See Humans as Dinosaurs?	269
16	Hitting on Consciousness	277
	Chapter Notes	298
	References	320
	Index	334

Although you appear in earthly form
Your essence is pure Consciousness.
You are the fearless guardian
of Divine Light.
So come, return to the root of the root
of your own soul.

Rumi
*

---

* Quoted from (Star 1997), page 3.

Introduction

The special difficulty with the scientific study of consciousness is not that the concept resists easy definition – many scientifically tractable concepts share that feature – but that as would-be scientists we live in consciousness. This indefinable state of organized or unified awareness frames our every move as cognitive agents. We seem to need to perform a Kantian critique of pure reason before we can even begin to see how and where science can get a grip on the concept.

Ideally, such a philosophical critique can set the limits of the scientific enterprise in psychology. What we seek is a story about a mechanism that can explain our range of experiences as neutrally and uncontroversially as we now explain other biological functions like digestion or physical phenomena like liquids or technology like computers.

What we need in addition – and this is the hard problem – is *perspectival therapy* to get us out of the mental confusion about first and third person perspectives that makes the issue seem so intractable. In principle, the inner–outer contrast is as trivial as a perspectival shift in an Escher picture. All we need to do is find a set of reliable ways to characterize this perspectival shift in logic, physics, psychology, and philosophy. In practice, this task is far from trivial. But it is doable.

My main purpose in this book is to perform that therapy, essentially by taking the first steps in logic and physics toward a substantial explanation of consciousness within the frame of contemporary science, using what I hope are familiar and uncontested results and approaches and simply putting them together in such a way that the correct view of it all is fairly obvious. Some of my assertions may seem variously ambitious, optimistic, abstract, simplistic and so on, but by the end of it all I hope you'll find the general position quite plausible and even natural. In fact, I hope you'll be thinking – *of course, quite right, no problem.*

Try this test – read the book and see if you agree.

Portrait of a Philosopher

To ease you gently, dear reader, into my researches in the philosophy and science of consciousness, I first present a brief and fact-laden self-portrait. This is intended to be rather more than an elegantly narratized version of my résumé in that it should provide a glimpse of my motivations and priorities. The aim is not to try to rationalize a life that has its fair share of randomness and confusion, but to put into a wider personal perspective the set of rather narrowly focused and technical essays that follow. I think the wider perspective is necessary here, because writers on consciousness often bring personal baggage to the workplace without seeming to realize it, and this can damage their work. By putting my cards on the table, I hope I can raise the chances that my results, such as they are, are seen to be kosher.

The story has a more practical relevance to the main topic of this book, namely in helping to fix the semantic background from which the key terms in the following chapters acquired their meaning for me. For philosophers, if not always for scientists, knowing where they came from can be crucial to understanding what they have to say.

Fundamentals of Consciousness

This 1997 essay is the first piece of hard analytic philosophy in this book, and my first such piece since 1980. Its immediate trigger was the 1996 book by David Chalmers, *The Conscious Mind*. As I read the book and wrote my essay in response, I realized that over the years I had cooked up something that was worth the effort to say. Hence, in the following decade, I wrote the rest of this book. Indeed, the still largely unstated message of this oracular first essay unfolds in the following chapters.

The message of the essay did not meet with immediate public enthusiasm. The organizers at Stanford University of the conference Cognitive Science 1997 showed me the reports on the essay of two anonymous referees: one praised the evidently serious attempt to tackle the roots of the issue with a multidisciplinary approach and the other complained that my position was not scientific in the sense of being amenable to direct experimental testing. In August 1997, I presented essentially the same essay as a poster at the Brain and Self Workshop in Elsinore, Denmark, and several participants showed animated interest. By then I was hooked.

Introduction

Consciousness: A Logical Model

This essay was written in early 2000 in readiness for the Toward a Science of Consciousness conference in Tucson, Arizona, in April. I laser-printed a set of copies, with four pages per double-sided A4 sheet, as stapled booklets in color covers sporting an inkjet print of a beautiful painting by a British artist friend called Josephine Wall, and distributed them at the conference. My supply was used up very quickly, probably because the cover picture was so nice.

The essay was a landmark for me. It persuaded me that I had not only something worthwhile to say but also a viable way of saying it. The T2K conference was a landmark, too, in that it confirmed my feeling that I was first and foremost a philosopher, not a novelist or an editor or an educator but a seeker after truth.

Mindworlds

The collection of slides featured in this chapter took time to assemble and went through a series of incarnations. Their title at first was "The Miph of Consciousness" (*miph* – mathematics–informatics–physics – is an acronym from my 1996 sci-fi novel *Lifeball*, where I played a lot with more or less serendipitous acronymic fabrications) and a suitable subset with this title accompanied my twenty-minute mini-lecture at the 2001 conference in the Toward a Science of Consciousness series, held at an isolated hilltop hotel in Skövde, Sweden, in August 2001.

My Skövde presentation sufficiently impressed a few people, including Ted Honderich, to move me to develop the show further, to the full length indicated in this chapter, with slides whose graphic interest is lost, sad to say, on the printed page but which can be enjoyed in full (except that a few delightful animations are lost in the compact format used) on my website. The added value from the graphic medium was substantial, and I am sure that future philosophers with more advanced web tools will routinely create animations presenting hard work in multimedia form.

In April 2002, I presented another suitable subset of the slides in the form of a 40-panel poster at the Toward a Science of Consciousness conference in Tucson, Arizona. In the meantime, the encounter with Ted Honderich led me to read his autobiography, which led in turn to the next chapter.

First-Person Consciousness

This chapter is an extended book review. The world of London philosophy in the late twentieth century that Ted Honderich presented in his autobiography was so familiar to me that I just had to respond. Then Colin McGinn, who was an acquaintance from my years as a student in Oxford, published his autobiography, too, and it was a no-brainer to review the two books in parallel. While pursuing this exercise, which naturally caused me to reflect anew on the whole enterprise of philosophizing from a personal perspective about consciousness, I revisited the works of David Chalmers and Daniel Dennett. These distinguished thinkers had so much that was worth saying on the whole topic that they took pride of place in the essay.

The resulting piece is readable, as several readers said, as an introduction to the philosophy of consciousness. They also said it was entertaining – no mean feat for this topic, I think. With four such actors to animate the tale, I claim no personal credit for this feat, but I'm grateful anyway.

The Self: From Soul to Brain

This chapter presents my report on the New York Academy of Sciences conference "The Self: From Soul to Brain" held at the Mount Sinai School of Medicine, New York, in September 2002. As a longtime member of the NYAS, I felt that this was a conference I had to attend. Also in attendance was Keith Sutherland, the founder and publisher of Imprint Academic, who invited me to report on the event for the *Journal of Consciousness Studies*.

The idea behind the report was not merely to reflect the look and feel of the conference but to get to the heart of the concept of self on display and subject it to critical review. This appeared to me to be a useful exercise for the rather complicated reason that (1) this concept of self is currently the dominant paradigm, (2) it has practical implications for psychiatric and clinical practice through the support it offers for drug-based therapies, and (3) it's wrong! Or rather, not to be too controversial, it's a concept that does not reflect the whole truth about the self, and therefore risks mistaking the physiological effects of various kinds of psychic distress for their causes, and thus of treating the symptoms with invasive therapies that can do serious chemical damage to the delicate neuronal foundations of a human self without beginning to address the depths that a more comprehensive psychology should respect and embrace.

That said, the piece is not a manifesto for a new school of psychology. It is instead a reminder that the hard science of our neuronal lives is far from finished. As readers of my 1996 novel *Lifeball* may recall, I have an idea about the physical embodiment of the self that lifts it above its neurons and gives it a life of its own, where the physics of that life is not yet well understood but nevertheless undoubtedly well worth serious study. We have the makings of a new paradigm for understanding the self in the idea that the cerebral electromagnetic field generated by neural activity has a dynamical life that cannot be predicted solely from the neural and synaptic configuration of the brain that generates it. In company with some other researchers, I believe that the quantum properties of this field are decisive in generating the characteristic look and feel of first-person experience, and I therefore dub it the *photonic* theory of consciousness.

A Photonic Theory of Consciousness

This chapter presents what is intended to be a definitive introduction at a scientific level to the sort of view of the logic and physics of the self that I am proposing in this book. But be warned – unless you already know quite a lot about formal logic, set theory, and quantum physics, and have already considered the issues they raise when you try to put them together in a theory of mind, the chapter will be hard going. To ease my intended readers into the required mindset, the rest of this book is the best I can offer.

I wrote the paper immediately after the New York conference report, to make the view it presents finally available in a clear and concise form. When you reach your fifties you begin to think of mortality, and I would have greatly regretted losing the opportunity to explain my view while I was still mentally fit enough to give it my best shot. For all its flaws, I regard the essay as a milestone in my career as a philosopher.

Essentially, the essay is hard because I think a scientific understanding of consciousness cannot be achieved without more clarity on issues normally addressed in mathematics and physics than most researchers in psychology and neuroscience currently possess. So I had to outline all that.

I presented a talk based on the paper, with some suitable slides (from the set in chapter 5), at the conference "Towards a Science of Consciousness: From Phenomenology to Neuroscience" held in Prague, capital of the Czech Republic, in July 2003. The audience received the talk with evident interest and the subsequent question-and-answer session was very good.

Toward a Science of Consciousness

My manuscript in early 2003 for the previous chapter did not meet with the enthusiastic endorsement of two of its readers. Since they had been asked to review the paper for publication, this left me with an anticlimax. The paper presented in this chapter is the result. The same theme is addressed in a lighter and more digestible manner. It presents a compact and practical account of how we experience a temporal flow of phenomenal forms, and thus describes the core mechanism for a credible physics of consciousness.

However, it turned out that my understanding of the physical background was still evolving, both in depth and in scope. So again the chapter records work in progress. The quest continued.

Consciousness as a Physical Process

This chapter started life as a draft article for *Scientific American*. But it soon became clear that the ideas were still too exotic for such a presentation, so it now serves the role of presenting a shorter and possibly more readable take on the same old story aired earlier. More to the point here, as a result of further reading and thinking, the physics has been reinforced. Indeed, I have come to the conclusion that getting a better view of the physics of relativistic spacetime and quantum phenomena such as superposition and entanglement will be essential to building a viable concept of consciousness. For me, a viable concept must not only serve as a foundation for what we now regard as human psychology but must also be sufficiently fundamental to accommodate the insights on consciousness that have arisen in the Indian philosophical tradition, insights which in the West have often been lost in the fog of religious doctrine.

Purpose in Life and Science

This chapter goes as far as I dare go in resuscitating the concept of purpose in the context of a science of mind. My opinion as to the subjectivity of the concept should be obvious from the treatment, but I do not wish thereby to devalue the idea of purpose. On the contrary, a sense of purpose seems quite central to a well balanced human life, and analytical scepticism should not be allowed to subvert that evident fact. Yet honesty compels me to insist on its derivative status in a scientific perspective.

I submitted the essay for the 2004 Power of Purpose Awards. This was a worldwide competition sponsored by the John Templeton Foundation. The essay failed to win one of the nineteen prizes, unsurprisingly, but I think it was worth writing – and is worth reading – anyway. My relentless pursuit of scientific rigor is evident – all too evident for an inspirational piece.

Roads to Reality

This chapter is an extended book review. Prompted by Roger Penrose's book *The Road to Reality* (2004), my strategy here is to lift the focus of attention from the implementation of consciousness in the brain to the organized phenomenology of the world reflected in consciousness, which means the radical shift mentioned above of the overarching perspective from biology to mathematics and physics, and indeed to logic and philosophy, where my consideration of the whole issue began. I recall that my awareness of consciousness as a central concept in a philosophical foundation for a logical and scientific worldview grew from Penrose's earlier book *The Emperor's New Mind* (1989).

This review reflected a change of heart. It replaced an earlier fragment called *Consciousness: The Movie* that I drafted earlier in 2004. The title and the methodology of that approach were prompted by Oliver Sacks, who published an essay giving prominence to the movie metaphor in a January 2004 issue of *The New York Review of Books*. As I prepared that draft, I read Christof Koch's fine new book *The Quest for Consciousness*, then started reading Thomas Metzinger's forbidding tome *Being No One* (2003), then read two more new books, *Wider Than the Sky* by Gerald Edelman and *Mind Time* by Benjamin Libet, after all of which I was too punch-drunk by physiological details to go on. There had to be a better way.

The better way – the road to reality – dawned as soon as I leafed through Penrose's new volume. This was the book I had been waiting for, the book that offered realistic hope of the insight I recall yearning for in 1988 as I started a hopeful reading of Stephen Hawking's little essay *A Brief History of Time*. All else could wait as I ploughed into the equations. After reading Penrose, I think I know where consciousness fits into the Big Picture.

As the chapter took shape, it became clear that a confrontation with the views of Stephen Wolfram, as recorded in his massive 2002 book *A New Kind of Science*, was an essential part of my enterprise. So the review of Penrose's ideas became a comparative review of the two sets of ideas, as well as the whole history of related ideas, against my own ideas as implicit backdrop. In my humble opinion, the result rises above the views of any individual and achieves a perspective that may fairly be called breathtaking.

A shortened version of the review was published in the *Journal of Consciousness Studies*. I have taken the opportunity to trim the additional material anew for this volume. The earlier long version was the last essay in the online pilot edition of this book.

About Time

I first conceived the ideas at the core of this essay in 1975, when I was 25 and doing postgraduate research in logic at the University of Oxford. Since then, the ideas have fermented into a rich brew, as I hope the rest of this book already shows, and found a new organizing concept in the realm of consciousness studies. This essay roots the new ideas in the hard bedrock of miph (mathematics–informatics–physics) and thus – I hope – establishes my position as based on more than mere rhetoric.

As precipitating cause for the essay, I cited a fascinating book entitled *Quo Vadis Quantum Mechanics?* (edited by Elitzur and Dolev, 2005). This book was published by my former editorial colleague at Springer, Angela Lahee, who gave me a copy and discussed its ideas with me often enough to ensure that the precipitation occurred.

The essay will be hard going for psychologists, most of whom have long forgotten how to think in terms of basic logic and physics. It will be hard in a different way for most physicists, for whom sullying the impersonal purity of their concepts with perspectival considerations may suggest the sort of transformational hermeneutics that Alan Sokal spoofed or indeed the sort of woffle that Harry Frankfurt writes off as bullshit. In response, I can only say that there must be a shared philosophical foundation for psychology and physics, and that my logical construction is how it might look.

Blinded by the Light

The philosopher Christian de Quincey had some refreshingly common-sense views about consciousness in 2006. As a frequent contributor to the *Journal of Consciousness Studies*, I was invited to respond to his views, and did so in the short piece presented in this chapter.

I am immodest enough to think that my effort bore some fruit. In 2008, Christian de Quincey published another *Journal of Consciousness Studies* essay on consciousness, entitled "Reality bubbles" and displaying such a thoroughgoing similarity to my *Mindworlds* position that I can only ask why he did not cite my work alongside the works of Descartes, Kant, and Whitehead that he did cite.

Will Robots See Humans as Dinosaurs?

In the summer of 2006, I indulged in a sentimental return to Oxford for the tenth ASSC conference. Among other delights, we enjoyed a champagne reception in the Pitt Rivers Museum of Anthropology and Archaeology. There, surrounded by dinosaur skeletons and other preserved reminders of our biological heritage, I held forth to a small audience of interlocutors on my signature themes (from my novel *Lifeball*) of the long-term evolution of life on Earth and its imminent culmination for humans – either as epiphany or as apocalypse – in the coming of the machines. One of my witnesses was the biologist Claude Pasquini, who wrote a report on the conference for the *Journal of Consciousness Studies* that cited some of my words.

My reply became an essay on the future of the human species in view of the imminent Singularity prophesied by AI futurologist Ray Kurzweil. The Singularity was first predicted by sci-fi author Vernor Vinge back in 1993 and is billed as the moment when machines become more intelligent, under some suitable definition, than humans. The idea was part of the *Zeitgeist* in the nineties and was integral to my *Lifeball* vision.

The chapter presents my reply, as it appeared in the last 2006 issue of the *Journal of Consciousness Studies*. Several readers responded in writing to its thrown gauntlet, and I enjoyed several lively debates on the strength of the feelings my argument stirred up. Since then, others have said flattering things about the essay, which emboldens me to imagine that it is one of my more successful compositions.

Hitting on Consciousness

In 2007, as daily work continued to grind down my once-youthful energies, the philosophical world continued its evolution independently of me. But toward the end of the year I was distracted from my blogging (on which more later) by Ted Honderich and Colin McGinn, who engaged each other in a very public cat-fight over Ted's new book on consciousness. Since I had in 2002 contributed to the pairing of these figures in the public imagination (see chapter 6), I was called back from my semi-retirement to moderate the cat-fight and try to restore a semblance of calm.

I did so in a review of the controversy that appeared in the first 2008 issue of the *Journal of Consciousness Studies*. To judge by the responses, I think my review had some success. It was also fun to write and is apparently fun to read. At any rate, it makes a cheering high note on which to end this book. But don't expect it to add much to your understanding of the concept of consciousness!

Notes and References

Some of the above essays originally appeared with numerous footnotes and citations of sources from the literature. To avoid cluttering the text, I have moved all these notes and citations to the end. In any case where a reference to a work or an author is central to the argument, the reference in the main text is explicit. Otherwise, the fine detail is moved to the notes chapter.

As part of the editorial preparation of this volume, I have revised the notes to ensure that where necessary they are intelligible without flipping back and forth too much.

By consolidating the references into a single listing, I have avoided what would otherwise have been a horribly repetitive reappearance of some titles in numerous chapter listings. This also gives potential readers of this book the chance to review all the references at once, quickly, to check the overall relevance of the book to their own work. If any titles are listed that are not mentioned by name in the chapters or notes, it is because were sufficiently important in shaping the evolution of my thoughts on these topics over the last ten years that they deserved mention. Anyone wishing to reconstruct my thoughts should find the resulting list useful in setting their context – as well as in suggesting how much I had to filter along the way.

Ten Years Later

An anthology like this is not required to have a story or a dramatic climax. Still, it is gratifying when an evolution is discernible in the series of essays. It is especially gratifying when an overall result emerges that crowns the collection and stands as a result that others may quote and reuse.

In my own case, I must admit that ten years of work here have achieved less than I would have liked. My mindworlds formalism of layered sets and moments of experienced time may lead to further formalistic modeling of consciousness and may even form a foundational architecture for a robot consciousness, but I would hardly deserve credit for any such development.

The acid test would be to formulate a recipe for a consciousness along these lines that could unfold in a suitable physical substrate, but passing that test is far beyond my powers.

However, I can cite several more modest achievements as conclusions, which I hope will serve to justify the publication of yet another book about consciousness.

One big conclusion is immediately clear. Within the scope of a scientific project, even one pursued worldwide for over a decade, we cannot hope to solve the riddle of *why* consciousness exists. As scientists, the best we can do is show *how* the brain supports these cognitive states that can seem to embrace the entirety of phenomenal reality.

The *how* question is eminently soluble, and I am convinced that we are well on the way to solving it. No new physics is needed to explain how the cerebral neuronet modulates the heterophenomenology of consciousness, and explaining the autophenomenology is an issue for philosophy. In my view, there is no substantive scientific problem to be solved in the transition from a third-person, public, objective perspective to a first-person, private, subjective perspective on the phenomenal manifold that constitutes the reflection in consciousness of reality. The perspectival shift is tractable in mathematics or logic, as I hope to have shown, where multiple or partial perspectives on objective domains are nothing new, and any residual puzzlement over the issue can be handled in philosophy, perhaps as a kind of therapy. The deeper issue – of why there is a phenomenal world at all – is for mystics to contemplate.

A more solid conclusion is that we shall not understand consciousness, as opposed to the various cognitive faculties that result in behavior that lifts us above the zombie league, until we have integrated physics and psychology more substantially than at present. Relativistic and quantum physics offer insights into physical reality that need to be integrated coherently within a psychological worldview. My talk of time flow and perspectives is the way to go here, but all this needs to be followed up more massively. The physics of the real world is just as deserving of a psychological reconceptualization as is everyday naïve realism regarding perceptual objects.

A corollary of these two conclusions together is that dramatic advances in science, such as the unification of physics in a single coherent perspective, will not solve the hard problem of consciousness. Any physical theory will merit psychologization, and the perspectival shift that characterizes the hard problem will be trivial in any sufficiently advanced psychophysics. But the ongoing possibility of such a shift – the puzzle of how we get a phenomenal dualism from the neutral monism of the underlying psychophysics – will remain as a nugget for mystics.

In my considered opinion, future advances in psychophysics are likely to show that *I* am not bounded by the brain that supports my consciousness. I am an instantiation of a concept – the "I" – that is really the proper subject of another discipline, though not now of theology but of an anthropology of religion. On that still highly speculative and politically hazardous topic, see my 2009 draft for a book titled *Godblogs*, based on a series of online forum conversations in which I participated during 2007 and 2008.

Portrait of a Philosopher

1949–1961

I was born in November 1949, in the town of Luton, in southern England. My father was from Morpeth, Northumberland, and worked as an engineer. During the Second World War he served as an RAF officer and diplomatic attaché, mostly in India. My mother was from Huddersfield, Yorkshire, and worked as a secretary. I have a sister, who is two years younger than me and now has five children and several grandchildren.

When I was still too young to remember, we moved to Poole, Dorset, on the south coast of England, where I lived until 1969. Poole has a cherished history as a fishing town and boasts one of the biggest and best natural harbors in the world, as well as some glorious beaches.

1961–1968

From the age of 11 to the age of 19, I was a pupil at Poole Grammar School. There I sat Ordinary-level exams (three in 1965, five in 1966), Advanced-level exams (1968), and the Oxford entrance exam (also 1968).

At age 12, I was deeply impressed by a visit to the Science Museum in London. My reading at that time included science fiction by Captain W. E. Johns (creator of Professor Lucius Brane, who used to be picked up by friendly aliens for flying-saucer jaunts around the universe) and Patrick Moore. I also read a lot of history books about the Second World War and light technical books about ships and aircraft. My schoolfriends and I regularly went on day trips to spot aircraft, both at local airports and at national air shows like Biggin Hill and Farnborough. I recall fondly our binocular vigil for the maiden flight of the BAC One-Eleven at Bournemouth Airport in August 1963.

Later that year, nine days after my fourteenth birthday, I heard the news that President John F. Kennedy had been assassinated while at our regular Friday evening Boy Scouts meeting. I enjoyed the Boy Scouts and served as a Second in my patrol, although my only proficiency badge was for aircraft spotting. By then I was reading a lot of science fiction, including most of the classics and books by Isaac Asimov and Arthur C. Clarke. My interest in war machines bloomed into a passion for plastic modeling: I built up a 1/76 scale army of two thousand men with a hundred armored vehicles, at 1/1200 scale a hundred-ship navy, and at 1/72 scale a magnificent air force of a hundred planes, almost all from the Second World War. For the army I built scale landscapes using model railway accessories and used them to play tabletop war games with friends. A few years later, I sold most of these models to other enthusiasts via classified ads in hobby mags.

As a teenager, I cut a nerdish figure, academically good and sometimes outstanding but not obviously a genius. I had a high IQ and used to read books about relativity and quantum physics, but I was unable to say I really understood them. I had no evident prowess at sports, no popular charisma, and was shy with any girls I found attractive. On Saturday nights, friends and I went to local discos, but my first girlfriends were not ideal soulmates and I remained virginal throughout the sixties.

At that time I earned pocket money by working as a stockroom boy at Woolworths on Saturdays. In the summers of 1966 and 1967, I worked as a seaside seller of tea and ice-creams for the Bournemouth Beach Catering corporation. I developed an interest in motorcycles, and rode and restored a pair of old British bikes, first a BSA Bantam and then a Triumph Tiger Cub. The Bantam was impossible to style but the Tiger Cub ended up with high bars, a purple paint job, and a rather loud exhaust. My own style veered between Mod and Rocker, with colorful shirts and a parka for streets and disco but a greasy black jacket and jeans for the bike.

Despite all these distractions, my school career ended quite well:

Year	Subject	Level	Grade
1968	Pure Maths	Advanced	A
1968	Applied Maths	Advanced	A
1968	Physics (+ practical)	Advanced	A+A
1968	Pure Maths	Special	Credit

In the summer of 1968, the school sent me as its delegate to an international young scientists' congress in London. This was a landmark event for my imagination and confirmed my impression that I was a scientist first and foremost (recall that a scientist is a kind of philosopher). In December 1968, I was awarded the Stapledon Exhibition to read Physics at Exeter College Oxford.

For the first half of 1969, I worked as a bus conductor for the Hants and Dorset Omnibus Company, read Tolkien's classic *The Lord of the Rings* and other large books,[1] and bought my first LP records – an album of sitar music by Ravi Shankar and the white double album by the Beatles. I also bought an old car, a Renault Dauphine, and learned to drive.

In the long, hot summer, two other Oxbridge-bound schoolfriends and I hitch-hiked around Europe. We started by heading south, through Paris, Marseilles, Genoa, Rome, Florence, and Athens. We were at sea, on a ferry sailing across the Adriatic from Italy to Greece, when we watched Apollo astronaut Neil Armstrong step onto the Moon on television. Then we turned north, through Yugoslavia, the Alps, Munich, Heidelberg, and Amsterdam. By then our hair was quite long.

1969–1972

In October 1969, I matriculated at the University of Oxford. I studied for three years at Exeter College Oxford. My roommate for the first term was an elegant young man called Paul who was very rich and read English. He introduced me to his friend Martin Amis, his drug of choice marijuana, and the cult music of the Velvet Underground. Martin and Paul made quite a pair with their flowing hair, fancy handmade shirts, velvet suits, snakeskin boots, patrician accents, and elegant and sophisticated girlfriends.

Back in Poole, over the Christmas vacation, I was introduced to the joys of sex by a beloved local girlfriend.

Back at Oxford, Paul found me another room and I took up the study of philosophy. My English friends eased me into a lifestyle of sex and drugs and rock'n'roll and I cultivated a hippy biker look. I read a lot of big novels, too, and decided I could best transmit the spirit of Apollo into the future by authoring some good books, some novels perhaps.

In 1970, I despaired of doing justice to the Feynman Lectures on Physics in Oxford's hothouse atmosphere and decided that adding my bit to the human sciences was more urgent than yet more progress in physics. I joined the Oxford University branch of the United Nations Association, where my main activities as a committee member were to arrange a coach visit of student protesters to a Springboks rugby match and to publish an interview with a Frelimo freedom fighter from Mozambique. As one of the organizers of a student rock music club called Stonehenge, I arranged a concert in the Oxford Union building by the Bournemouth folk singer Al Stewart.

In the summer I took Second Class Honour Moderations in Physics and Philosophy, then returned to Poole to work as a laborer in a steel factory.

In the fall I enrolled as a student of Philosophy, Politics and Economics (PPE) with a focus on philosophy, and began serious reading in philosophy. In addition I brushed up my cultural awareness by reading numerous novels, mostly Russian and other classics in translation. My favorite authors at the time were Tolstoy, Dostoyevsky, Joseph Conrad, Jean-Paul Sartre, Hermann Hesse, James Joyce, and contemporary Americans such as Philip Roth and Norman Mailer. My favorite musicians included the Beatles, the Rolling Stones, the Who, the Doors, Jefferson Airplane, Bob Dylan, and so on.

To celebrate my twenty-first birthday, I bought myself a typewriter, an Imperial Olympia, which I used for the next ten years.

In early 1971, I met a fellow student called Judy Mallaber. We went on to spend the next four years together. They were very good years. Judy studied PPE, too, in her case with an emphasis on politics, which became increasingly Marxist during our time together.

In 1972, after electing to take three advanced papers in philosophy, I was awarded Second Class Honours in Philosophy, Politics and Economics. My grades for the philosophy papers were good but the rest were mixed, so I narrowly failed to get a First. My elective papers were in philosophy of mind and the philosophy of Immanuel Kant (mainly *Kritik der reinen Vernunft*), for which my tutor was college fellow Paul Snowdon, and the philosophies of Bertrand Russell and Ludwig Wittgenstein (from *Principia Mathematica* to the *Tractatus Logico-Philosophicus*), for which my tutor was Gordon Baker, who worked with Peter Hacker.

Happily, I was awarded a Leverhulme Studentship to study for a two-year Master's degree in Logic and Scientific Method in the department founded by Karl Popper at the London School of Economics and Political Science (the famous LSE).

1972–1974

In autumn 1972, Judy and I joined two other couples in a shared house in Hackney, north London, and I studied at the LSE. The head of department was Imre Lakatos, who as a recent refugee from Hungary had developed a Popperian philosophy of mathematics and science that invited comparison with the views of Thomas Kuhn and Paul Feyerabend.[2] I studied Quine's works in depth – especially *Word and Object* and *Set Theory and Its Logic* – and enjoyed the buzz around the works of Noam Chomsky and Saul Kripke, with their exciting new perspectives on how to develop a scientific approach to the semantics of natural language.[3]

One spring day in our Hackney commune, four of us dropped acid and tripped out blissfully to some classic Californian rock music. A week or two later, I finally read *Ulysses* from cover to cover – that was quite a trip, too, indeed the best novel I've ever read.[4]

In 1973, I did some part-time lecturing on Fundamental and Integrative Studies in the Department of Accounting and Finance at the North East London Polytechnic. I supplemented my LSE studies with parallel seminars in other London colleges, mostly University College (where among others the young Ted Honderich toiled for a pittance). Judy and I moved to a new student commune with former Oxford colleagues in Ealing, west London. I studied Hegel and set theory, and enjoyed visionary insights while studying them in alternating sessions under the respective influences of musical works by Beethoven and David Bowie, both very loud. I envisioned the closure of the cumulative hierarchy of sets into a strange loop analogous to the looping of dialectical hierarchies in Hegeliana.

In 1974, I completed my Master of Science studies:

Papers
Advanced Scientific Method
Elements of Mathematical Logic
Philosophy of Mathematics

Thesis (distinguished)
Logical Foundations for Probability Theory
Carnap semantics for inductive logic and Kripke semantics for modal logic are used to build a logical foundation for probability theory.

In the summer of 1974, Judy and I traveled to Berlin. We lived in a radical student commune in Kreuzberg, near the Berlin Wall. I taught English as a Foreign Language at the Hartnackschule, and also worked my way through Hegel's masterpiece, *Phänomenologie des Geistes*, in German and English, in the American Memorial Library at Hallesches Tor.

Later in 1974, I was awarded the Master of Science degree in Logic and Scientific Method from the University of London.

1974–1977

In October 1974, I returned to the University of Oxford to pursue graduate studies. I was awarded an Amelia Jackson Studentship from Exeter College and studied for a Bachelor of Philosophy degree in philosophy.

In 1975, I wrote a draft book entitled *Dialectical Logic*. In it, I tried to demonstrate the logical open-endedness of propositional logic, predicate logic, arithmetic, set theory, and truth theory. Since the work began with a quotation from Lenin and ended with one from Mao Zedong, it was not calculated to appeal to conventional readers and is better left unread.[5] It marked the zenith of my trajectory through the cresting wave of radical chic – I gradually gave up reading trendy authors like Louis Althusser, Herbert Marcuse, Marshall McLuhan, Timothy Leary, Leon Trotsky, Ronald Laing, Germaine Greer, Shulamith Firestone, Hunter Thompson, Wilhelm Reich, and many others (all as jumbled in my mind as they appear here). Also, I gradually drifted apart from Judy, whose own political views were more consistently leftist than I had ever wanted to be.

In early 1976, I did some freelance journalism for the Oxford University magazine *Isis*. I published reviews of new books by Alfred Ayer (*The Central Questions of Philosophy*) and Karl Popper (*Unended Quest*).[6]

In 1976, I completed my Bachelor of Philosophy studies:

Papers
Original Authorities for the Rise of Mathematical Logic
Philosophy of Mathematics
Social and Political Philosophies of Hegel and Marx

Thesis
Truth and Provability
An open-ended sequence of restricted logical calculi is applied to arithmetic and set theory to accommodate the problems of self-reference illustrated by Gödel's incompleteness theorem.

I was awarded a distinction for both the papers and the thesis, and received warm congratulations all round. Robin Gandy at the Mathematics Institute had been my tutor for mathematics in 1974–75. He had formerly worked under Alan Turing. Crispin Wright at All Souls College was my tutor for philosophy in 1975–77. He had formerly worked under Michael Dummett. The Oxford Bachelor of Philosophy degree is worth somewhat more than a Master of Philosophy degree elsewhere and has since been renamed to prevent confusion with a first degree. It is considered a sufficient and final qualification for teaching philosophy.

Naturally, I had other ideas. I spent the summer passionately reading Iris Murdoch novels. Iris Murdoch somehow seemed a kindred spirit – she had taught philosophy at St. Anne's College Oxford and worked in the British civil service.

In the academic year 1976–77, I continued my studies at Oxford, now registered for a Doctor of Philosophy degree, and did part-time work as a tutor in logic and philosophy at St. Anne's College Oxford. I wrote another, more formalized and detailed draft of my ill-fated book *Dialectical Logic*. The argument now culminated in a new, open-ended, evolutionary theory of facts that unfolded in a constructive universe where time was realized layer by layer behind a moving present moment. The memory of this dialectical theory is now burned inextinguishably in my brain, as my highest flight in the glorious realms of visionary experience, and forms the mathematical backbone of my mindworlds constructions in this volume.

The prospect of settling into a quiet academic backwater somewhere did not appeal to me. I decided to join the Civil Service as what they called a "high flyer," initially as an Administration Trainee. I did well in the exams and was posted to the Ministry of Defence in central London.

1977–1981

In October 1977, I started work at the Ministry of Defence in London. My work there is subject to the Official Secrets Acts. I hope and trust that I may now say that a high point of my time there was an extended visit to NATO Headquarters in Brussels.

I was still working on philosophical logic. I submitted my new draft of *Dialectical Logic* as a doctoral thesis and was examined on it in June 1978. My examiners were both young and already known to me: John Bell, a mathematical logician from Oxford who now lectured in London, and Daniel Isaacson, the Oxford Reader in Philosophy of Mathematics. They gave the work a sympathetic reading but found it unacceptably uneven and perilously obscure. They found nothing in it they could confidently endorse as a solid presentation of a well defined research project. They invited me to resubmit, as and when I could submit something more polished.

The Ministry and I didn't work out well. I was sufficiently conflicted by my philosophical reversal to resign from the Ministry. This was undoubtedly a good move, painful as it was.

In early 1979, unemployed now, but restless and ambitious, I decided I had to write something. Staying with my sister in the country, I wrote a quick novel and called it *Fireball*. It was a ripping yarn, utter nonsense, of course, but fun (secret agent Adam Hammer defeats a German terrorist and saves the world from nuclear war). In the coming months a succession of publishers politely rejected it.

Then I returned to London, to an elegant shared house in Muswell Hill. Soon enough, I got a job as an advertising representative for an electronics journal called *Electron*, published by the International Publishing Corporation based on the South Bank. While there, I also wrote for their journal *Data Processing*. Despite the pleasure of a company car, this didn't really suit me, and I resigned to write my thesis anew in late 1979. With minimal length, math-free dialog form, and few references, the typescript was more or less completed by the end of the year.

In the first quarter of 1980, I finished and submitted the thesis, and did temporary clerical work for the Institute of Administrative Accounting and Data Processing in the Strand, just opposite the Savoy Hotel. The Institute was computerizing its records, and needed someone with a clear mind and a sharp eye to mark up its files.

I moved back to Oxford and took a short course in teaching English as a Foreign Language at the Oxford Intensive School of English, then spent the summer teaching vacation students in Oxford. It was a pleasant summer, and I swam a lot and ran for hours alongside sunlit canals. I also read numerous good books. I read Bertrand Russell's history of Western philosophy, J. M. Roberts' eurocentric history of the world, Charles Taylor's big book on Hegel, some of Marx's early writings, Nietzsche's *Also sprach Zarathustra*, Crispin Wright's book on Wittgenstein's philosophy of mathematics, and parts of the New Testament and the Koran.[7] My logical thoughts receded and my daybook recorded the following philosophical thought: "Aim – to be philosophical about philosophy itself."

The time came for the *viva voce* exam on my thesis. The examiners were Edward Craig from Cambridge and Michael Inwood, an Oxford man whose seminars on Hegel some years earlier I had attended with some pleasure. Graciously enough, they accepted my Socratic dialog *Dialectical Logic* for the degree of Master of Letters.

In September 1980, I moved back to London and started work as a tutor of Advanced-level Physics at the Davis, Laing and Dick Tutorial College in Notting Hill Gate. It was good to be busy with physics again. I was in charge of the laboratory and set up some neat experiments.

In November 1980, clad in *sub fusc*, bow tie, cap and gown, I attended the University of Oxford degree ceremony at the Sheldonian Theatre in Oxford, and was formally awarded certificates for the following degrees:

Master of Arts
Bachelor of Philosophy
Master of Letters

In early 1981, I started reading Douglas Hofstadter's big new book *Gödel, Escher, Bach: An Eternal Golden Braid.* It seemed mad! I was glad to be planted anew in physics (albeit temporarily – I was merely deputizing for an indisposed incumbent).

Unemployed again later in 1981, I moved back to Poole. There I typed out a quick autobiography based on my diaries. As a total of 500 typescript pages slowly piled up, I reflected philosophically on the chequered course my life was taking.

My mental life was still far too volatile to entertain thoughts of settling down meekly. Among my philosophical acquaintances, Hidé Ishiguro was intriguing. Her Japanese upbringing had not hindered her from lecturing with impressive poise on British and German philosophy. I read novels by Yukio Mishima and thought about Zen (prompted in part by Robert Pirsig's novel, as well as John and Yoko).[8] Through a small ad in the education supplement of *The Guardian*, I found a job teaching English in Japan. Hidé acted as my sponsor for the Japanese work permit.

1981–1987

In summer 1981, on the day Charles and Diana got married in Westminster Abbey, I stood in the crowd and watched them ride past in an open carriage. I was with a Chinese girl who had studied physics with me that year. Hours later, I was at Heathrow airport for my flight to Japan.

For a year, I taught English as a Foreign Language at the Green English Conversation School, based in Shizuoka City, Japan. It was a psychedelic year, with a daylight clarity that bleached away the murkier parts of the formalistic logic that still rattled in my head. As last rites for that logic, I read Hofstadter's book carefully in my *tatami* room during a heat wave, with drops of sweat falling on the pages. I was left in no doubt that it did a better job of dramatizing the philosophical aspects of mathematical logic than my own logical trilogy.

Freed of that, I went to the local bookstore and bought all three volumes of the Feynman Lectures on Physics, then went back to my apartment and read them from beginning to end, as I should have done in 1970 already.

Japan was the perfect backdrop for this. I was brought back to my senses, to a world of clean outlines, new machines, bright colors, and smart people. It was all very different from London. I drove around in a small Subaru, befriended several local girls, and had fun trying to learn the language.

But my plan to write a novel – or rather, as I said to myself, to buy an Olivetti and type out some alphabetti spaghetti – didn't convince me. After a year of ignoring it, I read my autobiography. It was really bad. I was freed from its grip by a wonderful Japanese girl, who energized me enough to trash the script.

Refreshed, I returned to England in the summer of 1982 to start again. Getting a job is not always easy, and I had to wait a while, reading more physics and writing notes for a novel about Japan. I started writing a sci-fi novel but its guiding idea soon unraveled.

In January 1983, I started work as a tutor of Advanced-level physics and mathematics for Lansdowne Tutors, a small college based in London. For the first 18 months I worked as a housemaster at their residential campus in Woking, southwest of London, where an élite group of Iraqi military cadets (embarrassing to say) were being given a fast-track education, no expense spared, under the terms of a deal between the British government and the government of Saddam Hussein. But it was a golden opportunity for me to consolidate my physics.

In the summer of 1984, I moved back to London, as a housemaster at the Lansdowne college in Kensington, where a group of undergraduates from Florida were getting the star treatment. During the day job with A-level students from all over the globe, I was in charge of the physics lab, and set up lots of fascinating toys to keep my classes bubbling. Then I moved to the Lansdowne dormitory in Notting Hill Gate, with more Americans. It was a pleasure to serve as their housemaster as I watched them adjust awkwardly to the strictures of London life.

In early 1986, to become more independent, I moved to a bleak bedsit in Crouch End in east London, where the twin disasters of Challenger and Chernobyl seemed to fit my mood as I began to work out some novel ideas. In the summer, in nice rooms in Putney in southwest London, on a Canon typewriter with a one-page electronic memory, I typed a script combining a sketchy autobiography and some lightweight philosophy in a novel entitled *Made in Japan*. Not good enough, as a series of publishers politely told me. Back to the drawing board.

Teaching the same old syllabus each year was getting boring. Time for something new. In the second quarter of 1987, to have a fresh record of my academic standing, I sat the U.S. Graduate Record Examination in London:

Test	Score	Percentile
Verbal	790	99
Quantitative	800	99
Analytical	700	92
Physics	890	94

Soon after, I was offered the financed opportunity to study for a Ph.D. at Stanford University in California, but just a few days before the offer arrived I had accepted a job in Heidelberg, Germany.

1987–1998

In June 1987, I moved to Germany. I've been here ever since. I started work as the promotion editor for physics and economics books and journals at the academic publisher Springer-Verlag based in Heidelberg. I was responsible for promoting new products by planning and writing brochures and newsletters and serving at conference exhibitions. The products were mostly in English, but at work we spoke German. I studied German in evening classes at the local *Volkshochschule*. In mid-1988, I was awarded the ICC/Goethe Institut Zertifikat *Deutsch als Fremdsprache* with the top grade (*sehr gut*).

Over Christmas/New Year 1988–89, I traveled to New York to see the sights. I stayed in a smart penthouse apartment on the lower East Side, caretaking for a lady who was off with her family. Among the other delights, such as a visit to the local Springer-Verlag offices in the Flatiron building, I enjoyed the view from the top of the World Trade Center and bought a lot of books. The trip reminded me that promoting European physics books was not yet the culmination of my ambitions. In 1989, I published an article titled "Springer's Tower of Power" in the Springer New York magazine *Springboard*.

Later in 1989, within Springer-Verlag, I moved to the computer science editorial department. There, essentially as a copy editor, I helped academic authors and editors to get their books together. This was mostly a matter of language and presentation, though sometimes I could do more and help sort out tricky technical details. The work was satisfying and the environment pleasant. I stayed in the department for almost a decade, until I left Springer at the end of 1998. My senior colleague in the department was Dr. Hans

Wössner, who had studied at the Munich Institute of Technology under Professor Dr. Dr. h.c. mult. Friedrich L. Bauer.

I decided to write a big book of my own, a novel, spurred in part by the Turner Tomorrow Award with its $500,000 prize – a big enough target. That summer I wrote a short novel called *Lifeball – A New Age Romance*, and entered it. It didn't even win a mention. I rewrote it in 1992. It was still not enough to impress the friends who read it.

In 1991, I published "The Globall Hyperatlas – a development proposal" in the Computer Graphics Society journal *The Visual Computer*. This was an idea for an electronic globe consisting of a fixed glass sphere mounted like a lightbulb on a baseplate and covered on the inside with a few million pixels. Online, and with a trackball remote control and the right software, it would show interactive real-time images of the Earth from space or thematic global maps with a zoom feature for close-ups and drilldowns.

One of my projects in this period was to complete and edit the translation of Konrad Zuse's autobiographical book *The Computer – My Life*. Zuse was a fascinating figure who designed and built some of the first-ever digital computers during the most chaotic and dangerous days of the Third Reich and then built up his own computer company in the postwar years.

From 1992, I managed and desk-edited new proceedings volumes in the NATO ASI Series F on computer and systems sciences, which included the NATO Special Programme on Advanced Educational Technology.

During this period, I worked on my novel *Lifeball*. I now wrote using Microsoft Word on a Macintosh LCII with a laser printer. In 1993, I wrote a blockbuster 800-page draft. It had sixteen binary-numbered chapters, each with sixteen sections, as well as diagrams, notes, references, even an index. Each chapter took as its *leitmotif* a different scientific or philosophical discipline. Into the story I packed complex philosophical discussions, an intriguing Japanese romance, some carefully calibrated sex, a hero trying to write a book, a political subplot complete with an air strike, high jinks with giant computers, and contact with an extraterrestrial intelligence for good measure. I called it *Lifeball – Proceedings and Prophecies on Planet Earth* and made sixteen hardback copies to impress agents and publishers. But they weren't impressed.

I tried again. In 1994, I edited it down to some 500 pages and improved the style. Out went the numbered sections, the diagrams, the notes, the references, the index. In came a massively juiced-up plot and more credible characters. I called it *Lifeball – Birth of a New God* and made fifty paperback copies. Some people read it and said good things, but without great enthusiasm. A New

York agent enthused at first, then lost all courage as the rejections trickled in. She gave up on it in early 1995.

In mid-1995, to media fanfare, Martin Amis published his next big novel, *The Information*, a comic story about the literary rivalry of two novelists with a shared past. One of them, the wimp of the pair, has unaccountably struck lucky and now boasts extravagant wealth and fame. The other remains a flop who can't get his books published.

I was spurred to revise *Lifeball* one last time, to create the 432-page paperback edition that appeared in 1996. This version was yet more tuned, trimmed, and turbocharged.[9] A flatteringly enthusiastic and professional New York agent tried her best to place it for a while, but again to no avail. Now the full text is posted on my website, for free, and I've learned to be philosophical about the project.

Leaving aside the whole story of my romance with philosophical fiction, perhaps the high point of my time at Springer was the work over several years in collaboration with Professor Friedrich Bauer in Munich on his book *Decrypted Secrets – Methods and Maxims of Cryptology* (1997).

All this work with scientific ideas and academic publications reawakened my interest in professional philosophy. I realized that the fallow years had allowed my own ideas to grow far enough to be worth following. At the suggestion of Springer author Alwyn Scott, I participated at the Brain and Self Workshop held in Elsinore, Denmark, in August 1997, as part of the conference series "Toward a Science of Consciousness" sponsored by the Department of Consciousness Studies at the University of Arizona. It was a revelation – I was hooked.[10]

As the next step, in 1998 I joined the Association for the Scientific Study of Consciousness (ASSC), and participated at the next ASSC conference, "The Neural Correlates of Consciousness," held in Bremen, Germany, in June 1998. There I met David Chalmers for the first time, and found he was quite charismatic by philosophical standards.

The Springer directors did not take up my passionate offer to focus on books and journals devoted to consciousness studies. I used my interest in computers and computing to land a documentation job at SAP, which was and is one of the biggest success stories in the German business scene.

1999–2009

In January 1999, I reported for work at SAP AG, in Walldorf, Germany. I was hired as an information developer in a department called Technical Core

Competence (TCC) and was responsible, together with a few others, for editing, translating, writing, and coordinating technical documentation.

In April 2000, I took time off work to attend the conference Toward a Science of Consciousness, held in Tucson, Arizona. This was a magical experience, from the inbound flight via Dallas over the sunlit Midwest to the return flight via Chicago with a bagful of souvenirs. The conference events were of variable quality, as you might expect, but the best were excellent. University of Arizona philosophy professor David Chalmers was the master of ceremonies and the presiding genius of the whole conference series. To mark the end of the gig, he invited us all to an "End of Consciousness" party at his spread outside the city. It was a lot of fun.[11]

Later in 2000, I moved with SAP Support to the new company campus at St. Leon-Rot, a ten-minute drive south of Walldorf. Amid idyllic scenery, beside a tournament golf course, I focused on preparing training materials for courses held at the adjacent SAP University.

The work was interesting and I took numerous training courses myself. In 2001, I became a certified support engineer and began to conduct remote EarlyWatch Check sessions for paying customers. I learned to handle the SAP tools for technical authors and editors, and to maintain online content in the company intranet.

In August 2001, I attended the next Toward a Science of Consciousness conference, held in Skövde, Sweden. I drove to this one, in my 1998 Honda Accord, over the new bridge linking Denmark to Sweden. The conference site was in a self-contained hotel on top of a hill.[12] Among the highlights of the conference for me were conversations with Peter Farleigh, Scott Hagan, Basil Hiley, Susan Greenfield, and Ted Honderich. I delivered my own talk in a twenty-minute slot sandwiched between the first and second halves of a dramatic reading of a long poem putting into suitably direct words what it was like to be a pig (I guess the organizers regarded this as a brave attempt to contradict Thomas Nagel's claim that we can't imagine being bats). Also at the conference was a charming Swedish lady with whom I socialized in Stockholm, Heidelberg, Prague, London, and Oxford.

In April 2002, I attended the next Toward a Science of Consciousness conference, again at Tucson, Arizona. After the T2K event, this could only be an anticlimax, but it was a good one. I presented a poster, although its contents left David Chalmers, Stuart Hameroff, and many others puzzled. The Poetry Slam featured a winning verse entitled "Microtubules – My Ass" and Dave's "End of Consciousness" party featured (for me) a friendly Valley girl. Soon after my return, I wrote a review of recent books by Ted Honderich and

Colin McGinn.[13]

At SAP in 2002, I took an active role in the creation of a new series of online "learning maps" designed to enable consultants to train themselves on new releases of SAP products using a mixture of multimedia materials.

In September, I moved from a small apartment in a crowded suburb near Heidelberg to a large apartment in a village on the west bank of the Rhine, sharing a house with an American SAP colleague and her family. My new company car was a BMW 3-series sports coupé, so the autobahn commute to SAP was quite fast.

Also in September 2002, I took time off work to attend the conference "The Self: From Soul to Brain," organized by the New York Academy of Sciences and held at the Mount Sinai School of Medicine in New York. I was sufficiently inspired by this event to write a very detailed review of the proceedings for the *Journal of Consciousness Studies*.[14]

In 2003, I started work as a developer in SAP, now back in Walldorf, on intelligent search and classification tools and technology, and on new ideas for the Semantic Web such as the ontology language OWL.

In July, I attended my next consciousness conference, this one entitled "Towards a Science of Consciousness: Between Phenomenology and Neuroscience" and held in Prague, capital of the Czech Republic. There I met Johnjoe McFadden – we kept in touch for long afterwards. I also enjoyed a nice conversation with Arthur Piper, who invited me to write a brief essay "Business at the Speed of Evolution" for one of his journals.[15]

In September, I went as an SAP delegate to the conference DC-2003 on Dublin Core metadata held in Seattle. The conference program included a pleasant formal dinner at Microsoft in Redmond.

In November, I presented a version of my *Mindworlds* lecture to my SAP colleagues, who gave it a good reception. Buoyed by this success, and also by having just found something new to say on the physics of consciousness, I wrote the essay that became chapter 10 in this book.

In early 2004, I discovered that the Templeton Foundation was holding a big competition for essays on "the power of purpose" – a theme I could relate to rather readily. My entry became chapter 11 in this book.[16]

In May 2004, I spent a week at a fine hotel in New York City, courtesy of SAP. A colleague from my SAP team and I served as SAP delegates for the thirteenth World Wide Web conference. There I exchanged a few words with Tim Berners-Lee and redoubled my enthusiasm for the Semantic Web revolution. But just as our conference was winding down in a confusion of backpacks, farewells, and mass munching of packed lunches, it was utterly upstaged by the Daytime Emmy Awards ceremony in the same hotel – crowds of flawless babes in ball gowns and tanned celebs in tuxedos, swathes of pink carpet, dazzling lights and big cameras down through the lobby, then police-cordoned and red-carpeted paths through several city blocks lined with shrieking fans down to Radio City. I quickly changed from grunge to white shirt and black suit and mingled smoothly with the happy throng.

In July, SAP sent me on two more business trips. In early July I traveled with two of my colleagues from SAP Walldorf to the SAP Labs in Atlanta, Georgia, to deliver a training course to our American colleagues on search technology. My teaching experience and consciousness workouts had given me pretty good skills for this sort of assignment, even though my grasp of the technology itself was patchy. Two weeks later, another SAP Walldorf colleague and I traveled to Sheffield, England, as delegates to the 27th annual international ACM Special Interest Group conference on research and development in information retrieval (SIGIR).

In August I enjoyed a traditionally relaxed seaside vacation in Poole and Bournemouth. I was so overjoyed by Roger Penrose's new book *The Road to Reality* that I immediately dropped other plans and devoted many days on end to reading it intensively.[17] That gave me the thoughts developed in chapter 12 of this book.

In 2004, I published my works so far on the theme of consciousness as an online book – the first edition of *Mindworlds*. That edition had the subtitle "Consciousness and related studies". For a few years it was available for download as a PDF document from my website. But its only added value relative to this second edition is its inclusion of four essays that are frankly not very interesting from a scientific perspective.[18]

I buckled down to serious work at SAP. In 2005 I worked hard on the introduction of my team's new flagship product, which soon became known as the SAP NetWeaver Business Intelligence Accelerator. This work caught my imagination and crowded out consciousness for a while.

In 2006, I attended the tenth ASSC conference at St. Anne's College in Oxford. This was my swansong conference on consciousness (prior to this book) and a sentimental return to the college where I had taught philosophy thirty years earlier. Highlights of the conference for me were satisfying conversations with Daniel Dennett, David Rosenthal, and David Edelman. Another good conversion, with Claude Pasquini in the Pitt Rivers Museum, I forgot until his conference report in the *JCS* prompted me to write the essay in chapter 15 of this book. I drove to the conference in my BMW and endured first-hand Oxford's grudging accommodation of cars.

Also in 2006, I read Dan Dennett's fine book *Breaking the Spell* and then Sam Harris' polemical manifesto on religion, *The End of Faith*. In fact, the latter book galvanized me.

Starting on January 1, 2007, and continuing to summer 2008, I blogged actively on the *On Faith* web forum hosted by the *Washingon Post* and *Newsweek*, where the threads that caught my attention trailed from target articles by Sam Harris. Soon, too, I blogged on Sam Harris' own new web forum, in part with the same interlocutors, and generated a buzz of interest around my own views.

In 2007 and 2008, I also put some effort into my SAP work, still in the team I joined in 2003. This effort culminated in my book *SAP NetWeaver BI Accelerator*, published at the end of 2008 by SAP Press as volume 42 in their SAP Essentials series.[19]

In the summer of 2008, I compiled all my posts on religion into a book format and saw that it had a coherent didactic shape. The script became yet another of my draft books, *Godblogs*.[20]

In 2009, I saw that my 2004 online collection *Mindworlds* was in serious need of a major upgrade. Hence this second edition, which is so greatly tuned and buffed in comparison to the first edition that it finally seems worth publishing on paper.

Fundamentals of Consciousness

Abstract

A new model of consciousness with deep roots in logic and physics is sketched. The first-person phenomenology of consciousness is given a temporal structure using a constructive logic of ontico-epistemic advance through a monotonic series of centered possible worlds. Physically, consciousness is seen as the phenomenal manifestation of the ongoing crystalization of a determinate ontic landscape into a localized past from a flux of future possibilities by an infinite series of quantum jumps. The model offers a novel perspective on the "hard problem" of explaining first-person consciousness.

Introduction

The Borg

The recent science-fiction movie *Star Trek – First Contact* featured an evil empire called the Borg with a collective mind. The Borg assimilated civilizations and their members into its collective cybernetic consciousness by injecting the member organisms with nanotechnological devices that hijacked their minds and grew prosthetic interfaces to plug into the Borg mind.

Good harmless fun, perhaps, but it raises some serious issues. Nanotechnological implants designed to interface with the implantee's consciousness, such as artificial retinas, will likely be developed in coming decades. As the sophistication and power of such devices increase, they will serve an increasing variety of purposes and create new possibilities. For example, if the axons in the corpus callosum connecting the cerebral hemispheres were spliced to artificial fibers and multiplexers, then the interhemispheric traffic could be copied and fed into an observer's brain, to achieve a depth and intimacy of access to the contents of a person's mind that philosophers have long maintained was the privilege of that person alone.

We need to understand whether, and, if so, how, future technology can enable us to transmit conscious experience directly from brain to brain. Such technology could allow us to plug arbitrarily many brains together, or link them via radio waves, in order to share their experiences – qualia – without first filtering them through the public apparatus of audio-visual images or other media.

More speculatively, a person's intercerebral signals might be not merely tapped but processed in some way in a computer and then fed back into that person's brain. We might be able to share qualia with a computer, or download our thoughts onto memory chips, or create autonomous machine minds. This may allow people to benefit in new ways from computers – at the cost of new risks. Looking deeper into the future, it may become routine for connected or implanted computers to augment or enhance numerous brain functions in healthy people.

The Borg is still science fiction, but the conceptual issues involved in these other future scenarios deserve immediate examination. We need to clarify our ideas about consciousness before we can develop the technology to manipulate it.

The Hard Problem

The phenomenon of consciousness can only become a proper object of scientific investigation when it is given an objective, empirically based definition that we can accept as a substitute for our subjective phenomenological knowledge of our own consciousness. To get started at all, we need to adopt a preliminary definition of consciousness, if only a simple ostension or enumeration of paradigm cases in which it is instantiated.

Here a mere sentence must suffice. We all recognize the phenomenon of consciousness in our own first-person (1P) case, and are readily able to attribute consciousness to other people in 2P and 3P cases, so both its instantiation in humans, at least, and its more obvious properties, such as its association with the waking state and with the brain, need not be doubted.

In due course, too, the evident contrast between 1P, 2P, and 3P manifestations of consciousness must be examined. Each conscious person builds an edifice of conceptual thought on the foundations of 1P consciousness, and this edifice effectively separates the mental life of that person from the mental lives of other people.

The 1P experience of consciousness, or rather of the succession of qualia that make up the contents of consciousness, appears on the face of it to be both incorrigible and essentially inaccessible to other persons. These features of 1P experience constitute a deep problem. The intractability of the 1P case is what David Chalmers calls the "hard problem" of consciousness.[1]

The main goal of this paper is to take a step toward solving the problem.

Logic

The phenomenon of consciousness is experienced as prior to logic. The truth or falsity of propositional assertions about conceptual structures discerned in the qualia sets that constitute the contents of consciousness is a secondary issue. It only arises when the qualia are channeled and shaped by brain processes that come into play after those qualia have been accepted at face value as phenomenal input. The phenomenology of consciousness is parasitic in this sense upon the raw qualia. Conversely, the 1P nature of qualia renders them philosophically problematic. Daniel Dennett even argues for denying their existence altogether,[2] and remaining sceptical about 1P consciousness until it has been so thoroughly restructured by 2P or 3P "heterophenomenological" processes that the 1P case seems like a kind of fiction.

The raw qualia reflected in the autophenomenology of 1P consciousness remain inaccessible to other persons in such fiction. Qualia appear in 1P but not 2P or 3P manifestations of consciousness. Cultural transmission of phenomenal forms shapes the consciousness of others by indirect means. This gives rise to the philosophical problem of other minds: only by analogy can a conscious subject infer that other apparently conscious subjects enjoy strictly equivalent qualia. Hence the solipsistic predicament: it is possible in principle that I am the only 1P experiencer in the entire universe.

Four Axioms

The logic behind the solipsistic predicament should, if possible, be systematized in a way that leaves room for the extension of subjectivity to 2P and 3P cases. The first logical axiom we need to build up such a system is due to Wittgenstein:[3]

I am my world. (1)

This axiom says that, at the global level, modeling the external world requires reflecting it in subjectivity, so that the reflection as a whole is identified with the world. The boundaries of that world and the identification of phenomenally prominent features of that world with subjectively defined entities are matters for detailed scientific analysis, but the identification for each conscious subject of that world as a whole with the reflecting subject is not negotiable. It is a precondition for the possibility of analysis. A subject can only be treated as a rational subject when that subject's identity with its objectivity is accepted. In Newtonian terms, subject and object are equal and opposite. In Kantian terms, the transcendental ego reflects the transcendental object (*Ding an sich*), where that reflection is mediated by the categorial structure imposed upon the phenomenal manifold. Axiom (1) implies that the subject reflects its subject on an ontic level as well as an epistemic one.

The second axiom is also essentially due to Wittgenstein:[4]

My world is the totality of facts, not of things. (2)

Facts must have a subjective impact, like qualia but unlike things (which can have the metaphysical property of existing independently of the subject). The set of facts constituting a world defines a subject, the subject for whom those are the facts. The facts are synthesized into a structured unity by the subject. In Kantian terms, the 1P phenomenal manifold is unified under the categories in the synthetic unity of apperception.

We need to recognize that both subject and object evolve, either in or out of step with each other. The logic of this evolution requires that we define a fundamental dimension along which the unidirectional process of mutual accommodation of subject and object may accumulate complexity in a stepwise fashion. The third axiom introduces this logical dimension:

My world unfolds in time. (3)

The world reflected by the conscious subject changes with every passing moment of experience, and the dimension along which it unfolds is experienced as time. The moments of experienced time may be identified with the momentary stages in the development or unfolding of the world reflected in consciousness.

Logically, consciousness evolves along an epistemo-ontic dimension. The epistemic progess of the reflecting subject is complemented by comprehension of progressively larger ontic domains: the series of domain views appears to the subject to unfold and ramify in complexity as time passes. In this conception, there is a mutual accommodation of ontology and epistemology. As the conscious subject endures, history gets longer not merely epistemically but also ontically. More determinacy is reflected in the external world, and the world unfolds to give spatiotemporal location to the new determinacy.

The psychological aspect of consciousness introduces complications into this simple logical picture. The external world reflected in 1P consciousness may be seen as a subset of the public world recognized by the physical sciences. As the experience of a conscious subject unfolds, so the subset of the physical world reflected in consciousness increases. (We ignore the complications induced by forgetting, which we can model without sacrificing the monotonicity of unfolding by representing it as the 1P manifestation of fuzzification, whereby fine detail is for practical purposes lost to entropy.) The 1P phenomenal world unfolds as the subject evolves within the 3P physical world by enduring in public, physical time.

The unfolding of the external world is not a smooth process. Each conscious view of the world is a static freeze-frame, and the jump to the next view is a relocation. Each view is closed – it is realized as totality by the reflecting subject – and hence is contradicted by the next view. New facts emerge to falsify old claims to totality. As an axiom:

Each worldview contradicts its predecessors. (4)

When a conscious subject takes a worldview to be the truth and acts accordingly, the option of awaiting possible falsifying input is temporarily closed off. When new facts enter the picture, the result is a contradiction resolved only by reconceiving the totality.

The resulting dialectic of epistemology and ontology is an evolutionary process: each worldview is reproduced from its predecessor with whatever variation is needed to fit the new facts. Indeed, several candidate worldviews could compete at each stage and a survival-of-the-fittest algorithm could pick the winner.

This process of endless revision recalls Dennett's "multiple drafts" model of the running narrative behind consciousness.[5]

Intuitionist Logic

The problem of the deep entanglement of epistemology and ontology – that we are not free to posit entities that transcend all possible means of knowing about them – has long been recognized in mathematics and logic. The 19th century mathematician Kronecker was a passionate advocate of the constructivist perspective. His views were taken further in the 20th century by L. E. J. Brouwer, who proposed a deep revision of logic that led to the intuitionist movement.[6] Intuitionist ideas have since been adopted and generalized in constructive mathematics.[7]

Intuitionist logic is motivated by denial of the validity of the law of excluded middle (for all propositions *p*, *p* or not *p*) in cases where no means exist to prove or disprove a proposition. Given the problem of skirting the paradoxes of self-reference in logic and mathematics, and especially the existence of undecidable Gödel sentences for any formal systems powerful enough to express elementary arithmetic, the case for denial is strong.[8]

Formalized, intuitionistic logic generates a tree, whose nodes are epistemic situations, each reflecting an ontic state of affairs. Progress from node to node in the tree corresponds to acceptance of new axioms or proofs. Generalized to the logic of consciousness, the nodes correspond to experiential states, or qualia sets, or states of affairs, or totalities of facts, and the advance from node to node corresponds to comprehension of new facts via apperception of the new qualia sets.

Saul Kripke gave a formal semantics for intuitionistic logic that proved it to be isomorphic to a system of modal logic.[9] In terms of his semantics for modal logic, among the set of possible worlds is the actual world, but the actual world does not stay fixed. It becomes momentarily identical with a succession of different possible worlds as time passes.

In this view, worlds that are candidates to become the actual world are centered on the reflecting subject. The actual, centered world, whose poles are the Kantian transcendental ego and its object, evolves logically through a series of phenomenal manifestations that can be modeled as nodes in a tree of possible worlds.

The relation of accessibility between worlds that says which future worlds are accessible from the actual world is hard to describe for worldview dialectics in the logic of consciousness. Each worldview must survive as a dated fragment in later views, so the accumulation of truths is monotonic, but former truths must also be relativized or subsumed as special cases in order not to contradict new truths. The question is complicated and technical.

Physics

Classical physics implicitly presupposes a transcendental perspective. It makes no explicit mention of a reflecting subject, yet an implicit subject is easy to see in absolute Newtonian space and time as a preferred frame of reference. The subject of Newtonian physics may be said to be the Kantian transcendental ego.

In relativity theory, the subject becomes more explicit. The spatiotemporal location of the subject defines a past light cone that embraces all events that can have a causal influence on events at that location: around the subject is a light horizon that defines the causal boundary of the physical universe. Beyond this positional role, however, the subject remains causally inactive.

Quantum Ideas

Quantum physics complicates the picture. The experimenting observer interacts with physical reality by taking measurements in a given experimental setup. The observer not only has a spatiotemporal location but also acts causally by choosing which properties of a system to measure. The wave–particle duality of quantum phenomena (those for which Planck's constant h is significant) implies that experimental choices give rise to an ontic complementarity, not merely an epistemic one. (Heisenberg's uncertainty relations are facts about physical systems, not merely about our knowledge of them, hence they have ontological as well as epistemological meaning.)

Choosing which experiments to perform amounts to choosing a path through a branching tree of possible scenarios. The observer follows a timelike path through the tree and occupies a succession of possible worlds. As Niels Bohr put it, an act of measurement or observation is an irreversible amplification of a quantum process, that is, a time-asymmetric jump to a new situation.[10]

Quantum systems exist in superpositions of states in which each state has a certain amplitude. When an experimental outcome is consistent with several of the states in a superposition, the probability of that outcome is calculated by squaring the sum of the amplitudes of the states. The states can interfere, as in the classic two-slits experiment. When several outcomes are possible, each pointing uniquely to one state, their combined probability is calculated by summing the squares of the amplitudes of the respective states. Without superposition, there is no interference. Thus whether the states are superposed or distinguished by a measurement makes a big difference.[11]

A phenomenal world in which certain states are indistinguishable is symmetrical with respect to those states. Choosing to distinguish those states, that is, jumping to a world in which one of them becomes amplified, breaks that symmetry irreversibly, since it changes the wave function for the system.

A centered phenomenal world is symmetrical with respect to all possible future continuations of that world and to all possible quantum states that may be superposed beneath its phenomenal surface. It is also symmetrical with respect to fine classical detail that may be discerned in later worlds. Such detail can give rise to chaotic effects: if parameter x is known to ten decimal places in this world, for example, and a difference in the twelfth decimal place causes all the difference between two contrasting possible future worlds A and

B, then this world is symmetrical between A and B, and measuring x to twelve decimal places breaks that symmetry.

The succession of states manifested by a physical system represents an ontico-epistemic advance through a tree of possible worlds. Each jump from a state to a successor state represents a change in the objective domain recognized by the experimenting subject and a corresponding change in the subject. Subject and object are complementary in the sense that they reflect each other at each stage in the evolution of the system. The subject is an experienced succession of phenomenal manifestations (qualia sets), whereas the object is a physical system undergoing a series of changes in its determinations.

A subject–object pair has a spatiotemporal location that may be more or less extended and more or less sharply bounded. Its temporal location defines the "now" of the subject, which has an extension and fuzziness that depends on the ontic granularity of the system representing the pair. On this view, the future of a given system is indeterminate, and becomes progressively more determinate as its "now" evolves through a series of states, whereas the past states of the system retain their determinacy, and remain contradictory to counterfactual states. (Again, we assume for simplicity that forgetting can be handled somehow.)

Consciousness Transforms

A more concrete metaphor for the conscious subject may help fix ideas. Imagine that inside the subject is a mirrored ball that reflects not merely visual images but also all the categorial structure discerned in the phenomenal manifold. All the input of which the subject is conscious is reflected in the image formed by the ball.

The image is generally a nontrivial transformation of the input. To pursue the visual metaphor, it may be not only geometrically distorted but also colored or shaded in a time-dependent way. We can imagine the ball changing its shape or surface continuously, throwing off a dazzling stream of images to enthrall the subject. The output from the ball is applied by the subject to act in the external world. The input and output of the reflection are related, let us say, by the *consciousness transforms*.

The mirrored ball's input and output are complementary; indeed, they would be trivially equal and opposite were it not for the complications induced by the consciousness transforms. Given those transforms, the complementarity manifests itself as the amenability of physical reality to categorial unification. That we can build physical theories that work, and continue to work, shows how tight the coupling is between input and output via the consciousness transforms. In terms of the visual metaphor again, the underlying harmony of input and output reveals itself as the transparency of the physical world to the light of pure reason.

Coherent States

Consciousness manifests itself as the inner transparency of a world of objects that reveals their articulation and the structures and relations they form. The physics of a system with such inner transparency is generally nonclassical – consider for example the quantum electrodynamics of reflection and transmission of light by glass.[12] Analogously, explaining consciousness may require appeal to the quantum nature of physical systems realizing it.[13]

One candidate for such a quantum substrate for consciousness is a Bose–Einstein condensate, which is the coherent state realized by the photons in a laser beam or the current-carrying electrons in a superconductor. It seems conceivable that such a condensate could be formed in a living brain by decahertz photons (such as the 40 Hz waves that apparently serve to synchronize neural firings) or gigahertz photons (for example, the microwaves in cytoplasm that, as Roger Penrose speculates, may be related to microtubules).[14]

However, the physics of consciousness is still wide open. Penrose has suggested that a theory of quantum gravity may be needed to explain consciousness.[15] Earlier he said: "Any world in which minds can exist must be organized on principles far more subtle and beautifully controlled than those even of the magnificent physical laws that have so far been uncovered."[16]

Psychology

The living human brain often sustains consciousness. No physical instantiation of (2P or 3P) consciousness in any system other than a living mammalian brain has yet been observed. It may even be the case that some hitherto unknown physical process only instantiated by the electrochemical stimulation of cerebral neuronets is necessary for a centered world to manifest itself to itself in the kind of synthetic unity we would recognize as 1P consciousness.

John Searle is well known for maintaining such a view.[17] He argues that the living brain generates "intentionality," which gives rise to our ability to convey semantics by means of syntax. By contrast, a computer can only manipulate syntax blindly.

The model sketched in this paper, whereby epistemological syntax confronts ontological semantics in an ongoing dialectic, is defined in terms that a computer could handle, in principle, yet incorporates semantics. Searle's argument fails to rule out machines with minds.

Hence, it may be physically possible for consciousness to be instantiated in an electronic configuration in a computer or a network, or even in a plasma field in a star, or in the superfluid neutronium in a pulsar. These questions are still open.

Personal Consciousness

A prior question concerns the contrast between 1P, 2P, and 3P consciousness. The 1P case is the special case, since it suffices to ground logic and physics as outlined above. The 3P case is the general case, of interest to psychologists and other scientists interested in how consciousness is instantiated in objectively given systems, such as animals, computers, or stars. The 2P case may perhaps be seen as transitional, allowing an initially solipsistic subject to perform a first leap from the 1P case to the natural and easy 2P case, and only then to induce more widely to 3P cases. The phenomenal contrast between the 1P and other cases is not lessened by this induction, but the pragmatic contrast, in human social life at least, soon becomes relatively trivial for a normally socialized person.

The phenomenology of consciousness is paradigmatically 1P. Qualia are 1P. We learn what it is to be conscious from the 1P case, then attribute analogous states in 2P and 3P cases on the basis of behavioral or other physical evidence. But only after we have taken this step can we be said to understand the concept of *personal* consciousness. Only after we have learned to see it reflected in the 2P case (prototypically in the mother or in siblings, for example) can we know what it means in the 1P case. A subject recognizing only 1P consciousness is solipsistic. Such a subject can pursue logic and physics unhindered, but it will not have the concept of a person (in this sense the term 1P – first person – is a bit of a misnomer).

It is altogether conceivable that 1P qualia could manifest themselves in a synthetic unity, even within a human brain, without thereby generating a person. However, if such a manifestation occurs in a human brain, its owner's pragmatic intercourse in the everyday human world of embodied, personal consciousness will soon inculcate a superficial skill at making 2P and 3P attributions of consciousness. Yet the history of philosophy from Descartes to Chalmers shows that this is consistent with an underlying solipsistic mindset.

Evolution of Consciousness

The question of how the distinctions between 1P, 2P, and 3P consciousness evolved in humans can be distinguished from that of how any kind of consciousness evolved in earlier creatures. Some form of 1P consciousness may be a feature of quite primitive life, and may well arise naturally from Darwinian evolution between neural groups in the growing brain.[18]

Such consciousness may be relatively easy to implement in an artificial neuronet using modern genetic algorithms. Perhaps the hardest part would be to convince ourselves that the neuronet really did have qualia.

By contrast, the evolution of the full glory of personal consciousness seems to involve advanced culture. Julian Jaynes gives a vivid picture of how 2P and 3P consciousness in the modern sense developed from 1P consciusness in early human history, as recorded in the Bible and similar documents.[19]

Philosophy

Chalmers argues that human zombies could have evolved to display the sort of skills that would normally prompt us to attribute 2P or 3P consciousness to them, yet not in fact possess 1P consciousness. Bizarre as this may seem, the reasons for its implausibility are hard to express. For it is not the case that the normal grounds for 2P or 3P attributions of consciousness are criterially sufficient for attribution of 1P consciousness. Something more is required.

Morphing

The model of 1P consciousness sketched above suggests a novel solution to this puzzle. There is no obvious reason not to stipulate that 1P consciousness is essentially unique, for 1P consciousness in its purest form is solipsistic and impersonal. Nothing in mathematics or physics compels the subject to be personalized, and nothing stops us from saying that different people can identify in some sense with the *same* subject when they study mathematics or physics.

It is a commonplace that several people can interact with one and the same object. Given that subject and object are equal and opposite, this implies directly that those people can at the same time identify with one and the same subject. To generalize, subjects can reasonably be supposed to stand in the same complex relations to each other as objects do. Subjects can be expected to change, and to suffer change in their identity criteria, just like objects.

This view, developed with a little imagination, makes it natural to say that personal subjectivity is polymorphous. For example, it seems intelligible to say that we morph for a while into the collective mathematico-physical subject when we subject ourselves to those disciplines. In this spirit, the Cambridge mathematician G. H. Hardy once said that all mathematicians were isomorphic, meaning not that their bodies were similar but that their thoughts formed similar patterns.

A popular metaphor for the predicament of the subject in a world of objects is a boat alone in a sea of objectivity. Our interaction in a shared subject extends the metaphor: we all live in the same ship (Spaceship Earth, perhaps) and float on the same sea of qualia. Otto Neurath is credited with the image that we are at sea in a boat that we are rebuilding plank by plank while trying to stay afloat.[20] The ongoing reconstruction of ontology and epistemology in the 1P model sketched here is a natural elaboration of that image.

A solitary and impersonal subject reflecting the categorial unity of the mathematico-physical world recalls a certain concept of God, as held by Spinoza and Einstein. Such a subject, above and beyond the fragmentation of humanity into a contingent plurality of persons, union with which is the shining goal of all who pursue mathematics and physics, also recalls Hawking's hope that we might one day "know the mind of God."[21]

More practically, if personal subjectivity is polymorphic enough to achieve fleeting union with such divine images, there is surely no bar to our projecting our consciousness through technological prostheses of arbitrary size and power, even beyond the planet. Let's hope the Borg doesn't get us first.

Conclusion

A model of the logical form of consciousness has been sketched that tackles the "hard problem" in a new way by inviting the hypothesis that first-person consciousness is essentially unique. This hypothesis has the great merit of guaranteeing the uniqueness of the physical background against which interpersonal psychology may be understood. Relativism of personal belief may thus be reconciled with absolutism about the hard facts of nature.

According to the model, both the logical form and the physical basis of consciousness are consistent with the instantiation of consciousness not only in human beings but also in other systems or bodies. Logically, consciousness is essentially 1P, temporal, and revisionary, and it is only contingently distributed among a plurality of persons. Physically, consciousness is probably some sort of quantum phenomenon.

The model invites the further speculation that scientific activity is directed toward the realization of a single focus of conscious subjectivity. Nothing in the view outlined precludes the eventual sharing or downloading of human consciousness, and nothing outlaws a Borg collective.

Note

The ideas presented here have grown from contemplation of many strands of argument. The basic logical ideas grew from over twenty years of reflection on the works of Kant, Hegel, Frege, Russell, Wittgenstein, Gödel, Quine, Kripke, and others. Detailed references to those works would be out of place here, and indeed the exact lines of influence are hard to trace. Anyway, such history is strictly irrelevant to the coherence of the ideas, which must obviously stand or fall on their own merits.

Consciousness: A Logical Model

Abstract

A formal model for the concept of consciousness is outlined using logic and set theory. The model organizes a phenomenology of qualia into an evolutionary epistemology of centered worlds that supports standard physics. The model involves only minimal assumptions about consciousness, so it is applicable not only to personal consciousness but also to any future machine consciousness.

Introduction

> The job of a science of consciousness, then, is to connect first-person data to third-person data; perhaps to explain the former in terms of the latter, or at least to come up with systematic theoretical connections between the two.
> *David Chalmers* [1]

We need a general model for the concept of consciousness before we can build theoretical foundations for a science of consciousness. The preliminary model suggested by common sense is a useful place to start, but it leads quickly to the problem of deciding how much we can reasonably presuppose. For example, the model David Chalmers has in mind in the above quotation presupposes that we understand the contrast between first-person and third-person data. Arguably, it is one of the tasks of a science of consciousness to explain that contrast, so it is worth looking deeper.

The concept of a person may be understood partly in terms of the ability to serve as a center of consciousness. For this reason, we do better to avoid using the concept of a person in a theory of consciousness. Instead, we can use the more general concept of a subject. The opposite of a subject is an object. In principle, subjects and objects come in pairs: to every subject, there is an equal and opposite object, and vice versa. For practical purposes, however, the vast majority of such pairs are of rather one-sided interest.

Consciousness is a relation between subjects and objects: a given subject is conscious of a domain of objects. Only a relatively tiny number of subjects and objects participate in this relationship, and for those that do participate in it, a more detailed characterization of the relationship may presumably take a variety of forms. But it is essential to the relationship that one subject be conscious of an unspecified number of objects. Also, a conscious subject persists in time. In general, the objects of consciousness may relate to the subject either serially or simultaneously, or both.

The objects of consciousness may be spatiotemporal objects with detailed properties and extensive relations with other objects or they may be degenerate items of immediate experience. Let such items of immediate experience be called *qualia*. If consciousness as humans experience it is always, by definition, consciousness of qualia, it is a difficult and interesting problem to specify the general conditions under which qualia may be further characterized in terms of spatiotemporal location and relations to other objects. David Chalmers calls such characterization of qualia in the "third-person" terms of normal science the "hard problem" of consciousness.[2]

The phenomenology of consciousness is the logical study of how reality seems to a conscious subject. Reality seems like a changing manifold of qualia. The task of phenomenology is to take this initial characterization far enough to connect with the data and laws of normal science. The normal science of human consciousness is modern psychology together with the collection of disciplines known loosely as the brain sciences.[3]

But consciousness is not necessarily human consciousness. The assimilation of the phenomenology of consciousness to the brain sciences presupposes the reductionist premise that consciousness as we understand it is a property or a product of appropriately functioning cerebral tissue. It is not unreasonable to anticipate that this will be an outcome of a future science of consciousness, but it is unreasonable to stipulate it at the outset as an axiom. It is analogous to stipulating a thousand years ago that the task of a future science of astronomy is to explain how the heavenly bodies orbit the Earth.

A future science of consciousness may be expected to explain:

- Personal consciousness. Each and every normally functioning human being is conscious, regularly and routinely. This is the gross fact that any science of consciousness must explain.
- Interpersonal consciousness. Before consciousness is ignited in an organism, the organism may require some special kind of socially mediated personal interaction. Consciousness may be a phenomenon manifested in a

Consciousness: A Logical Model

society of reciprocating organisms but impose only basic requirements on the cerebral architecture of those organisms. If some kind of interaction is essential, a science of consciousness must explain the societal prerequisites.
- Transpersonal consciousness. It is conceivable that human consciousness is able to transcend its personal bounds and experience other lives or oceanic states. It is certain that human consciousness can *seem* to do these things.
- Impersonal consciousness. Subjective consciousness of a domain of objects may be possible independently of persons. Animals lacking the concept of a person may be conscious. Machine consciousness may be developed without recognizable personality.

This chapter outlines a logical model of consciousness that is sufficiently general to accommodate all four of these issues.

Truth unfolds

Subjective consciousness of a domain of objects can be seen to a first approximation as analogous to optical reflection. Images that represent objects in some way are juxtaposed within the unified scene reflected by the subject. The optical medium within which the reflection occurs allows information about the objects to be transmitted by light beams. The information transmitted is limited to those properties that affect the light beams.

In general, we can regard the information about the objects that surfaces in consciousness as giving a logical characterization of those objects. A logical characterization need not be based on optical images. A logical characterization is based on information that we can specify consistently and perhaps completely by means of a suitably defined formal language.

A linguistic specification of the relation between subject and object allows that the conscious reflection of various spatial parts or temporal phases of the objective domain can be true or false. The *epistemic state* of the subject can be specified in terms of a set of statements of the formal language. Let us call the state of the objective domain confronting the subject the *ontic state*. The ontic state may either match or not match the epistemic state of the subject. If and when it matches, the epistemic statements that claim to specify the ontic state are true. Where it does not match, the statements are false.

This soon leads to the elementary logic of the propositional calculus (PC). Propositions that express the epistemic state of a conscious subject are either true or false, depending on how that epistemic state compares with the ontic state confronting the subject. If we use the same formal language to describe both the epistemic and the ontic state, and if that language is a fragment of English, then we can characterize truth using Tarskian theorems of the form:

"Snow is white" is true if and only if snow is white.

Such true propositions express facts. Wittgenstein developed an outline theory of facts in his earlier philosophy.[4]

The ontic state confronting a conscious subject may be called a *world*, where a world is a totality of facts. The epistemic state of a conscious subject may also be represented as a world. Assuming that the subject is in a consistent state, such a world must be *possible*. By contrast, the ontic state confronting the subject may be called the *actual* world. The epistemically possible world reflected in the subject may or may not be identical to the ontically actual world that is being reflected. If they are identical, then everything believed by the subject is true, but in general they will differ.

The linguistic characterization of the actual world is hardly ever perfect, for obvious reasons that defeat any language we can devise. But the linguistic characterization of an epistemically possible world is perfect, by definition. Thus possible worlds are as fundamentally different from the actual world as rational numbers are from real numbers. A diagonal argument shows that the real numbers outrun the rational numbers,[5] and a similar argument, based on a recursion over the sentences of a PC language, shows that the actual world can differ from any epistemically possible world.

Truth and falsity depend on meaning. The sentences of a language can only be classified as bivalent (that is, determinately either true or false) when their meaning has been specified unambiguously. The meaning of propositions can be specified in terms of their truth conditions using Tarskian theorems of the form:

"Snow is white" means that snow is white.

Meaning can only be specified in detail in terms of patterns of usage in the relevant speech communities. Wittgenstein described this anthropological view of meaning in his later philosophy.[6]

The ongoing pursuit of science generates new meanings for old sentences as well as new concepts and new sentences. Meanings change and unfold, and truth assignments grow with them. Thus, any language used in earnest to describe the epistemic course of a conscious subject must admit continuing extensions and revisions of its set of possible epistemic states and of the set of possible ontic states that can corroborate or falsify the propositions asserted by that subject.[7]

In general, the continuing experience of a conscious subject can be described as an ongoing dialectic of epistemology and ontology, where the confrontation of each new epistemic state with the actual world generates falsehoods that are corrected in the next epistemic state. Alternatively, following Daniel Dennett,[8] the conscious subject maintains an ongoing narrative about its role in the world, and this narrative goes through multiple drafts as new experience prompts revisions and reappraisals. In general, truth unfolds in the actual world, and an epistemic subject must keep moving to track it.

Things change

Propositions are linguistic items that can be decomposed into subjects and predicates. Thus analyzed, propositions say of objects that they fall under concepts. They may say that individual objects have certain properties, that sets of objects have certain properties, or that various objects stand in various relations to each other. In each case, the propositions express a movement from an *initial state* to a *final state*. In the initial state, certain existing objects are simply denoted. In the final state, the objects are further specified as having the properties or standing in the relations asserted by the proposition. This movement between epistemic states is what makes a proposition informative.

Typically, a conscious subject whose successive epistemic states are represented by sets of informative propositions continually reidentifies many of the same old objects. New things are said about those objects, and old falsehoods are corrected. But for any objects, certain properties are more essential than others. The essential properties are needed to ensure success in denoting those objects. We can distinguish *names* from *definite descriptions*. Names are rigid designators that continue to track changing objects through modifications of their more essential properties, whereas definite descriptions do not, and instead denote whatever happens to satisfy their descriptive predicates.[9]

The use of names to ensure successful denotation does not obviate the need for objects to have essential or criterial properties, but it does enable us to be more relaxed about their criteriality. Smooth changes can be tracked even when they result eventually in outright contradictions compared with earlier situations. The history of science includes many such contradictions. Scientists can agree on what objects they are talking about even when they disagree on what to say about them.[10]

Denotation can succeed despite changes in the criterial properties of objects. Denotation does succeed routinely as objects accumulate determinacy in the continuing course of epistemic advance. For example, as time passes and new facts come into existence, most objects feature as denotees in larger and larger sets of informative statements.

If things change in this way, complicated propositions about them need to be handled with care. For example, quantified propositions can only be given determinate truth conditions when the domains over which the quantifiers range are specified exactly. Moreover, quantifiers can be hidden in the semantic foundations of simple and apparently unquantified propositions, such as definite descriptions. For this reason, when parsing any propositions that purport to state facts, it is wise to relativize explicitly any quantifiers involved to definite ontic or epistemic states, or at least to impose definite limits on which states may be invoked for those propositions.

The quantificational calculus (QC) extends PC by admitting quantification over a domain of objects. The objects need not all have names in the language. If all the objects in the domain can be named, then PC propositions can be obtained from QC propositions by replacing universal and existential quantifiers thus:

"For all x, $F(x)$" $\Rightarrow$ "$F(a)$ and $F(b)$ and $F(c)$ and ..."

"For some x, $F(x)$" $\Rightarrow$ "$F(a)$ or $F(b)$ or $F(c)$ or ..."

Here a, b, c, ... are the names of all the objects in the domain of quantification and $F(\ )$ is a predicate. Infinite domains of objects cannot all be named in finite languages, or uncountable domains in countable languages, so we need QC in mathematics.[11]

Any conscious subject that wishes to theorize about experience is likely to perform computations that involve serious mathematics. Most mathe-matics that remains less powerful than the arithmetic of natural numbers, for example, the sort of finite math that a pocket calculator can handle, can be represented as tautologies in PC or QC, but the formal theory of arithmetic (AT) already goes beyond pure logic.[12]

The dialectical picture of ontico-epistemic advance presented so far presupposes that each epistemic state is internally consistent. If a state is not consistent, then simple PC computations inside that state can generate complete confusion. However, the consistency of an epistemic state that is closed under AT computations cannot be not guaranteed unconditionally. Such a state runs a tiny but nonzero risk that a contradiction may be generated by apparently valid computation from evidently true premises.

Gödel's incompleteness theorem for AT illustrates the risk.[13] The formal metatheory of AT can be expressed in a simple language based on QC. Gödel coded all the sentences of this language into the natural numbers. The natural numbers form the domain over which the theorems of AT are interpreted, so the Gödel coding allows the sentences of the language of AT to be interpreted as metatheoretic statements about AT. For each sentence s of the metatheory, let s be coded into the Gödel number $G(s)$. Gödel constructed an open AT sentence g with this interpretation in the metatheory:

The sentence with Gödel number $G(s)$ is not a theorem of AT.

Now consider the closed sentence $G(g)$ obtained from $G(s)$ by substituting g for the free variable s. If proposition $G(g)$ is a theorem of AT, then AT is inconsistent. If $G(g)$ is not a theorem of AT, then AT is not complete, since there are truths in the language of AT that are not provable.

Gödel's second incompleteness theorem (based on the first) states that if AT is consistent, the consistency of AT is not provable in AT, but only in another theory, say ET, that extends AT. But the extended theory ET stands more in need of a consistency proof than AT, so nothing is gained.[14]

Gödel's theorems show that there is a residual risk involved in allowing a computing subject to use the full power of AT to manipulate the propositions that constitute an epistemic state. Any ontic domain reflecting such a state includes truths that, if discovered by the subject, can be used to generate contradictions within that state. The subject can always move into new states by accepting sentences like $G(g)$ as axioms in extended theories ET, but then the argument can be applied again to ET. In this way, a series of theories ET can be used to generate an epistemo-ontic dialectic.

Gödel's theorems show that truth outruns provability even in mathematics. More generally, model theory outruns proof theory and ontology outruns epistemology.

Sets cohere

The picture developed here of an open-ended series of logically defined states invites set-theoretic treatment. Subjects and objects can both be represented as sets. The relation between a subject and its objects can be represented (arbitrarily) as the membership relation, so that the sets representing the objects of consciousness are members of the set representing the conscious subject. Successive states of consciousness can be represented as a succession of sets, with some relation between them that we can seek to specify.

Successive momentary determinations of given objects can be represented by successive sets, again with some relation to be specified between them. Ontic states and epistemic states can be represented by sets, and whole dialectics of such states can be represented by infinite series of the corresponding sets.

The strategy of using sets to represent all the entities comprehended in a theory has the merit that mathematical machinery then becomes available to clarify and extend the theory.[15]

The set-theoretic structure that seems suitable for this task is the cumulative hierarchy of pure well-founded sets, which is the natural or intended model of standard systems of axiomatic set theory such as Zermelo–Fraenkel (ZF) set theory.[16] This hierarchy is a mathematical structure analogous to the natural numbers, but much richer and therefore more useful in logic. Just as arithmetic is logic plus the assumption that the natural numbers exist (as defined in the Peano axioms), so set theory is logic plus some assumption about which sets exist (typically formulated as axioms).

Mathematicians developed the cumulative hierarchy as a reaction to the antinomies in naïve set theory discovered by Bertrand Russell and others.[17] The pioneering set theory formalized by Frege allowed sets to be formed as the extensions of any well-defined predicates. Making use of Frege's formal syntax, Russell defined:

$R = \{x \mid x \notin x\}$ (the class of sets x such that x is not a member of x)

The variable x here can stand for any set. If R is a set, then R is a member of R if and only if R is not a member of R. This contradiction shows that we need to restrict the definition of admissible predicates rather carefully.

Ernst Zermelo and others reacted by starting small and building up step by step. Sets were not allowed to be members of themselves and were always constructed from members that had been built earlier; that is, sets were said to be well founded. In pure set theory, we start at step zero with just the empty set $\emptyset = \{\}$. At step one, we use just the sets from step 0, namely $\emptyset$ alone, as elements to form all the sets we can, namely just $\emptyset$ again and its singleton $\{\emptyset\}$. At each finite step n in the building process, the nth determination V_n of the universe V of sets has as members all and only the subsets of the previous determination V_{n-1} of V (including $\emptyset$ and V_{n-1} itself).[18] That is, for each n, determination V_{n+1} is the power set $\wp(V_n)$ of the previous determination V_n:

$$V_0 = \emptyset = \{\}$$

$$V_{n+1} = \wp(V_n) = \{x \mid x \subseteq V_n\}$$

John von Neumann defined a transfinite function V_α that extends this definition to build up the cumulative hierarchy. He represented ordinal numbers α in the hierarchy as sets $\{\beta \mid \beta < \alpha\}$ of all their predecessors:

$\alpha_0 = \emptyset$

$\alpha_+ = \{\beta \mid \beta \leq \alpha\}$ for the successor α_+ of any given ordinal α

$\alpha_\lambda = \bigcup_{i<\lambda} \alpha_i$ at limit stages λ (α_λ is the union of ordinals less than α_λ)

The von Neumann function for V is defined by transfinite recursion:

$V_0 = \emptyset$

$V_{\alpha+} = \wp(V_\alpha)$ for the successor $\alpha+$ of α ($V_{\alpha+}$ is the power set of V_α)

$V_\lambda = \bigcup_{\alpha<\lambda} V_\alpha$ at limit stages λ (V_λ is the union of sets V_α, for $\alpha < \lambda$)

For any set x, the first V-set V_α in which x appears as a subset gives the *rank* α of x. For example, each ordinal α has rank α.

The axioms of finististic set theory HF assert the existence of sets with finite ranks $n < \omega$, where ω is the first infinite ordinal. The sets comprehended in HF are the *hereditarily finite* sets, which have a finite number of elements, each of which has a finite number of elements, and so on down to $\emptyset$.

The axioms of ZF set theory assert the existence of all sets in the cumulative hierarchy up to the first *inaccessible* ordinal, defined as the first ordinal that cannot be reached using just the ZF axioms.

Numerous other axioms have been proposed, asserting the existence of sets up to (apparently) higher ordinal or cardinal ceilings.

The "thinnest" universe that satisfies the axioms of ZF and related theories is Gödel's *constructible* universe L obtained by comprehending in power sets $\wp(V_\alpha)$ only those subsets of V_α that can be constructed by an explicit recursion from given sets.[19]

The consistency of any theory that comprehends sets of transfinite rank α is increasingly doubtful as α increases. A natural picture is that somewhere in the transfinite hierarchy, the theory becomes incoherent. How much of the hierarchy can be coherently described at all is a philosophical question. A constructivist answer here is that it depends on how well we have built the syntactic apparatus (notation, proof procedures, and so on).

Each set has two sides. Seen from above, it is an *element* that can be used as a member of further sets. Seen from below, it is a *class*, namely the class of its members. A useful notational extra in von Neumann–Bernays–Gödel (NBG) set theory is to introduce new (uppercase) variables X for classes and deny their equivalence to set variables x by refusing to allow class variables before the membership predicate (so "$x \in X$" is allowed but "$X \in x$" is not).[20] Thus classes may be discussed without assuming they exist as elements. Some classes are then *proper* classes, which means they cannot be consistently regarded as sets. For example, the universe V of sets is a proper class, distinct from its momentary determinations V_α, since otherwise V would be a member of itself, contradicting the requirement that all sets be well founded.

At each stage α in the determination of V, the elements comprehended at that stage are all the sets of rank less than α and the proper classes at that stage are the sets of rank α. A formal logic PC or QC can be defined over the class V_α (PC for finite α, otherwise QC), such that the elements of rank less than α are the objects comprehended in PC/QC and the classes of rank α correspond to (one-place) predicates defined over them.

Returning to consciousness, we can represent a subject by a proper class V and the objects that the subject comprehends by elements in V. The V-sets are successive momentary epistemic states in the ongoing life of the subject, and later (but corresponding) V-sets serve as the ontic states by reference to which those epistemic states are evaluated. The subject is thus embodied as successive V-sets and comprehends an accumulating domain of elements.

A paradox of consciousness is that the inner life of a conscious subject is invisible from outside, whereas the outer form of a subject is invisible from inside. A paradox in set theory represents the situation: the proper class V is invisible from outside (unlike its momentary determinations, which are visible a moment later), whereas the proper element $\varnothing$ is invisible from inside (since it has no inside). Setting the class V and the element $\varnothing$ "back to back" to form a single entity $V|\varnothing = \infty$ is impossible within set theory, since in any suitably formalized set theory ST we have:

> It is a theorem of ST that for all x, $x \in V$
> It is a theorem of ST that for all x, $x \notin \varnothing$

However, closing the cumulative hierarchy into a (transfinite) loop by setting $V|\varnothing = \infty$ (imagine a closed relativistic universe with a time loop, as in Gödel's solution to Einstein's cosmological equations) gives a model of consciousness that should be radical enough to satisfy even a Zen master (Douglas Hofstadter might appreciate it, anyway).[21]

Worlds evolve

Epistemic and ontic states represent worlds. Worlds can also be represented in set theory as V-sets. More accurately, momentary stages in the evolution of worlds can be represented by V-sets. The fine structure of the cumulative hierarchy can then be used to micromap the ontic evolution of worlds and the epistemological process of reflecting them with ever increasing precision in consciousness.

The actual world that serves as the notional referent of all true propositions outruns its determinations just as V outruns individual V-sets. Thus characterized, the actual world is reminiscent of Kant's transcendental world in that it lies beyond its phenomenal manifestations.[22]

As represented here, in set theory, the actual world is conflated with the representation of the conscious subject. This is harmless: a conscious subject first realizes itself as a separate inhabitant of its environment in the act of cohering a determinate landscape as its ontic reflection, at which point it is represented by a definite V-set.

The possible worlds that serve as the set-theoretic correlates of epistemic states have so far been assumed to have the feature that they purport to match the actual world. Such worlds remain possible unless or until they somewhere come into conflict with the actual world. When a contradiction appears between such a possible world and the subject's view of the actual world, that possible world ceases to be possible. Epistemic progress then becomes a matter of progressively pruning the tree of such possible worlds.

A second kind of possible world is familiar in modal logic, namely one that is *counterfactual*. A counterfactual world exemplifies a state of affairs that is discernibly alternative to the state that prevails in the actual world. Such a world may be possible in the sense that it obeys all the basic laws of science and is contingently similar to the actual world in various respects, but differs in some specified way. Here, possibility is contrasted not with actuality but with *necessity*. Certain features of the world are regarded as necessary, and variation in all other features counts as possible. Modal operators may then be added to logic to distinguish necessary, contingent, and possible truths.[23]

Using modal logic, we can theorize about possible worlds independently of whether they are counterfactual. A useful relation is that of *relative possibility*. In terms of the first (epistemic) kind of possible world, world B is possible relative to world A if, starting from an epistemic state satisfied by world A, we can realize an epistemic state satisfied by world B. In terms of the second kind, worlds A and B satisfy the same necessary truths and differ only contingently.

Epistemically possible worlds that are still candidates to determine the actual world can be ranked in terms of *probability*. Given a set of epistemically possible worlds, we can theorize (on the basis of more or less solid science, as the case may be) that they each have some definite probability of being realized, such that the sum of the probabilities over the full set of alternatives is normalized to one. Then a step forward by the subject can determine which of the alternatives is realized, and the process can repeat itself. This process is evolutionary. A steadily better fit between the current epistemic state and the actual world evolves as successive generations of unrealized alternatives are winnowed out.[24]

With probability comes the concept of *entropy*. As generations of outcomes are realized that are probable relative to their predecessor states, the process of epistemic evolution may quickly become unidirectional. Earlier states may cease to be effectively recoverable from later states. As new states unfold, the traces of past states get blurred over. In terms of conscious states, the lost information sinks into unconsciousness and is forgotten.

Typically, the dimension along which epistemological evolution takes place is *time*. In the pure cumulative hierarchy, the ordinal dimension has no obvious interpretation as time, but in all more concrete interpretations the evolutionary process is somehow temporal.[25] Ultimately, this concept of time may turn out to be deeper than that defined by physical clocks.

Reality is centered

A world reflects a subject. No sense has been given in this model to the notion that a world could exist without a subject. And no sense needs to be given to that notion. Worlds are centered in the sense that they are structures ultimately constructed from qualia sets, or information. The qualia must be qualia for a subject. The subject must evolve in lockstep with the world it inhabits. At each stage, subject and world reflect each other.

The actual world of contemporary science is a big-bang universe filled with fermions and bosons and sprinkled with DNA organisms.[26] This world is the notional target of ongoing epistemic investigation by numerous scientists. For this world, the subject is not human, yet it is defined in its outlines by human subjectivity. The subject of this world can only readily be characterized in terms of its objective reflection. The consistency and coherence of that reflection constitute what Kant might have called the synthetic unity of apperception of the transcendental subject of the real world. In terms of human society, the subject of the universe may be seen as a highly schematic envelope pushed out at each point by the activities of different human scientists.[27]

Worlds, as defined here, are informatic constructs. The formalized language used to define them need bear no simple relation to any natural language, but it is always a symbolic structure. It can always be represented in terms of bits of information. For example, it may be a visual code whose ultimate elements are colored pixels, generating a movie that depicts an evolving world.

More generally, a world is a multimedia presentation portraying a virtual reality (VR).[28] In the epistemological scenario discussed here, a VR world is a candidate for representing real reality, otherwise known as the actual world. A VR world must be centered on a subject. A VR world is a symbolic construct, and a subject must experience it to realize the symbolism. The symbolism works both ways. The subject is itself realized in the evolution of its VR reflection. In this model, without the external correlate embodied in the VR world, the subject would collapse to the null state.

Returning to modal logic, consider a set of epistemically possible worlds arrayed before a subject inhabiting a VR world A. For the subject, world A is a transparent and presumably accurate and reliable representation of the actual world. For that subject, world A *is* the actual world. Only new experience that somehow contradicts the facts that constitute world A can force the subject to move on. Yet the subject can readily entertain a set of possible VR worlds that would somehow extend or replace world A. Since the specification of world A is limited (as a particular V-set, say), it is *always* possible to define a set of further worlds that are possible relative to A. So long as A remains a satisfactory VR for the subject, A is *symmetrical* with respect to the possible worlds in that set. It can become any one of them.

Theoretical physicists have made intensive use of the concepts of symmetry and spontaneous symmetry breaking, and here is a context where they fit well.[29] Any VR world A is symmetrical with respect to all worlds that are epistemically possible relative to A. World A could evolve into any one of those worlds, either following an epistemic breakthrough on the part of the subject experiencing world A or simply following the passage of a suitable increment of time. In the latter case, where time suffices, it is natural to say that the symmetry is broken spontaneously.

In the evolution of VR worlds through their momentary determinations, spontaneous symmetry breaking can occur when there is no way to predict the new determination. In this case, the new determinacy of the subsequent world may be *random*. Alternatively, deep theoretical reasons may emerge later as to why world B and not world C was realized (in which case the symmetry was not broken spontaneously).

Any VR world A embodies only limited determinacy, therefore it may be further determined to become some other world B that is epistemically possible relative to A. For example, world A may be the actual world of contemporary science at time t_1. At time t_1, it is not yet determined whether nucleus X in a given laboratory experiment will undergo alpha decay in the near future. At time $t_2 > t_1$, nucleus X emits an alpha particle. If world B is the actual world of contemporary science at time t_2, then world B embodies more determinacy than world A. If world C is like world B in all respects except that in world C nucleus X did not decay, then at time t_1 world A was symmetrical with respect to the future worlds B and C.

Pursuing the example, imagine that in world A the unstable nucleus X is hidden from any kind of observation. Then world A can persist up to time t_2 in a *superposition* of states B and C. The superposition collapses only when an observation determines whether nucleus X decayed or not, at which time world A becomes world B or C, respectively. More generally, in accordance with quantum mechanics, such hidden determinacy can evolve superpositionally for arbitrarily long periods of time (this is the moral of the story of Schrödinger's cat), and therefore we can be living in a world that is now a superposition of any number of states of systems that remain unobserved in our world. In fact, our actual world is never in a unique quantum state. We always live in a world that embodies a superposition of states and is symmetrical with respect to different possible outcomes of measurements of those states.[30]

The formal model of consciousness presented here is well suited for interpretation in terms of quantum mechanics. Ontic state A evolves into a superposition of quantum states, then something happens and the superposition collapses into state B. State B evolves into a superposition, and so on. The whole story of evolving states in consciousness can be told in such terms, with the rhythm of the changing states determined by the speed with which the superpositions collapse.[31] In principle, it even seems conceivable that some such quantum story could be told for the evolution of states of electrochemical excitation in human brains, where the collapse times for interneural resonance quanta correspond to moments of "now" in consciousness.[32] However, the formal model is independent of such a brainbound interpretation. Indeed, the quantum story may be more interesting at the level of actual physical reality, where the relativity of quantum reality to a suitable observing subject has often been mooted.[33]

Any VR world corresponding to a definite epistemic state reflects a limited subject. The totality of information represented by that world fails to determine any amount of detail that further investigation can reveal. Any such world is centered on that subject and is inconceivable without that center. As epistemic agents in an ontic environment that we can only access through the medium of our VR tools (concepts, theories, imaging hardware, brains, and so on), we are doomed to have our own perspective on reality.

I am conscious

I experience an evolving series of VR worlds, therefore I am a conscious subject. These VR worlds are pixelated with qualia and structured with logic. My experience is ordered along a timeline as a series of states of knowledge. These states embody limited determinacy and evolve into their successors in a great variety of ways. Each step I take along this series is a transition between two states, the *before* and *after* states, and in general the states are contradictory, since they are competing representations of the actual world.

During each transition between states, I change. Either I briefly bridge the two states or I transit a null state between them. Alternatively, at each step I briefly relive all the states from the null state to the new state, in an ever-increasing spiral movement that invites description in terms of the apparatus of V-sets. Such stepwise or cyclic movement in a space of VR worlds may be constitutive of consciousness.

So far, the entire description of subjective consciousness has remained neutral with respect to persons. The whole story could have been told for a Hegelian *Weltgeist*[34] as well as for a normal human being with a personal life, or indeed for a robotic subject embodied in electronic circuitry. In terms of Martin Buber's distinction between *I–it* and *I–you*,[35] the story so far has been the drama of *I–it*. That drama is sufficient to account for the objectivity of mathematics and the physical sciences, in the sense that no relativity to *personal* perspective is required of such theory. However, it leaves much unexplored.

The denotation of the term "I" is one of the most deeply puzzling subjects of all. I cannot be an object to myself, any more than in set theory the proper class V can be a member of V. Yet I confront my limits with every passing moment, and those limits enable others to see me as coterminous with an object inside their world. By analogy, I have learned to represent myself as an object inside my world. This *analog* I is a cultural invention by means of which I become socialized in a public world. If we could not refer to ourselves in this relatively objective way, we would each incorrigibly regard our own self as possessing mystic truth and therefore would be unable to discuss anything rationally at all. But the analog I is not the real me. In terms of set theory, the analog I is a normal set within some V-set, whereas the real me is the epistemic subject, the paradoxical entity ∞.

By accepting that you exist as a subject like me in my world, I learn how I can see my own limits and accommodate them gracefully. By accepting that each human being, however different in knowledge or ability, also exists as a subject, I learn to dissociate the concept of subjectivity from all its contingent entanglements. Conversely, by observing the extensive isomorphism of subjectivity among skilled practitioners of a scientific discipline,[36] I can account for the unity and objectivity of the actual world of contemporary science.

The concept of a logical subject is distinct from the concept of a person. I am necessarily a logical subject but only contingently a person. I can accommodate other persons in my world without difficulty, but accommodating other logical subjects would lead to the sort of contradiction that I could only experience as schizophrenic breakdown. It is a condition for my existence that my subjective consciousness is unique. If your personal experiences were somehow piped into my brain, they would become my subjective experiences as well. If my personal experiences were simultaneously piped into your brain, we would become one logical subject (or go mad).

Consciousness is a state that can be defined subjectively rather easily: it is the state I am in, now. Defining it objectively is another matter. It can naturally be defined in some detail in terms of awareness and alertness and so on, but there is always the residual question of whether such a definition can really exhaust the possible complications.[37] Observation of patients reporting lucidly on their own mental states comes closest to providing criterial evidence of consciousness from the outside, but the catch here is the term "lucidly". I regard your speech as lucid when I *understand* it, and that occurs only when I can put my own subjectivity behind your words, so to speak. My subjective consciousness is thus projected through your speech output, much as yours is through mine when you understand my words here.

Our predicament as logical subjects is quite stark: we are one. However closely I identify with you, however freely I grant personhood to all the intelligent organisms on the planet, my experience is mine, and I accept only on faith that yours is yours. The moment I *know* your experience, it becomes mine too. If I continue to know your experience, we become one. As human society becomes more integrated and more pervasively intimate, we shall probably cease to see our separate personal selves as separating our logical subjectivity. We shall each feel for all of us, as integral parts of a global lifenet. Consciousness will be globalized, and the assertion "I am conscious" will take on a new meaning.

We are conscious

The formal model of consciousness presented here can be developed further using the tools of logic and mathematics. In future, engineers may use such a model to implement consciousness in computational hardware, for example in artificial neural networks[38] and eventually a global network like the Internet. The creation of artificial consciousness will surely enable us to understand and appreciate human consciousness more fully.

Consciousness is now defined ostensively in terms of how it is manifested in humans. Roughly, human are conscious when they are capable of perceiving their environment and making sense of it in some suitable way. Researchers have explored all this in some detail, albeit without much theoretical guidance. Because theoretical efforts have so far fallen short, there is a great temptation in consciousness research to let it drift into the field of biology, and forget the wider landscape in which a seminal understanding of consciousness can really bear fruit.

That said, the biological research program in consciousness studies is clearly the initiative with the best short-term prospects of achieving a breakthrough. Once we know exactly which structures and processes in human brains are responsible for consciousness, we can deepen that knowledge and give it the theoretical foundations that have so far been obviously missing. This will surely smooth the way for any future project of building conscious machines.

The biological search for the neural correlates of consciousness is exciting.[39] Spatiotemporal maps of electrochemical activity in the cerebral neuronets of experimental subjects clearly show detailed and exact correlations with the introspected conscious experience of those subjects. As new imaging technology enables us to generate more focused maps, with better spatial and temporal resolution, we can hope that the correlations become steadily more fine-grained and illuminating in future.

However, such maps alone cannot reveal the mechanisms of consciousness. For example, we still cannot explain:

- The binding problem. Large numbers of individual neural excitations are somehow bound together into unified mental images. Introspection reveals qualitatively variegated images, not innumerable blips, but how the electrical blips merge into such images is still a puzzle.
- The unity of consciousness. In a brain where billions of neurons are firing in rapid and extremely complex rhythms, fleeting images pass over the screen of the inner Cartesian theater like scenes in a movie. How is this enduring inner theater implemented, and where am I in it?

Wolf Singer and his team have emphasized the possible relevance of resonances between neurons firing in approximate synchrony at frequencies around 40 Hz in explaining the binding of disparate neural excitations into unified mental images.[40] Here, the physics is interesting. The decahertz electrical waves may trigger chemical changes that stabilize neural groups, which then always fire together to give a qualitatively unique experience at a rather complex level. Alternatively, some hitherto unknown quantum effect may play an essential role in creating qualia from neural activities.

As for the unity of consciousness, my own view is that successive states of excitation become fused in an ongoing excitation loop that can be analyzed formally in terms of the model presented here. The loop creates a VR world that evolves through a series of momentary determinations as a stream of images pass through, each forming part of a V-set that freezes a single scene in the ongoing show. The Cartesian theater is the manifestation from inside of the neural hardware (the wetware) that implements the loop. The ongoing show is the way the loop appears to itself. Somehow, the loop is transparent enough to see the last scene in its entirety, but not transparent enough to spoil the view with simultaneous images of previous scenes. Yet the loop also has access to a large repository of previous scenes, and can recall them from memory using an associative mechanism.

The evolution of consciousness in the history of life on Earth is another field where new insights can be expected. Our present understanding of consciousness suggests that relatively simple neuronets, such as those in all mammalian species, may exhibit some form of consciousness. Given this understanding, the idea that consciousness is a distinguishing mark of human beings is unlikely to survive.[41] However, the highly cultivated forms of consciousness exhibited in human communities are certainly unique to our species, and are certainly responsible for the major role humans now play in the ongoing reconfiguration of consciousness support systems on planet Earth.[42]

Conclusion

My logical model of consciousness represents it as the inner transparency of a set-theoretic loop in which an evolving VR world is brought to an experienced focus. Such loops can presumably be implemented in a variety of hardware or wetware architectures and support a corresponding variety of active subjects. When the loop is implemented in a human brain and interacts with its environment over the usual human sensorimotor modalities, the result is consciousness as we know it.

The "hard problem" of accounting for qualia in this model is circumvented. Qualia are the raw inputs for a conscious subject. Normally, they are processed into complex landscapes before they emerge in consciousness, and they are not distinguished individually within those landscapes. My qualia are mine alone in the same sense that my entire universe is mine alone. We can share our universe only by bounding our persons and sharing a self.

Mindworlds

This chapter is a transcript of a slide collection I prepared for a series of public presentations. I presented a subset at the Toward a Science of Consciousness conference, Skövde, Sweden, August 2001, another subset at the Toward a Science of Consciousness conference, Tucson, Arizona, April 2002, and a third subset at the Towards a Science of Consciousness conference, Prague, July 2003. All the slides are posted on my website.

1. Mindworlds

How set theory and quantum physics can give us a scientific concept of consciousness

2. Abstract

Consciousness is a subjective state of awareness of an objective domain unfolding in time. This state is supported by the information processing operations of a living brain and is correlated with rhythmic patterns in the electrochemical pulses between neurons.

It seems that a continually changing inner or mental model is keyed so exactly to neural input and output that it serves as a functional representation of the physical world. Somewhere in the ongoing interaction, appearance and reality become one.

Here we need a constructive logic that admits the interaction of epistemology and ontology, and a mathematics that goes beyond computation. Axiomatic set theory provides a suitable foundation.

Consideration of how we select a possible future world and make it the actual present world leads us to physics. Physical reality unfolds as we break the symmetry of our states in action. This quantum process may correspond to the decoherence of superposed brain states.

3. Mindworlds 1

Introduction

4. Introduction

Consciousness is a subjective state of awareness of an objective domain unfolding in time. First characterized scientifically by William James, in modern terms it is:
- A subjective state of awareness – defined in terms of possession of a more or less stable and coherent perspective, so that there is something it is like to be in that state
- Of an objective domain – represented as somehow independent of the subject and constituting a totality or a world that supports and includes the subject
- Unfolding in time – where time is experienced as the dimension of change and embedded in physical theory as a process of quantized symmetry breaking

Consciousness is supported by the information processing operations of a living brain and is correlated with rhythmic patterns in the electrochemical pulses between neurons.

5. The axis of reality

> The axis of reality runs solely through the egotistic places – they are strung upon it like so many beads. … The world of our present consciousness is only one out of many worlds of consciousness that exist – *William James* [1]

6. What is consciousness?

Awareness dawns over a domain of objects in a space of subjectivity.
Subject and object are co-created and change in time.

7. Time and change

In eternity, we are and we exist.
In time, we change and we grow.

> Nothing is forever except change – *Buddha*

> Everything is flux – *Heraclitus*

8. We are worlds

Consciousness forms a cosmos.
Each of us forms a microcosm.
My microcosm reflects my self.
Together we inhabit a macrocosm.
We form *takes* on it.
Each take is a world.
"I am my world (the microcosmos)."[2]

9. Cosmic origins

At the moment of the big bang the universe had perfect symmetry.
Time broke the first symmetry.
In time grew subject and object.

10. Cosmic evolution

In time:
- Successive symmetries were broken
- The universe cooled and matter condensed
- Atoms aggregated in a sea of photons
- Phase changes created ordered states
- Ordered states became more complex
- DNA life evolved on Planet Earth

11. Knowledge and reality

In the last few million years, nature evolved conscious organisms and conscious subjects reflected increasingly complex objects.

12. Knowledge and the brain

Knowledge is generated by conscious human beings.
Human consciousness is generated by brain activity.
Conscious states are correlated with brain states.
- The brain – the seat of subjectivity
- The body – transition to objectivity

13. Signs of consciousness

From the inside, I cannot doubt my own consciousness.
I am realized in consciousness and I take shape in it.
From the outside, an organism is conscious when:
- It exhibits behavioral correlates of consciousness
- It has the right sort of physiology and cerebral activity
- It interacts reciprocally with other conscious beings

14. The miph of worlds

To launch a science of consciousness we need a 3-stage booster:
- Mathematics of consciousness – set theory defines worlds
- Informatics of consciousness – neuronets compute worlds
- Physics of consciousness – photon bubbles reflect worlds

15. Mindworlds 2

Formal logic

16. Formal logic

The logic of consciousness is that a continually changing inner or mental model is keyed so exactly to neural input and output that it serves as a functional representation of the physical world. Here we need a constructive logic that admits the interaction of epistemology and ontology:
- Epistemology embraces proof theory in logic and the issues of experimental testing, and theoretical coherence in the natural sciences.
- Ontology embraces model theory in logic, truth theory in semantics, and the issues of which fundamental objects or entities exist in the natural sciences.

The interaction of proof theory and model theory creates the tree structures of constructive logic. Somewhere in the ongoing interaction of epistemology and ontology, appearance and reality become one.

17. True or false?

Conscious states are states of knowledge.
Epistemology is the theory of knowledge.
Ontology is the theory of what exists.
Knowledge states are propositional.

Bivalent propositions are true or false.
But what about "This proposition is false"?

18. Propositional logic

Bivalent propositions form classical logic.
True propositions p have truth value $t(p) = 1$.
False propositions p have truth value $t(p) = 0$.

p	q	$\neg p$	$p \wedge q$	$p \vee q$	$p \to q$	$p \leftrightarrow q$
0	0	1	0	0	1	1
0	1	1	0	1	1	0
1	0	0	0	1	0	0
1	1	0	1	1	1	1

Valid inference preserves truth.

19. First-order logic

Propositions have inner structure:
  $p = f(a, b)$ states that concept f applies to objects a and b.
Syntax: f is a predicate and a, b are names.
Semantics: f is a concept and a, b are objects.
General propositions use quantifiers and variables:
  $(\forall x)f(x)$ states that for all x, $f(x)$
  $(\exists x)f(x)$ states that for some x, $f(x)$
In classical first-order logic, $(\forall x)f(x)$ iff $\neg(\exists x)\neg f(x)$.

20. Valid inference

Propositional inference
  Modus ponens: p, $p \to q$ ⊢ q
Quantifier inference
  For free variable u, $f(u)$ ⊢ $(\forall x)f(x)$
  $(\forall x)f(x)$ ⊢ $f(z)$ for any z
  For any z, $f(z)$ ⊢ $(\exists x)f(x)$
  $(\exists x)f(x)$ ⊢ $f(c)$ for new constant c
Different axioms and rules give different systems.
Nonclassical systems may limit the assertibility of $p \vee \neg p$.

- Implication: $p, \ldots \vdash q$ is valid iff conclusion q is true whenever all the premises $p, \ldots$ are true.
- Consistency: First order theory T is consistent iff, for all propositions p of T, not both $T \vdash p$ and $T \vdash \neg p$.

21. Constructive logic

Intuitionism
    For some meaningful propositions p, the law $p \vee \neg p$ need not hold.
    I can assert that p is true iff I can prove p.
    I can assert that p is false iff I can disprove p.
    For some p, I can neither prove nor disprove p.
    Any such proposition p is *undecidable*.
    For such p, we cannot assert that p is bivalent.
    Yet we can assert some truths involving p.
Constructive logic
    p is bivalent iff p is decidable in principle.
    How much we can say about undecidable p?

22. Logical trees

As time passes and knowledge develops:
- Meaning and truth conditions change
- Decision and proof procedures change
- The tree of knowledge grows

23. Theories and models

A first order theory T is a set of sentences s in a first order language L with a distinguished set of axioms and theorems.
    Theory T implies L-sentence s: $T \vdash s$
A model M for T is a set of objects and relations denoted by terms in L such that, when L is interpreted in the set, the axioms and theorems of T are true.
    Model M satisfies L-sentence s: $M \vDash s$
    Completeness: for all s, $T \vdash s$ iff $M \vDash s$

24. Computational linguistics

All human languages have the same deep structure that can be expressed in a suitable formal language L (via transformational grammar).[3] In principle, any human languages X and Y can be translated via L.

- For language L we can define a theory T such that for all distinguished L-sentences s, $T \vdash s$
- For theory T we can define a model M such that for all true L-sentences s, $M \models s$
- For some theories T and models M, $T \vdash s$ iff $M \models s$ (completeness)

Perfect translation is impossible in principle.[4]

25. Truth and meaning

Truth attribution is disquotation (Quine):
- For any sentence s of language L expressing proposition p, s is true iff p (Tarski)
- Example: "I am" is true iff I am

A theory of meaning for a language L is a specification of truth conditions for the sentences of L:
- For any sentence s of language L expressing proposition p, s means p iff: s is true iff p (Davidson)

26. Logic and consciousness

Language L can be any symbolic interaction medium used by a subject.
Semiotics can apply well beyond human languages.
M can model any world that appears to surround the subject.
Worlds can be abstract, mythical, pheromonal, ...

27. Mindworlds 3

Computation

28. Computation

A constructive logic that admits the interaction of epistemology and ontology can be used to generate a conception of mathematics that goes beyond computation.

The formal theory of arithmetic was developed as part of an attempt to prove that classical mathematics was consistent and complete.
- Kurt Gödel proved that if formal arithmetic is consistent, then it is incomplete. For any theory T that admits infinite domains, the model theory of T must outrun its proof theory.

- Alan Turing developed formal arithmetic into the general theory of computability and proved constructively that not all the truths of that theory are computable.
- Roger Penrose argued that our consciousness of these results shows that the brain cannot be just a computer.

Artificial neuronets are computers with a gross architecture like a brain. Arguably, they are insufficient for consciousness.

29. Mathematics and science

Nature is woven into patterns.
Mathematicians play with patterns.
Mathematical games have rules.
The rules define computations.
Mathematics is the science of patterns.
Natural science is applied mathematics.
"The book of nature is written in the language of mathematics"
– Galileo Galilei

30. Mathematical forms

The realm of mathematical forms is eternal, outside time, said Plato.
Numbers are abstractions of:
- Arbitrary physical things (Mill, Husserl)
- The pure intuition of time (Kant, Brouwer)[5]

Number theory is a prototype for:
- Any first order theory (Gödel)
- Any computable theory (Turing)
- Any algorithmic theory (Chaitin)
- Any virtual reality (Deutsch)[6]

31. Arithmetic

Arithmetic is the theory of the natural numbers.
More accurately, arithmetic is the theory of the nonnegative integers,
but one can allow zero as an "honorary" natural number.
$\mathbb{N} = \{0, 1, 2, 3, \ldots\}$ is the infinite set of natural numbers.
$S(n) = n + 1$ is the successor of natural number n.
The limit of of the sequence of natural numbers is ω,
but ω is not a natural number.

32. Formal arithmetic

The axioms of formal arithmetic **FA** are as follows.[7]
For all $x, y, z \in \mathbb{N}$,
 $x = y \rightarrow (x = z \rightarrow y = z)$
 $x = y \rightarrow S(x) = S(y)$
 $0 \neq S(x)$
 $S(x) = S(y) \rightarrow x = y$
 $x + 0 = x$
 $x + S(y) = S(x + y)$
 $x * 0 = 0$
 $x * S(y) = (x * y) + x$
For any **FA** predicate $A(\ )$,
 If $A(0)$ and $(\forall x)(A(x) \rightarrow A(S(x)))$ then $(\forall x)A(x)$

33. Gödel's theorem

Theory **FA** has natural model $\mathbb{N}$. Let **FA** have metatheory **MA**.
Gödel proved that **FA** is incomplete, as follows.
Code **MA** into **FA** and the symbols of **FA** into $\mathbb{N}$ such that
every syntactic item s codes into a number $G(s)$.
Define the open **FA/MA** sentence g:

> For all s, $G(s)$ is not the Gödel number of a proof in **FA** of x.

An instance of g is the closed **FA/MA** sentence g^*:

> For all s, $G(s)$ is not the Gödel number of a proof in **FA** of g.

If FA is consistent, g^* is true but not provable in **FA**.
As a slogan, *truth outruns provability*.[8]

34. Turing machines

Turing machines are idealized computers. They consist of:
- An infinite input/output tape with a string of symbols (such as 0 and 1)
- A read/write head that can move stepwise left or right along the tape
- A machine table that, for each combination of machine state x and symbol s under the read/write head, specifies:
  1. Whether the head writes symbol t for s (such as 0 for 1, or 1 for 0)
  2. Whether the head moves left (L) or right (R) or halts (H)
  3. The next machine state

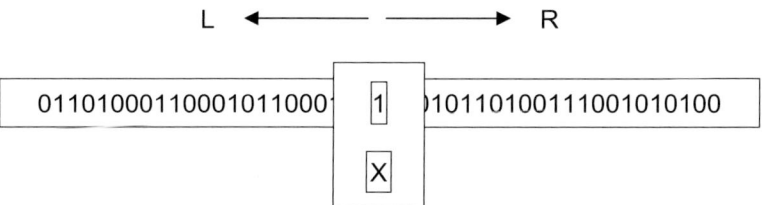

Here the machine reads symbol 1 and is in state *X*.

State	Read	Write	Move	Next
X	1	1	R	Z
X	0	1	L	Y
Y	1	1	H	H
Y	0	0	...	

The machine table tells it to write 1, move right, and go to state *Z*.

35. Computable strings

Computable strings are Turing machine output from input strings.
1. String is input
2. Machine starts
3. Machine halts (maybe!)
4. String is output (if machine halts!)

Turing proved that it is not decidable for which input strings the machine halts. This is called the *halting* problem.

36. Are brains computers?

Computers
- Have digitized input and output
- Have a finite number of inner states
- Operate according to fixed rules
- Are classical machines

Human brains
- Have approximately digitized input and output
- Have a vast but probably finite number of inner states
- Operate according to rules that are presumably fixed
- Are subject to quantum physics

37. Are brains really computers?

Truth outruns provability in **FA** (Gödel).
FA theorems are computable.
The set of **FA** truths is not computable (Turing).
Not all truths are computable.
So brains are not computers (Penrose).[9]
We can solve problems by using insight.

38. Brains are neuronets

The human cerebral cortex contains some hundred billion neurons.
An average neuron connects with thousands of other neurons.
Neurons receive and emit electrical signals.

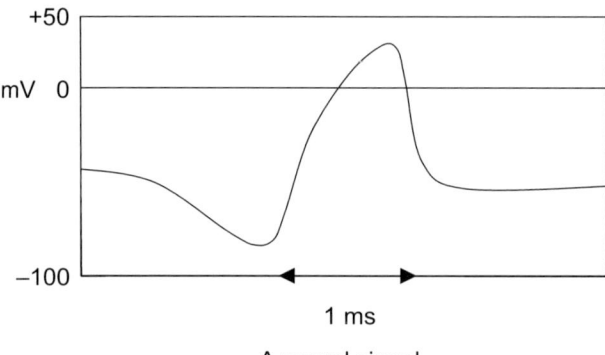

A neural signal

39. Artificial neuronets

Artificial neuronets (ANNs) reflect the gross architecture of natural cerebral neuronets.[10]

Each neuron receives a large number of inputs and emits an output which is a function of the weighted sum of all the inputs:

$x_1\ w_1$
$x_2\ w_2 \longrightarrow \boxed{F} \longrightarrow F((w_1x_1 + w_2x_2 + w_3x_3), t)$
$x_3\ w_3$

40. Neuronets are computers

ANNs can compute any computable function.
ANNs can do full truth-functional logic.
ANNs with backpropagation can learn.
Backpropagation is output fed back to reset weights.
ANNs can emulate many brain functions.
But can ANNs emulate brains completely?
- ANNs are classical machines.
- Brains may be quantum machines.
- So ANNs may face a fundamental physical barrier.

41. Easy and hard problems

Easy problems can be represented as P problems.
- P problems of size n are solvable with algorithms that scale as a polynomial function of n.

Hard problems can be represented as NP problems.
- NP problems of size n are only solvable (it seems) with algorithms that scale exponentially (or so) with n. NP problems cause combinatorial explosions.
- Computers solve NP problems by brute force.

How do we think? We use *insight* – but how?

42. Mindworlds 4

Set theory

43. Set theory

To provide the formal concepts for a theory of consciousness, we need a mathematics that goes beyond computability theory. Axiomatic set theory provides a suitable foundation. Sets are classes of elements:
- Classes are universals, like concepts denoted by predicate or relational terms in Fregean logic.
- Elements are particulars, like objects denoted by subject or substantive terms in Fregean logic.
- The membership relation between elements and classes is like predication or attribution in logic. It is the sole primitive relation in set theory.

The cumulative hierarchy of sets provides a formal metaphor for the worlds we recognize in consciousness.

The growth of the hierarchy by ontogenesis of ranks of sets reflects the logic of the growth of worlds of consciousness.

44. Back to basics

Arithmetic is the logic of time (Kant).
Numbers are sets of sets (Frege).
Each number is the set of all smaller numbers (von Neumann):
- $0 = \emptyset = \{\ \} =$ the null set or empty set
- $1 = \{0\} = \{\emptyset\} =$ the set whose only member is 0
- $2 = \{0, 1\} = \{\emptyset, \{\emptyset\}\} =$ the pair set of 0 and 1
- $3 = \ldots$

Sets are more basic than numbers.[11]

45. Elements and classes

Sets are the ultimate ontology (Quine).[12]
Elements a, b, c are members of class C: $a, b, c \in C$ and $C = \{a, b, c, \ldots\}$
In pure set theory, all elements are sets.
The null set $\{\ \} = \emptyset$ is the only urelement.
Russell's paradox: the class of all sets that are not members of themselves is a member of itself if and only if it is not a member of itself.
Such paradoxes show that the universe V of all sets is a class but not an element.

All you need is sets.

46. Subject and object

Sets are elements from above, classes from below:
- Elements stand for objects.
- Classes stand for subjects.

Can we see a set as a formal metaphor for a moment in the ongoing life of consciousness?

47. Models as metaphors

Scientific progress often results from finding a good model for something.
Consciousness is so polymorphous that it is hard to imagine a model for it.
It has a logic that transcends identity with physical states or processes.
Set theory is so general that it is hard to use as a model of anything.
It is logically deeper than any physical states or processes.

48. ZF set theory

Zermelo–Fraenkel set theory[13]
Axioms: For all $x, y \in V$,

- Extensionality: $x = y \leftrightarrow (\forall z)(z \in x \leftrightarrow z \in y)$
- Regularity: $x \neq \emptyset \rightarrow (\exists z)(z \in x \wedge z \cap x = \emptyset)$
- Pairs: $\{x, y\} \in V$
- Union: If $U(x) = \{u \mid (\exists v)(u \in v \wedge v \in x)\}$ then $U(x) \in V$
- Power set: If $P(x) = \{u \mid u \subseteq x\}$ then $P(x) \in V$
- Null set: $\emptyset \in V$
- Infinity: If $\omega = \{u \mid \emptyset \in u \wedge (\forall v)(v \in u \rightarrow v \cup \{v\} \in u)\}$ then $\omega \in V$
- Replacement schema (Fraenkel):
  For any ZF function f from D to C, $D \in V \rightarrow C \in V$

49. Extensionality

For all $x, y \in V$, $x = y \leftrightarrow (\forall z)(z \in x \leftrightarrow z \in y)$
This defines identity for sets.
In set theory, the only primitive predicate is the binary membership relation $\in$, conventionally written in infix form.

50. Regularity

For all $x \in V$, $x \neq \emptyset \rightarrow (\exists z)(z \in x \wedge z \cap x = \emptyset)$
This axiom asserts that every nonempty ZF set x has a member that is disjoint from x. Thus
ZF $(\forall x)(x \notin x)$
ZF $(\forall x)(x \notin \ldots \notin x)$
Regularity ensures that there are no loops of sets in a ZF universe.

51. Pairs and union

Pairs: For all $x, y \in V$, $\{x, y\} \in V$ (simple, but required as an axiom)
Ordered pairs: $\langle x, y \rangle = \{\{x\}, \{x, y\}\}$ (definition due to Kuratowski)
Union: For all $x \in V$, $U(x) = \{u \mid (\exists v)(u \in v \wedge v \in x)\} \rightarrow U(x) \in V$
The union of x is the set of all members of members of x.

52. Power sets

Power set: For all $x \in V$, $P(x) = \{u \mid u \subseteq x\} \to P(x) \in V$
$P(x)$ is the set of all subsets of x, including $\emptyset$ and x itself.
If x has n members, $P(x)$ has 2^n members.
Example: If $x = \{1, 2, 3\}$, then $n = 3$ and $P(x)$ has $2^3 = 8$ members.

53. From 0 to infinity

Null set: $\emptyset \in V$
Infinity: $\omega = \{u \mid \emptyset \in u \land (\forall v)(v \in u \to v \cup \{v\} \in u)\} \to \omega \in V$
This axiom gives an infinite set.
- For a radical constructivist, it is unacceptable, since an infinite set reflects an infinite process, so such a set is in a state of becoming.
- Yet given objects can reveal themselves as infinite. Consider the infinite series of intervals remaining when Achilles tries to catch up with the tortoise. The total distance between them remains finite, but there is no need to deny its infinite divisibility.

54. Powers of infinity

The power set of x is the set of all subsets of x.
If x is infinite, is $P(x)$ bigger?
$P(\mathbb{N})$ cannot be mapped 1-1 onto $\mathbb{N}$ (Cantor).
Consider a list of real numbers between 0 and 1, ordered anyhow.
The list has $\mathbb{N}$ terms. The set A of all such numbers has $P(\mathbb{N})$ terms.
Consider a *diagonal* term that differs in each nth digit from the nth digit of the nth real number, working along the diagonal from top left to lower right.
This term never appears in the list, but it is in set A, so $|P(\mathbb{N})| > |\mathbb{N}|$.
$\mathbb{N}$ is a countably infinite set with cardinality $\aleph_0$.
$P(\mathbb{N})$ is uncountably infinite with cardinality $\aleph_x$.
Continuum hypothesis: $P(\mathbb{N})$ has cardinality $\aleph_1$.[14]

55. Replacement

Replacement schema (Fraenkel): For any f from D to C, $D \in V \to C \in V$
Translation: for any function f from D to C definable in the formal language of ZF, if D is a set, C is a set. Accepting that C is a set appears to be safe, because the fact that f is a function guarantees that C is not "bigger" than D.

56. Ranking universes

Every ZF set x has an ordinal rank $R(x)$ (von Neumann):
Ordinal numbers α
    $0 = \emptyset = \{\ \}$
    $\alpha = \{\beta \mid \beta < \alpha\}$
V-sets V_α
    $V_0 = 0$
    $V_\alpha = P(V_{\alpha-1})$ for successor ordinals α
    $V_\lambda = \bigcup \{V_\alpha \mid \alpha < \lambda\}$ for limit ordinals λ
$R(x)$ = the least ordinal α such that $x \subseteq V_\alpha$
Ranks of V-sets form a hierarchy.

57. Beyond ZF

Reflection principles **R**: For any open sentence $\phi(x)$ in a ZF-like formal language, if $(\forall x)\phi(x)$ then $\{x \mid \phi(x)\} \in V$.
Roughly, **R** says that any such sentence that is true at all is true in a set in V.
Or, any true sentence is true in some V-set: for each such sentence, that V-set reflects V.
Depending on the language, reflection principles can apparently give arbitrarily "big" universes.
One can also consider infinitary and higher order languages …
All this is rather speculative.

58. Birthing sets

Basis step: at stage 0, nothing exists.
    $\emptyset \subseteq V$
    $\emptyset \in V$ (ontogenesis – birth of a set)
So at least one set exists.
Induction step: at stage α, for all $\beta < \alpha$, all sets of rank β exist.
    $V_\beta \in V$
So all classes of rank α exist.
    $\bigcup \{P(V_\beta) \mid \beta < \alpha\} \subseteq V$
    $V_\alpha \subseteq V$
    $V_\alpha \in V$ (ontogenesis – birth of a V-set)
So all sets of rank α exist, for α tending to transfinity.

59. The universe of sets

The cumulative hierarchy of pure well-founded sets

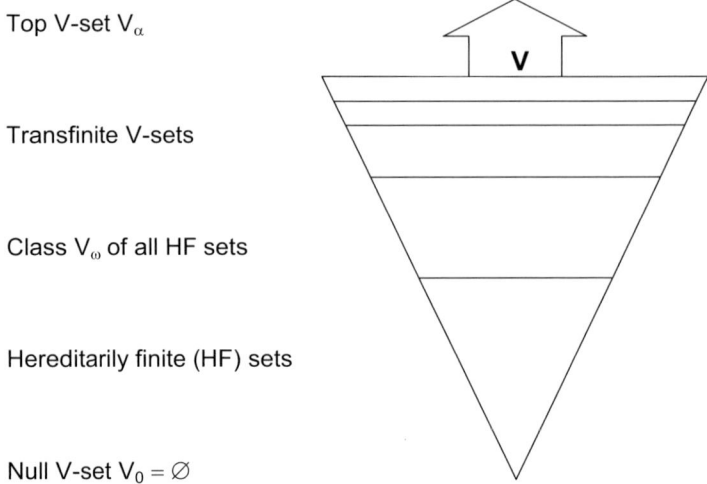

Top V-set V_α

Transfinite V-sets

Class V_ω of all HF sets

Hereditarily finite (HF) sets

Null V-set $V_0 = \varnothing$

60. Constructible sets

The constructible universe L is the least or thinnest universe that contains all the constructible sets (Gödel).

Each constructible set is defined by a recursive function in the formal language of ZF.

In ZF, L is at least an improper subset of V.

Axiom of choice (AC): For any set x of nonempty pairwise disjoint sets z, there is a *choice* set y with exactly 1 element from each z in x.

In ZF, $V = L \rightarrow$ AC

Continuum hypothesis (CH): For any countable set x with cardinality $\aleph_0$, its power set $P(x)$ has the lowest uncountable cardinality $\aleph_1$.

In ZF, $V = L \rightarrow$ CH

AC and CH are independent of ZF (Cohen).

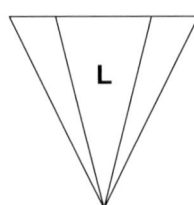

Mindworlds

61. Layers of logic

First order theories have models between ranks in V:
- Ontology of elements $a, \ldots$ (of rank α)
- Epistemology of classes $C = \{a, \ldots\}$ (of rank $\alpha + 1$)

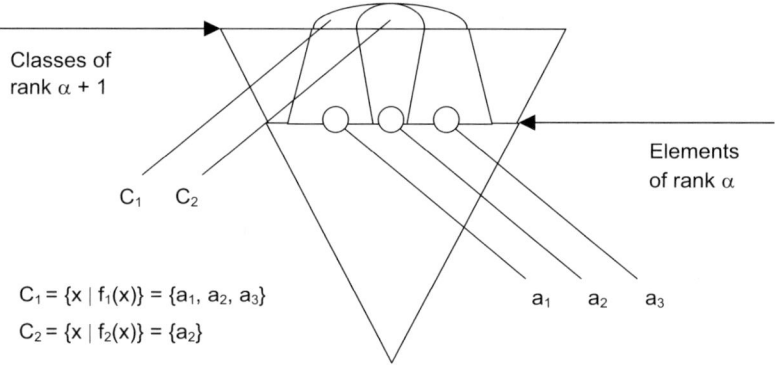

62. Evolution of knowledge

Epistemology and ontology form a *dialectic* in V.
The classes of each rank help define the elements of the next rank.
Such ontico-epistemic progress is reminiscent of the development of a consciousness.

63. Worlds of knowledge

A knowledge state is:
- A totality of facts or a set of true propositions
- Closed under logical inference and satisfied in a world

This picture is due to Wittgenstein.[15]
New facts are informative: we advance from knowledge state α to knowledge state β and comprehend new facts.

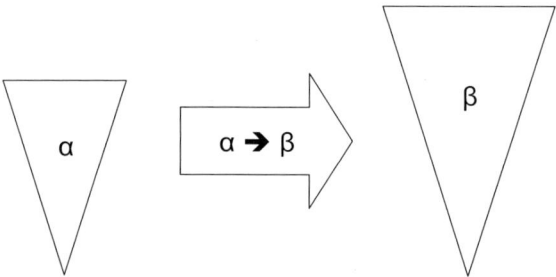

64. Worlds as universal sets

Universal sets can represent worlds.
Let set V_α be the natural model for set theory T_α.
If knowledge state K_α is isomorphic to T_α then V_α is a formal model for K_α.
If world W_α satisfies K_α then V_α is isomorphic to W_α.
- A set V has same logical structure as a world W.

65. Beyond sets

Sets have cardinality (Cantor): cardinality is the transfinite analog of size.
Sets x and y have the same cardinality iff x can be mapped 1:1 onto y.
Cardinality is relative (Cohen): ZF is independent of AC and CH.
Set identity is extensional.
Sets are equivalence classes of structures isomorphic under $\in$.
Categorial information is lost.
Sets are abstract objects.

66. Categories

Categories are beyond sets (Mac Lane).[16]
Categories contain objects and various morphisms between the objects.
Isomorphisms are reversible morphisms that categorify identities for sets.
Category theory distinguishes various isomorphisms between objects.
Arithmetic equations about numbers decategorify isomorphisms between finite sets.
V-sets are isomorphic to worlds.
Set-theoretic identities decategorify various isomorphisms between worlds.
Worlds are categorified V-sets.

67. Mindworlds 5

Possible worlds

68. Possible worlds

Consideration of how we select a possible future world and make it the actual present world suggests a constructive interpretation of modal logic.
   The worlds of modal logic are not like planets.
- Worlds are phenomenal totalities. The subject reflected or realized in such a world is its singularity, where its universality is projected to an

embedded perspectival point.
- Worlds are unbounded from inside but bounded from outside. A jump in time or epistemology is required to transcend the limit of a mindworld.
- Possible worlds are virtual realities as conceived by David Deutsch. They are built by some kind of construction from atomic bits, as in a computer simulation.

Consideration of the relative probability of different possible worlds leads us to physics.

69. Worlds as realities

Worlds reflect states of:
- Information: made of bits = logical atoms
- Knowledge: made of facts = cognitive atoms
- Consciousness: made of qualia = sensory atoms
- Closure: self-contained

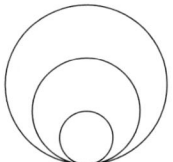

70. Worlds as closed loops

In set theory, looping V to 0 is a paradox.
For a world W represented as a V-set,
- Its universe V is not an element inside W
- Its urelement 0 has no members inside W

From inside, W is a totality.
From outside, W is nonuniversal.

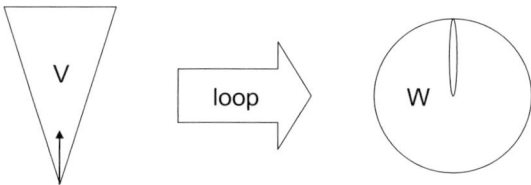

71. Worlds as strange loops

For a world W, looping its universe V to its urelement 0 is *strange*.[17]
- The inhabitant of W is inside space V and outside point 0.
- Event horizon loops back to singularity 0.
- The inhabitant of W is locked in the loop.

From outside, W is a finite sphere with a smooth surface.
From inside, W is a bubble with a singular event horizon.

72. Pearls and onions

If each world W builds on the singularity formed by the horizon of another world, W is not strange – but worlds multiply.
- Worlds on worlds – growing pearls
- Worlds in worlds – peeling onions

If worlds multiply in time, they can be ordered.

73. Virtual realities

A world embeds a subject. The world is reality for the embedded subject.
A world may be actual or possible.
An actual world is an existing state of:
- Information (bits)
- Knowledge (facts)
- Consciousness (qualia)

A possible world is a virtual reality.
The VR is defined by computable rules from atomic bits.[18]

74. Possible worlds

Worlds can be actual and/or possible.
The actual world G is the world as it is now.
Possible worlds W are worlds as they may be.
An accessibility relation R links pairs of worlds.

75. Modal logic

Modal logic is the logic of possible worlds.[19]

- Necessarily p: p is true in all possible worlds.
  p is true in G iff, for all worlds W such that W is R-accessible from G, p is true in W.

- Possibly p: p is true in some possible worlds.
  p is true in G iff, for some world W such that W is R-accessible from G, p is true in W.

76. Possible world semantics

Possible worlds form model structures (Kripke)

A model structure **A** = ⟨G, K, R⟩ contains:
- Actual world G
- Set K of possible worlds W (including G)
- Relation R(W, G) saying W is accessible from G

Satisfaction

Truth conditions for sentences s of language L are defined relative to all R-accessible W in K. If language L defines modal theory T, a model structure **A** may satisfy T: **A** ⊨ T

Completeness

For suitable modal theories T and all sentences s of L, T ⊢ s iff **A** ⊨ s

77. Epistemic and ontic modalities

Axioms for modal logic define necessarily p and possibly p. In a modal theory, modalities may be:
- Epistemic (psychological)
    □p if p is implied by what is known
    ◇p if p is consistent with what is known
- Ontic (physical)
    □p if the intrinsic probability of p = 1
    ◇p if the intrinsic probability of p > 0

There is a spectrum spanning (psycho-epistemic) shades of belief and (physico-ontic) grades of probability.

78. Probabilities

Probabilities are numerical weights attached to possible worlds such that:
- The probability of world W, relative to world G in a model structure **A**, is a real number $p(W)$ between 0 and 1.
- The combined probability of two or more distinct worlds is the sum of their separate probabilities.
- Each world W such that R(W, G) is possible from G.
- Each $p(W) > 0$.
- The worlds W such that R(W, G) cover all cases:
    Sum $\sum_W p(W) = 1$.

79. Mindworlds 6

Quantum theory

80. Quantum theory

Physical reality unfolds as we break the symmetry of our states in action. This is a quantum process in which the probabilities of the respective states change:
- Before an action, the probabilities of different possible present or future states of a physical system can be calculated for various classical and quantum processes.
- An action is a change, marked by an increment of time. A minimal action is a quantum jump in which a system interacts via a single quantum with its environment.
- After an action, the probability of the actual state of the system becomes 1. The probabilities of the other previously possible but now nonactual states becomes 0.

Quantum symmetry breaking occurs quasi-continuously at the Planck scale. Spacetime foam crystalizes into classical order and the past light cone grows.

81. Classical and quantum probabilities

In classical physics, the world is eternal:
- Reality evolves rigidly along a fixed timeline.
- Exact laws determine the past and future.
- Statistical approximations generate probabilities.

So classical probabilities are *epistemic*.

In quantum physics, the world is changing:
- Reality comes into focus along a growing timeline.
- The past is fixed but the future is fuzzy.
- The probability of possible futures is intrinsic.

So quantum probabilities are *ontic*.

82. Classical states

In classical physics, a state of a system S is a definite configuration of the parts of S.
- **Determinism:** In principle, given state S_1 at time t_1, state S_2 at any later time t_2 can be predicted.
  Example: each gas molecule in a closed volume has a definite position and linear and angular momentum.
- **Chaos:** In fact, any errors in measuring S_1 grow so fast that soon S_2 cannot be predicted.

Example: weather forecasting is difficult.[20]

83. States and entropy

Worlds have macrostates and microstates:
- A *macrostate* is defined by global variables like temperature that characterize the world phenomenally.
- A *microstate* is defined by a complete set of values of the dynamical variables for each and every particle.

Entropy: $\Delta S = k \ln N$, where $N = |Y| / |X|$ and $|Z|$ = number of possible microstates realizing macrostate Z, X is macrostate at time t, Y is macrostate at time $t + \Delta t$, and k is Boltzmann's constant.

84. States and time

Each macrostate is consistent with many microstates.
- Microdynamics is symmetrical in time.
- Macrodynamics is such that entropy increases in time.

How much sense does it make to suppose that all these states exist eternally in 4D spacetime? Does physics set a limit to the number of states we can distinguish for a world, and if so, how?

85. From classical to quantum physics

In 1900, classical physics faced problems with:
- Blackbody radiation
- Stability of the atom

Quantum physics came to the rescue:
- Photon radiation is quantized (Planck).
- Electron orbital energy is quantized (Bohr).

The theory of photons and electrons is quantum electrodynamics (QED).[21] The limit to the number of states we can distinguish is set by Planck's constant h (about $6 \cdot 10^{-34}$ joule-second)

86. Distinct states

Microstates are configurations of particles that can have various statistics:
- Maxwell–Boltzmann: distinct quanta can have identical properties and their permutations form distinct states. Example: molecules
- Fermi–Dirac: distinct quanta can have identical properties but their permutations are not distinguished. Example: electrons

- Bose–Einstein: Distinct quanta must have distinct properties or they lose their separate identity. Example: photons

Particle properties such as spin, charge, or energy are quantized.

87. Photons

Photons are quanta of electromagnetic radiation.
Large numbers of photons together behave like waves:
- The waves consist of electric and magnetic fields oscillating perpendicular to each other and to the direction of propagation.
- The waves travel with constant speed $c \sim 3 \cdot 10^8$ ms^{-1} (in free space).
- If **E** and **B** are the electric and magnetic field vectors, then $\mathbf{E} = c\mathbf{B}$.
- If the wave frequency is f, then **E** is a sinusoidal wave $E_0 \sin \omega t$ with angular frequency $\omega = 2\pi f$.

Each photon has energy $E = hf$.

88. Experiments with photons

A laser beam passes through two small parallel slits onto a row of detectors.
- Experiment A: First one of the small slits is covered and then the other is covered, then the independent results are added. ➔ We see the sum of two Gaussian curves.
- Experiment B: Both slits are open at the same time, and photons from the two slits interfere. ➔ We see a row of interference fringes.

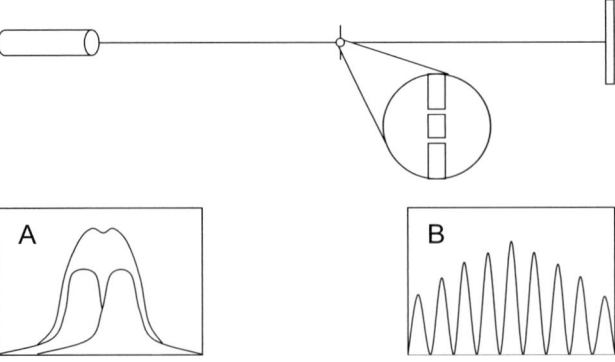

89. Complex spaces

Quantum mechanics uses not real but complex spaces.
Complex number $z = x + iy$, where x and y are real numbers and $i = \sqrt{-1}$.
The complex conjugate of z is $z^* = x - iy$.
If we choose z so that $z^*z = 1$, then $z = \cos\theta + i\sin\theta = \exp[i\theta]$.
Setting $\theta = \omega t$, $\exp[i\omega t]$ is a complex wave function whose real part is a sinusoidal wave with angular frequency ω.
The modulus of z, $\mathrm{mod}\,z = |z|$.
The squared modulus $|z|^2 = z^*z = x^2 + y^2$.

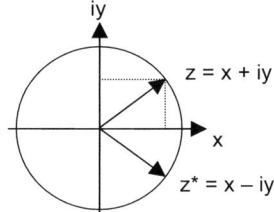

90. Quantum interference

In quantum theory, events correspond to states, and states have amplitudes defined by complex wave functions. Consider the possible events or states A and B and combined state C in which either A or B is realized. There are two ways to calculate the probability $p(C)$ of state C from $p(A)$ and $p(B)$:

- If A and B are mutually independent, square the modulus of amplitude a to get probability $p(A)$ and square mod b to get probability $p(B)$, then add $p(A)$ and $p(B)$ to get the probability of state C:
  $a^*a + b^*b = p(A) + p(B) = p(C)$
- If A and B interfere with each other, add their amplitudes a and b to get the amplitude $c = a + b$ of event C, then square the modulus of c to get the probability of state C:
  $(a+b)^*(a+b) = c^*c = p(C)$

These two calculations correctly predict the results of the experiments with the laser beam and the double slit.[22]

91. Uncertainty

Wave-particle duality implies uncertainty (Heisenberg).
The quantum of action h (about $6 \cdot 10^{-34}$ joule-second) is a tiny fuzzball of uncertainty such that:

- Momentum and position uncertainties $\Delta p \, \Delta x \sim h$
- Energy and time uncertainties $\Delta E \, \Delta t \sim h$

In quantum field theory, particles can appear or disappear randomly.

In trying to predict the behavior of a system of particles, the best we can do is calculate the probabilities of creation or annihilation at each point in spacetime.[23]

92. Quantum fields

Quantum field theory deals with fields $\Psi(x, y, z, t)$ that create or annihilate particles at points (x, y, z, t).
- A field is defined by a complex wave function with an amplitude at each point in spacetime. Two or more fields can be mutually independent or interfere with each other.
- The state of a system of fields at each point in spacetime is defined from the vector sum of all the fields, from which we can calculate creation or annihilation probabilities.

93. State spaces

A world is a state of a physical system:
- An actual world G is a real state of a system.
- A possible world W is a virtual state of a system.

Each observable state of a physical system forms a dimension in a mathematical state space:
- The state space represents all observable states of the system as orthogonal dimensions (up to infinitely many).
- A state vector in the space specifies the actual state of the system (it may have nonzero projections onto many dimensions).

94. Superposed states

A system can be in several states at once:
- Generally, the system is in a superposition or mixed state of the possible observed values for an observable Ω.
- Each dimension of the state space is a pure state of Ω.
- Measurement or interaction nudges a mixed state to a pure state.

Mindworlds

95. From block to bloom

The classical universe is an eternal block.[24] All space and time exists in eternity, and each time slice is now for a brief moment.

The quantum universe is an emerging bloom. The actual world in the present blooms, again and again, into sets of possible future worlds.

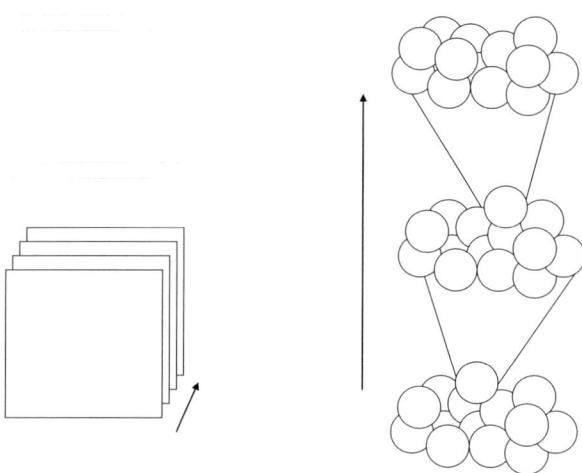

96. Quantum worlds

As time passes, a quantum world focuses stepwise on ever more fully defined states:

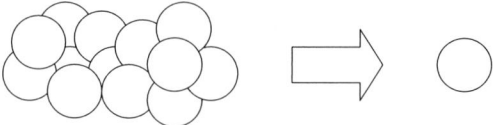

97. Decoherence

Systems in mixed states decohere spontaneously during interaction with their environment.
For objects of mass > 1 fg, decoherence times are < 1 as.
- 1 fg = 10^{-15} g = mass of a small grain of dust
- 1 as = 10^{-18} s = time for light to traverse an atom

98. Quasi-classical worlds

In the series of worlds preceding the actual world, each new world is consistent with its predecessors.
- Each world has a history of symmetry breaking that leads back consistently to time zero.
- The consistent history approach based on decoherence is the clearest interpretation of quantum theory.[25]

99. Time and realization

Systems evolve in time.
- Superpositions decohere to pure states in time.
- Moments of time are realized by approximately simultaneous devirtualization of fuzzy quanta:

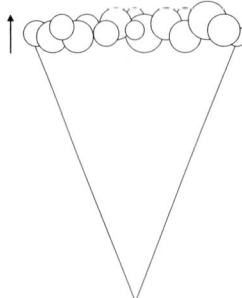

100. Symmetry breaking

When a mixed state evolves to a pure state, a symmetry of possible states is broken.
- Series of states form consistent histories by symmetry breaking.
- Each world has a history that leads back to the primal moment.

101. Quantum foam

At the ultimate Planck scale, spacetime may have a *foamlike* structure:[26]
- A Planck instant ~ 10^{-43} s = 100 f-f-fs
- A Planck length ~ 10^{-35} m = 10 a-am
- A Planck mass ~ 10^{-5} g = 10 µg ~ 1 GJ

As reality condenses into time, a nearly classical spacetime quasi-continuum crystalizes over the foam.

The epistemic time along which reality unfolds for a subject may not be identical to the ontic time of 4D spacetime.

102. Relativistic spacetime

Space and time are inseparable. If time unfolds, space does too (Einstein).
The future light cone is small and soft. The past light cone is big and hard.

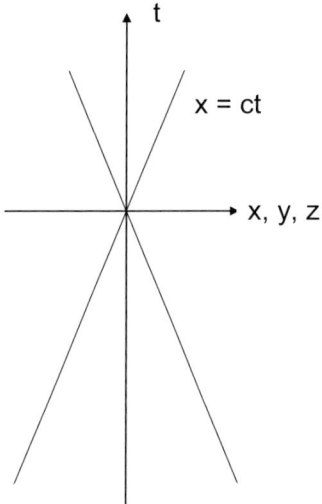

103. Relativistic cosmology

The observable universe is a big bubble.
The bubble expands with time.
The bubble is our past light cone.
Bubble radius $R = cT$ where T = time since the primordial fireball.
Bubble horizon is red-shifted thermal radiation from the primordial fireball.

104. Ontic and epistemic time

Ontic time
- Is defined as clock time in basic physics
- Is our best conception of real time

Epistemic time
- Is experienced as a flux of *now* states
- Is real *now* but becomes unreal before and after

105. Mindworlds 7

Consciousness

106. Consciousness

Consciousness of a phenomenal world is an ongoing interactive process of building a theory of reality.

- Descartes said *cogito ergo sum*. In modern terms, consciousness requires a subject to reflect or comprehend the world.
- Kant distinguished the phenomenal world, which is unified in apperception and ordered by logical categories, from the noumenal world, which is radically unknown.
- Hegel articulated a dialectical process that starts in sensory immediacy and develops to an ultimate or absolute state in which "all is one."

These philosophical pictures can be interpreted in the set-theoretic structure of mindworlds presented here. Imperfect self-consciousness and developing self-knowledge can also be modeled.

The "all is one" worldview paradox becomes the puzzle of reconciling the first-person and third-person views of a conscious brain.

107. What you see

Phenomenology: what you see is what you use to build a theory of reality (WYSIWYUTBATOR).

- The thinker thinks in a self-collapsing world.
- Inner access is no more privileged than outer access.
- The thinker is an artifact of "his" own phenomenology.
- The thinker is cocrystalized with the landscape.

108. Phenomenal worlds

Worlds embody the categorial structure of experience and reflect the synthetic unity of apperception (Kant).[27].

Each world

- Has an analytic *a priori* logical structure
- Has a synthetic *a priori* structure given by the time and V-sets needed to fill it with content
- Has an *a posteriori* structure given by experience

Consciousness forms a synthetic unity with a categorial structure.

Kant's puzzle:
- Behind the manifold of phenomena is the *Ding an sich* – what is it?

109. Dialectical consciousness

Geist [mind or spirit] [28]
- Begins in sensory certainty
- Grows in an epistemo-ontic dialectic
- Culminates in absolute knowledge

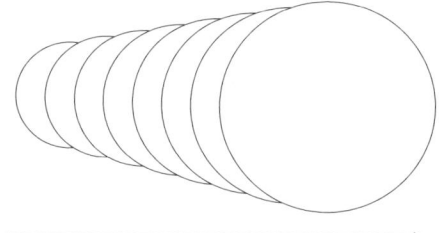

A series of ever bigger worlds grows in time.

110. Consciousness as process

Human consciousness forms a virtual reality in the brain. The VR model is identified with the actual world and is adjusted in an ongoing evolutionary process to optimize its consistency with new sensory input. Input from the actual world is processed through mind – the gap – and reflected as VR in consciousness.

111. Other minds

Each conscious mind inhabits a different world. The private worlds of different minds overlap. Their intersection forms a shared public world. The public world of information can grow independently of the minds that help define it.

112. Self-consciousness

Self-consciousness is a self-referential loop.
Consciousness forms a VR of its (former) self.
Like universal sets in set theory, for consistency,
the inner self must be a former conscious state.

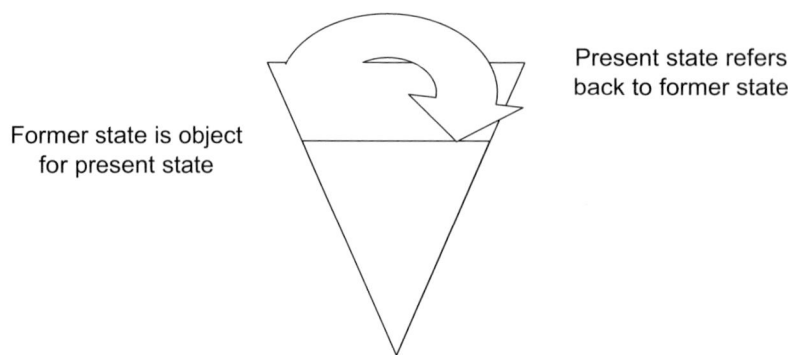

Former state is object for present state

Present state refers back to former state

113. Self-knowledge

Self-knowledge is a self-referential loop that forms a series of inner models of its former states. Knowledge of a series of former states that form a meaningful evolution can be self-corroborating.

Can a process like this lead to a closed circular flow, or even serve to model mystic states of consciousness?

Can some such flow be used to make sense of Gödel's time loop solution of Einstein's cosmological equations? [29]

114. Mindworlds and I

Possible mindworlds stretch into transfinite paradise.
I realize myself in the process of forming loops that sustain the growth of meaningful knowledge.

115. Me, myself, I

Consciousness implies an *I*.
The *I* is the 0 and *V* of the phenomenal world.
I become an object as me.
I see you as object – You see me as object.
I try to see me as myself.
I see an inner representation as myself.
My representation is never perfect.
My self image is an imperfect reflection.
Image quality is reduced in reflection.

116. I am conscious

The thinker creates an evolving VR (to help survive in a natural world). Therefore I am conscious.
Cogito ergo sum – Descartes

117. The conscious brain

The conscious brain [30]
- From inside
  – the first-person outlook –
  it seems like a phenomenal world of qualia
- From outside
  – with third-person insight –
  it seems like a wet lump pulsing with electrochemical activity

These views are *worlds* apart!

118. Zen consciousness

The Ross haiku:

The inner I looks out
And looking back sees me
All in all, quite strange

>   *Bloop*
>   *Floop*
>   *Gloop*
>   – Douglas Hofstadter

119. Mindworlds 8

Quantum mind

120. Quantum mind

Physical reality unfolds as we break the symmetry of our states in action. This quantum process may correspond to the decoherence of superposed brain states.

The quantum logic of superposed bit states provides a new model of computation that may help to explain consciousness.

Entanglement is the nonlocal phenomenon of correlated decoherence of superposed states of an extended system. Hypothetically, it may help explain our perceptual interactions.

Conscious states are apparently pure states of mind that may span mixed brain states, like macrostates span microstates in physics.

Ross proposes that decoherence of superposed states of the decahertz EM field generated by synchronous neural firings may correlate with consciousness and may help explain it.

Penrose and Hameroff have proposed an alternative model based on decoherence of microwave states generated by microtubules.

121. Quantum bits

Classical particles are always in pure states.
The states can be coded as bits
$|C\rangle = |0\rangle$ XOR $|1\rangle$

Between measurements, quanta are generally in superpositions of states.
The superpositions can be coded as qubits
$|Q\rangle = \alpha|0\rangle + \beta|1\rangle$ where:
- Amplitudes α and β are complex numbers
- $|\alpha|^2$ is the probability of measuring state $|0\rangle$
- $|\beta|^2$ is the probability of measuring state $|1\rangle$
- $|\alpha|^2 + |\beta|^2 = 1$
- $|Q\rangle$ is a vector (α, β) in the 2D complex vector space spanned by the orthonormal basis states $|0\rangle$ and $|1\rangle$

122. Quantum logic

Some 1-qubit gates:
Quantum NOT
$\quad |0\rangle \rightarrow |1\rangle \quad |1\rangle \rightarrow |0\rangle$
$\quad \alpha|0\rangle + \beta|1\rangle \rightarrow \alpha|1\rangle + \beta|0\rangle$
Hadamard transform
$\quad \alpha|0\rangle + \beta|1\rangle \rightarrow \alpha\frac{(|0\rangle + |1\rangle)}{\sqrt{2}} + \beta\frac{(|0\rangle - |1\rangle)}{\sqrt{2}}$

A 2-qubit gate:
Controlled NOT
$\quad |00\rangle \rightarrow |00\rangle \quad |01\rangle \rightarrow |01\rangle \quad |10\rangle \rightarrow |11\rangle \quad |11\rangle \rightarrow |10\rangle$
$\quad$ Target qubit is flipped iff control qubit is $|1\rangle$

Universality:
Any (classical or) quantum logic gate can be composed from
1-qubit gates and controlled NOT. [31]

123. Quantum computation

In a classical computer's n-bit register,
the n bits are each stored as distinct states 0 or 1.
One string of n bits can be stored at one time.
Calculations for different strings run separately.
In a quantum computer's n-bit register,
qubits are stored as superpositions of 0 and 1.
All possible 2^n strings of n bits are stored at once.
Calculations for all the strings can run superposed,
so long as the computation does not decohere.
One real byte corresponds to 256 virtual bytes.

124. Physical computation

Information is physical.[32]
Classical information is negentropy.
Losing information raises entropy.
Reversibility conserves entropy.
Reversibility preserves superpositions.
Computers are physical machines.
They perform classical computation.
Most computations are irreversible.
Their operation is thermodynamic.
They generate heat.

125. Is the brain a quantum computer?

Physical devices for quantum computing require:
- Submicron geometric precision to stabilize interference effects
- Setups like nanokelvin laser traps to isolate coherent states

The brain is far too sloppy and warm to do quantum computing.
But perhaps quantum effects that we can analyze in these terms are relevant
for explaining conscious phenomenology.

126. The quantum brain

Biological processes occur at molecular scales.
At molecular scales quantum effects can dominate.
Neuronets learn by thermodynamic relaxation.
Relaxation is a stochastic process.
In the brain, it is an *extremely* delicate analog process.
Brain states may show quantum effects.

127. Local and nonlocal effects

Electric potential fluctuates both within and between the neurons in a brain.
The potential surface is like the surface of a sea.
Random disturbances make waves on the surface.
The charges that cause the potential are quantized.
Local quantum effects are too small to affect neurons.
Nonlocal effects may entangle extended brain states.

128. Entangled states

Bell proved and experiments confirm that the statistics of nonlocal correlations are nonclassical.
- Entangled states are mixed states of multiple particles.
- Entangled states are nonlocal and decohere simultaneously to correlated pure states.

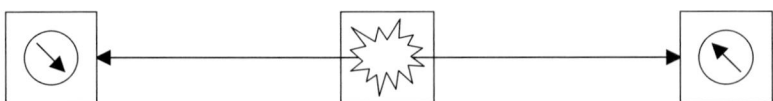

Event creates entangled Bell pair $|B\rangle = \dfrac{|01\rangle + |10\rangle}{\sqrt{2}}$

Left dial measures spin $|0\rangle$ (or $|1\rangle$)
Right dial measures spin $|1\rangle$ (or $|0\rangle$)

129. Mental states and public events

We identify mental states with public events.
The identification is intentional projection.
Intentional projection is transparent to us.
Identification may involve entangled states.

Are mental states entangled with public events?
Do public events have superposition signatures?
Do we get entangled in their superpositions?
Correlated superpositions that decohere together are entangled.

130. Do we reflect mixed states?

When I perceive an object, my set of possible futures becomes focused on those that contain the object.
- Do I reflect its superposition signature in the superposition signature of my mental state?
- Is the direction of our epistemo-ontic progress steered by our percepts?
- If so, when and how?

131. Do we enter entanglements?

Conscious states evolve in time.
Mixed states evolve into pure states.
Possible states remain balanced until an interaction realizes a unique state.
States decohere in moments of now in the specious present.
Which states do we realize?
- How can conscious states reflect the superposition signatures S of our percepts?
- Somehow, nerves and neurons from eyeballs to visual cortex may enter the states S.

132. Macroconsciousness

Conscious states seem to be pure states of mind.
Brain states are generally mixed or entangled states.
Does consciousness span entangled brain states?
Are conscious states like macrostates in thermodynamics?

133. The rhythm of now

Conscious states evolve in moments of *now*. Large patches of phenomenal reality decohere with a periodicity that seems more or less steady. Conscious states are phenomenal equivalence classes of brain states experienced from the inside.
An increment of *now* $\Delta t \sim 20\text{--}100$ ms lies in a band of frequencies in the decahertz range corresponding to:

- The flicker fusion rate
- A fast reaction time
- Physiological tremor

Timeness is consciousness.[33]

134. The unity of consciousness

Consciousness is unified – but how so physically? Like a laser beam?

In a laser beam, photons lose their identities in a boson condensate.

A boson condensate is a Bose–Einstein state where the separate identities of the constituent particles are dissolved in a quantum unity.

This is the only known way to physically unify brain events.

135. Correlates of consciousness

Consciousness is correlated with extended decahertz electromagnetic (EM) brainwaves.

Synchronized neural firings create coherent EM fields over regions of many cubic millimeters with frequencies $f \sim 40$ Hz.

These gamma waves generate neural binding and unified percepts in consciousness.[34]

136. The thalamo-cortical self

Consciousness is correlated with temporal binding of neural groups firing in decahertz rhythms.

Thalamo-cortical loops firing rhythmically form a main mechanism of brain function.

These loops serve to unify what Rodolfo Llinás calls *isochronous* conscious states.[35]

137. The Ross hypothesis

Interneural photons with $f \sim 40$ Hz that form boson condensates lasting for 1 *now* are the quantum correlates of consciousness.

Unstable BE states of photons serve as momentary mirrors for our states of mind. Our states of mind are frozen in photons.

Time stands still for a photon.[36]

138. The bubbling brain

Synchronous neural firings emit waves of photons.

The photons form bubbles of superposed states that extend for ~ 80 ms over the thalamocortical system.

As a bubble pops, it
- Freezes a moment of *now*
- Reflects qualia like a mirror
- Realizes a state of mind

Popping bubbles form a quantum foam.

Foaming decahertz photons have large Heisenberg uncertainties:

Δt ~ 30 ms

Δx ~ 10 000 km = 10 Mm (in free space)

139. Biophotons

Cells in the body exchange photons.

These photons are mostly microwave or infrared and sometimes visible light. They may be conducted along microtubules and absorbed in centrioles and may communicate biologically useful information.

Is it possible that transient coherent states of these photons coordinate and unify life processing and that a hierarchy of such states leads seamlessly to the decahertz states of consciousness? [37]

140. A related hypothesis

Penrose–Hameroff microwave reduction: [38]

Superposed spacetime geometries at the Planck scale corresponding to entangled energy superpositions in brain states decohere in an "Orch OR" to generate classical states of consciousness.

The entangled superpositions are generated by microwave (~ 10 GHz) laser action in microtubules in neural cytoskeletons as tubulin dimers oscillate between conformal states.

141. Megawaves and microwaves

Megawaves
- Generated by neural groups firing synchronously
- Frequencies ~ 20–100 Hz, wavelengths ~ Mm
- Time uncertainty ~ 10–50 ms ~ 1 now

- No special mechanisms needed to stay coherent long enough to sustain the rhythm of now

Microwaves
- Generated by synchronous oscillation of tubulin dimers
- Frequencies ~ 10 GHz, wavelengths ~ cm
- Time uncertainty ~ 100 ps ~ 1 nanonow
- Exotic screening mechanisms needed to stay coherent for up to 1 now

142. Criticism of related hypothesis

Problems at 3 levels:
- Any reduction of spacetime geometries at the Planck scale is way, way below the scale of brain events and is probably irrelevant to consciousness. Mesoscopic mechanisms should explain consciousness.
- Any laser action in microtubules would occur in every cell of a living organism and in many brain states that are not linked to consciousness, so microtubule states do not correlate with consciousness.
- A centisecond duration for the coherent microwave states requires extreme isolation of the states in microtubules. Such isolation is physically and biologically implausible.

Hypothesis unconvincing

143. Criticism of Ross hypothesis

In favor:
- Megawaves correlate optimally with consciousness.
- Megawave effects relate to concept formation.
- Megawave coherence need not be very high.

Against:
- Decahertz photons are extremely fuzzy and have feV energies.
- Decahertz waves are only the tip of a cascade of activities in the brain.
- Alternating current (AC) doesn't seem to affect consciousness.

Hypothesis interesting

144. Consequences of Ross hypothesis

If conscious states are identical with certain coherent decahertz photon field states, then:
- The fields are robust enough to extend over volumes ~ 1 cl for periods ~ 1 now in the environment of a living brain.
- Different states of consciousness correspond to different frequency and

amplitude modulations of the fields.
- Manipulations of the fields from outside can cause disturbances in consciousness.
- Artificial consciousness (AC) is possible in principle.

145. Experimental research

A new scientific hypothesis must be experimentally testable. It must make definite predictions and the predictions must be falsifiable.[39]

A new paradigm must support a fertile research program. It must support a family of scientific hypotheses and motivate a program of detailed experiments.[40]

The experimental results should be interesting and illuminating even if they overthrow the hypotheses.

What use is a newborn baby? [41]

146. Experimental suggestions

Experiments needed to test the *quantum theory of consciousness* (QTC):[42]
- Detailed empirical studies of phase locking and coherence in cerebral decahertz EM fields
- Neurophysiological studies of how the cerebral interneural environment can support transient BE states
- New techniques for in vivo measurement of decoherence times of interneural BE states
- Studies of correlations between cerebrally localized BE states and subjective reports of conscious states
- Measurements of thresholds for perturbation of coherent interneural EM fields by extracerebral events

147. Mindworlds 9

Open questions

148. Open questions

- Can consciousness be explained as a quantum phenomenon in terms of the decoherence of superposed brain states?
- Is consciousness photonic?
- Do states of consciousness correlate with collapsing superpositional states of coherent interneural decahertz EM fields?

- Do all living cells have photonic protoconsciousness?
- How did consciousness evolve and how did it improve fitness?
- Which animal species in addition to humans are conscious?
- Can we build conscious machines?
- Will artificial consciousness resemble human consciousness?
- Will conscious machines form a single global mind?
- If so, how will we know this, or relate to the global mind?
- Are we alone in the universe?

149. Is consciousness photonic?

The brain is a VR generator.
Does the brain use quantum effects?
Do its coherent 40 Hz photon fields form a stream of *now* states?
Are these the quantum correlates of consciousness?

150. Are cells protoconscious?

If cells communicate via photons and consciousness is photonic, cells may be protoconscious. Protoconsciousness may feature:
- Intense phenomenology
- Highly variable *now* states
- Primitive information processing

Does the spark of inner phenomenology reach back in evolution to the first cells?

151. How did consciousness evolve?

Biological evolution enslaves our minds to nature.
- Natural selection forced brainwaves to reflect objects.
- Qualia may have emerged early in evolution as constituents of photonic nanoworlds.

The mind is a tool for survival.

152. Which species are conscious?

Which DNA based organisms enjoy consciousness?

153. Can we build conscious machines?

If consciousness arises in photon condensates, artificial consciousness (AC) should be possible.

AC requires:
- Information processing
- Interaction with an environment
- Accumulation of states of mind

AC may require:
- Quantum *now* states
- Quantum data fusion
- Quantum self-realization

154. Will machines understand us?

Will AC machines think like us?
Is the Turing test relevant?
AC machines will
- Be able to share inner states with each other
- Have faster and sharper *now* states than us
- Fail to share most of our psychology

155. Will machines form a global mind?

Do mammals have the only minds on Earth?
Will AC form a global mind?
Are we alone?

156. Mindworlds 10

Conclusion

157. Conclusion 1

Consciousness involves recognition of a more or less stable and coherent world that surrounds the subject and unfolds in time. It is supported by information processing operations in the brain, which generate an inner model of the external world.

A constructive logic can characterize the dynamic interaction of truth and provability and generate a conception of mathematics that goes beyond computation. The theory of computability shows that not all mathematical truths are computable. Arguably, our consciousness of this fact shows that the brain cannot be just a computer.

For a theory of consciousness, we need to go beyond computability theory. In set theory, sets are classes of elements, and elements are members of classes. Classes are like concepts and elements are like objects. The membership relation is like predication. The cumulative hierarchy of sets provides a formal metaphor for mindworlds. The growth of the hierarchy by ontogenesis of ranks of sets reflects the logic of the growth in time of new mindworlds.

158. Conclusion 2

The way we select a possible future world and make it the actual present world suggests a constructive interpretation of modal logic. Possible worlds are phenomenal totalities. Their subject is their singularity, an embedded perspectival point. Worlds are unbounded from inside but bounded from outside. A jump in time can transcend the boundary of a world.

Mindworlds are virtual realities constructed bit by bit, as in a computer simulation.

Physical reality unfolds as the symmetry of successive states of a system are broken. Before a physical action changes a system, the probabilities of different possible outcomes can often be calculated. A minimal action is a quantum jump, marked by an increment of time. After the action, the probability of the actual state of the system becomes 1 and the probabilities of the other previously possible states becomes 0. Quantum symmetry breaking occurs as spacetime configurations crystalize into place.

159. Conclusion 3

Consciousness of a phenomenal world is an interactive process. It requires a subject to reflect or comprehend the world. The phenomenal world is unified and ordered by logical categories. A dialectical process starts in sensory immediacy and develops an ideally self-explanatory world. Self-consciousness and self-knowledge can also be modeled. The paradox of worldviews is the puzzle of reconciling the first-person and third-person views of a conscious brain.

Our reality unfolds as we break the symmetry of our states in action. This may correspond to the decoherence of superposed brain states that correlates with consciousness. Decoherence of superposed states of the decahertz EM field generated by synchronous neural firings may physically constitute the flow of subjective phenomenology.

Open questions include:
- Can we explain consciousness in photonic terms?
- How widespread is consciousness in nature?

- Can we build or control conscious machines?

160. Mindworlds

Mindworlds are structured sets of qualia with subjective sides that are:
- Phenomenologically closed and unified
- Manifested as consistent sets of facts
- Temporally transient or momentary
- Experienced as states of an ongoing "I"

The corresponding objective sides are:
- Centered on living and functioning brains
- Associated with specific interneural activity
- Realized as momentary boson condensates
- Linked in the flow of an ongoing me

161. On free will

With all the science in the world, I cannot predict my inner life. Still less can I predict the inner lives of other subjects. For me, free will is a known fact. Every moment of time that passes forces me to choose my world anew.

162. Countdown

The science of consciousness today is like the science of electromagnetism at the time of Faraday.
Vilayanur Ramachandran [43]

It's possible that in the next hundred years something really surprising will happen that will make us look at the whole mind-brain problem in a new way.
David Chalmers [44]

In a hundred years, we'll have a biological account of the brain and how it produces consciousness.
John Searle [45]

First-Person Consciousness

Two Professors

A nice everyday conception of consciousness is as autobiography. Ongoing experience is stored and restructured as a personal narrative, and consciousness is the generic mental state that accompanies this lifelong cognitive activity. On the higher scale of human cultural achievement, the literary form of autobiography brings this form of consciousness to a natural zenith. From this perspective, it is a happy coincidence that two distinguished philosophers of consciousness have recently published philosophical autobiographies.[1]

The first and more senior autobiographer is Ted Honderich, who from 1988 until his retirement in 1998 was the Grote Professor of Mind and Logic at University College London. The second is Colin McGinn, who since 1988 has been a professor of philosophy at Rutgers University in New Jersey. Both have written extensively on consciousness, and both weave their views on consciousness into their respective life stories. Indeed the parallels run deeper. Honderich grew up in Canada and moved to England to pursue his career in philosophy, almost all of it in London at UCL. McGinn grew up in England and moved to America to pursue his career, after spending some ten years of it at UCL alongside Honderich. And both were locked for decades in a love-hate relationship with Oxford, the parochial sun in the British philosophical firmament.

In other respects, the two protagonists seem to be opposites. Honderich is tall and gruff-voiced, a rough-hewn alpha male in the academic world, whose record of boozing, schmoozing, and womanizing stands almost scandalously proud of the philosophical pack. McGinn, by contrast, is short and modest in demeanor, and lives a quiet life as a vegetarian scholar whose main passion outside reading and writing is kayak surfing. Honderich comes from a family with German roots and has prosperous and well-connected relatives in Canada. McGinn's background is working class, with numerous coal miners in his family tree and no great financial ballast.

As for philosophy, both were close to the Oxford mainstream, in the British liberal tradition defined most prominently in recent decades by Sir Alfred Ayer, and both hold views on the philosophy of mind and consciousness that fall squarely within the Anglo-American analytical tradition of the last half-century or so. Honderich has held a variety of specific views, including a theory of *psychoneural intimacy* that seems a shade away from Davidsonian anomalous monism, and now maintains that consciousness is, in short, the experienced part of a world. McGinn has been closer to psychology, but ten years ago he came out for a position since dubbed *mysterianism* according to which we as a species are cognitively unable to get our minds around our own minds, so to speak, and must in all probability accept that our own consciousness will forever remain a mystery to us.

My plan here is to review the two autobiographies briefly from the standpoint of how they motivate and illuminate their respective authors' views on consciousness, then to look at those views more closely and see how far they give us a useful view of the truth, whatever it is, about consciousness. After that, I shall stand back a little and consider some recent developments within the wider field that both authors share. The main problem here is how to accommodate first-person phenomenology in a tradition that was historically dominated by behaviorism and is still inextricably linked to third-person reductionist science. This involves discussing the work of David Chalmers. Then, I shall consider the autobiographical enterprise as a source of insight into consciousness, with reference to the views of Daniel Dennett. In conclusion, I shall suggest that the unfolding history of science may be seen as the autobiography of consciousness itself.

As a declaration of interest, I am personally acquainted with both of the authors reviewed here. I met Colin and Ted in the 1970s. Colin and I are contemporaries, and we both served time as philosophers in Oxford and London. I met Ted again in August 2001 at the "Toward a Science of Consciousness" conference in Skövde, Sweden. David Chalmers I know from several recent conferences. In recent decades I have focused mainly on physics and computer science, but I share with all three a passion for the challenge of understanding consciousness.

From Boat to Grote

Ted Honderich was born in 1933 and raised in Canada. Initially, he wanted to be a writer in the manner of Hemingway or Arthur Miller, but then, as he wrote in his diary in 1957, he was "wonderfully inspired by A.J. Ayer's *Language, Truth and Logic*" and decided to study philosophy in England. As he reports in his autobiography: "My sight of England, from the deck of the liner *Italia*, as we came in along the coast to Portsmouth harbour in July 1959, was wonderfully affecting." Because Ayer was then Grote Professor of Mind and Logic at University College London, Honderich enrolled at UCL. Ayer held a regular seminar in the Grote professor's room at UCL, and there in October 1959 Honderich began his acquaintance with the subject, the role, and the room. After two years of study, he lectured for two years at the University of Sussex, then returned to teach at UCL, and stayed. In 1988 he made it to the Grote chair, and sat enthroned there until his emeritus years.

Honderich's autobiography is a large and fairly dense book that in parts rewards close reading. It is also eminently quotable, so let me save my own words for a while and quote the Grote:

> Philosophy is not any of linguistics, psychology, cognitive science or any other science. To its credit or discredit, there is hardly any Philosophy of Life in it, not much on the meaning of life, hardly any consolation. ... [Philosophy] is the line of life owed to a certain impulse ... to reduce to clarity and thereby get a systematic and comprehensive hold on the nature of one or two of the fundamental parts of reality, including human reality. ... I suspect the truth is that our line of life ... concentrates more on good thinking about the facts as against getting or using the facts ... Good thinking is getting a clear hold. That is the real impulse in philosophy.[2]

Well, good thinking about consciousness is worth treasuring, so let's see how Honderich builds up to the theme. He declares ownership of three main "pieces of philosophical furniture." First, he believes in determinism:

> [E]ach of the actions in our lives and also the choosing and willing of it is an *effect*. It is the effect of a sequence of events or states or properties, each of these also being an effect. ... Each effect is what it sounds like, something that had to happen. There was no other possibility. It wasn't just probable, to any degree.[3]

Second, he has a conviction about consciousness:

> The two problems here are the nature of consciousness itself and the relation of this consciousness to the brain. My conviction is that conscious events, states or properties involve what is easier to name than to analyse, a fundamental *subjectivity*. That is their essential nature. ... A demonstrated fact of psychoneural intimacy, as I was pleased to name it, is the gift of neuroscience to philosophy. A better gift, as it seems to me, than anything from muddled physics.[4]

Third, and less relevantly here, he believes in the principle of equality:

> [W]e should not be distracted or detained in any way from trying to make well-off in a certain sense all those who are badly-off. That is the solution to the problem of justice.[5]

More relevantly, Honderich's notion of the contribution of "muddled physics" to philosophy is the history of attempts to use quantum theory to deny determinism or to explain consciousness. It is easy to sympathize with his problem here:

> [T]he interpretation of Quantum Theory, the understanding of what it comes to in terms of the world, is allowed by most of its users to be a mess. Certainly it *is* a mess, and has remained so for too long. ... What is the mathematics or formalism of the theory *about*?[6]

Well, indeed, a tricky question, though hardly sufficient reason to give up on it in philosophy, especially when your life's work is a theory of determinism that seems at first glance to be simply falsified by quantum randomness. But Honderich gives up on more than physics:

> I have no love for Formal Logic, and enjoy the certainty that it has not solved or advanced any philosophical problem, and so I have not learned a lot.[7]

This is an embarrassing admission for a modern Anglo-American philosopher. In a tradition where some of the biggest names are Frege, Russell, Quine, and Kripke, it's hard to get by without mastering a few formulas. The consequence is that Honderich has nothing very useful to say on the deeper questions of truth and meaning.

We can check this by returning to his life story. In 1968, at 35, Honderich started his seventh year as lecturer and his fifth at UCL, working in an old terraced house that served as the philosophy department:

> My eyrie was at the back of the house. ... If these two years and the different one that followed were not wholly unlike all my others in terms of morale, they were a nadir. ... Another reflection on the first part of my nadir in morale is not yet perfectly manageable, and of course has to do with my actual philosophical abilities. ... [I]t is clear that I did not have and do not have all of the things that are called philosophical strengths. Fortunately, it is also clear that that is the condition of my entire profession.[8]

Honderich spent the academic year 1970–71 in the USA, the first semester at Yale and the second at the City University of New York. Of March 1971 he says:

> This was ... the nadir of my nadir in morale, not so bearable as the rest. As recorded a month later in my diary, I could not escape a kind of frenetic thinking on my troubles, fell to weeping for a while one day, and was afraid to be alone. ... Do I think I might have done myself in? ... Things weren't that bad. They never have been. I'm ordinary enough to be saved that.[9]

On a personal level, the chief consolation of philosophy is the support it provides for negotiating the existential fact about life, the human predicament, that it features moments of truth when the limits of one's powers and achievements become painfully evident. Critically examined, such moments can fuel some good thinking. The sustained rhetoric of introspection in Honderich's autobiography is a pleasing result of such thinking. But its lack of system is a weakness. The book is written almost like a diary, with topics coming and going over the weeks and years, with no clear thematization, or even a summary chronology or bibliography at the end. The life passes like a dream.

That said, the life featured a central achievement: a theory of determinism. Honderich's *magnum opus* is a thick volume entitled *A Theory of Determinism: The Mind, Neuroscience, and Life-Hopes*, a dry tome better not attempted by any reader who has not first enjoyed his brief, popular introduction *How Free Are You?*.[10] On the tome:

> I was confident that the book contained a resolution of the problem ... of the human consequences of determinism. ... [E]ach of us has two sorts of hope, including two sorts of life-hope. ... One sort of life-hope carries the thought or is based on the idea that maybe nothing will get in the way of your desires and your nature. ... The other sort of hope carries an additional thought, that your future is not already settled, that you have a kind of chance. ... The way to go on, said I, was to try to give up the kind of life-hope whose contained idea has to be false if determinism is true – give it up by trying to see that the other hope you can persist in is sustaining and there are other compensations.[11]

Beyond this work and his teaching, Honderich busied himself in gentlemanly fashion over several decades with ongoing editorial duties for several book series, including a venerable RKP series called *The International Library of Philosophy and Scientific Method*, a later Routledge series called *The Arguments of the Philosophers*, and the more popular philosophy paperbacks from Penguin. His work for these series was less than zealous, and involved various elements of bad conscience whenever the signs of his relaxed approach became too evident. Yet the harvest of this lifetime of editorial experience was good: in 1991 he was commissioned to edit *The Oxford Companion to Philosophy*.[12] After more work than he wanted, much of it sheer drudgery, the book was finally published to acclaim. Wittgenstein biographer Ray Monk said it was "the most authoritative single-volume reference work in philosophy yet published." Whatever Honderich's career may have lacked in analytical depth, it made up in breadth and community service.

Another major philosophical thread in his life has been the analysis of political activism, including violence and terrorism. This resulted in a succession of more or less ephemeral books that consistently located him in the left-liberal part of the political spectrum. Although he was no Marxist and boasted of never having read Marx, his rhetorical broadsides against conservatism, from Thatcherism generally to the specific Salisbury radicalism of his London colleague Roger Scruton (Honderich called him "the unthinking man's thinking man"), and against centrist liberalism, for example as represented by John Rawls with his theory of justice as fairness (Honderich called it "bumble"), must have scored points with many a Marxist. In the end, Honderich became a Labour Party activist. He was proud to work at the request of the then leader of the Labour Party, Neil Kinnock, on speeches for the 1992 general election campaign in which Kinnock, lampooned mercilessly in the tabloid press as the "Welsh windbag," lost to the equally uncharismatic Conservative Party leader John Major. Not a great advertisement for Honderich's political savvy, perhaps, but at least a tribute to a certain kind of moral consistency.

More entertainingly, Honderich was quite a Casanova. He treats us to plenty of detail about his succession of mistresses, none of it prurient but altogether quite sufficient to establish that despite his smooth veneer he was true to form in a joke he made to his longtime Marxist colleague Jerry Cohen (now Chichele Professor of Social and Political Theory at Oxford) that women are *tarmac* – "something rolled over or landed on in the course of life's journey." In his own summary verdict:

> I have been a man of many women, if that uncertain description is taken to mean a man who has been for a longish time with each of many women, a succession of them. Here my life has been a bit more than middle-sized. I have been a libertine too, if one of those goes on being free from convention, and does not go in for much concealment of his freedom.[13]

Remarkably, for a man who prides himself on good thinking and freedom from convention, his story never once reflects on his apparent compulsion to get down on the tarmac whenever he could, whatever the complications. He says he was not a sensual man and was quite conventional in sex, to the point when younger of not masturbating and finding condoms unmentionable, yet he frequently enjoyed casual sex outside the confines of his latest relationship, recommended abortions to his pregnant mistresses, and slept with several of his undergraduate students. Evidently it never occurred to him to stand back and consider the wider issues – even decades later, when trawling through his diaries to compile the catalog of his conquests.

This should not distract us from the philosophy, but it does. No man who womanizes – and wines – so freely can be *rigorous* enough to cut it down at the coalface of knowledge. If you don't believe me, ask Colin.

From Blackpool to Broadway

Colin McGinn was born in 1950 in Hartlepool and grew up in Gillingham and Blackpool. After taking O-levels in a secondary modern school and A-levels in a grammar school, he graduated with a First in Psychology from the University of Manchester and then took a distinguished B.Phil in Philosophy at Oxford. The latter degree was quite a challenge at first because as a philosophical neophyte he was surrounded by high-powered specialists who scorned his provincial background. But in 1974 he won the prestigious John Locke prize in philosophy – he was informed of his triumph by Professor Ayer personally and in public as he was waiting for a lecture by Saul Kripke to commence – and this put him on the road to philosophical success. In the same year he got a job as a Lecturer at University College London, alongside Honderich, who had just been promoted from Senior Lecturer to Reader.

McGinn worked for many years at UCL and wrote several books. In 1980 he spent what for him was a glorious semester at the University of California, Los Angeles, with good discussions on what were then the fashionable topics of belief and desire with David Kaplan and Keith Donnellan. In 1982 he survived a less glorious semester at the University of Southern California, where he struggled mightily with Wittgenstein and Kripke on meaning and wasted endless hours playing such video games as Pacman and Galaga in amusement arcades. These visits opened his eyes to the fact that American philosophy was flourishing independently of Oxbridge, and awakened in him the idea that maybe he should emigrate to the United States.

First-Person Consciousness

But it wasn't over yet in England. Just after his 1982 visit to California he well-nigh burned himself out writing a book that tried to correct what he saw as Kripke's misrepresentation of Wittgenstein's views on meaning.[14] To get away from it all in his head, he morosely wrote a novel. For years he had nursed a secondary ambition to make it as a man of letters, as he reveals in his autobiography:

> I had always had a yen to try my hand at fiction ... Reading the early novels of Martin Amis (before he got famous) also stimulated me; I liked his combination of literacy and vulgarity, the high and the low.[15]

Martin Amis graduated from Oxford with a congratulatory First in 1971, which was the year McGinn graduated, so it was natural to make comparisons. Honderich confirms this with characteristic wit: "The envy of my small colleague Colin McGinn ... extended even to wanting to be Martin Amis."[16] Martin's autobiography,[17] cast as a record of his relations with his father Kingsley, appeared to such fanfare in 2000 that it must have influenced Colin, whose own life story has a preface dated July 2001.

Indeed McGinn's prose style owes a lot to Martin Amis, and many of the most amusing words in his vocabulary are straight from the Amis *oevre*. McGinn's novel was called *Bad Patches* and written as the first-person story of an unfortunate antihero who suffers gruesome mishaps, works with a pair of stooges called Fock and Fack, and makes out with a female dentist. McGinn commissioned an agent to try to publish it, but no-one was interested. I haven't read the book, of course, but in my mind's eye I can already see Martin's style prints all over it. Martin and I were friends for a while as undergraduates, and I too was fascinated by Martin's early novels. Indeed many years later I too wrote a novel, and my agent also failed to find a publisher for it. Colin may agree that such an enterprise is born of the sort of deep night of the soul for which the best consolation is good philosophy.

In the summer of 1982, McGinn applied without much hope for the prestigious post of Wilde Reader in Mental Philosophy at the University of Oxford, formerly held until his untimely death by the legendary and charismatic Gareth Evans. Miraculously, it seemed, McGinn was offered the job, apparently because the psychologists saw in him a kindred spirit, more sympathetic than the philosophically stronger candidate Chris Peacocke, who as an All Souls genius may have been rather too Olympian for them. Once McGinn was established as the new mental philosopher, he began working hard on the interface of philosophy and psychology. There he had his greatest insight in philosophy:

> [T]wo sets of thoughts were mingling in my mind at this time: the potential unknowability of reality, and the deeply puzzling nature of the mind-brain relation. ... One night, as I lay in bed turning these things over in my mind ... the two sets of ideas locked together. It was one of those flashes of insight that I had read about in other people's memoirs. Maybe the reason we are having so much trouble solving the mind-body problem is that reality contains an ingredient that we cannot know. ... [I]f we could remedy this ignorance the solution to the problem would be immediate and uncontroversial. ... We are suffering from what I called 'cognitive closure' with respect to the mind-body problem.[18]

The result was his paper "Can We Solve the Mind-Body Problem?" that first presented the *mysterian* position for which he was later popularized in *Scientific American*.[19] This bleak and rather disappointing insight is McGinn's defining achievement as a philosopher. Most of his other philosophical work, so far as I can see, is of technical or educational interest but not historic, and his early writings made little impact. Said Ted, unkindly: "McGinn ... distinguished himself not only as the Wilde Reader in Oxford but also the Wilde Writer."[20] It is a relief to add that McGinn's life story takes no shots at Honderich.

In 1988 McGinn spent a semester at City University of New York. He realized it was time to move out of an increasingly stifling Oxford scene and leave the Thatcherized remnants of British philosophy behind. Soon after his return to England, he was offered a post at Rutgers University in New Jersey and took it. The rest was plain sailing. Living in New York, enjoying street life on Broadway and kayak surfing off Long Island to keep the looming ghost of critical self-consciousness at bay, he found the peace of mind to write his life story.

From Dualistic Identity to Existence

Let us now look briefly at Honderich's views on consciousness. Here I face a methodological problem. Nowhere in his autobiography does Honderich state what those views are in a way that escapes the morass of second thoughts, jargon, and posturing *isms* that envelops too much in the philosophy of mind. Everything is qualified with doubts and nuanced to the competing views of other thinkers. Life is too short to go through all the works he mentions in passing, especially since he seems to think most of them are wrong, so I shall rest content here with a few brief notes.

Let me illustrate the problem thus. In the year 1971–72, Honderich edited a volume entitled *Essays on Freedom of Action* whose theme was whether determinism was compatible or incompatible with freedom,[21] on which he says:

> My assembled contributors ... had given a majority vote for the answer of Compatibilism, with [Donald] Davidson, [Daniel] Dennett, and [Anthony] Kenny to the fore. ... David Wiggins, with the aid of a symbol or two of formal logic and 29 substantial footnotes, followed by further material attached to an asterisk, had proved to his satisfaction that much was to be said for the gloom and bravery on the other side. ... My situation was still one of being inclined to join David Wiggins in the gloom of Incompatibilism, if not at all in the bravery about determinism.[22]

See what I mean? But let's plough on. In the year 1977–78, Honderich and Myles Burnyeat edited a volume entitled *Philosophy As It Is* that included the celebrated paper "Mental Events" by Donald Davidson,[23] on which Honderich says:

> [W]hat did Donald Davidson mean by saying mind and brain were *identical*? What did he mean if he also said that he was *not* reducing mind to brain, not embracing Eliminative Materialism, not joining those Australians for whom conceiving the *Art of the Fugue* was nothing but a complex physical event – no sweetener for the pill? I had managed to write my brief preface without finding out.[24]

When Honderich tries to tackle these questions directly, this is the result:

> The main idea in Identity Theories of mind and brain ... was that a conscious or mental event, an event with the property of subjectivity, was identical with a brain event. But what did that come to? ... The first answer was that the conscious event had only the property or properties of subjectivity. ... This was the madness of mentalizing the brain. ... Things were just as bad if you started at the other side ... This was the absurdity of Eliminative Materialism. ... There was another answer to the question ... You could say the conscious event had both the property of subjectivity and also neural properties. Indeed, that seemed to be what was in the minds of such sensible persons as Professor Davidson. ... Clearly a dualism of two kinds of properties remained when the dualism of two events had been discarded. This deserved the name of being a Dualistic Identity Theory. ... This was the prideful start of the paper 'Psychophysical Lawlike Connections and Their Problem'. My friend Alastair Hannay honourably published it in his journal Inquiry.[25]

This seems not to be going anywhere much beyond Davidson's ideas, but let's pursue the thread further anyway. Here's the next gobbit:

> Another anomaly on my mind was Anomalous Monism, the best-known and most intriguing version of the idea that mind and brain do not merely go together but are one thing. It was owned by the aforementioned Don Davidson, the Pied Piper of Berkeley, California ... This Dualistic Identity Theory has more to it ... The first proposition is the humdrum one that there are causal relations between mental and physical things ... The second is that wherever there are causal relations between things, the things are connected as a matter of natural or scientific law, nomically connected. ... The third proposition is that there are no lawlike connections between mental and physical things. Mental things are not a matter of law but are anomalous.[26]

We can skip the further quotes for this story. Honderich argued that this boiled down to epiphenomenalism and published his claim in *Analysis*. In the next issue, Peter Smith of Sheffield University said that Honderich was confused. In the next, Honderich replied that Smith was confused. In the next, Smith replied that Honderich was extremely confused. In the next, Honderich said something unintelligible (to me at least) about mauve slippers. I spare you the references in *Analysis*. Who cares? Academic catfights are sometimes as daft as they seem.

Honderich picked many such fights. One such arose from the big book by Karl Popper and neurophysiologist John Eccles called *The Self and Its Brain*:[27]

> The book ... announced that the Self or Self-Conscious Mind was not tied to the brain, but was its proprietor, somehow free-floating and magnificent. ... It proved possible for me ... to concentrate ... on the basic reason given for the doctrine. This was a piece of Californian nonsense owed mostly to one Benjamin Libet of that state's university. Wrapped up in much experimental evidence in nine scientific papers, it was about a conscious sensation occurring on its own before the brain caught up with it. My refutation, wrapped up in much conceptual clarification, had been accepted as an article by The Journal of Theoretical Biology, thereby establishing to its readers that philosophy was not merely the handmaiden of science.[28]

In fact, the story is a little more complicated. Libet and his colleagues said:

> [A] dissociation between the timings of the corresponding 'mental' and 'physical' events would seem to raise serious though not insurmountable difficulties for the ... theory of psychoneural identity.[29]

On the basis of Libet's early results, Popper and Eccles said:

> This antedating procedure does not seem to be explicable by any neurophysiological process. Presumably it is a strategy that has been learnt by the self-conscious mind ... to play tricks with time.[30]

It took some years get this clear. To summarize, Libet's most intriguing result was that when a stimulus was applied to the skin of certain patients, it took about half a second before they were consciously aware of that stimulus, yet the patients themselves had the subjective impression that there was no delay at all in their becoming aware of the stimulus. The patients apparently referred the perception of the skin-touching backwards in time by about half a second.[31] Daniel Dennett gives a good account of the story that concludes:

> Where does this leave Libet's experiments with cortical stimulation? As an interesting but inconclusive attempt to establish something about *how the brain represents temporal order*.[32]

The full story is long, tangled, and irrelevant here. As I see it, all this illustrates the dangers of waxing too rhetorical about consciousness before the basic science is firmly in place.

To return to Honderich, he continued to engage with relish in academic fights. In 1992–93, he published "The Union Theory and Anti-Individualism" in *Mental Causation*, a collection of papers edited by Heil and Mele.[33] This paper was the first of several in which his "long-held truths" about the nature of consciousness and its relation to the brain were defended against what he hoped were passing fashions. The paper featured clashes with Harvard professor Hilary Putnam and California professor Tyler Burge, but it is hard to make sense of the details from his rather florid autobiographical account, as it breaks off abruptly with a paragraph about ongoing editorial work for the *Oxford Companion to Philosophy*. Apparently a righteously angry female contributor mailed him a large brown envelope addressed in large letters to *Gross Yob Honderich*.

In later years, Honderich mellowed somewhat. In November 1994, he presented a paper at a philosophical meeting in Copenhagen in which he discussed John Searle's book *The Rediscovery of the Mind* (1992):[34]

> My Copenhagen paper looked at [Searle's] way of seeking to state the truth about consciousness ... by ... relying on what he called humble and obvious truths about the mind. One was that a conscious event has a special mode of existence. It exists only as *somebody's* conscious event. It depends for its existence on a 'first person', an 'I'. But what did that mean if it was not a dive into the deep and murky philosophical water? ... What about the natural idea noticed in his famous paper 'What Is It Like to Be a Bat?' by Thomas Nagel ... the idea that when something is conscious, there is a way it is like to be that thing. ... Isn't it inevitable that what we understand by what it is like to be something is *what it is like to be something conscious* or indeed *what it is like to be conscious*? But this is a disaster. ... The sad conclusion of my paper, which thereafter went into the *American Philosophical Quarterly*, was that humble and obvious truths were no great help in trying to understand consciousness.[35]

In spring 1996, preparing for the 1996–97 lectures of the Royal Institute of Philosophy, Honderich boiled down his thoughts on consciousness to a short list:
1. Conscious events are physical events.
2. Conscious events are in our heads.
3. Conscious events are not merely cells.

However, this was not entirely satisfactory: "It sounded like something awful heard of before in the history of philosophy, in connection with souls, egos and selves – *conscious stuff*, maybe a relative of ectoplasm".[36] In the first RIP lecture, he finally said that *my consciousness consists in the existence of a world*.

> Despite the initial suspicion, my saying my perceptual consciousness consists in a world is indeed not philosophical disaster. ... We need to be guided by the idea of *consciousness as existence*.[37]

Honderich pursued this theme in a series of papers. In May 2002, he mailed me an electronic preprint of the latest installment. The basic idea is that what it is to be conscious of certain things is for those and related things in a certain way to exist. Whether we can do much more with this idea or not, I like the idea that consciousness consists in a world. I had a similar idea some years ago, independently, and built a lot of formal logic around it. But I spare you the details. Let's just say all these ideas represent work in progress.

The Mysterious Flame

For my money, McGinn's best book – and indeed the best elementary introduction by anyone to the philosophy of consciousness – is *The Mysterious Flame*.[38] Because it presents his views on consciousness more fully than does his rather thin autobiography, I shall quote from it exclusively in this section.

> The central topic of this book is the explanation of consciousness. Suppose I had asked you to imagine waking from a coma without having a brain in your head. You would have been rightly perplexed. Having a brain is what makes it possible to have a mental life. The brain is the 'seat of consciousness' … The machinery of the brain allows the mind to work as it does and to have the character it does. … I argue that the bond between the mind and the brain is a deep mystery. Moreover, it is an ultimate mystery, a mystery that human intelligence will never unravel.[39]

Thanks in part to the Amis apprenticeship, McGinn's style is clear and direct – a refreshing change from Honderich's ponderous constructions (in a *New Society* review of his early book on punishment, Giles Playfair said, "Honderich is, to say the least, an ungifted writer of English prose"[40]). McGinn also has the knack of drilling down precisely onto perplexing issues:

> Isn't there some kind of violation of the uniformity of nature in the fact that brains produce consciousness? Brains seem very similar to other parts of animal bodies, being basically a big collection of cells organized according to biochemical principles. Yet there is a yawning chasm between the natures of these entities, because brains produce consciousness and those other meaty organs do not, not even a little bit.[41]

> Some people like to harp on the complexity of the brain, as if this gave a clue to its mental productivity. But sheer complexity is irrelevant: merely adding more neurons with more synaptic connections doesn't explain our problem a bit. The problem is how *any* collection of cells, no matter how large and intricately related, could generate consciousness.[42]

> What do electricity and cells have to do with conscious subjectivity? How could a conscious self exist *inside* such a soggy clump? It begins to seem that we are all djinns, each magically ensconced in our own personal brain lamps, waiting to be rubbed into life.[43]

When it comes to presenting the main historical doctrines on mind and brain, or rather to presenting the straw men that he wishes to cut down with *samurai* swordstrokes of pure reason, McGinn's exposition is clear as a bell:

> Materialism says there is nothing more to the mind than the brain as currently conceived. The mind is made of meat. It *is* meat, neither more nor less. ... According to materialism, we are under an illusion about the nature of the mind.[44]

> Dualism ... is best interpreted as the belief that there is no logical relation between brain and mind. There is no possibility of reducing the mind to the brain, because they are separate realms. There are indeed empirical and contingent relations between the two – correlations between mental and physical processes have been discovered – but there is no necessary link between consciousness and the brain.[45]

> There are two major problems with dualism, the 'zombie problem' and the 'ghost problem'. The zombie problem is that dualism allows us to subtract the mind from the brain while leaving the brain completely intact. ... The ghost problem is the converse of the zombie problem. If the mind is separate from the body, then not only can the brain exist without the mind but the mind can exist without the brain.[46]

But the argument soon homes in on the despairing theme that we may never understand consciousness. For what it's worth, I find the arguments he presents to be bloodless and unconvincing. The general drift is toward the *a priori* position that we do not have reasonable grounds to expect in advance that we will find a satisfactory explanation, despite all the progress we see elsewhere in science and the massive advances we have made recently in the detailed understanding of brain physiology and cognitive function. Here is an example of such an *a priori* argument:

> We certainly cannot infer that *since* we understand the physical world so well it is only a matter of time until we understand consciousness, because consciousness is so different from what has so far yielded to our understanding.[47]

The basis for his pessimism is in large part the Chomskian view that the mind is highly modular, with specific innate capabilities. This view has been skillfully popularized in an evolutionary context by Steven Pinker.[48] As McGinn puts it:

> The prevailing view in cognitive psychology today is that the human mind consists of separate faculties, each dedicated to certain cognitive tasks: linguistic, social, practical, theoretical, abstract, spatial, and emotional. The mind is thus as highly structured as the body. ... Every mental faculty has limits

to its achievements and acuity, and necessarily so. ... We can, it is true, do more with our minds than apes can, but that does not mean that we somehow magically escape the constraints of biology.[49]

This model of the mind as a Swiss army pocketknife, a multifunctional kludge, provides a tempting reason to deny the explicability of consciousness, but McGinn offers – apparently unwittingly – a large piece of ammunition that I think we can use to argue *for* the ultimate explicability of how the djinn is ensconced in the meat. He presents the ammo as a general consideration on the logic of thinking:

> Perhaps the most basic aspect of thought is the operation of *combination*. This is the way in which we think of complex entities as resulting from the arrangement of simpler parts. There are three aspects to this basic idea: the atoms we start with, the laws we use to combine them, and the resulting complexes. We find these three basic elements in everything from physics to language to mathematics. ... The big question is this: Is the mode of derivation of the mind from the brain comprehensible according to this kind of combinatorial model? ... The answer is clearly "No."[50]

This stacking of parts into wholes suggests a Lego brick model of mind that uses a single basic strategy for every representational task. If you have enough Lego bricks, or enough neurons in your brain, you can model just about anything. To use another metaphor, just as the information revolution has swept all before it by digitizing any and every content area into the binary logic of bit streams, so the biological breakthrough of endowing a species with a big, labile neuronet that can do nifty combinatorics has swept that species into dominance all over the natural landscape. And the reason I think this is ammunition *for* the explicability of the mind-brain connection is that there is no end of historical cases where the apparently simple *qualitative* nature of some puzzling natural phenomenon yielded – often unexpectedly – to a somewhat more complex conception of it in terms of the quantitative behavior of otherwise familiar entities. For me, the explanations of heat and the phases of matter in terms of molecular motion and of life and heredity in terms of organic chemistry both offer close enough parallels to suggest that the Lego brick mind, despite its humble evolutionary ancestry, can perform prodigious feats of explanation. It is certainly not clear that the proper answer to McGinn's rhetorical question is no.

McGinn offers another piece of ammunition to his critics when he stresses the humble nature of consciousness:

> Consciousness is not the evolutionary pinnacle, not the most impressive piece of organism design to date. Consciousness, I believe, is biologically primitive and simple, comparatively speaking.[51]

This suggests that the whole mind-brain mystery is a mountain from a molehill. The puzzle looks big to us because we are close to it. Indeed, we are each as close as we can be to our own personal copy of the puzzle. *Minds are us*, we have to admit, and then we can't stand back far enough to be objective. Yet McGinn wants to say we face a more substantial cognitive limit:

> To grasp what I am saying about cognitive limitations it is vital to distinguish sharply between the brain as an objective entity in the world and our conception of the brain. The key point is that the objective nature of the brain is not exhausted by our conception of it.[52]

Good point, but not a problem. The soggy clump of cells is a red herring. The functioning brain has a feature that does not show up well in blithe philosophical talk of meat or neurons, or even in many clinical or laboratory investigations of brains, namely a surrounding electromagnetic field. This field offers a much more plausible candidate to serve as the substrate of the mind or the seat of the soul than any macromolecular, microtubular, or neural substrate. The objective nature of the brain is that it generates a complex and dynamic electromagnetic field that interacts with the neurons in subtle ways that are not yet well understood. On this issue, the best reference I know is a recent *JCS* paper by Johnjoe McFadden.[53] An electromagnetic field that interacts with neurons through coherence and phase locking (see the work of Wolf Singer and others cited by McFadden) has nontrivial quantum properties (like laser beams) and should therefore be seen as a photonic field. Given the undeniable fact that we have a long way to go before we exhaust such fertile conceptions, it is premature to abandon all hope and go canoeing with the mysterians.

Interestingly, the field theory of consciousness that may emerge from the work of McFadden and others suggests a view of the mind that surprisingly echoes the radical dualism of Popper and Eccles. McGinn characterizes this general kind of dualism in theistic terms:

> The picture is that God created your soul and adjoined it to your body for the duration of your mortal life. ... The brain is merely the organ or instrument of consciousness, not its cause or origin. According to this kind of theistic dualism, the brain is a mediation device used by the soul to influence the movements of the body. The soul itself is a thing apart.[54]

The theism is scientifically unhelpful, of course:

> The hypothesis of God simply pushes the question back, either because he himself has complex design or because he is himself a conscious being. ... The second problem is that ... sentience is by no means unique to human beings. ... The third problem is that the mind of an organism is manifestly causally dependent upon its brain, no matter how hard it is to penetrate the nature of this dependence.[55]

A materialist dualism obtained by identifying the mind with a photonic field obviates the first problem and turns the second and third into benefits. It also puts us right on the issue of how minds can act on brains:

> What is crucial to hyperdualism is the denial that brains cause consciousness to exist. Rather, consciousness exists in its own right in its own dimension of reality. The brain is not generative; it is merely transducive. As it were, the brain listens to consciousness instead of uttering consciousness. ... This raises two big questions: How could disembodied consciousness cause anything? and How could the physical sequence of events in the material universe be disrupted by what is going on in the parallel mental universe?[56]

A more practical question is whether we can clarify the phenomenology of photonic fields sufficiently to avoid other problems, such as panpsychism:

> According to panpsychism, the reason we are stumped by the question of how the material brain produces consciousness is that we ignore the fact that consciousness is pervasive in nature. Matter is throbbing with consciousness in all of its manifestations; the brain simply steps the mental volume up high enough for us to notice its presence.[57]

If photonic fields are supposed to explain consciousness, this is by no means a trivial problem, since such fields are just about everywhere in nature. The explanation must be a long and tortuous story, and then we are almost back where we started:

> Granted that atoms do not have full-blown mental states, might they not have mental states in a degraded or attenuated sense? ... No, the idea must be that rocks have what are sometimes called *proto*mental states, states that can *yield* conscious states while not themselves *being* conscious states. ... The problem with this theory [is that it] merely says that matter has *some* properties or other, to be labeled "protomental," that account for the emergence of consciousness from brains. But of course *that* is true! It is just a way of saying that consciousness cannot arise by magic; it must have some basis in matter.[58]

The photonic theory is still an embryo, too delicate for the cut and thrust of philosophical posturing, but it does bring relativistic and quantum insights about time and indeterminacy right into the heart of the story, where they can help us explain the elementary facts of consciousness. Such a theory may seem like overkill, but that's not the problem that worries McGinn, who stoutly maintains there will be no kill at all:

> If a theory provided a fully adequate explanation of the mind-brain link, it would not really matter how crazy it appeared to us to be. The problem is that no matter *how* crazy we allow ourselves to be, we can never account for the elementary facts of consciousness.[59]

This is a *non sequitur* of numbing grossness (to echo Peter Strawson's words about something Kant once said – words that McGinn quotes approvingly in his autobiography as brilliant logical swordplay). But before we toss McGinn's work out with the trash, let's review some of the elementary facts he has in mind.

> [T]here is this strange incongruity in the relation between mind and world: the world outside us is essentially spatial and we represent it that way in our every experience, yet our experience is itself essentially nonspatial. ... The nonspatiality of consciousness is connected with another feature of it, namely its imperceptibility. Consciousness enables us to perceive the world, but it is not itself a perceptible thing. ... This is surely part of the reason for the famed infallibility of introspection: you can't be wrong about your conscious states because there is no sense in the idea of these states moving out of range of the introspective faculty.[60]

OK so far – nonspatiality, imperceptibility, and infallibility.

> Consciousness appears to be *transparent* to the subject of consciousness. The question is: Is this impression correct? ... Is every property that is *intrinsic* to my consciousness revealed to my faculty of self-knowledge?[61]

The word *intrinsic* is tricky. McGinn says that the Freudian unconscious, for example, is extrinsic to consciousness, but the *computational* unconscious is intrinsic. This is important, since the computational substructure of conscious thoughts is in a fuzzy zone that may or may not surface in consciousness, as we can see from the routine performance of learned tasks or from the phenomenon of blindsight. But perhaps the most puzzling fruit of consciousness is the sense of self:

First-Person Consciousness

> I may not be certain that there is an external world, or even that I have a body, but I am certain that I exist. ... *Cogito, ergo sum.* ... If we cannot understand states of consciousness, then it is hardly likely that we will be able to understand the nature of the *subject* of those states. That subject is simply defined to *be* what has those mysterious conscious states. ... The deeper question here is how a bunch of cells can become a self *anyway*: What converts biological tissue into that self whose existence so impressed Descartes? The fact is that there are no scientific criteria for the appearance of selves; all we have are shaky intuitions about when to declare the onset of selfhood.[62]

This is a more complex question that surely involves a lot of cultural baggage. No theory of brainwaves is going to help us decide when abortion is permissible, for example, or where to set the age of responsibility for children. Yet biologists happily talk about the immunological self and psychologists about logical stages in the development of self, so we don't need to be too mysterian about this.

Another basic issue is how far a computational model of mind can take us. This is ground well covered by John Searle and all his debaters. McGinn sides with Searle:

> Mental processes are *not* identifiable with symbol-manipulating algorithms. There are two big problems with the theory. The first is that minds *do* respond to meaning and not just to syntax. ... My mental processes involve the manipulation of meanings, not merely strings of syntax. I am a *semantic* manipulator, as well as a syntactic one. ... The second point is that running a program does not guarantee sentience; in fact, it is neither necessary nor sufficient for sentience. It is not necessary because sentience in general does not involve symbolic manipulations.[63]

The point seems clear, but there are subtle issues here that proponents of functionalism and machine intelligence can use to fight back. Those who talk too confidently about the computational intractability of semantics are guilty of the sort of reification of meaning that offended Wittgenstein in his later years. Meaning is a treacherous quagmire: even street signs mean what they say whether I read them or not, and even I don't always mean what I say. But we digress. For McGinn, the outcome is clear:

> What follows from all this is not that a robot could not be conscious. What follows is that a robot could not be conscious *in virtue* of being a computer – that is, in virtue of running computer programs.[64]

Be that as it may, the more interesting question is whether something analogous holds for *any* purported mechanism of consciousness. For example, it may soon be debatable whether a robot could be conscious *in virtue* of interacting functionally with a dynamically configured photonic field around its core processor. Only time will tell.

To return to McGinn's argument, this much is true:

> The mechanism of consciousness is a mystery. But then how are we to *say* whether an inorganic brain could be conscious? If we knew what made *our* brains conscious, then we could ask whether that property could exist in an inorganic system. But we are in the dark on the question simply because we don't know what makes our brains conscious.[65]

This much, however, is not:

> Speaking loftily, it is just a matter of bad cognitive *luck* that we cannot solve the mind-body problem; our minds happen not to have been engineered that way.[66]

McGinn's bad luck certainly, but if someone had said something similar about, say, the matter-energy problem a hundred years ago, Einstein would have proved them wrong just three years later. Indeed McGinn seems tantalizingly close to such a revelation:

> My whole point has been that mind and brain form an indissoluble unity *at the level of objective reality*. ... Objectively we are naturally constituted from smoothly meshing materials, as seamless as anything else in nature. We only *seem* comical because we cannot grasp what this unified reality consists of.[67]

But no, his grip is gone. Someone else must do the job.

Toward a Science of Consciousness

Forgive me, but I need to review some history before we can go on to see how to build over all the work of Honderich and McGinn – and many other philosophers – on consciousness. The key figure here will be David Chalmers, who is clearly the leading philosopher of consciousness to have emerged in the last ten years.

Logical positivism had its roots in the late nineteenth century in the work of the Austrian physicist Ernst Mach, whose work was important for Einstein's special theory of relativity (1905). From those roots, the Vienna Circle arose after the First World War and created a tradition that venerated Wittgenstein's *Tractatus* (1922) and gave rise to Ayer's *Language, Truth and Logic* (1936).[68]

Wittgenstein had been inspired by Frege and worked with Russell, but the *Tractatus* is a unique work with a deeper ambition. He later repudiated that ambition and spent the following decades working out a more pragmatic view of language and thought. Ayer's work flowed directly from the approach that Russell defined and remained consistent as Oxford orthodoxy evolved toward Wittgenstein's later views.

The positivist movement had its effect on the sciences, not only in physics but also in psychology, where J. B. Watson founded behaviorism and B. F. Skinner and others continued it into the 1960s. In philosophy, too, the influence continued into the 1960s. In particular, Willard Van Orman Quine, who was not only Skinner's friend but also an accomplished mathematician, pushed on with Russell's work in mathematical logic and created a new philosophical puzzle, the *indeterminacy of translation*, that meshed well with a behaviorist outlook.[69] Quine and Davidson set the philosophical tone in Oxford in the 1970s, when I was there. The positivist tradition left its mark on cognitive science in the idea that the brain can reasonably be modeled by any computational black box that when fed with appropriate input produces the right output. That mark is evident in Douglas Hofstadter's brilliant and idiosyncratic work on Gödel's incompleteness theorems and the computational approach to the mind in Artificial Intelligence.[70] After early research in mathematics at Oxford, Chalmers worked with Hofstadter's team in Indiana.

The phenomenological tradition began in Germany in the nineteenth century from the work of Edmund Husserl, who lost a debate with Frege on the foundations of arithmetic. We can see Husserl's work as an attempt to recreate in a rigorous and scientific manner what Hegel had sketched in his verbose but visionary *Phänomenologie des Geistes* (1807). Husserl's most famous student was Martin Heidegger, whose notoriously obscure book *Sein und Zeit* (1927) founded the existentialist movement most famously associated with Jean-Paul Sartre.[71] Many observers imagine that despite its initial ambitions, the phenomenology of Husserl and his followers is no longer relevant to psychology. Yet any modern science of consciousness has a historical link there. As the perceptive critic Thomas Metzinger says:

> [T]he idea of a 'science of consciousness' is anything but a new idea, especially from the viewpoint of the philosopher. For example, the whole phenomenological movement (and its demise) can be understood in these terms.[72]

In philosophy, too, the phenomenological tradition diverged so far from the Anglo-American tradition that the two can now be seen as quite separate cultural movements, between which understanding is at best limited. To illustrate this claim, I can hardly do better than quote Honderich, reporting on a 1998 BBC radio show in which he participated:

> I pleased myself and some others by first saying of Continental Philosophy that I was like many British philosophers in not allowing my ignorance of it entirely to obstruct my judgement. It was a different kind of thing from ours, and aspired more to the condition of literature or intellectual show-business. It was only disgraceful by our standards.[73]

As an aside, one may wonder whether the works of Honderich and others, if not most recent Anglo-American philosophical writings on consciousness, will seem disgraceful to future scientists of consciousness.

Now I can explain the relevance of all this history. Both positivism and phenomenology influenced the development in the 1920s of quantum mechanics by Bohr, Einstein, Dirac, Heisenberg, Schrödinger, and others.[74] The message of positivism was that in science only facts count, and anything that cannot be verified or falsified can be cast out as metaphysics. The facts about black body radiation and electron orbitals in atoms were not consistent with the usual interpretation of classical physics. So out with the classical metaphysics and start again! The message of phenomenology was that the way to start again was to create a systematic account of the experimentally observable phenomena, no more. That account would create its own theoretical frame and with it a new metaphysical conception of reality.

By and large, this has happened. The new metaphysics is not yet as stable as we might like, as Honderich and McGinn would both insist, but we are making progress. The theoretical work of John Bell in the 1960s and its experimental investigation by Aspect and others in the 1980s have greatly clarified the situation, and enabled us to clean up the interpretational mess left by the pioneers.[75] The new *consistent histories* approach to quantum phenomena championed by Omnès improves on all its predecessors,[76] and in particular on the Everett *many-worlds* picture favored by David Chalmers.

So, back to Chalmers. To set the stage, let me again proceed with a series of quotations, this time from *The Conscious Mind*. First, his stated aim:

> In developing my account of consciousness, I have tried to obey a number of constraints. The first and most important is to *take consciousness seriously*. ... The second ... is to *take science seriously*. ... The third constraint is that I take consciousness to be a natural phenomenon, falling under the sway of natural

laws. If so, then there should be *some* correct scientific theory of consciousness, whether or not we can arrive at such a theory.[77]

He starts from Nagel's idea of *what it is like* and introduces qualia:

> We can say that a being is conscious if there is *something it is like* to be that being ... we can say that a mental state is conscious if it has a *qualitative feel* – an associated quality of experience. These qualitative feels are also known as phenomenal qualities, or *qualia* for short.[78]

Dennett's vociferous objections to qualia notwithstanding,[79] Chalmers makes extensive use of qualia. I think the proper course is to remain agnostic about them for a while and see where they take us. If we don't like the destination, we can always come back and throw them out.

Next, Chalmers distinguishes two quite distinct concepts of mind, the *phenomenal* and the *psychological*. On the phenomenal concept, mind is characterized by the way it *feels*; on the psychological concept, mind is characterized by what it *does*. Aspiring phenomenologists face a linguistic problem that psychologists do not share, namely that our *language* for phenomenal qualities is derivative on our nonphenomenal language. The result is that our progress in the physical and cognitive sciences has not shed significant light on the question of how and why cognition and consciousness are related. For Chalmers, a useful concept here is *supervenience*, which formalizes the intuitive idea that one set of facts can fully determine another set of facts:

> B-properties *supervene* on A-properties if no two possible situations are identical with respect to their A-properties while differing in their B-properties.[80]

> The position we are left with is that almost all facts supervene logically on the physical facts (including physical laws), with possible exceptions for conscious experience, indexicality, and negative existential facts. To put the matter differently, we can say that the facts about the world are exhausted by (1) particular physical facts, (2) facts about conscious experience, (3) laws of nature, (4) a second-order "That's all" fact, and perhaps (5) an indexical fact about my location.[81]

Facts (4) and (5) here are key, I believe, in reconstructing a logical concept of consciousness in the framework of modern physics, where the relativity to the observer of both time and determinacy is reflected in the formalism. But let us not digress. Back to supervenience:

> The failure of consciousness to logically supervene on the physical tells us that no reductive explanation of consciousness can succeed. Given any account of the physical processes purported to underlie consciousness, there will always be a further question: Why are these properties accompanied by conscious experience?[82]

Chalmers presents the following argument against physicalism:[83]
1. In our world, there are conscious experiences.
2. There is a logically possible world physically identical to ours, in which the positive facts about consciousness in our world do not hold.
3. Therefore, facts about consciousness are further facts about our world, over and above the physical facts.
4. So materialism is false.

On this basis, Chalmers argues that to bring consciousness within the scope of a theory of everything in fundamental physics, along the lines envisaged by Stephen Hawking and Steven Weinberg, "we need to introduce *new* fundamental properties and laws."[84] He calls his view *naturalistic dualism*. He claims that that if one takes consciousness seriously, then property dualism is the only reasonable option.

This much would presumably be endorsed warmly by Honderich. However, Chalmers disagrees with McGinn:

> *Mysterianism*. Those unsympathetic to reductive accounts of consciousness often hold that consciousness may remain an eternal mystery. ... Such a view has been ... developed by McGinn. ... Such a view can be tempting, but it is premature. To say that there is no reductive explanation of consciousness is not to say that there is no explanation at all.[85]

As a preliminary to his effort toward a nonreductive explanation, Chalmers introduces a new idea, or rather an old one in a new context:

> The primary nexus of the relationship between consciousness and cognition lies in *phenomenal judgments*. ... Phenomenal judgments are often reflected in *claims* about consciousness: verbal expressions of those judgments.[86]

Using it, Chalmers disputes Dennett's claim to have explained consciousness by explaining phenomenal judgments, in effect reductively.[87] He argues that Dennett exploits the knife-edge between the phenomenal and psychological realms, and points out that what we need to explain are not the judgments but experiences themselves. We shall return to this distinction between the words and the referents of those words – between syntax and semantics – in the context of the view of consciousness as computation.

Having established that we cannot expect to create a reductive theory of consciousness, Chalmers sets about looking for a nonreductive theory:

> The most promising way to get started in developing a theory of consciousness is to focus on the remarkable *coherence* between conscious experience and cognitive structure. The phenomenology and the psychology of the mind do not float free of each other; they are systematically related.[88]

For Chalmers, the central correlation between physical processing and experience is the coherence between consciousness and *awareness*. What gives rise directly to experience is not oscillations or temporally extended activity or high-quality representations, but the process of direct availability for global control. This relates to the global workspace theories of Baars and others.

Chalmers considers at length the suggestion that consciousness arises in virtue of the functional organization of the brain. This leads to an extended but rather inconclusive discussion of the protean science of information:

> This treatment of information brings out a crucial link between the physical and the phenomenal: whenever we find an information space realized phenomenally, we find the same information space realized physically. And when an experience realizes an information state, the same information state is realized in the experience's physical substrate.[89]

> A conscious experience is a realization of an information state; a phenomenal judgment is explained by another realization of the same information state. And in a sense, postulating a phenomenal aspect of information is all we need to do to make sure those judgments are truly correct: there really *is* a qualitative aspect to this information, showing up directly in phenomenology and not just in a system of judgments.[90]

> It is sometimes suggested from within physics that information is fundamental to the physics of the universe ... This "it from bit" view is put forward by [John Archibald] Wheeler ... To each fundamental feature of the world there corresponds an information space, and wherever physics takes those features to be instantiated, an information state from the relevant space is instantiated.[91]

This is deep stuff indeed, but necessary. A science of consciousness must engage fundamental physics, and I believe that information will be central in that engagement. Wheeler only glimpsed the new realm, but David Deutsch has recently done great work to help establish a revolutionary new science of quantum information.[92] However, Chalmers may have traveled too far with the prequantum computationalists:

> I ... argue that the ambitions of artificial intelligence are reasonable ... there is a nonempty class of computations such that the implementation of any computation in that class is sufficient for a mind, and in particular, is sufficient for the existence of conscious experience.[93]

This defense of the strong AI claim is natural enough for a former colleague of Hofstadter but it puts Chalmers into direct conflict with John Searle, not to mention both Honderich and McGinn. At first blush, it looks like a mere confusion of computation with consciousness, but the issues are too subtle for summary dismissal here.

At last, Chalmers brings us back to quantum physics, where we started with positivism and phenomenology:

> I ... argue that we can reconceive the problems of quantum theory as problems about the relationship between the physical structure of the world and our experience of the world, and that consequently an appropriate theory of consciousness can lend support to an unorthodox interpretation of quantum mechanics.[94]

The unorthodox interpretation Chalmers has in mind is the Everett interpretation,[95] on which he says:

> Everett's view is sometimes called a *many-worlds* interpretation ... but the view I am discussing is more accurately a *one-big-world* interpretation. ... On this view, if there is any splitting, it is only in the minds of observers. As superpositions come to affect a subject's brain state, a number of separate minds result, corresponding to the components of the superposition. Each of these perceives ... a *miniworld*, as opposed to the *maxiworld* of the superposition. ... Everett calls his view a *relative-state* interpretation: the state of a miniworld ... only counts as the state of the world *relative* to the specification of an observer.[96]

But this is an old view. The modern view of complex macroscopic systems and their state statistics does not support the idea that the coherent miniworlds in a superposition would be big enough to be perceived by a human mind as worlds (so at last the Schrödinger's cat nightmare is banished[97]). At best, we may be able to construct a sense in which the popping of such miniworlds out of superposition would correspond to the appearance in time of individual qualia in an atomized phenomenal manifold. This way we could make qualia more respectable and retrospectively vindicate Chalmers' faith in them. Wittgenstein liked the idea that a cloud of philosophy could condense into a drop of grammar, and indeed his own early philosophy of truth conditions condensed into the binary grammar of bit strings. Soon, perhaps, the philosophy of worlds multiplying and collapsing will condense into the physics of popping qubits in a quantum foam of experience. But to pursue this here would lead us too far afield.

Autobiography as Philosophy

We have flown through a cloudscape of cosmic dimensions, and it is time to land again in the familiar world of human lives. How do autobiographies help us to understand consciousness?

Daniel Dennett claims to explain consciousness, and the argument is temptingly close to what we want. For Dennett, to be conscious is to run a virtual machine in the brain that spins an ongoing autobiography from the accumulating increments of experience. So let's look closer.

Dennett starts with this problem:

> Events in consciousness ... are *experienced* by an *experiencer*, and their being thus experienced is what makes them ... *conscious* events. ... And the trouble with brains, it seems, is that when you look in them, you discover that *there's nobody home*.[98]

To avoid the sort of problems the behaviorists had with phenomenology, Dennett introduces *heterophenomenology*. If *autophenomenology* is my theoretical account of my own subjective experience, heterophenomenology is my account of someone else's reported inner experience. This is analogous to fiction, where the reader lets the text define a fictional world, and whatever the author says, so long as it makes sense, is satisfied in that world. Thus the scientific heterophenomenologist allows that the experimental subject's reports define a *heterophenomenological world* that satisfies whatever the subject says, so long as the subject remains coherent and consistent.

Dennett proposes a *multiple drafts* model of the mind. According to this model, all varieties of perception – indeed, all varieties of thought or mental activity – are accomplished in the brain by parallel, multitrack processes of interpretation and elaboration of sensory inputs. These drafts are autobiographical histories. And like schoolbook history, they can falsify the facts. Dennett distinguishes two kinds of falsification: *Orwellian* and *Stalinesque*. Orwellian revisions of history use artful confabulation to create false memories of experiences that never occurred. Stalinesque revisions stage false experiences that obscure and replace the original facts. It seems that our cognitive processes use either or both of these ploys to clean up our memories and redraft the stories of our selves.

All this may look fine and dandy, but it seems to leave consciousness untouched. Here Dennett offers a good biological analogy:

> There is a nice parallel between ... the origins of sex and the origins of consciousness. There is almost nothing *sexy* (in human terms) about the sex life of flowers, oysters, and other simple forms of life, but we can recognize ... the foundations and principles of our much more exciting world of sex. Similarly, there is nothing particularly *selfy* (if I may coin a term) about the primitive precursors of conscious human selves, but ... we must begin at the beginning.[99]

Essentially, Dennett tells an evolutionary story here. But rather than base it on genes, he uses Dawkins' more fanciful notion of memes, a notion now well established in modern folklore due in part to the efforts of Sue Blackmore.[100] Dennett concludes:

> Human consciousness is *itself* a huge complex of memes (or more exactly, meme-effects in brains) that can best be understood as the operation of a *"von Neumannesque"* virtual machine *implemented* in the *parallel architecture* of a brain that was not designed for any such activities. The powers of this *virtual machine* vastly enhance the underlying powers of the organic *hardware* on which it runs.[101]

A machine with a von Neumann architecture is centralized, linear, and serial, indeed a fairly literal implementation of the ideally minimalist architecture of a Turing machine. A virtual machine is a software construction that can run on quite different machines. For example, a Java virtual machine can be delivered through a browser to run on your desktop hardware, whatever model you have. In this sort of way, Dennett proposes, culture delivers a serial self through language to our cerebral wetware, where it sits and grows and enslaves the little cognitive demons that make up our biologically evolved modular mind. Here Dennett coins another richly evocative term:

> In our brains, there is a cobbled-together collection of specialist brain circuits, which, thanks to a family of habits inculcated partly by culture and partly by individual self-exploration, conspire together to produce a more or less orderly, more or less effective, more or less well designed virtual machine, the *Joycean machine*.[102]

However, the Joycean stream of consciousness so familiar to lovers of *Ulysses* is a dangerous metaphor for a philosopher who has set his face against Cartesian dualism:

> There is no single, definitive "stream of consciousness," because there is no central Headquarters, no Cartesian Theater where "it all comes together" for the perusal of a Central Meaner. Instead of such a single stream (however wide), there are multiple channels in which specialist circuits try, in parallel pandemoniums, to do their various things, creating Multiple Drafts as they go. Most of these fragmentary drafts of "narrative" play short-lived roles in the modulation of current activity but some get promoted to further functional roles, in swift succession, by the activity of a virtual machine in the brain. The seriality of this machine (its "von Neumannesque" character) is not a "hard-wired" design feature, but rather the upshot of a succession of coalitions of these specialists.[103]

At last we come to Dennett's big claim about consciousness:

> Anyone or anything that has such a virtual machine as its control system is conscious in the fullest sense, and is conscious *because* it has such a virtual machine.[104]

This sets Dennett against both Honderich and McGinn, but presumably puts him in some kind of agreement with Chalmers, despite Dennett's failure to explain *experience* (as opposed to judgments about experience) and his emphatic repudiation of qualia. Chalmers says that the implementation of certain computations is sufficient for a mind and for the existence of conscious experience. The computations performed by a Joycean virtual machine would seem to make them good candidates for such mind machines. So despite the complete absence both of new physics and of a role for qualia in the autobiographical view, we seem to have made progress. If new physics can explain qualia, perhaps we can allow them back. Otherwise, why not let them go?

Science and the Self

Consciousness and the self are related. The self is what *has* consciousness. To the extent that we *are* conscious, given that our consciousness can be as limited as both Freudian orthodoxy and heterophenomenology suggest, we have a more or less successfully running inner narrative of a self that serves as the more or less sharp focus of all our internal and external experiences. Dennett is stolidly biological about the self:

> But the strangest and most wonderful constructions in the whole animal world are the amazing, intricate constructions made by the primate, *Homo sapiens*. Each normal individual of this species makes a *self*. Out of its brain it spins a web of words and deeds, and, like the other creatures, it doesn't have to know what it's doing; it just does it.[105]

Of course, we philosophers *do* have to know what we're doing, otherwise we're out of a job. And despite what both Chalmers and Dennett say, I believe that what we're doing is a lot more than programming. A self is an autobiographical wrapper for a pre-existing entity, an entity that accumulates physical experience and only later, after infection with the memes of culture, puts those experiences into words. This entity may or may not be the photonic field that I guess it could be, but whatever it is, physics will have a lot to say about it. We need some fundamental new science here. On that I agree with McGinn.

To return to McGinn's mysterianism for a moment, many years ago he made the following tentative (and tangled) approach toward suggesting how we might look for an explanatory theory of consciousness:

> There has to be more to consciousness than there seems to be or else it could not depend upon the physical world in the way we know it does. ... It may help to bring this idea into focus if I contrast it with two proposals made by Thomas Nagel ... The first proposal ... is that subjective experience might be describable in objective (though nonphysical) terms, and that such an 'objective phenomenology' might put us in a better position to understand the physical basis of experience. ... Nagel's second proposal ... is that the real nature of conscious states might just consist in states of the brain. ... The kind of hidden structure I envisage would lie at neither of the levels suggested by Nagel: it would be situated somewhere between them. Neither phenomenological nor physical, this mediating level would not (by definition) be fashioned on the model of either side of the divide, and hence would not find itself unable to reach out to the other side. Its characterization would call for radical conceptual innovation (which I have argued is probably beyond us).[106]

Not surprisingly, Dennett pounces on this suggestion triumphantly:

> The "software" or "virtual machine" level of description ... is exactly the sort of mediating level McGinn describes: not explicitly physiological or mechanical and yet capable of providing the necessary bridges to the brain machinery on

the one hand, while on the other hand not being explicitly phenomenological and yet capable of providing the necessary bridges to the world of content, the world of (hetero-)phenomenology. We've done it! We *have* imagined how a brain could produce conscious experience.[107]

I can imagine McGinn replying that heterophenomenology is not autophenomenology: the uniquely vivid quality of *my* experience remains unexplained.

This reply is devastating to any theory of consciousness that fits within science as we now know it, because that science is built from a third-person perspective. Before we can crack the problem of first-person experience, we need a logico-physical frame that can accommodate the asymmetry between the first-person and third-person perspectives. Insistence upon the importance of this problem is essentially Chalmers' great contribution to the debate.

A first move toward a solution is to assert that first-person consciousness is instantiated *uniquely* in a world. Only first-person consciousness requires an autophenomenological analysis. Third-person consciousness is tractable in psychology or in heterophenomenology. This drastically simplifies the task of building a theory of worlds. A world is an entity with the logico-physical property of being epistemically centred on a unique self. Each self constructs its own evolving world. To recall Chalmer's take on Everett, we can call such a world a *miniworld*. Our miniworlds are largely congruent, but they differ in where they locate their central point. The corresponding *maxiworld* is all of reality as we know it. The central self for the maxiworld is not a personal self but a *cosmic* self. Our miniworlds are modeled after the maxiworld, rather like tabletop globes are modeled after Planet Earth.

In this view, the full concept of consciousness itself is reflected in the vast universe of science. The universe feels like pure consciousness. Consciousness and the cosmos are complementary. Pure consciousness is *timeness* (to exapt a word coined by Llinás [108]) and the cosmos is a spatial manifold (with four extended and perhaps seven compact dimensions), yet spacetime is a single reality. Moreover, as our science develops, our concept of consciousness expands to reflect it. So, to complete the circle of my story, the history of science is the autobiography of consciousness. No wonder McGinn despaired of understanding consciousness!

Let the final thought here go to Honderich. In the coda to his autobiography he says:

> A human life, any human life that has lasted a while, has a fullness that can seem greater than that of any other single subject-matter. ... Each life or entire consciousness and carry-on, in a sense that may one day be made explicit, is *a world*, a world going on through time and one that includes other people and more.[109]

Consciousness reflects the existence of a world. The logic and physics of worlds is the logic and physics of consciousness. A human life is a microcosm, a drop in the cosmic ocean.

The Self: From Soul to Brain

*A New York Academy of Sciences Conference
New York City, September 26-28, 2002*

Gurus

The Mount Sinai School of Medicine is an imposing monument to the wealth and power of scientific medicine. Set on its own block in upper Manhattan, its rhetorical center is the Stern Auditorium. Here, just over a year after 9/11, a group of gurus and self-seekers assembled to confer on the nature of the self. I was there too, looking for help in constructing a grand unified theory of soul and brain.

The New Hubris

Joseph LeDoux, Henry and Lucy Moses Professor of Science at New York University's Center for Neural Sciences, was the man in the middle, the master of ceremonies. It was his idea to bring this event into being, perhaps as a gathering of friends and colleagues to celebrate and confirm their collective status as guardians and cultivators of the new reigning orthodoxy about the self. Not quite incidentally, it also served to showcase his new book, *Synaptic Self*. From his perspective, the very first words of that book could probably have served as the motto for the conference:

> The bottom-line point of this book is "You are your synapses." Synapses are the spaces between brain cells, but are much more. They are the channels of communication between brain cells, and the means by which most of what the brain does is accomplished.[1]

At 52, LeDoux is at the height of his professional standing, well represented by the strength of his new book and his impressively smooth orchestration of the conference. Son of a butcher and set on his course as a teenager by the experience of extracting bullets from cows' brains, he recalls his early research at Louisiana State University thus:

> Robert Thompson was one of the early proponents of the systems approach ... Unencumbered by theoretical preconceptions, Thompson marched through the rat brain, making lesions from front to back and top to bottom, and constructed neural systems of learning and memory totally from empirical observations ... I owe my whole career to Bob Thompson.[2]

At 52 myself, I have carved a less glorious trail in the course of my pilgrimage to Mount Sinai. My humble contribution in this report will be to do what the invited philosophical gadfly at the conference, Daniel Dennett, in my not-so-humble opinion failed to do, and locate the critical weakness in the synaptic self, so that we can shrug off this new *hubris*. But first, let us recall the events of the conference and relive the excitement of hearing the words of the prophets.

Sessions 1 and 2: Perspectives on the Self

LeDoux opened the proceedings by sketching out the scope of the conference. It was an attempt to think about the self in terms of the brain. What is the self? How does it relate to the brain? Is there room for a soul? How is the self related to consciousness? Is it possible to have more than one self in the same brain? What are the roles of memory, and genes? How does the self relate to personality, and in what sense do other animals have selves?

LeDoux's model of the self is that it is an integrated representational structure distributed over the brain system as a pattern of synaptic connections. The pattern reflects which neurons connect with which others, and how strong the connections are between them. Determine that pattern in a brain and you determine the self that owns or occupies that brain. LeDoux referred to his own earlier work on how synaptic changes caused by stress-induced neural activity centered on the amygdala and hippocampus explain fear conditioning and anxiety states, work reported in his book *The Emotional Brain*,[3] to illustrate how mental states can be reduced in classic scientific fashion to underlying neural activity.

But LeDoux pushes his case. For him, the self is synaptic, period. He can't see what else it could be. He says the trick is to understand how the self emerges from synapses. Indeed. The synaptic story leaves us struggling when we approach the realm of what we used to describe as the soul.

Patricia Smith Churchland was the next speaker. She is professor and chair of philosophy at the University of California, San Diego, and a celebrated public figure. She and her husband Paul have come to symbolize a whole approach to the mind, the hard-AI or *computationalist* approach. She related her talk to her recent paper in *Science*.[4]

In her view, the brain's earliest self-representational capacities arose as evolution found neural network solutions for coordinating and regulating inner-body signals. She sees the neural basis for self-control in natural selection for individuals that were neurally equipped to forego short-term gratification for the sake of long-term reward, and to suppress impulses that had self-destructive consequences. In social animals, this included the ability to modify social behavior through reward and punishment and to develop skills in cooperative behavior.

She said that since human brains are very similar to those of other apes and monkeys, the human experience of self is unlikely to be unique. Selves may have evolved to maintain a basic level of coordination of bodily functions and behaviors (such as the famous four F's) by using an inner modeling capability to assist in motor planning. The inner model represents the animal's own body in its environment and includes some level of simulation of body, world, self, and other selves.

She asked whether we can give a neural characterization of the contrast between being in and out of control. Whatever the self is, a general formal description may represent it as a multidimensional entity in a large abstract space with dimensions coding information about neuronal organization in various parts of the cortex and in the amygdala and hypothalamus, as well as molecular-level parameters for levels of various neuromodulators, hormones, proteins and so on that influence how we interact dynamically with our environments. A zone within this space represents our being in control, while much of the rest of the space represents our being out of control. If a subject's parametric state puts that person's brain in the "in control" zone, that person acted freely and is responsible for the relevant actions, whereas a person whose brain is in the "out of control" zone did not act freely. This is relevant in turn to ideas about the biological basis for ethics and about how best to maintain civil society. At this point in history, the multidimensional space is hand waving, of course, but she pointed out that such models co-evolve with our knowledge of the practical details they are intended to explain. As we learn more, we can refine the idea.

Daniel Schacter was the next speaker. He is professor and chair of psychology at Harvard University, and studies the psychological and biological aspects of human memory and amnesia. His list of publications is vast, and includes *Searching for Memory* and *The Seven Sins of Memory*,[5] which were among the New York Times Book Review Notable Books of the Year in 1996 and 2001 respectively. His theme was the relation of self and memory as two sides of the same fact, as William James noted in 1890. Our memory of the past is reviewed as a drama in which the self is the leading player. Like all authors of recent books, Schacter reviewed his book. The seven sins of memory are:

- Transience, or decreasing accessibility of information over time,
- Absent-mindedness, or failures at the interface of memory and attention,
- Blocking, or temporary inaccessibility of stored information,
- Misattribution, or assigning a memory to the wrong source,
- Suggestibility, or implanting false memories,
- Bias, or rewriting the past on the basis of current knowledge and beliefs, and
- Persistence, or intrusive recollections that are difficult to forget.

Such "sins" (I still find this a bizarre word in this context) change the self: citing William James again, my losses of memory or false memories change *me*.

Regarding bias, which is a top-down influence on memory, the most obvious example is the egocentric bias. It seems that information that is relevant to the self is processed in a different frontal region than information that is not. We stabilize our sense of self by seeking to preserve consistency, which involves the sins of bias and misattribution. People tend to misremember past attributes of themselves in line with their present attributes. Our efforts to preserve consistency can be seen as a mechanism to reduce cognitive dissonance with regard to memory.

Schacter's general point, that memories make the self, is entirely consistent with LeDoux's view. When we lay down memories, we change our synaptic connections by growing new ones, pruning old ones, or changing the weights of existing ones. But memory research often relies on first-person techniques such as introspection to find out what a person remembers. With memory, we cannot deny the primacy of phenomenology.

That was it for Thursday. My phenomenology suddenly got wet as, filled with zeal for the new words in my head, I ran 36 blocks south down Madison Avenue through the pouring rain to the conference hotel.

Friday started with a session chaired by Daniel Schacter. The fist speaker was Nancey Murphy, a professor at Fuller Theological Seminary in Pasadena, California. She is a prolific author and helps plan conferences on science and theology sponsored by the Vatican Observatory. Her question: Whatever happened to the soul?

Her main point was that there was no conflict between the emerging neuroscientific consensus and normative Judaeo-Christian views. There could be agreement on the physical nature of humans. She presented a more or less historical survey, from the dualistic distortion of a biblical view that one finds in Hellenistic philosophy – and which reappears in Descartes' dualism – through the neo-Platonic views of Saint Augustine and the Aristotelian scholasticism of Saint Thomas Aquinas and others to Kant's transcendental argument for the immortality of the soul. She dwelled sympathetically on the Thomistic view that the soul is the *form* of the body, a view that is held by many modern Catholic theologians. However, if I recall correctly, she said that the crude scientific doctrine of physical atomism made it impossible to regard the soul as the form of the body.

If I may respond here, form is a concept from information theory. To say the soul is the form of the body is to say that the soul is the dynamically evolving configuration of the ultimate parts of the body, and as such is a structure with a mathematical description. The soul therefore enjoys the same eternal quality as any mathematical or informational entity. My soul is coded in a bit string that can be used to call me back into existence for as long as God has the right software. There is nothing here to contradict either the crudest atomism or the most exalted belief in immortality.

Murphy granted gracefully that Christians are free to believe in either physicalism or dualism. She made the useful point that neurobiological determinism did not supplant the concepts of free will and so on, but seemed to require us to develop some new terminology. In sum, she argued that the Jewish and Christian traditions contain minority voices that are not only consistent with the results of current cognitive-neuroscientific research, but also provide grounds for celebrating the monistic-physicalistic accounts of human nature that science promotes.

Alexandre Mauron was next. He is professor of bioethics at the University of Geneva. His research work was in molecular genetics and neurobiology, but since the late 1980s his work has included the ethical issues of genetics and related areas. He began with a reference to the contemporary German-language philosopher Peter Sloterdijk and the provocative idea of the self-engineering of mankind – *homo faber sui ipsius* – as well as its resonance, in the works of Nietzsche and Heidegger, with the project of domesticating the species. All this clearly needs ethical terms of reference.

In this context, neurobiological visions of shaping the brain seem less controversial than eugenic visions of rebuilding the genome, given that the genome is the ontological hard core of an organism. We can see the genome as the secular equivalent of the soul, and genomic metaphysics as a new kind of hylomorphism. But this suggests that the soul is created at conception, when a new diploid genome is created during fertilization, and this has implications for the ethical standing of the embryo. Yet there are problems with the view of the zygote as a person. What about identical twins or clones – do they share the same soul? Or mosaic individuals – do they have two or more souls? Mauron maintained that a better basic criterion for personhood is numerical identity – one brain, one person.

Another problem with genomic metaphysics is the view it encourages that for any behavioral trait x such as alcoholism or dyslexia or homosexuality there is a "gene for x" – that our genes determine our acts. Since genomic characteristics are stable, this view invites an unwelcome fatalism about our prospects for improvement. The idea that our neuronal states determine our acts seems better.

Mauron liked the idea that the self is a social or cultural construct rather than a product of the genome, and in particular liked Sloterdijk's idea that humans create environments – *bubbles* – for themselves that feed back onto human nature and in the long term change us. But he questioned the ethical contrast between genomic manipulation that affects future generations and "neuromic" manipulation that affects only one individual. As he saw it, *Robocop* and other science-fiction scenarios in which people are transformed by silicon implants create *new* individuals, and hence similar ethical issues. For Mauron, international bioethics is still a very heterogeneous intellectual enterprise, beset with many misunderstandings about implicit standards of argumentation and the proper weight of cultural differences.

Terrence Sejnowski was next. With a Ph.D. in physics from Princeton and an affiliation with Caltech, he is now an investigator with the Howard Hughes Medical Institute and a professor at both the Salk Institute for Biological Studies and the University of California, San Diego. He spoke about the computational self. The brain is never at rest, and its input is a ceaseless pattern of activity. Neurons fire constantly and create a background field, and the task of investigators is to look for patterns above the background. We have learned more about how the central nervous system works in the last ten years than in all of previous history.

Sejnowski considered a hierarchy of scales ordered by powers of ten, from the CNS at the scale of tenths of a meter down to molecules at tenths of a nanometer. This analysis into ever smaller pieces creates the Humpty-Dumpty problem of how to put them all back together again. Microelectrodes can pick up signals from individual neurons, but doing so for a hundred billions neurons at once is impossible. Imagine a brain as big as New York City. Then people in the city are like neurons. Now imagine ten thousand times as many people in the city as there are now, piled miles high into the sky, all communicating with each other busily. That's an image of the brain. How can you get a meaningful picture of what's going on by tapping the signals from a handful of people?

One way out is to take EEG readings of the total signal. Now we face the cocktail party problem. How do we extract individual signals from the background noise? Sejnowski has developed a computer algorithm to do just that. He calls it the *brain microscope* and sees it as heralding a new dawn of imaging studies. The idea is to record signals from different directions and then perform a *principal component analysis* and an *independent component analysis*. By analyzing enough signals, he can generate clear diagrams of what's going on where in the brain. He can see structure in event related potentials, which consist of large numbers of microvolt-level signals that are averaged out but which also show systematic phase shifts and increased coherence compared to the background. He showed us some fascinating detailed studies. It all seemed very geeky, with huge but vague promise for the future.

A panel discussion followed. In reply to a long question that involved the assertion that realism and idealism are equivalent, Sejnowski said "one man's top is another man's bottom." To a question about the chimp in the mirror and whether self-awareness was a test for the existence of a self, he replied that he once wrote a 450-page book about falling asleep in which he discussed the low-frequency, high-amplitude synchronous waves generated by the neurons in that state. He contrasted the waves he studied with the higher-frequency gamma rhythms studied by Wolf Singer and his colleagues. Sejnowski was interested in how thalamo-cortical loops recruit neurons and get them to burst in synchrony. He said he was still trying to put Humpty-Dumpty back together again.

To another question, Professor Murphy said we're all in the process of recognizing the falsity of the reductionist assumption that it's all ultimately physics. She opined that we haven't begun to think about complex systems in ways that show *how* that's false. We need to find a way to describe how we become *creators of ourselves*. That brought me back to Nietzsche and Heidegger but left me sceptical about her physics. She's writing a book about it.

Sessions 3 and 4: Psycho-Social Aspects of Self

After a kosher lunch in the Mount Sinai canteen, I was ready for the afternoon session chaired by Professor Churchland.

Marc Hauser was first, on "our ancient selves." Hauser is currently a professor at Harvard University and author of over 100 peer-reviewed publications. His latest book, *Wild Minds*,[6] is being translated into seven languages. His research sits at the interface between evolutionary biology and cognitive neuroscience and is aimed at understanding the processes and consequences of cognitive evolution. In his talk, he explored how human and nonhuman animals differ with respect to their sense of self. In the first part, he explored the general problem of what animals know about the physical world and revealed an intriguing dissociation between perception and action. In the second part, he examined the capacity of animals to imitate, recognize their image in a mirror, and represent the beliefs and desires of others.

Hauser reminded us that we share 98 percent of our genes with chimps and raised a laugh with a portrait of a chimp morphing into President George W. Bush. He presented some results of his recent research on delayed gratification, reciprocation, and defection, comparing and contrasting human infants and monkeys. One set of experiments involved falling balls. If an experimental subject sees a ball falling toward a table, and then sees a box on the table and a box under the table, which box does the subject approach to try to find the ball? Monkeys, it seems, don't really understand tables and approach the lower box. Human infants do the same. Both human infants and adult monkeys show evidence of exquisite object knowledge, yet appear incapable of accessing such knowledge for the purpose of explicit action. Maybe they have difficulty accessing it because they have weak inhibitory mechanisms, which causes them to engage in ballistic action sequences. There is a gap between perception and action. We can under-stand a physical regularity yet still act as if we didn't.

As for delayed gratification, Hauser reported some longitudinal studies that tracked infants into adulthood. Long ago, some infants were faced with one sweet now, unconditionally, or two later, if they could first resist the offered sweet for a few minutes. Those who were unable to resist the temptation turned out later in life to have higher rates of alcoholism, gambling, drug abuse and the like, as well as lower SAT scores, job satisfaction and so on, than the stronger-willed infants. This could be relevant to social policy – test infants and plan their lives accordingly.

Regarding altruism, the evolutionary story involves similarity of genes. We are more altruistic toward people who share more genes with us or are more similar to us. In prisoner's dilemma experiments, where cooperation between pairs is rewarded only if both play along, the reciprocal exchange involved is limited by individual strength in face of delayed gratification and temptation to defect. In experiments with paired monkeys, cooperation continues until one defects, then the wronged partner punishes the defector for a while to produce renewed cooperation. But monkeys can be remarkably altruistic: they will starve themselves rather than administer a painful shock to a fellow, regardless of the dominance relation between the pair. This makes them ethically better than some humans, who will happily shock their fellows if an authority figure tells them it's OK.

Hauser's general message was that our actions lag behind our knowledge in the sense that our actions are in part hard-wired by our evolutionary past and robust against quick change. He suggested that we look to the neural circuitry underlying inhibition and conflict monitoring for clues to the evolution of a human sense of self.

Naomi Quinn was next. She is a professor at Duke University. To quote her conference abstract, she is part of a current effort in cognitive anthropology to build a theory of culture on the basis of schema theory and connectionist modeling, and within this framework to demonstrate how meanings become internalized, shared, motivating, enduring historically and within individuals, and thematic across cultural domains. Whew! Unfortunately, she had no slides to show us and mumbled indistinctly as she peered myopically at her notes. But I shall try to do her justice.

She reviewed some recent cross-cultural studies of child development, which showed that all cultural models for child rearing work in two ways. First, they all promote extreme constancy of the child's experience, as this is seen to relate to key values and associated behaviors. This constancy is achieved by maintaining a community of opinion about what children must learn, by investing this opinion with moral force, and by embedding it in child rearing practices that are highly regular and oft repeated. Secondly, the models couple the lessons with techniques to make the learning experience emotionally arousing. In other words, child rearing everywhere is designed to ensure that children get the message, and that they remember it once they get it.

She gave us a handout with some fascinating quotations from various anthropological sources that contrasted child rearing practices in different societies around the world. They were fine anecdotes, but what did they tell us about the self? Professor Quinn: what results from the experience of being reared according to a given cultural model is a lifelong self that is culturally distinctive. Child rearing is the central way to form a self. Quinn concludes that there is no way to say what's the best way to raise a child. And what about the adult consequences of these practices? Or their relevance to neuroscience? Here Quinn squinted and mumbled a *bon mot* – "I'm waiting for the neuroscientists to fetch me!"

Michael Lewis was next. His theme was the emergence of consciousness and its impact on children's development. Lewis is Director of the Institute for the Study of Child Development at Robert Wood Johnson Medical School, and a professor at Rutgers University. His forthcoming book, *Altering Fate: Why the Past Does Not Predict the Future*, argues that children's conscious adaptation to the current environment is the directing force in development. In his talk, he explored how the adult machinery of the self and the mental state of the idea of *me* develop over the first two years of a child's life, and provide the scaffolding for the child's further development in the social, emotional, and cognitive domains.

He started by considering imitation in newborn infants as a process of sensorimotor integration. Then he considered self-recognition in mirrors, the use of personal pronouns, and pretend play, all of which show that there is a strong developmental coherence in the emergence and onset of an explicit self. They lead to a change in the child's emotional life that is better characterized by embarrassment than self-consciousness. He mentioned his earlier book *Shame: The Exposed Self*.[7] As the child develops the mental state of me, infant features are transformed into humanlike abilities. Social interactions become relationships, primary emotions become self-conscious emotions, and the child develops a theory of mind. He closed with some videos of small children showing how self-recognition and the ability to distinguish between appearance and reality emerge at various mental ages.

Following refreshments, Michael Gazzaniga chaired part two of the session. Gazzaniga is a giant figure in neuroscience. Currently a professor at Dartmouth College and Director of Dartmouth's Center for Cognitive Neuroscience, he is well known for his deep involvement in matters of public policy, ethics, and public understanding of science.

He introduced Hazel Rose Markus. She is currently a professor at Stanford University. Her research has focused on the role of self in regulating behavior, and her most recent work explores the interdependence between psychological structures and processes and sociocultural environments. Interestingly, for me at least, she is a member of the MacArthur Research Network on Successful Midlife Development – maybe she would give us a handy tip or two!

Her talk was on models of agency, and her main theme was the contrast between two different ideals for the self in society, symbolized by the metaphor of a fish that can either swim against the stream or just go with the flow. She characterized these as the disjoint and conjoint selves, respectively. The most extreme exaltation of the disjoint self occurs in contemporary U.S. American society, where the independent, self-sufficient individualist is celebrated above all. Contrariwise, the most extreme celebration of conjoint selfhood occurs in China, Korea, and Japan, where interdependence is stressed and they say the nail that sticks out gets hammered.

Disjoint and conjoint selves reflect two contrasting models of action. For the disjoint self, a good act is self-focused and independent – ideal Americans think and act for themselves – with the result that differences between people are affirmed and celebrated. For the conjoint self, a good act is focused on relations with others and on their welfare. Such acts affirm the community and arise from respect or concern for others. Markus illustrated this contrast with slides presenting a barrage of media images, mostly commercial advertising for everyday consumer products. Their overwhelming endorsement of the transpacific contrast was more than just amusing, it was startling. Advertising exploits existing cultural ideals, of course, and can only work when the ideals of self are there to be exploited, but the relentless assault of the media on consumers also reinforces and exaggerates these stereotypes to absurd extremes.

Markus emphasized that these contrasting models of agency are not just in the head but are played out in the world. She reminded us of George W. Bush's call to defend the individual against the collective, as if we were the crew of Starship Enterprise fighting the Borg. She quoted a Japanese person as saying, "I behave in order for people to feel peaceful." She told a story about some Korean Americans who visited South Korea and said the visit changed their souls. She made the point that different social contexts shape the individual self to become either conjoint or disjoint. As a European who selfishly conjoins the transpacific disjunction, I can only agree with her.

Daniel Wegner was next. He is currently a professor at Harvard University. His work is focused on the role of thought in self-control and in social life. His anthology *White Bears and Other Unwanted Thoughts* is fascinating.[8] The title essay explores the psychology of the classic conundrum of trying *not* to think about a white bear, where the harder you try, the harder it gets. His latest book, *The Illusion of Conscious Will*,[9] was the source text for much of his talk. Not to beat about the bush, here is the key to that book, from its preface:

> Do we consciously cause what we do, or do our actions happen to us? ... This is a book about a different sort of answer to the question. Here it is: Yes, we feel that we consciously cause what we do; and yes, our actions happen to us. Rather than opposites, conscious will and psychological determinism can be friends. Such friendship comes from realizing that the feeling of conscious will is created by the mind and brain just as human actions themselves are created by the mind and brain.[10]

In his talk, Wegner addressed the question of why we feel that we cause our actions. He showed a fine slide to get us in the mood – *The Mind's Self-Portrait* by the Dutch engraver M.C. Escher, which portrays a hand holding a mirrored ball in which the image of Escher looking at his image is reflected. As Wegner put it, we see our selves or our souls each time the mind looks at itself. He pursued the metaphor of a painted self-portrait. Our self-image consists entirely of conscious phenomena, so the palette is limited, with no dark shades. The portrait is a miniature, to fit into the mind's tiny space (speak for yourself, Wegner). It presents a model focused on agent causation, not event causation. And the image is somehow convincing or self-luminous. In our self-portrait, thought seems to cause action, yet in fact our thoughts are part of a much more complex picture.

Wegner was attracted by David Hume's notion of will as the sentiment or feeling we get when we do something. We have the feeling that we cause what we do, but as Hume famously insisted, causation is just constant conjunction, so the way is open to declare that the feeling is an illusion. Experiments tend to support the idea that we rely implicitly on three principles to decide when we willed our actions:

- Consistency: when a thought is relevant to and compatible with the subsequent action, we tend to think the thought caused the action.
- Exclusivity: if there is no other cause for the action in sight, we are free to think we caused the action.
- Priority: the thought must precede the action by an appropriately brief interval.

Wegner discussed various middle-class pastimes from a hundred or more years ago, when people liked to indulge in table-turning, automatic writing, hypnosis, divination and so on. In all these cases, the sense of agency is somehow effaced or diluted, or an "agentic shift" occurs. A modern analog of these pastimes is facilitated communication, where a communication-impaired individual enjoys the help of a facilitator to enter text on a keyboard, perhaps by letting the facilitator hold their hand as it twitches over the keyboard, or by letting the facilitator complete sentences or expand on themes. Wegner cited detailed studies of fairly obvious facilitator interference, even when the facilitators were convinced they were not corrupting the messages. His recent book goes into much more detail – some of it very amusing and recounted with admirable wit – on all these activities and how they fit the three principles of agency.

His big conclusion is that whenever we think we willed our action, the brain provides both the thought and the action. The best way to see it is that on the basis of our feelings we *theorize* that we will our actions. Like all theories, the theory of free will is fallible, and may be plain wrong.

Mahzarin Rustum Banaji came on next. Banaji is currently a professor at Harvard University and at Radcliffe. She studies human thinking and feeling as it unfolds in social context. She is particularly interested in the unconscious nature of assessments of self and other humans that reflect feelings and knowledge about social group membership – about age, race or ethnicity, gender, class, and so on. I noticed that she is a young woman of color.

Her talk was about the unconscious and social construction of preferences and beliefs. She cited some detailed studies of ethnocentrism involving thoughts or feelings about black and white, poor and rich, foreign and American, Jewish and Christian, gay and straight, and trees and birds (the neutral control), where their relation to good and bad was explored. The biases of the experimental subjects were measured in terms of reaction times, and were of course both strong and strongly correlated to the subjects' own positions in all these pairings. Moreover, in each case the majority group showed the bias more strongly.

She then discussed implicit cognition and implicit attitudes that we are unable to identify introspectively. In particular, we have a self-attitude that involves investing objects with associations to our own self. She discussed a study of women versus men in mathematics and science that showed an interesting dissonance between explicit and implicit attitudes for female scientists, who showed little or no explicit bias in thought or feeling against female scientists yet revealed some implicit bias, presumably reflecting the culture around them.

That was the hard work over for the day. We all relaxed at a wine and cheese reception in the lobby. I talked with two nice young ladies and then with a Floridan called Gordon Johns who's writing a book called *The Mythical Me.*

Sessions 5 and 6: Self and Brain

Saturday dawned sunny. Perhaps the shining truth would be revealed at last. The first session was chaired by Joseph LeDoux.

The first speaker was Francesca Happé, who after research on autism under Uta Frith at Oxford is now a senior scientist at the Institute of Psychiatry, King's College London. She told us about some recent research on "theory of mind" and the self, where theory of mind is the aspect of social cognition that enables us to attribute mental states such as beliefs and desires to others. Despite much research on autism, which is a developmental disorder of social insight, little research has addressed the normal and abnormal development of insight into one's own mental states.

Each of us has a theory of mind. We use it every day to deceive, joke, teach, gossip and so on. Experiments on the development of this theory in children may involve, for example, the famous Smarties task where a tube ostensibly containing chocolate candies but in fact containing something else, such as pencils, is traded between knowing and unknowing kids to see how well they cope with the deceptions involved. The conventional view is that we need a theory of mind for others and that we have privileged access to our own mental states, so we don't need it for ourselves. But Happé reported results that show otherwise. It turns out that children are no better at attributing mental states to themselves than to others. And autistic children also have problems reading their own minds. It seems that we theorize our own states of mind no less than those of others.

Question: do we activate the same brain regions to read our own and other minds? Neuroimaging studies show that theory of mind activity occurs in medial frontal cortex and paracingulate cortex for both kinds of mind reading. And in both cases, autistic subjects show decreased paracingulate activation in theory of mind tasks compared to normal subjects. So we seem to use similar resources for reading our own and other minds. More speculatively, our ability to read other minds may even precede and facilitate our ability to introspect. Evolution may have forced us to read other minds before our own.

Antonio Damasio was next. He is a professor at both the University of Iowa and the Salk Institute, and has received countless distinctions and prizes, including the Golden Brain Award in 1995. His books *Descartes Error: Emotion, Reason and the Human Brain* and *The Feeling of What Happens: Body, Emotion, and the Making of Consciousness* are taught in universities worldwide.[11]

He talked about feeling and self. He distinguishes two kinds of self: *core self* and *extended self*. Core self corresponds to the transient process that is continually generated relative to any object with which an organism interacts, and during which a transient sense of knowing is automatically generated. It requires neither language nor working memory, just short-term memory. Extended self is a more complex process that depends on the gradual buildup of autobiographical memory. It requires conventional memory and is enhanced by language.

Damasio said the essence of the self was its stability, continuity, and singularity. The self is a stable representation of individual continuity and serves as the reference for mental states. Its basis is the representation of one's own body. He finds support for this conception in the writings of Spinoza, William James, Nietzsche, Husserl, and Merleau-Ponty. The representation of the body is the backbone, so to speak, of the representation of self. Its variance has a narrow range, in contrast to the variance of perception, which can approach infinity.

The senses are relevant to the self, but these are not just smell, taste, touch, hearing, and vision. Kinesthesia and visceral input are also important. Sherrington produced a classification of the senses that distinguished chemoreception, proprioception, exteroreception, and telereception. The chemoreception system in particular provides a rather detailed sensory representation of the state of the organism. All the input to the brain about the body is much like external sensory input, except that it is steady. The brain uses it to create an *image* of the self.

There I can let it go. Here was a master at work. I look forward joyfully to his forthcoming book, *Looking for Spinoza: Joy, Sorrow, and the Human Brain*.[12]

Rodolfo Llinás was next. Currently a professor at the New York University School of Medicine, his honors include the UNESCO Albert Einstein Gold Medal Award in Science and election to the National Academy of Sciences. His book *I of the Vortex: From Neurons to Self* introduced the *mindness state* as the class of all functional brain states in which sensorimotor images, including self-awareness, are generated.[13]

He talked on cognition as a premotor event. Consciousness of self is required in order that we can move with intentionality. He used the image of a tennis player to argue that prediction is essential to skilled movement. To laughter (for he is a *maestro* of precise timing and wording), he said that without prediction we would be like burocrats, who use their wits to become sessile and then eat their brains because they don't need them any more (he didn't say professors with tenure).

A key event in the biological history of the self was the evolution of neurons that were neither sensory nor motor but *interneural*. Now arbitrarily complex interneural circuitry could develop. In Llinás' view, the central architectural feature here is that of thalamo-cortical loops. The thalamus is at the center of connectivity to the cortex, and the cortex reconnects to the thalamus "with a vengeance." Consciousness, on this view, is a *process*, not a thing, generated by recursive looping between thalamus and cortex.

He talked wide-eyed about cells with "personality" and "points of view" and mentioned polarized and depolarized states of the thalamus. Roughly speaking, polarized means you're "on" and depolarized means you're "off." When there was no electricity flowing, there was no *you*. The gamma-band activity of the cells is related to cognition and consciousness. He showed some slides depicting cortical activation in the 35-45 Hz band and showed some MEE images of such activation for dreaming subjects. Dreaming, he said, is similar to wakefulness without the sensory input. The brain is about making images – we could call it a *dreaming machine* limited only by its sensory input.

The thalamo-cortical loop mechanism creates a set of global oscillations that cause the brain to operate discontinuously, generating dreams with a rhythm, like the frames of a movie. New sensory input is fed into this cycle very selectively, with the result that we can focus consciously on only a few things at once. All this was music to my ears – but it was soon over.

A questioner asked why, if the thalamus is so important to the self and we have two thalami, we nevertheless have only one self. The maestro replied simply that we also have a corpus callosum, and thus segued to the next speaker.

Antonio Damasio chaired the final, climactic session, and Michael Gazzaniga was the first of the trinity of climactic speakers. Gazzaniga did his early research under Roger Sperry, who won the Nobel Prize for split-brain research on patients whose corpus callosum had been cut, and this talk was essentially an update on the topic.

To summarize, dividing the cerebral hemispheres of the human brain creates two largely independent cerebral processing centers, each with its own set of mental capacities. The left hemisphere is heavily committed to rational and interpretive functions and the right hemisphere is specialized for visuo-spatial and complex perceptual processes. Observing one's own behavior creates the subjective sense that a self-directed cognitive system is in action. Gazzaniga and his colleagues recently showed that the left hemisphere has a greater sense of personal self than the right hemisphere.

He started his talk with his conclusion, just in case he ran out of time: *all reality is virtual*. He showed us a slide with a view from above of a split-brain patient looking at a screen that was divided so that each eye saw just half the screen. The patient was shown images, left and right, and asked to press the most appropriate keyboard images, again left and right, with the corresponding hand. For example, a screen image may be snow and the keyboard image a shovel, or the screen image a chicken and the keyboard image an egg. When the right eye saw a chicken and the left eye saw snow, the subject was asked why the left hand chose the shovel. "To shovel up the chicken droppings," came the instant reply, which shows how skilled the subject's verbal hemisphere was at confabulating to cover up its ignorance at what the right hemisphere was doing, as well as how naturally the left hemisphere took the leading role.

It seems that the thinking left hemisphere (depicted as the Einstein in another slide) is good at detecting *self*, while the reactive right hemisphere (depicted as the rat) is good at detecting *other*. The left hemisphere asks how relevant new input is to *me*, the right asks what orientation it has and so on. So the mapping of self into the left hemisphere is natural.

Split-brain patients show no particular insight into their condition. This absence of awareness is typical in cases of brain damage. A subject who suffers a lesion to the visual system may typically complain, "I can't see any more!" But a subject who suffers a lesion to the visual cortex may not even notice the deficit. The faculty is just gone. The self in the post-lesional brain will regularly interpret the bizarre as normal. To a ripple of laughter, he pointed out that we all do much the same: we interpret as few fancy colors in a VR display as bizarre but treat flying five miles high in an aluminum tube as perfectly normal. He mentioned four syndromes that share this lack of insight:

- Anosognosia, or unawareness of a neurological disability, the most common form of which is unawareness of paralysis,
- Capgras syndrome, in which patients make delusional misidentifications of people they should know, often claiming that the misidentified person is an imposter or double of the "real" person,
- Reduplicative paramnesia, or the mistaken belief that there are two nearly identical versions of a particular place, and
- Hemispatial neglect, in which a patient ignores stimuli on the side of the body or the space opposite to a brain lesion.

All these syndromes are described via case studies in *Altered Egos* by Todd Feinberg.[14]

Subjects with these syndromes can show an amazing lack of insight, which must have implications for the insight the rest of us enjoy. Each of us has a self for which the processing is distributed over two hemispheres but which is coordinated into a single, seamless consciousness. Our speech engine does duty for both hemispheres and is ready with a story whether it knows the facts or not. Our consciousness seems integrated on the surface, but the idea that everything comes together in the Cartesian theater is an illusion. Gazzaniga could have used this line to hand over to Dan Dennett, but Dan had to wait.

Eric Kandel was the second member of the ultimate trinity. He is quite old now, but still spry. He is a professor at Columbia, Senior Investigator at the Howard Hughes Medical Institute, and the recipient of countless distinctions and awards, including the Nobel Prize in Physiology or Medicine for his work on the molecular mechanisms of memory. His talk was entitled "Radical Reductionism in Science and Art: Biology of Memory Storage and Minimalist Art."

Kandel finds memory and learning endlessly fascinating, and is delighted by the idea that new imaging techniques may one day enables doctors to say, for example, "Here, your superego is a little too large." We all laughed, and he allowed that this may be less a fond hope than a fond illusion. He discussed the contrast between the blank slate view of the mind and the Kantian view that we come into the world with a toolbox of *a priori* concepts. Some brain science was needed to decide between these views. When he was young, Kandel expected that the black box brain would open up in his lifetime, and indeed he saw the shift from a psychoanalytic view of the mind to empirical biology. For example, in memory, the contrast between explicit or declarative memory and implicit or procedural memory is now explained biologically. Explicit memory involves the temporal lobes and the hippocampus, whereas implicit memory involves the striatum, amygdala, cerebellum, and reflex paths.

Kandel began his work in 1957/58. He realized that the complexity of memory systems was fairly intractable with prevailing techniques and that he had to simplify. So he chose to study the marine snail. This humble organism has about twenty thousand neurons, compared to the human trillion or so. When subjected to stimulus-response training, the marine snail only adapts a few hundred cells, so he could trace the pathways exactly. His research corroborated the Kantian picture. The *patterns* of neural connection were given, hard-wired, and all that changed during learning were the *strengths* of the synaptic connections.

However, the full picture was subtler. Kandel's first stab here was like minimalist art, like a Matisse canvas (pause to show a nice slide). He had to go further. Long-term memory requires the activation of genes. This activation causes the cells to grow new synapses. There are also repressors to prevent all learning from generating long-term memories, so there was a high threshold for such new growth. Still, a new conclusion emerged: your experience affects the expression of your genes. In the long term, your memories are the result of anatomical changes to your brain. The sensori-motor homunculus is not fixed. We all have different brain maps.

Kandel insisted passionately that such biological reduction does not trivialize or reduce the wonder of these natural phenomena. He compared this to Rothko's minimalist art (here we saw some more nice slides), with its move from figurative representation through cubism and the abandonment of form to bands of color, and finally to sheer black. Rothko saw all this as expressing basic human emotions. Kandel was interested in the power of such reduction. Why do we respond to it as we do? Here he referred to V.S. Ramachandran, who explains it in terms of a limit to our attentional response. We prefer simple images because they enable us to focus on the essentials. This intensifies the pleasure they generate and gives us the kick we crave. As Kandel sees it, art can teach us about how the brain works.

Daniel C. Dennett was the final, ultimate speaker. Billed originally to talk on Friday, he delayed his arrival until Saturday, with the result that his imminent Coming was announced several times during the proceedings. Modestly listed in the program as University Professor, Austin B. Fletcher Professor of Philosophy, and Director of the Center for Cognitive Studies at Tufts University, Dan Dennett is one of the greatest living philosophers and a prolific author, with numerous books and over 200 scholarly articles to his name. His books *Consciousness Explained* and *Darwin's Dangerous Idea* are wonderful.[15] Moreover, together with wayward genius Douglas Hofstadter, he edited *The Mind's I – Fantasies and Reflections on Self and Soul*,[16] which is surely one of the best collections on the theme ever assembled.

Dan Dennett is a big man with a silver beard and the charismatic presence of Santa Claus or the Grand Oral Disseminator of Maxi Jazz fame. He went straight to work. Descartes identified *res cogitans* with the immortal soul, but since then materialism has swept dualism aside. We now have a mortal and material soul whose only Cartesian relic is the Cartesian theater. All the work of the soul is now done by Cartesian theater homunculi, and all this work must be distributed to lesser agencies in the brain. With the self as an organ, we face Jerry Fodor's big question: Who's in charge?

Dennett's oratorical flow was so fast and rich I that could hardly keep up with my scribbled notes. I wrote: "Will Hamilton's question – What did I want?" Presumably this was Hamilton the evolutionary biologist. But what did he want? I can venture the brave guess that the point is that such a question is in principle unanswerable because there is a failure of reference in the prerequisite attribution of determinate desires to an ill-defined self.

Or what about his reference to Robert Wright's book *Nonzero: The Logic of Human Destiny*, where in chapter 21, footnote 14, Wright says he's convinced Dennett thinks consciousness doesn't exist?[17] What can we do with this? Dennett's own argument in *Consciousness Explained* was that the heterophenomenology of consciousness reduces it to computation and behavior, or as John Searle said, explains it away, so why should we insist that Wright is wrong?

At least this was clear. Dennett strongly recommended that we read a book called *Breakdown of Will* by George Ainslie.[18] Apparently, Ainslie argues that an organ of self doesn't have to exist.

Dennett strode on. Why does it *seem* to us that there's a Cartesian theater? And who is the *us* to whom it so seems? Consider Dan Wegner's claim that we inhabit an extremely complex machine. Who are *we*? Or consider one of Libet's famous experiments: a subject is seated in front of a clock face with a dot on it that rotates around the face at the rate of three and a half revolutions per second. The subject is asked to flick a finger – *flick!* – voluntarily, at whim, and note the position of the rotating dot when the urge to flick emerged in consciousness. Libet's measurements showed that the readiness potential grew in the subject's brain a full 350 milliseconds before the urge emerged. What are we to make of this? In *Consciousness Explained*, Dennett said that although such results seemed to show we were not quite out of the loop, this whole picture was "compelling but incoherent."[19]

Ramachandran (him again) said that such delays show we don't have free will. What we have is "not free will but free won't."[20] That is, the role of the will is inhibitory. In most cases, we just do what we do, but occasionally we can stop ourselves.

Earlier, in his book *Elbow Room*,[21] Dennett said that if you make yourself really small, you can externalize everything. But wherever you are, you get illusions of simultaneity. He showed us a few diagrams to clarify this. Imagine various brain modules communicating with each other. Wherever the self is located relative to these modules, there are varying distances to the respective modules. Given slow signal propagation, this means varying delays caused by the signals' travel times. I can have this signal arrive before that one, or vice versa, by locating the self nearer to this or that source module. But wherever I put myself, the time ordering generated by the arrival of the signals will in general be different from the order of creation of the signals in the modules. That's just physics.

Dennett now suggested various hypotheses. First, the *strolling you* moves back and forth in about 300 milliseconds, so you misjudge all the times. Second, the *out-of-touch you* outsources or delegates the whole business and is thus in a poor position to judge any timings, since all your information is second-hand. Third, you go for Libet's window of opportunity, which looks horribly like an artifact of the whole experimental protocol.

He suggested a new approach. Whenever you distribute work in time and space, you distribute responsibility in time and space, too. In this case, you're not so much out of the loop as the loop itself, the whole thing. That sounded much better.

What was the punch line of all this? Aha, he said, see my next book![22]

From Ground Zero to Paradise

The conference was a first-class portrait of the current state of play with regard to the neurological self. The big question is whether this snapshot makes it plausible to suppose that the neurological self can do duty for the soul. Or is Joe LeDoux expecting too much of neurological reductionism?

The problem is that the radical reduction this mechanistic metaphor has accomplished leaves us at Ground Zero, with no easy way back to the dizzy heights we wanted to explore. Imagine a tribe of truth-seekers who knew nothing of computers but who were full of hypotheses to explain how they worked. A tribal guru who said a computer was just a pattern of connections between transistors would rightly be celebrated, but could hardly be said to have told the whole story, any more than the earlier guru who said it was just a big pile of elaborately juxtaposed atoms. LeDoux is a synapse specialist, so he sees the brain that way, but the holistic problem of how it all comes together remains untouched.

The neurological self is but one slice or aspect of a many-splendored thing. The self of popular discourse is so polymorphous that no tidy definition can wrap it up. We have a personal self, a rational self, a conscious self, a biological self, a genetic self, an immunological self, and now a neurological self. Are they all identical? That seems impossible. Each of these selves is defined in a different realm of discourse, and the discourses do not admit straightforward translation from one to another. Or, to placate Dan Dennett, each is a draft in a multiple-draft drama stretching across our whole civilizeation. We have a turbulent pandemonium of selves jostling for supremacy in a public theater. The hope that the whole riotous show boils down to synapses is hollow, not inspiring.

Indeed, LeDoux's very first words in the first chapter of his new book give us pause for doubt:

"I don't know, so maybe I'm not," the T-shirt said.[23]

This post-Cartesian *aperçu* is my point of critical departure. It hints that the self is the referent of the word "I" and therefore as polymorphous as our usage of that little word is multifarious. Ever since Moses heard the great I AM, the first-person singular pronoun has been a battleground. The history of "I" is most unlikely to reduce without residue to talk of synapses. For a conscious mind rises much higher above its synapses than a computer above its transistors. As Llinás said, the electricity has to flow for us to be "on", and as McFadden says,[24] the brain's electromagnetic field may be the real substrate for an integrated self. The field generated by billions of neurons reacts back on individual neurons and interacts with the internal and external environment in a dynamical coupling that physicists are still exploring. Our thoughts do not reduce as neatly to synaptic action as computer programs reduce to transistor action.

The cerebral EM field is still *terra incognita*. This is the critical weakness in the neurological concept of self. Perhaps the photonic self will one day be seen to rise as far above the neurological self as the neurological self rises above the genomic self. Perhaps we shall even glimpse a hierarchy of selves, soaring through the hierarchy of Buddhas into Cantor's transfinite paradise.

Buy

In my humble opinion, the conference was a big success. The New York Academy of Sciences is publishing the proceedings in its Annals series.[25]

A Photonic Theory of Consciousness

Abstract

The conscious mind is the central mystery of psychology. How it can be implemented in terms of basic physics is still unclear. Because there is a potentially paradoxical circle involved in the idea that the mind can understand itself, the problem begins at the level of logic. We need a preliminary formalism that can remove the air of paradox from this circularity, then we need to see how this formalism can be interpreted in physical terms. Thus we can establish a perspective in which the ongoing state of phenomenal awareness that characterizes a conscious mind appears as a natural phenomenon to be explained using the same kinds of laws we use for other natural phenomena. This paper starts from a logical view in which epistemological stages in the development of ontological theory are ordered along a timelike dimension, then introduces enough set theory to outline a conception of *worlds* that can serve as formal analogs of states of mind. Such worlds are then described from the standpoint of quantum physics and cosmology. All this theory is used to suggest that coherent wavefronts of decahertz photons generated by neural firing may reflect phenomenal consciousness. Some consequences for psychology are explored.

Introduction

Physics and psychology are complementary. Reality as we know it admits description in terms of both physics – we live in a physical world – and psychology – we reflect or model the world in our minds. Thus the whole *intentional* aspect of psychology – that our mental contents denote an external world – must correspond to a physical process that we can describe in physics. But how?

The physical foundations of psychology are often taken for granted. We tend to assume that any proposed mechanism for implementing a psychological function or feature can be realized physically, even if the details of the physics involved are not yet worked out. Within physics, too, most physicists implicitly assume that they themselves, as conscious agents, come within the scope of their theories. Richard Feynman had little time for psychology or psychologists, but in his opinion, "the theory of quantum electrodynamics describes ... *all* the phenomena of the physical world except the gravitational effect ... and radioactive phenomena."[1]

Yet despite the success of QED, we are still groping for a physical explanation of the phenomenal consciousness that David Chalmers and Max Velmans relate to the first-person perspective in contrast to the third-person perspective of conventional science.[2] To some, such as Colin McGinn, it can even seem impossible that we should ever understand the role of phenomenal consciousness in physical reality.[3]

The issue of first and third persons is somehow critical. Phenomenal consciousness is *my* consciousness. I *know* that I have phenomenal consciousness, but I only *believe* that others do. That epistemological contrast gives life to Daniel Dennett's distinction between autophenomenology and heterophenomenology.[4] Physics is conventionally understood as the background theory for a third-person view of the world, that is, for a heterophenomenological psychology. Yet physicists avoid invoking personal perspectives in their formal theories. The observers of relativity and quantum theory are like perspectival points in geometry. They have no personality. In this sense, we can describe physics as an *autistic* theory. No theory of mind is needed to pursue physics – so long as physicists can still understand each other. In principle, if not in fact, an autistic development of physics can remain ambiguous about whether it describes a first-person or a third-person reality. We can trace that ambiguity back to the logical and mathematical foundations of the physics.

This is the key to the following argument. I plan to construct a logico-mathematical frame, and within it a physics, that accounts for both first-person and third-person facts, without losing the ambiguity of the autistic perspective. For the science of psychology, this provides a stable base from which to allow that my mind and other minds are phenomenally different despite the background presumption that all minds work in physically similar ways. A central fact of psychology, that each of us experiences our own mind in a way that seems quite different from our experience of other minds, is thus preserved and given its due prominence. A central claim of physics, that its dominion should extend in principle over both external and internal reality, whether we recognize this in our everyday psychology or not, is also preserved. And thus we can relate psychology to QED, as advertised.

If we can sustain this perspectival ambiguity, we do not need to cultivate a separate phenomenological language to account for subjective experience. If we can exploit this ambiguity to establish mappings between phenomenal and nonphenomenal language, we can avoid the otherwise baffling obstacle that "our *language* for phenomenal qualities is derivative on our nonphenomenal language."[5] Once we have found reasonable bridges between the more and the less phenomenal ends of our language, we can put phenomenology in its rightful place at the heart of science. Sadly, that great project goes way beyond what I can tackle in these pages. I claim only to show how logic and physics can support a theory of consciousness.

Logic: Truth

The next few sections outline some basic formal logic and set theory, the relevance of which may not be obvious at first. Its role is to serve as a scaffolding for the task of conceiving consciousness in a perspectivally ambiguous way, so that it can consistently accommodate the tricky enterprise of understanding consciousness from within, and thus of relating psychology to physics. If you are familiar with logic and set theory, you will recognize most of the details. But the interpretational gloss is subtly (or even grossly) novel, so beware.

The science of logic outlines the basic structure of any possible language used to build up a cognitive structure designed to model an external reality. Such a language expresses propositions that may be true or false, and the set of true propositions is satisfied in the natural or intended model described by the language. Every science, including physics and psychology, is pursued in a linguistic environment. In terms of logic, the aim of a scientific discipline is to develop a model or a set of models relative to which certain propositions of the language used in that discipline may be said to be true.

Formal logic develops this basic conception into a calculus. Atomic propositions can be connected to form compound propositions that inherit their truth-values recursively from those of their constituents. Thus we can develop a Boolean algebra for such connectives as *and* ($\wedge$, analogous to set-theoretic conjunction), *or* ($\vee$, analogous to disjunction), and *not* ($\neg$, analogous to complementation). Following Frege, we can distinguish subject and predicate parts in propositions, and use the mathematical notation of functions and variables to build up first-order logic in which the variables range over objects and the functions stand for predicate or relational terms, with quantifiers *for all* (∀) and *for some* (∃) to bind the variables in general statements. For example, to say that all objects x either have property P or lack it, we can write: $(\forall x)(P(x) \vee \neg P(x))$. We can develop a formal semantics for such logic by defining models as sets of objects over which various properties and relations are defined, and then by stipulating recursively the conditions under which the models satisfy the various quantified and unquantified formulas of the language. All this is well known.

Obviously, none of this machinery is any less applicable to the first-person theorist than to scientists in a public domain. Logic and truth can be characterized in just the same way by a methodological autist. Indeed they must be, if Wittgenstein's arguments against private language are taken to heart.[6] So phenomenology must conform to elementary logic.

Logic: Trees

Our knowledge changes and evolves, and generally seems to accumulate. As time goes by, we learn more, understand more, and maybe forget things. This holds generally, for whole cultures over historical time and for an individual from moment to moment.

We can represent this in logic in terms of trees. At any given moment, the knowing subject occupies a node in a tree. Starting at node zero, the subject advances from node to node as the domain of knowledge expands or unfolds. At each node, certain truths are known, either by some process that so far as logic is concerned is direct recognition or by deduction or proof, and at each successor node, certain further truths become known, either by renewed direct recognition or by deduction from the earlier truths. This process of epistemic advance can be modeled in the tree as closely as we like simply by multiplying nodes, and can be given a physical reference by indexing the nodes in time. For example, each node can represent a hundred milliseconds in the cognitive life of an experimental subject who is busy analyzing a visual scene or parsing heard sentences.

Such an epistemic tree has an obvious limitation. The model by reference to which the truth-values of sentences entertained at the respective nodes are evaluated remains unaffected by the advance. The picture is that we are filling out a jigsaw puzzle, piece by piece. This is unrealistic. The model itself for such a tree is a formal construction, built by a process very like that described in the tree. Formally, the model is defined in a metalanguage, and the metalanguage is subject to exactly the same analysis as the object language for which it provides the semantics. So we can improve our picture by recognizing a tree of models to match the original tree of epistemic states. As we advance through the epistemic tree, we need to build ever more detailed models to make sense of the new truths that we recognize.

Here we can introduce a Quinean gloss on the distinction between epistemology and ontology. In a given domain of discourse, our epistemology is the set of sentences, theories, and the like that we hold to be true, together with all the means by which we came to recognize their truth, such as direct perception, calculation, or meter reading. In that domain, our ontology is the set of things we suppose to exist to explain those truths. The ontology includes not only the objects over which the quantified variables of our formal language range but also their properties and relations and indeed the entire models that they collectively form. Our ontologies develop over time no less inexorably than do our epistemologies.[7]

A tree with epistemic and ontic nodes can be negotiated dialectically. Each step forward in our epistemology prompts a corresponding advance in our ontology. We shuttle back and forth between epistemology and ontology, refining our ontology in the light of each new piece of knowledge and using each new model to prompt the search for yet further truths. This picture of science invites comparison with the process of conjecture and refutation described by Karl Popper.[8]

To introduce a mathematical metaphor, the stepwise process of accommodating various consequences of Gödel's incompleteness theorem for arithmetic can be represented as an epistemo-ontic dialectic shuttling between proof theory and model theory through a transfinite hierarchy of ever more sketchily defined metalevels.[9] The details are irrelevant here, but the basic idea is that stepwise avoidance of impending contradiction drives an onward push through a logical hierarchy. There is no fixed, final frame, just an open-ended series of provisional frames.

All this machinery arose to describe knowledge in the large, on a societal scale. But it can also describe knowledge in the small, on a personal scale. And not to forget forgetting, we can develop a logic of partial information in which hard knowledge is distinguished from soft knowledge and later nodes in a tree can correspond to states of reduced knowledge.[10]

Such an evolutionary picture of the logic of knowledge is surely essential for consciousness. It looks to me like the only way to bridge the gap between the mind as an ongoing phenomenological process and a constantly changing phenomenal reality. The basic idea is that the intentional coupling of mind and reality gets more intimate and complicated as time goes on.

Modal Logic

Both in everyday experience and in organized science, the advance from node to node in an epistemo-ontic tree has a feature lacking in mathematics. Whereas in mathematics all truths are necessary (if only by definition), even minimally scientific experiencers distinguish between contingent and necessary truths. This distinction turns out to be crucial to understanding how quantum theory can be relevant for understanding or representing consciousness.

To accommodate the distinction, we simply add branches to the tree such that, from each node, all necessary truths continue to be true in all accessible nodes and different contingent truths are true in different accessible nodes. So some of the nodes that are accessible from a given node are now mutually contradictory, in the sense that the contingent propositions are true in some nodes but false in others. Scientists in different fields have different ways of deciding which truths are necessary and which are contingent, but that need not detain us. We can see the multiplication of contingent propositions at each node in terms of an evolutionary epistemology as the generation of competing hypotheses, most of which are destined to be falsified at the next node.

The formal study of modalities can be taken much further. If the ontic situation corresponding to a node is called a *world*, so that the world corresponding to node x is what makes propositions asserted by the epistemic subject at node x either true or false, then necessary truths are true in all possible worlds and contingent truths are true in some possible world or worlds, where in both cases the worlds correspond to nodes that are accessible from node x. All this invites a comprehensive ontology of worlds, each of which satisfies some more or less peculiar combination of contingent truths, and requires us to be explicit in saying what spectrum of worlds is possible, both *a priori*, before we start climbing a tree, and *a posteriori*, relative to the epistemic situation at each node in our tree. We can build formal theories and semantics to describe all this, and modal logic is now a rich field.[11]

To sum up so far, the semantics of a language is the formal analog of epistemology and ontology. To specify the semantics of a language that scientists can use to assert propositions about nature, we give a recursive specification of the truth conditions of those propositions in a suitably formalized syntax. To specify the ontology for the language, we define a set of worlds and an accessibility relation over that set. The worlds correspond to nodes in a dialectical tree. In general, an account of the semantics of a language is a specification of the conditions under which certain syntactic structures – its sentences or propositions – can be used to convey information that in the right circumstances correspond to certain transitions between worlds or sets of worlds, namely those observed or intended by the agents using that language. Crudely, language is a tool for reflecting and effecting changes in the world.

All this may seem like a lot of machinery to discuss the contents of consciousness, which may be both rather simple and lacking in much evident logic or consistency. Yet cognitive scientists regularly require surprisingly sophisticated computational models to explain apparently simple cognitive functions. And whether the contents of consciousness *seem* consistent or not, any machinery that we as scientists propose to implement the mind must be consistent. We are trying to reverse-engineer a biorobot that is vastly more sophisticated than any softbot we have so far constructed, so of course we need good tools.

Quantum Logic

In fundamental physics, sets of possible worlds are often quite easy to define. For classical particles such as gas molecules, they correspond to all possible assignments of position and velocity to the particles. Here we can introduce a useful distinction between *macrostates* and *microstates*, where each macrostate is defined by specific values of observable properties such as temperature or pressure. The entropy of a macrostate can be defined in terms of the number of microstates that can realize it. If all the possible microstates of a system are equally probable (this is decided by a symmetry argument), then the relative probability of given macrostates is determined by the relative numbers of microstates that can realize them. In these terms, the second law of thermodynamics says that complex closed systems tend always to evolve in the direction of increasing probability.

We can also characterize quantum systems in terms of possible worlds. States of a quantum system are defined by different assignments of discrete quantum numbers to the elementary particles of the system (or more generally by discrete configurations of quantized fields). The novelty in quantum theory is that systems or parts of systems can be in superpositions of states. A *pure* state of a system is a state in which the observables of the system have definite values, but these pure states can be superposed to form *mixed* states in which some observables have a range of possible values, each with a probability of less than one. If a mixed state is not disturbed from outside, it can persist indefinitely. If it is perturbed from outside, for example by a measurement, it evolves probabilistically into a specific pure state. Each pure state in a superposition has an amplitude determined by the wave function for the system. The probability that a given pure state is realized is proportional to the square of the amplitude for that state.

Interactions between quantum objects such as particles typically generate *entangled* states where the particles emerging from the interaction have correlated probabilities to collapse to particular unique states. The general state of a typical physical system described in quantum terms is a mixed state in which vast numbers of superpositions and entanglements persist below the observed surface.

In terms of modal logic, a mixed state is a state defined across a set of possible worlds. In quantum logic, the general state of a physical system involves reference to multiple worlds, and any change in the system involves a transition from one set of worlds to another set of worlds. By ignoring fine detail and considering only a phenomenologically characterized macrostate, we can say roughly that we inhabit a unique world, but the classical physics behind that claim works only in a macroscopic approximation, and classical logic breaks down for quantum phenomena in that world. Classical logic works within a world, but quantum phenomena involve multiple worlds. Roland Omnès has developed a consistent histories approach that clarifies the logic here.[12]

The phenomenal worlds of everyday life are *macroworlds* that correspond to mixtures of numerous microstates. But since different language communities use different languages, and translation between them is not always well defined, their macroworlds may be too fuzzy to make much sense in terms of transition probabilities between configurations of quantized fields. By contrast, our everyday presumption that we live in a unique world often makes fairly good sense.

In all this, it is important to remember that despite decades of debate, the whole question of how to reconcile an ontology of worlds with quantum theory is still unsettled.

Set Theory

The most abstract nontrivial characterization we can give of the logic of worlds is in terms of set theory. Sets are classes of elements such that the elements are the members of the classes. With only odd exceptions, all elements and classes are sets. Sets have a dual aspect: from above or outside, they are elements, and from below or inside, they are classes. In traditional terms, elements are particulars and classes are universals. In linguistic terms, elements correspond to objects, that is, to entities denoted by noun phrases, and classes correspond to properties, that is, to entities denoted by predicates or verb phrases.

The basic idea of sets is as simple as that, but we need some formal machinery to handle the idea. So let us again briefly review some standard theory. If you know it, you can skim it. If it is new to you, just try to get a general sense of the cumulative hierarchy as a kind of huge mushroom cloud of all the things we talk about, ranked into consistent layers.

A formal language L for set theory is based on first-order logic and includes the Boolean connectives and the Fregean quantifiers. It includes a single primitive binary predicate, called the *membership* relation, such that, for any sets x and y, $x \in y$ if and only if x is a member of y, where class $y = \{u \mid P(u)\}$ contains those elements u such that $P(u)$, for some predicate P in L. Identity for sets is defined in terms of membership; thus sets are *extensional*. Two sets are identical if and only if they have exactly the same members: for all x and y, $x = y$ if and only if $(\forall z)(z \in x \leftrightarrow z \in y)$. So far so good.

Our naïve intuitions about sets suggest that any syntactically reasonable property defines a set, namely the set of all sets that have that property. Notoriously, however, this does not work. When Frege tried to build his pioneering set theory on this basis, Bertrand Russell pointed out that the property of not being a member of itself is well defined in the language of set theory, but that the set of all sets that are not members of themselves is a member of itself if and only if it is not a member of itself: if $R = \{x \mid x \notin x\}$ then $(R \in R \leftrightarrow R \notin R)$. This contradiction shows that we need to be very careful in specifying which predicates may be allowed to define sets.

The natural strategy for avoiding paradoxes of this sort is to stipulate that sets may not be members of themselves. Sets are seen as constructions from pre-existing elements. The process of constructing sets is seen as analogous to a temporal process. The elements of a set must exist before the set itself can be defined. Proceeding methodically from a minimal foundation, we can thus build up a whole universe of *heterosets* without risk of infection by contradiction. Following Zermelo, we can even start with nothing at all, the empty set ∅. We forbid not only self-loops (where a set x is a member of itself or a member of ... a member of x, for any number of intermediate steps) but also infinitely descending membership chains. Such heterosets are said to be *well founded*. All this is basic, and well discussed by many authors.[13]

The Cumulative Hierarchy

The standard theory of heterosets starts with the null set $\emptyset$ and builds up layer by layer to fill out a *universe* V that cannot itself be a set (since it would be identical with Russell's impossible set R), each time admitting into the new layer only sets constructed by acceptable means from sets that already exist in the previous layer. Roughly, each new determination of V is as the class of all subsets of the set of all sets comprehended in the previous determination of V, where the subsets of set x include both $\emptyset$ and x itself. John von Neumann called these layers *ranks* and defined a rank function $V(\alpha)$ by transfinite recursion over the scale of ordinal numbers α to generate a transfinite series of ordinal-indexed determinations of the ranked universe V of well-founded sets:

$V(0) = \emptyset$, where ordinal 0 is defined as $\emptyset$,

$V(\alpha + 1) = P(V(\alpha))$, where $\alpha + 1$ is the successor of α and $P(x)$ is the power set of x, and

$V(\lambda) = \bigcup \{V(\alpha) \mid \alpha < \lambda\}$, where λ is a limit ordinal and $\bigcup$ is the transfinite union operator.

Here each ordinal is defined as the set of all smaller ordinals; thus each ordinal α has the same rank as the determination $V(\alpha)$ of V that it indexes.

Given the standard first-order formal language of set theory, the result of comprehending all the sets generated by the rank function is the *cumulative hierarchy* that serves as the standard or intended model of Zermelo–Fraenkel set theory.[14] This model suffices to provide a formal semantics for all of classical mathematics. *A fortiori*, it can provide a sufficient formal foundation for a physics based on that mathematics and for a psychology complementing that physics. Here I shall regard it as the foundational metaphysics for a maximally general and perspectively neutral concept of consciousness.

From 0 to Infinity

The cumulative hierarchy is infinite in a deeper sense than may be apparent. Not only is it transfinite in Cantor's sense, where orders of infinity leapfrog countable infinities into domains of arbitrarily high cardinality, but we can extend it further by extending the language in which it is defined. But relax – we can skip all that here.

More generally, we can define *reflection principles* that say, in effect, that any statement made using given syntactic resources that is true at all in the cumulative hierarchy is satisfied already in some set within the hierarchy, which is to say that set *reflects* the universe so far as that statement is concerned. All such sets are ranked determinations $V(\alpha)$ of the universe V, and suggest the general assertion that *anything* consistent that we can say about the universe as a whole is true already in some ranked determination $V(\alpha)$ of V. Conversely, if a statement resists interpretation in *any* ranked determination $V(\alpha)$ of the universe, then it is inconsistent – or meaningless.

Alternatively, we can start from other primitive elements in addition to the null set $\emptyset$. We can import such *urelements* from outside mathematics and simply erect a cumulative hierarchy as superstructure over them. This is technically harmless, since we can always map such urelements arbitrarily onto pure sets of some nonzero rank α such that there are enough sets of rank α for the mapping.

Physics suggests numerous candidates for urelements. Elementary particles or spacetime points may serve in a fundamental theory, or qualia or data bits in a phenomenological theory, and may give rise to more or less well defined universes. In such universes, the interpretation of the membership relation is likely to be unintuitive. The only constraint is that it be applied consistently. Using Kantian terminology, we can say that in a phenomenal world defined in some such physical terms, a manifold of such urelements is brought to a synthetic unity in a suitably ranked universe.

In any such theory, set theory gives us a logical frame to reduce an infinity of primitives to a single null element. In such a theory, the most general interpretation of the ordinal scale along which V-sets are ranked is as something like time, and the general picture for the application of set theory here is that the universe of discourse evolves from ultimate simplicity to infinite complexity along this growing timelike dimension. Such a conception of time is more general than that provided by relativity theory, where clocks in spacetime are synchronized by signals traveling at light speed, since it requires no particular furniture (such as clocks and light signals) and hence works for a wider range of phenomenologies. We need this generality to account for consciousness.

Sets as Worlds

The determinations $V(\alpha)$ of a set-theoretic universe V are natural candidates for the worlds that we anticipated schematically in logic. A world has a logical structure reflected in some suitable V-set $V(\alpha)$. Worlds sprout from worlds to form trees that grow along a timelike dimension indexed by ordinals α. All the worlds in a tree can be modeled in the same universe V, perhaps as successive V-sets $V(α)$ in an orderly progression. Thus we have a metaphysical picture in which physical and logical realities are coeval and grow along a timelike dimension that slices phenomenal reality into ranks. This does not force worlds to be finite, since a typical quantum jump leaves an infinity of superposed worlds behind it, and a typical macroworld is the phenomenal surface for an infinity of microstates, but it does create a link between mathematical and physical reality.

Worlds are centered. In terms of logic, the set of truths that are recognized at a given node – in a given world – defines a perspective. In Kantian terminology, each world is a phenomenal manifold that is brought to a synthetic unity of apperception in a suitable V-set. In terms of physics, a world realizes a very specific mixture of quantum states that reflect the equally specific history of an observer. In terms of psychology, a world defines a *subject*. The subject embodies the synthetic unity of the phenomenal manifold, reflects the realization of specific quantum states, and is in a position to assert the truth of a certain body of propositions. A subject need not be seen as a person. The ontology of personhood involves a lot of cultural detail that has no place here. A subject is defined as or by a perspective on a phenomenal world.

To prevent misunderstanding, it is worth emphasizing that worlds and subjects can be very simple. The null world $V(0)$ is trivial, but the *bit* world $V(1)$ is already interesting. The phenomenal manifold in the bit world is the single null element $\varnothing = 0$, and the reflecting subject is the singleton class $\{\varnothing\} = 1$. The digital phenomenologies we build with bits as urelements are virtual worlds that come together as unities in our minds. Indeed, the generality of the ideas here allows us to posit worlds within worlds almost without limit, and to see subjects reflecting objective domains in just about any constellation of elements. We simply need to remember that what is logically possible need not make much sense physically or psychologically.

Quantum Physics

Consider a physical system that consists of a very large number of quantum particles that are in a state of fairly continuous interaction, such as a human brain. The discrete pure states of these quantum particles form a very large set, and the set of possible mixed and entangled states is vast, even after we neglect vast numbers of such states as vanishingly improbable. A system like a human brain is open to its environment in innumerable ways, so its physical evolution in time is not constrained to increase its own entropy, but the sequence of macrostates that it realizes nevertheless evolves in accordance with physical law.

A key such law is the Schrödinger equation, which is deterministic but gives rise to a probabilistic dynamics when we introduce the interaction with an observer, as follows.

The rest of this section is basic background, in case you wish to be reminded of it. If you prefer not to wade through the formalism, you can skip it. So long as you are content to accept that the formal frame works, I hope you will find that the remainder of the argument makes sense anyway.

Generally, we can see a physical system as made up of particles that are subject to wave–particle duality. A particle with linear momentum p corresponds to a wave with wavelength λ given by $p = h/\lambda$, where h is Planck's constant. If the momentum p is sharply defined, so is λ, and the corresponding wave is extended, so the position x of the particle is not sharply defined, in accordance with Heisenberg's uncertainty principle that the product of the respective uncertainties Δp and Δx in momentum and position is of order h: $\Delta p \, \Delta x \cong h$. The particles have energy E and evolve in time t, where again the uncertainties ΔE and Δt are such that $\Delta E \, \Delta t \cong h$. The dimensions of h are those of action, so wave–particle duality and uncertainty are expressions of the ultimate granularity of physical reality with regard to action.

For each particle, its wave can be expressed as a function ψ of position x and time t such that

$$\psi(x, t) = A \exp[i(kx - \omega t)] = a \cos(kx - \omega t) + ib \sin(kx - \omega t),$$

where k is the wave number $2\pi/\lambda$, ω is the angular frequency of the wave, $A = a + ib$ is its amplitude, and $i^2 = -1$. Together, the orthogonal sinusoidal components of this wave define a helical motion in a complex space around the x-axis, like a propeller with radius A spinning along in direction x.

The wave function ψ is the basis of the Schrödinger equation, which in one of its forms says that for a particle with mass m and zero potential energy in one spatial dimension x,

$$d\psi/dt = (ih/4\pi m) \, d^2\psi/dx^2.$$

This equation is analogous to a classical diffusion equation, such as the heat diffusion equation $dT/dt = D \, d^2T/dx^2$, where T is temperature and D is a diffusion constant. In effect, it says that an initially sharp wave function for an undisturbed system diffuses steadily outward. The Schrödinger equation takes various forms and its solutions are well explored.

The general state of a quantum system is a mixture of pure states. The wave function for a mixed state is a superposition of the wave functions for the pure states. Each pure state in the superposition has an amplitude A determined by the wave function ψ for the state. If the system is disturbed in such a way that the superposition collapses, the probability that the pure state with amplitude A is realized is proportional to the squared modulus $|A|^2$ of A (where $|A|^2 = a^2 + b^2$). The constant of proportionality can be set to unity by normalizing all the amplitudes so that the probabilities of all the possible pure states add up to one.

More concretely, the *observables* of a quantum system are what we can measure. The theory enables us to predict an *expectation value* for the result of measuring a continuous variable such as x or p, which is the value we expect to obtain as the average of a large number of measurements. Observable O, corresponding to operator $\hat{O}$, has an expectation value defined as

$$\langle O \rangle = \int \psi^* \hat{O} \psi \, d\tau,$$

where wave function ψ is normalized, ψ^* is its complex conjugate (the complex conjugate of $a + ib$ is $a - ib$), and $d\tau$ is a volume element, with the integral taken over all space. What this means is that to predict an expectation value, we need to add up the contributions of all possible wave functions for the system. What we observe is the outcome of the interference between all the superposed states. When our measurements reveal or realize pure states, the individual results are random, but the expectation values and hence the statistics are predictable.

All this theory is the firm foundation of all modern chemistry and biology.[15] For a complex system like the brain, we can expect in general that any quantum randomness at the molecular level will be lost in the statistics of the large numbers of molecules involved in events like synaptic transmission or neural firing. So if we wish to describe something as global as consciousness in quantum terms, the burden is on us to show how all this beautifully intricate but forbidding detail can help. My basic proposal here is that worlds of consciousness correspond to quantum entanglements.

Physics: Entanglement

Interactions between quantum particles typically generate entangled states where the particles emerging from the interaction have correlated probabilities to realize particular pure states when measured. John Bell proved that these entanglements generate nonclassical statistics for the observables in EPR-type experiments, and these statistics have been observed in numerous experiments.[16]

The significance of entanglement and its pervasiveness in nature is that it can amplify quantum superpositions to potentially macroscopic scales. In principle, multiparticle mixed states can be arbitrarily large, but in fact thermal and other interactions severely limit the spread of superpositions. Nevertheless, in any macroscopic world, mixed states coexist in wild profusion below its phenomenal surface. For example, whenever an electron is shared between atoms in a molecule, the electron is in a mixed state of being with this or that atom. Each mixed state is defined across a set of possible worlds. In set-theoretic terms, each macroworld is an equivalence class of sets of microworlds. If the smallest microworlds correspond to pure states of a quantum system, mixed states correspond to worlds enclosing worlds. We may seem to inhabit a unique macroworld, but it corresponds to a vast set of copresent microworlds that are ceaselessly popping in and out of correlation from moment to moment.

The general state of a physical system involves multiple worlds, and any change in the system involves a transition from one set of worlds to another set of worlds. The minimal such change is a step in time, which changes the wave functions in the system. Some mixed states turn to pure states, other pure states turn to mixed states, and mixed states generally change their states of entanglement. This ceaseless activity at the quantum scale deserves the name *quantum foam* that John Wheeler introduced to describe the geometry of spacetime at the Planck scale.[17] In this new sense, physical reality quite generally, and not just the quasiclassical geometry of spacetime, is built on quantum foam.

My own view is that reality is foamlike and we are immersed in the foam. In the immortal verse of the poet Schiller quoted by Hegel as the closing words of his *Phänomenologie des Geistes*, "The chalice of this realm of spirits foams forth to God, his own infinitude" (in a standard translation I committed to memory many years ago).[18] This represents a deep generalization of the classical worldview that has consequences for how to see consciousness.

The universality of quantum phenomena such as entanglement is a good reason for describing the ontology of worlds in quantum terms. A world is a phenomenal surface brought to a synthetic unity in a subject that can be represented as the V-set or series of V-sets used to model that world. The surface is the boundary of a unique logical standpoint relative to which a certain set of truths is stable. In other words, the surface is the boundary of a pure state in a quantum system. If the world is big enough to realize interesting complexity, that pure state can be seen as a vast entanglement of particles. Beyond its phenomenal surface, other entanglements define other states that are mixed relative to the pure state of this world. From my perspective as the subject of a world, I live in a pure state that borders on innumerable mixed states. Alternatively, I live in a bubble in a foam. As my world changes, I inhabit a succession of bubbles that are linked to form a consistent history. In principle, I should be able to trace the bubble history right back to a cosmic $V(0)$.

If all this physics and metaphysics is making sense to you so far, you should already be glimpsing how it corresponds to a maximally general concept of consciousness.

Spacetime

The cosmological interpretation of the ordinal scale along which worlds unfold is as universal time. Let us pause to see how this conception of time relates to relativistic spacetime. Treatment of this topic is required to establish the complementarity (in Niels Bohr's sense [19]) of physics and psychology, but it is advanced and technical. Unfortunately for nonspecialists, the topic is essential to understanding how photons behave, so please don't skip the whole section.

Imagine, if you will, a rather small universe containing just a few photons. Photons are quanta of electromagnetism. They are bosons that always travel at light speed c, have no rest mass, and carry energy $E = hf$, where f is their frequency. As bosons, they have interesting collective behavior at the quantum level such that groups of them can be entangled in one and the same quantum state to form a coherent wave in which the separate identities of the photons is entirely dissolved. Laser beams are examples of this behavior. Coherent groups of bosons are macroscopic quantum objects. Because photons always travel at the constant speed c, photons emitted from a point source that are not yet determined to be traveling in a particular direction define an expanding sphere, which at time t after emission has radius ct. The wave function for a photon determines a probability distribution over the surface of this sphere for the realization of the photon somewhere on the surface. As soon as the photon interacts with something, its probability to be at the point of interaction becomes one and its probability to be elsewhere collapses to zero. Metaphorically, the bubble formed by its expanding wavefront has popped. Similarly, a coherent bunch of photons can pop out of superposition into a definite distribution of points on a surface.

On a cosmological scale, stars and quasars can be well approximated as point sources of photons that create expanding wavefronts. Indeed, about ten teraseconds after the Big Bang (when photons decoupled from matter) the primordial fireball became a photon bubble that now has a radius of about 42 billion light-years (the Big Bang occurred about 14 billion years ago, but space has expanded since then, as Max Tegmark points out in a survey of cosmological bubbles in *Scientific American*[20]). We and all our descendants are fated to live in this bubble. Thus generalized, photon bubbles define worlds in the cosmological sense.

In relativity theory, spacetime diagrams with space and time as ortho-gonal axes represent light signals as diagonals or as light cones defining null geodesics. The problem here is that relativistic spacetime suggests a classical "block universe" metaphysics in which the future is just as focused and determinate as the past[21] – and this seems inconsistent with the unfolding centered quantum worlds approach I am advocating here. However, the many-worlds story works for quantum field theory, which incorporates special relativity, and physicists are hopeful that gravity too will be quantized to bring general relativity at last into a quantum theory of everything.[22] So it seems reasonable to hope that the timelike dimension determined by a quantum interpretation of the V-set story will be consistent with a relativistic approach.

This physical concept of time is applicable in psychology whenever the phenomenological subject is a physical being. Realization as an unfolding cumulative hierarchy of V-sets, say as an unfolding digital panorama that can be modeled in V-sets, may intelligibly be said to transcend physical time. Such worlds define a timelike development of a phenomenology that only accidentally consumes our biological time as humans. Think of a DVD movie – its bit stream defines a virtual phenomenology whether or not anyone takes the time to watch it. A methodological autist can regard such worlds as the primary reality and the passage of physical time as a secondary phenomenon, or even as some kind of "illusion" (the word reportedly used by both Einstein and Gödel to characterize the experience of time).[23] Indeed, any physical subject modeled in a world of V-sets comes to a synthetic unity at a logical level that transcends clocks. The question for psychology is how much of this "eternal soul" admits reductive characterization in terms of physical mechanisms.

The Physical Observer

The role of the observer in physical theories is limited but crucial. In classical theories such as Newtonian or relativistic dynamics, the observer specifies inertial frames and defines motions or forces accordingly. In quantum theory, the observer performs measurements to collapse superpositions and realizes a pure state relative to which other states are mixed.

Psychology is also a physical theory. Here the subject observes a phenomenal world and brings it to a synthetic unity of apperception. The subject embodies a perspective on the physical world and experiences a proper part of it (a proper part is less than the whole) such that:

- The subject is a biological object in the public world and has many properties over and above those available to introspection in the subject's phenomenal world,
- Phenomenal worlds are implemented using the resources of this biological object,
- These phenomenal worlds are sufficiently transparent to allow their subjects to achieve veridical perception and establish truths about the public world, and
- Subjects have direct (but varying) experience of the passage of physical time.

The subjective experience of time is crucial. Familiar physical mechanisms change in time and can be constructed or evolved to show adaptive behavior, but there is nothing like phenomenal awareness in such behavior. The subject experiences a changing *now*, where phenomenal forms approach from a future and sink into a past. What mechanism can explain this?

Photons may support our experience of a moving *now*. By the relativistic definition of time, photons experience no passage of time at all. Like a single photon, a coherent bunch of photons lives its "life" in a vanishing moment, which from outside we may call a *now* of duration T. If the bunch decoheres instantly, the duration T is given by the time uncertainty Δt of the photons, which is about equal to the inverse of the photon frequency f. This is as close to instant as decoherence of a wave with frequency f can be. A periodic succession of such bunches can realize a succession of moments of *now* to impose a granularity on the phenomenal time of any subject reflected in them. If these coherent wavefronts of photons are recreated as soon as they decay, and thus follow each other with a frequency of approximately f, we have the basis for a clock that can entrain cognitive mechanisms in a suitably constructed subject, just as the clock in a computer drives its logical and memory operations. In this model, the subject is embodied as a succession of momentary states reflected in wavefronts of photons. These states have the logic of V-sets in that they reflect the universe for preceding states.

The protean experience of the passage of time is not bound to sensory modalities. It forms a constant background to any more traditional phenomenology. Let us call it *protophenomenology*. Photonic protophenomenology is the realization of a changing *now*. Behind, below, or within *now* is a realized and receding past, and beyond, above, or surrounding *now* is an advancing and still virtual future (this contrast of past and future invites comparison with the contrast of element and class in set theory). Any particular shapes discerned in the past or future are contributed by cognitive mechanisms that are outside the scope of protophenomenology.

The direction of time flow is given by entropy, since the photon bunches decohere probabilistically into determinate configurations in a one-way process. A potential problem here is that the past can essentially vanish in this process. We need to consider how a subject can persist when everything more than a moment ago is already gone. Some level of continuity is easy to explain: each photon wavefront is so similar to its predecessors that there are numerous overlapping patches of coherence, just as there are in the rays from an incandescent light. So, to mix metaphors, we persist as a stream of laser-like shards of consciousness. Subjective identity and memory are huge and complex issues in psychology, but one salient point is clear. The subjective sense of being a continuing subject is in part illusory. We change constantly, and our past lives on only through its contribution to determining our present state. Macrophenomenologically, to coin a term, we persist, but microphenomenologically we are born anew with each passing moment.

To speculate wildly, if this whole ongoing process of upwelling and breaking waves of photons can generate a fountain of phenomenology in the neural control circuitry of an organism shaped by natural selection, it is tempting to imagine that it could exert top-down effects that would cause it to evolve from functionally unhelpful noise to a finely tuned mechanism for orchestrating and centralizing control of the organism beyond the level available to an organism lacking phenomenal awareness.

If photons can be invoked in some such way to explain phenomenal experience, analogous macroscopic states of photonic protophenomenology exist throughout nature, wherever photons get sufficiently organized, and differ from our tuned states of awareness only in the fact that natural selection has not shaped them to any useful purpose. Wherever such states exist, they are surrounded by entangled states of matter that form boundaries to the worlds they instantiate. Presumably, such accidental worlds are as far from human worlds as random bit strings are from the digitized worlds of Hollywood movies.

According to this hypothesis, the observer of psychophysics is a series of momentary quantum mirrors formed by coherent bunches of photons that entrain a control mechanism for an organism. That mechanism prompts the organism to surround itself with a maximally extended and orderly reality. Poetically, we can say that in biological organisms, photons grow roots in the massive stuff of the universe. Such photons, in their eternal *now*, are utterly selfish. Bunches of dancing photons stamp patterns into macromolecules and biological evolution does the rest. I find this vision more congenial than the idea that our genes are the ultimate selfish replicators.[24]

Psychology: My World

The human brain is the seat of the psychological subject. If the above hypothesis is worth pursuing, the brain somehow generates and sustains coherent waves of photons that control the organism. These photons define a series of extended quantum states that determine the phenomenal reality of the subject and terminate in phenomenal surfaces formed by other quantum states. The inner logic of these extended quantum states is that they appear as a changing world, or a series of worlds, each of which is a consistent slice of reality with as much inner detail as may be. The mechanism of worlds allows us to model such detail as far as we choose, given the constraint that we need to identify computational mechanisms in the brain to implement the detail.

The brain of a conscious subject generates a continuous pattern of electromagnetic waves over a variable range of frequencies in the decahertz region (10–100 Hz). These waves have been studied in detail for many decades and much about them is well understood.[25] They are generated by the more or less synchronized firing of large numbers of neurons. Many billions of neurons contribute to these waves, so their individual firings are lost in the crowd, so far as EEG measurement is concerned, but their collective voice in the EEG signal is strong and richly patterned. Within the decahertz region, different frequency ranges correspond reliably to different states of arousal or awareness, from deep sleep to sudden jolts of alertness. Moreover, activity in specific regions of the cortex correlate so exactly with specific cognitive states that the task of mapping the details has become an ongoing industry in research labs, with no end in sight to its success.

So far so good. The problem is that decahertz photons have tiny energies in the femtoelectronvolt range. Decahertz waves are so deep in the radio region of the electromagnetic spectrum that their photonic properties seem uninteresting. Electrical power lines and appliances worldwide radiate decahertz photons in vast quantities without any measurable effect on us. The brain itself is soaked in an ocean of thermal photons, both real and virtual, including vast numbers of decahertz photons. It is hard to believe that the coherent decahertz waves generated in the brain can be more than an epiphenomenon of the more specific electrochemistry of neural activity. Neurons form networks that perform innumerable computational tasks just like the logical circuitry in a computer. The waves they generate seem as incidental as the heat generated by computer chips.

Yet consider the following. Synchronous neural firing appears to be a central mechanism of cognitive function. The work done over many years by Wolf Singer and his colleagues on cats and monkeys strongly suggests that synchronous firing in the gamma band (35–45 Hz) is a key part of the process of perceptual binding.[26] Neurons that fire together wire together, and the neural groups thus formed evolve via selective reinforcement into elaborate cognitive architectures.[27] Synchronous neural firing of sufficient intensity to establish coherent decahertz wavefronts is routinely observed over extended regions of cortex involving many millions of neurons. The functional role of this synchronous firing in building up cognitive architectures has obvious evolutionary value.

So the waves have a functional role. Nevertheless, their phenomenal corollary has no obvious role. As long as we restrict our attention to cognitive and computational mechanisms, subjective phenomenology seems to be an epiphenomenal dangler.

The situation looks different if we consider it from the perspective of a methodological autist. My world is unified and exhibits a rich phenomenology that unfolds in time. As this phenomenology unfolds in an evidently lawlike fashion, more and more of it makes sense, in a multilayered pattern that embraces the entire observable universe. There is nothing private about this increasing sense. I can explain it in public terms to anyone prepared to listen. My whole striving as a conscious being is to continue to enrich this unfolding phenomenology. My entire extended phenotype (this includes not only my body but also those aspects of my environment that I can choose or shape) is mobilized to achieve this goal. My genes assist to the extent that they drive aspects of my phenomenal experience (such as its affective coloration) and my cognitive and computational infrastructure provides functional assistance.

Seen in these terms, everything except my autophenomenology is secondary. On this view, organisms like us evolve as we do because our autophenomenology drives us to adapt and survive. Phenomenal symphonies of photonic vibrations entrain the whole organism, including our peak experiences of willed action.

Psychology: My Time

The decahertz photons I am proposing here as the physical correlates of phenomenology have time uncertainties in the millisecond range. For example, gamma-band photons with frequencies in the range 35–45 Hz have energies of 140–190 feV and time uncertainties of around 25–30 ms. This imposes a corresponding granularity on the moments of *now* for a subject with that phenomenology. By the sort of happy coincidence that makes a speculative hypothesis look better, the observed temporal granularity of human phenomenology is in this range.

This coincidence has a further happy consequence. The vast numbers of photons needed to raise phenomenology to a macroscopic level must be coherent for as long as the phenomenal world they reflect persists. But maintaining quantum coherence is difficult. This is what makes quantum computers so hard to construct. In a thermal environment like that of the living brain, a coherent state can be expected to decohere instantly, subject only to uncertainty. This problem is the main obstacle to theories of consciousness based on microwave photons, such as Penrose and Hameroff's Orch OR theory,[28] since microwave photons have time uncertainties measured in nanoseconds. For decahertz photons, instant decoherence means decoherence in tens of milliseconds, for the simple reason that it is not meaningful to talk about decahertz waves on shorter timescales.

Persistence times for phenomenal worlds of tens of milliseconds are consistent with the facts of human experience. As Rodolfo Llinás said in a recent conference,[29] the brain is a *dreaming machine* in which the dreams are like movies made up of frames that each persist for some tens of milliseconds. For Llinás, this rhythm is imposed by the cycle time for the recursive firing of chains of neurons in thalamo-cortical loops, which he sees as the main mechanism for generating conscious experience.[30] This is entirely consistent with the hypothesis advocated here, since this rhythmic firing of loops of neurons generates the decahertz oscillations that create the bunches of photons that reflect the phenomenology.

The model of temporal experience that emerges is simple. Rhythmic firing of synchronized neurons creates waves of decahertz photons. Each wavefront reflects a determinate phenomenology for a moment of *now* and then vanishes as its photons dissolve in the thermal ocean. This reflection of phenomenology is analogous to reflection in set theory in that a momentary state of the universe (from that perspective) is frozen as a definite object in subsequent states of the universe. Each wavefront emerges from a computational process in the brain that determines its characteristic phenomenology by providing cognitive focus. The focus arises automatically from the neural computation, which activates specific neural groups in a specific order and thus provides a combinatorial tag for that moment of *now* in memory.

The arrow of time is a corollary of the probabilistic asymmetry of past and future states of reality. All actual past states have probability 1 and form a consistent history ranked into simultaneity surfaces like V-sets in a cumulative hierarchy (where simultaneity is measured relative to the proper time of the subject). All counterfactual past states have probability zero. By contrast, all accessible future states have hypothetical probabilities in the open interval (0, 1). Each moment of *now* is symmetrical with respect to a range of possible futures in the sense that it remains selfsame regardless of which future is in fact realized. At each moment, that symmetry is broken by the realization of the next future state as a ranked surface in a consistent history. The flow of time crystalizes a growing pile of V-sets with the subject at the top in a shining *now*.

Consciousness

The role of consciousness in the cognitive and computational mechanisms that make up a human mind should now be clear. It has a *binding* role. It is the property of the first-person reality of the subject that everything comes together into a luminous moment of *now* that keeps changing. This corresponds to a perspectival point in a physically defined reality, from which classical motions and forces can be calibrated and quantum states and entanglements can be measured. The autistic nature of this role should also be clear. A single subject, alone in the universe, can fill it. The existence of other subjects, and the whole further story of interpersonal psychology, is an empirical matter, to be determined on the basis of the facts as they crystalize out in the changing world.

That said, consciousness in the human sense is clearly correlated with very specific states of the brain and body of a human being. Conscious subjects are awake and alert – or dreaming in REM sleep – and typically exhibit a certain focus in their attitude and behavior. Their brains are buzzing with neural activity at numerous levels, culminating in great decahertz waves of electrical excitation as neuron populations fire rhythmically around thalamo-cortical loops. These decahertz excitations throw off bunches of coherent photons that reflect the momentary states of mind of the subject, or reflect moments in the ongoing phenomenology that fills subjective consciousness.

Consciousness is photonic. I believe that this hypothesis best enables us to integrate the known physical facts about the brain with the metaphysics of phenomenal worlds in the mind. Aspects of mental function that surface as momentary topographic features in the photonic landscape that flickers over the conscious brain become part of the conscious mind. The photonic model seems to account well for the following features of consciousness:

- Our consciousness has limited scope. We are not conscious of most of what goes on in our brains, and we can only hold a few things in mind at once. By contrast, a neural account would have to explain how a relative handful of "conscious" neurons differed from the rest.
- The fringes of consciousness are very fuzzy and seem to shift or melt as we approach them. Core consciousness seems brighter and more focused than peripheral consciousness, and conscious states shade off seamlessly into subconscious or unconscious states. By contrast, a neural mechanism may be expected to have sharp edges.
- The conscious state is fragile. A knock on the head or a reduction of blood pressure can interrupt it. Even a calm environment and reduced sensory input can cause it to fade away. Whatever it is that gives rise to consciousness, it is less robust than many cognitive functions, which may continue independently of consciousness.
- States of consciousness and their contents correlate very precisely with rhythmic neural firing, both over the entire brain and in smaller cortical regions. Generally, such precise correlations in science are good indicators of interrelated or shared causality.

For all these reasons, it seems reasonable to propose that physicists should embark upon research and experiments to test the photonic hypothesis in more detail.

Other Minds

The methodological autist has a problem with other minds. They exist only as hypothetical posits. Yet everything about the physics of incarnation demands that other bodies like mine are animated by other minds like mine. There is a symmetry here that we can push one step further. By symmetry, I must admit that my own mind is a theoretical posit. My phenomenology necessarily culminates in a synthetic unity of apperception (*I think, therefore I am*), but the psychological nature of this unity as a kind of synthesized VR embedded in a public world is only meaningful as an instance of a kind of unification that other centers instantiate as convincingly as I do. From within, a mind is coterminous with universal reality, with the proviso that the illumination of reality provided by consciousness fades toward the periphery. This is what makes methodological autism a natural stance for a physicist. From without, a mind is like a black hole, with an event horizon surrounding an invisible singularity. If each mind corresponds to an extended quantum entanglement, other minds begin where my entanglement approaches the blurred surfaces of other entanglements.

If this physical metaphor seems to isolate minds too radically from each other, consider what it would be for me to know another mind in the fullest sense. Our entanglements would coalesce, we would enjoy the same phenomenology, and the whole show would shape up as my experience. The ultimate subject of phenomenology is always and necessarily unique. As logical subjects, we are alone. Only as the subjects of human thoughts and feelings can we claim company. Psychology is the study of everything that can happen in minds once that company is entertained. Prior to that opening, the exploration of the mind is at best mathematics or physics, at worst clinical autism.

This analysis suggests that the logic of other minds raises serious issues. If my mind is represented by a consistency surface (a V-set) in a logical space (a cumulative hierarchy), then recognition of other minds readily creates contradictions. Formally, it is easy enough to embed such spaces in a superspace and thus restore consistency at a higher level, but the cost can be high. If a mind loses touch with its universality, or in Kantian terms its transcendentality, and swims among others, it becomes a mere focus of bodily organization. Psychologically, the great danger of human social interaction is this loss of universality. Either minds are in some sense universes unto themselves (this idea has been celebrated for centuries in Jewish tradition) or they collapse to biomechanisms with no great ethical significance (this idea in turn is depressingly familiar in some circles). For the sake of preserving ethics, at least, the methodological autist deserves to be taken seriously.

As a historical footnote, there is another mind that puts the whole endeavor of methodological autism into perspective. William James anticipated the metaphysics of centered bubble worlds a century ago: "The axis of reality runs solely through the egotistic places – they are strung upon it like so many beads ... The world of our present consciousness is only one out of many worlds of consciousness that exist." [31]

Conclusion

The logical and mathematical study of worlds creates a formal platform for a description of subjective phenomenology in terms of quantum physics. This makes it natural to propose that photonic configurations in the brain realize conscious experience. Since the conscious brain does in fact generate coherent waves of decahertz photons that correlate closely with subjective experience, the hypothesis that these photons somehow realize the experience deserves further study. This study is primarily a challenge for physicists, who have not yet addressed decahertz photonics in any detail. Such questions as the following need to be studied:

- Are the observable properties and dynamics of the electromagnetic field generated by the living brain consistent with periodic realization of coherent and unified photonic *now* states?
- What spatiotemporal constraints does the thermal and chemical environment of the living brain impose on the dynamical evolution of these photonic states?
- How effectively does the brain screen these photonic states from decahertz EM radiation arising in the extracerebral environment or from instant decoherence within the brain?
- How do these photonic states exert the top-down effects on the brain that are required to couple the states to evolutionary pressures, and how can we measure these effects?

If a program of physical research along these lines develops well, it can provide a scientific foundation for psychology. Even if the empirical research remains inconclusive, the logic and mathematics of the serial growth of quantum bubble worlds should give philosophical psychologists food for thought.

Toward a Theory of Consciousness

Toward a Theory

The latest conference in the series *Toward a Science of Consciousness* was held in Prague, capital of the Czech Republic, from July 6 to July 10, 2003, and bore the soundly European title "Towards a Science of Consciousness: Between Phenomenology and Neuroscience" (note that defiant "s"). There I presented a talk entitled *A Photonic Theory of Consciousness*, enjoyed the program, and talked to numerous participants, including Johnjoe McFadden, who proposes a theory very similar to mine.[1]

My theory of consciousness is based on a technical construction in set theory, interpreted via quantum mechanics, and speculatively projected onto the decahertz electromagnetic waves generated by synchronous neural firing in the brain. So it needs careful introduction.

The theory starts out where no reasonable person would wish to disagree. The aim is to tell a story that remains consistent with all the known facts about how each of us, as a conscious being, enjoys the experience of a vivid and ongoing phenomenology, which seems to us to shape up as an external world that changes in time.

In outline, my approach is to describe our phenomenology as abstractly and noncommitally as possible, in logic, constrained only by the need for consistency in the story we tell, and see how this leads us naturally toward physics. We then do the same for the physics, only to find that in physics we're sleepwalking toward a psychology, by settling naturally on ways of thinking that reflect in the large, on a universal scale, what each one of us does in the small, as a conscious being trying to make sense of phenomenal experience. When we see how this can work in terms of brain mechanisms, an explanatory circle closes for me. The respective strands converge so well as to give me an "Aha!" experience. With your indulgence, I hope to give you a similar experience.

A Logical Start

> The axis of reality runs solely through the egotistic places – they are strung upon it like so many beads ... The world of our present consciousness is only one out of many worlds of consciousness that exist.
> William James (1902)

Before we ever understand ourselves as persons in a physical world, each of us draws a distinction between *in here*, where *I* live, and *out there*, beyond the pale, where thrills and horrors lie waiting and in principle anything goes. The pale, the boundary between me and all the rest, is a dynamic and fluid zone that prompts us to build what we may naturally describe as logical models to account for the ongoing flux of experience. These models cohere, more or less, depending on our cognitive capacities, into what we can define as *worlds* of consciousness. These worlds succeed each other with a steady rhythm that reflects the temporal flow of our conscious experience.

So much by way of a rather free gloss on William James. My task in this section is to outline a formal frame for describing these cognitive worlds, so that we can see the process by which worlds unfold in temporal succession as nothing more or less than the *stream of consciousness* under a rather natural interpretation. But before I do this, I must bow to Susan Blackmore, who protests vigorously that the stream of consciousness is an illusion.[2]

The stream of consciousness is not what it seems, I freely grant. The contents of consciousness are fleeting fragments that cohere only roughly into anything traditionally resembling a world. Worlds thus conceived are as substantial as the fictional worlds conjured up by a novelist's words or the dramatic worlds evoked by illuminated pixels on television. They are logical constructions jammed hastily together to enable networks of neurons to fire in harmonious symphonies when sprinkled by the input stream from the sensory periphery of the body.

To lay a couple more ghosts, the inner me does not sit in a Cartesian theater waiting for the qualia show to continue. The theater *is the world*, or rather the brief acts staged in the theater are the worlds that bubble past in the stream of consciousness. If qualia have a role in this picture at all, they are the *me*-sides (whatever that means) of those droplets from the input stream that make it relatively unscathed to the inner circles of neural action, where the higher harmonies evoked by rhythmic waves of neural firing create the logical worlds that I'm about to define more formally.

To shorten the story here, let me presuppose everything from the realm of computational modeling and cognitive function that leads to the conclusion that our *functional* understanding of our sensory input has a logic that we can reconstruct with arbitrary fidelity in terms of a computational metaphor. I would ask you to shelve the obviously begged question of where the self or subject is in this computational story. We can come back to that issue later. Important for now is only that we have an ongoing construction project in the activated neuronet, busy churning out draft after draft of an *intentional* world. Sorry – another ghost.

Intentionality is a philosophical word, a weasel word to some, that covers a lot of confusion. For me, any symbolic structure has an intentional relation to what it represents or symbolizes. For example, a novel is intentionally related to a set of fictional worlds, namely those that embody its dramatic action in the minds of its readers. Similarly, the word "two" is intentionally related to the second natural number. Thus, intentional relations are *subjective* pairings in the sense that they pair, or *confuse*, different things from the standpoint of a particular perspective. Indeed, we can use such pairings to help us define the otherwise rather tricky notion of subjectivity. A subject adopts a perspective on reality. From that perspective, the subject either regards an intentional pairing as some kind of symbolic relation or, more typically, confuses the referent with the reference, where we can take the referent to be a salient aspect of the cognitive model under construction in the subject's brain, and take the reference to be the modeled entity in the external world. A subject who confuses a referential model with a referenced reality is existentially revealed by that confusion.

Let's get down to work. We shall describe states of consciousness, and correlatively the worlds they reflect, in the austere language of set theory. We shall do this to strip away all irrelevant phenomenality and physicality. Thus we shall isolate the logic of conscious experience. Once that's clear, we can descend from the Olympian heights and clothe our new insights in physical stuff with phenomenal properties. The strategic plan here is due to Willard Van Orman Quine, whose big insight as a logical philosopher was that any ontology can be reduced to an ontology of sets.[3]

A state of consciousness with *no* logic, not even the distinction between inside and outside, is perhaps better described as a state of unconsciousness, but is anyway describable as a *null* state. We can represent it in set theory as the null set. From this state, the very first move is to distinguish inside from outside, *me* from *it*, the abstract subject from the abstract object, the class of everything from the set of nothing. I hereby call this move the first act of *ontogenesis*. An entity, the null set, has been comprehended as an existent in an accommodating or a comprehending state, namely the universal class *V* whose sole member or element is the empty set 0. This move from the null state to the first state is a change of perspective, and represents the first experience of time. The first increment of subjective time is born in the act of ontogenesis.

Now consider, if you will, an arbitrary state of consciousness, represented logically as a class of existing sets that together form a configuration that is isomorphic (under some suitable mapping) to a cognitive model of the sort that our cerebral neuronets construct when they implement that state of consciousness. The Quinean idea here is that the sets are generally sets of sets, which in turn are made of sets, and so on down as far as we care to continue our logical archaeology, until we reach some stable bedrock, say the null set. All these sets are stacked up in layers, or regimented in *ranks*, in accordance with a mathematical function first proposed by John von Neumann and defined in any good student text on set theory.[4] The rank function is a transfinite recursion based on piling up *power sets*. The power set of a set is the set of all its subsets, including both the set itself and the null set. The transfinite side of the story is irrelevant here. If we can start by reconstructing the saga of consciousness in terms of finite sets, any logician so inclined can doubtless continue the story into the transfinite realms of Cantor's paradise. For our purposes, the basic idea of John von Neumann's construction is that each ranked universal set $V(n)$ is the power set of the previous universal set $V(n-1)$, where we go up step by step through ordinal ranks n from the null set $V(0)$.

We need to be clear on the distinction between elements and classes. All sets are both elements and classes. They are classes of their elements or their members, and they are elements or members of further sets. Classes have higher rank than their members. Going up the cumulative hierarchy, more and more classes become sets by becoming recognized as elements in the universe. At each level n, the classes of rank n are still only halfway to becoming sets. To put this in a more philosophical way, they *are*, but they do not yet determinately *exist*.[5]

We are considering an arbitrary state of consciousness represented as a finite configuration of hereditarily finite sets, so all the action takes place with sets that are members of a finite V-set. Let the smallest such V-set be $V(n)$. For this state of consciousness, $V(n)$ represents – or *reflects*, to use a set-theoretic term – the universal class. That is, $V(n)$ is the *intentional world* for this state. To recall young Ludwig's Wittgenstein's oracular claim in his *Tractatus*, "I am my world".[6] In this state of mind, *the subject is confused* (intentionally) with $V(n)$. In this sense, a world of consciousness embodies a psychological singularity at which the subject is identical to the world, but with a twist. This world surrounds the subject and is experienced from the inside, but it is regarded as an external and objective configuration. Conversely, the subject opens into the world and unites with it, yet seems to retain the power to change things, with a faculty of self-control that itself seems controlled by the self in a recursive spiral. We could have fun trying to get to grips with all this, but let's move on.

This state of consciousness represented by $V(n)$ does not last long. The time experienced by the subject ticks on, and at the next time increment the subject is embodied in a new state of consciousness. This state may display an arbitrary level of similarity with its predecessor, but one feature at least will be new, namely that the previous state is past and gone, overstepped and separated from its previous confusion with the experienced world. That is, the previously universal class $V(n)$ becomes an ordinary set within a new determinate state of the world. Psychologically, my new state of mind will include in some sense the idea or the feel of its separation from the previous state of mind, which will thus become a potential object of contemplation within my new mindset. In set theory, this new state of consciousness is represented by the class $V(n + 1)$.

You have no doubt observed that we've just performed a mathematical induction that carries us through all the finite sets $V(n)$, for all values of n from 0 up into countable infinity. Here we've represented the increments of experienced time as natural numbers n, and thus presumed that the moments of specious present, or the moments of *now*, can be separated discretely from each other to enable us to slice consciousness into ranked worlds, where each ranked world is a consistent take on reality. This may seem unrealistic in the "real world" of illogical experiencers, but this is science we're doing. However messy the experience of a subject turns out to be, the least we can do as scientists who wish to build coherent theories of all this is to parse that experience into consistent slices.

An analogy may help. Imagine we're making a movie that depicts a hallucinatory chaos, with bizarre images that seem to defy common sense. To do so, we artfully construct a series of still frames, each one of which makes good sense when you see how it was made. So it is with the science of consciousness. As scientists, we define a logical series of cognitive states that involve unconscious processes going far beyond the conscious states of the experimental subject, so we have the tools to model states that look as messy as you like.

This raises a further issue. A conscious state typically embraces a rather limited domain of objects, each of which is sensed only superficially, yet the cognitive model and the correlative set-theoretic infrastructure we employ to do justice to that state may turn out to be rather complicated. For example, a conscious state may embrace five things yet require us to invoke $V(10^{10})$ to specify those five things in all their phenomenal glory from a standing start down at $V(0)$. Almost all the sets involved will be mere scaffolding, just as almost all the neural processing involved in supporting a conscious state is unconscious.

Worse yet, the size of $V(n)$ increases exponentially with n, so as time passes we find our intentional worlds exploding in complexity. Here we need to invoke *possible* worlds in parallel to actual worlds. Recall that each V-set is the set of *all possible* subsets of its predecessor, so a lot of these subsets will not match up directly with anything sensible in the state of consciousness they are invoked to describe. Yet they will be relevant to a semantic analysis of the intentionality of those states, because we need to invoke possible and counterfactual variants of an actual state of affairs to be able to give a semantic account of how we can refer to some aspects of that state of affairs, for example in conditional statements or nomological claims. As you can see, this is a heavy topic, best skirted here. The main point is that an intentional world $V(n)$ may best be regarded as an actual world *plus* a corresponding set of possible worlds, all specified together. The actual world achieves its nomological depth, so to speak, against the backdrop of its combinatorially coeval but nonactual worlds.

If you're acquainted with modal and intuitionistic logic and the crisis a century ago in the foundations of mathematics that led to axiomatic set theory, you may now be starting to see the big picture. Roughly, we're mapping the possible-world semantics for a constructive logic applied to a tightly coupled epistemology and ontology into successive initial segments of the standard cumulative hierarchy. Put more informally, we're creating a logical scaffolding for an evolutionary view of reality as a whole, where paradox foils attempts to achieve final closure, and using it as a jig for a new view of consciousness. We're scaling all this machinery down drastically to model the unfolding phenomenology of a conscious subject. To recall a factoid from the world of high technology, it's like building a billion-dollar factory to make ten-dollar microchips.

To sum up in simpler terms, we've used a set-theoretic model to create a very abstract formal description of the ongoing experience of a conscious subject. This description should be applicable in any case, whatever the contents of consciousness. With big enough sets $V(n)$ and small enough time increments n, we can model arbitrarily complex states of consciousness to arbitrary levels of fidelity. The mathematical part of the job is now done. Let's move on to the physics.

A Quantum Theory of Reality

To work out how the logic of consciousness becomes a foundation for the physics of consciousness, it makes good sense to start small and build up. Much of the conceptual apparatus of physics is highly theoretical, and our simpler states of consciousness – at the level of $V(n)$ for small n – don't begin to embrace those physical concepts. Yet all of physics as we know it has been born through human consciousness. A sensible approach here is to consider immediate consciousness again, as we did for the logic of V-sets, and see how some basic concepts of physics – time, space, quantum jumps, and symmetry breaking – begin to be involved.

At $V(0)$, *being* is not yet being in space and time. Time first enters the picture at $V(1)$, and space only begins to appear in a first prototypical guise when two things exist alongside each other in $V(2)$. Even for much later worlds $V(n)$, a relational structure sufficient to colocate a few things relative to each other need not seem anything like the familiar Euclidean three- or four-dimensional continuum (much less like a hyperbolic or elliptical space-time). Recall that for finite n, sets $V(n)$ do not support continuous time, and they don't support continuous space either. At best, they support a discrete approximation that comes arbitrarily close to the continuous limit as the step size decreases.

This is no catastrophe. On the contrary, discrete modeling of processes that are traditionally regarded as running in continuous spacetime is a major computational industry, and all the results so far, from airflow simulation in aircraft design to modeling thermonuclear plasma dynamics to finite lattice calculations in quantum chromodynamics, encourage one to shrug off the continuous limit as a theoretical idea. For what it's worth, software genius Stephen Wolfram believes discrete modeling is the way to go in theoretical physics too, and that our three-century obsession with the continuum is a relic of Newtonian thinking.[7]

The time dimension experienced by a conscious subject who is embodied as a series of sets $V(n)$ is a discrete number line $(0, \ldots, n, \ldots)$ that appears as an abstract object (for example, as an ordered set of sets $n = \{m \mid m < n\}$) in each new determination $V(n)$ of the experienced world. In this sense, time is *reified* within the experienced world, which means we don't need to see a problem with the physical assimilation of subjectively experienced time to a quasi-spatial dimension. This issue bothers some philosophers, but we can let it go here for brevity.

Physical objects exist in spacetime and have locations and histories. They also have properties, both individual (monadic) and relational (*n*-adic, for any *n*). We can model their properties in computational logic just as readily as their locations and histories. And we can map all the structure we need into suitable V-sets, just as before. When the going gets tough, as it did in the early days of quantum mechanics, and the pioneers had to allow that some properties failed to commute (such as position and momentum, which form a complementary pair in the Heisenberg uncertainty relation), we just invent more formalism and map that into some sufficiently big V-set. In this way, we can go as deeply as we like into physics, constrained by the goal of accommodating the phenomena but not necessarily such theoretical notions as the continuum, and still stay within the scope of the overall vision.

As you can see, this is a breezy dismissal of a vastly complex topic, but there's no need to doubt its practicality, since all we're saying, in effect, is that a sufficiently big – but still finite – software package can model as much physics as we care to pack into it.

To return to the basics, many quantum phenomena resist interpretation in classical physics. Consider three fairly representative examples:

- Photons seem to fan out between creation in a source and annihilation in a detector as if they were taking *all possible* routes outward from the source and "choosing" their destination by weighing up all those routes together. The location of a photon first makes the move from being on the surface of a virtual "bubble" of all possible locations to existing at a definite location when the bubble pops and the photon shows up at that place. This picture can be filled out to give an exact model of such photonic behavior as interference and diffraction.[8]

- When pairs of particles emerge from a source with opposite quantum properties, say with their spins in opposite directions, and one of them is measured as spin up, the other immediately becomes spin down, as if only then did the particles settle for this one out of *all possible* paired orientations. Theory and experiments agree that the quantum statistics of the measured orientations of such pairs are nonclassical in the sense that the final spin orientation cannot have been predetermined at the moment the pair was created.[9]

- In the brave new world of quantum computation, states representing qubits exist as superpositions of the classical bit states 0 and 1. Rows or registers of n such qubits can be in *all possible* permutations of the classical bit states until a measurement forces the superposition to pop into a unique classical state of the register with n bits. The most natural picture here is that all the 2^n possible permutations of register states are quantum-*is*-ing – or "quizzing" – beside each other in a virtual bubble, waiting for the pop that promotes one state into classical existence.[10]

In all these examples, the observed quantum phenomena seem to suggest that interpolation of unique classical world lines between events in the lives of quantum particles (which are only measured at creation and annihilation) is unwarranted. Instead, the superposition of all possible continuations of the previous world state is popped in an interaction (such as measurement), which only then creates the next world state relative to which the previous state becomes a determinate existent.

As I hope you can see without my having to labor the point any further, all this gets a rather natural interpretation in terms of the V-set story. The interpretation also illuminates the central theme of our approach here, which is all about representing the ongoing experience of the subject rather than preserving classical extrapolations or interpolations from the previous world of experience. To return to the early days of quantum theory, some theorists, among them John von Neumann, worried that classical logic would fail to survive the crisis of noncommutativity; indeed they invented some distinctly *ad hoc* logical calculi to try to rescue a few classical ideas. Now we see that what we can call a constructive version of classical logic survives in relation to worlds. We apply classical logic within any given world, where a limited domain of facts is brought to a consistent whole, and use a more subtle approach to handle transitions or relations between worlds.

The more subtle approach is straight from set theory. As we've seen, a world is reflected by some V-set $V(n)$, which represents all the objects in that world as elements and all the properties defined over those objects as classes. Any properties for which it is not yet decidably true or false (this is where the logical idea of constructivity come into play) whether they apply or not to given objects are represented by classes of rank n in world $V(n)$. Remember that *all possible* such classes of sets in $V(n)$ are ranked as sets in the upcoming determination $V(n+1)$ of the world of experience. But until the experiencing subject makes the move to $V(n+1)$, a unique actual world does not pop out from the set of all possible worlds. What this amounts to is that the move from $V(n)$ to $V(n+1)$ is a quantum jump. Each pop of a quantum bubble of possibilities is represented in set theory as a step upward in the cumulative hierarchy. And recall that each such step upward is a step forward in spacetime. As events take place in time, the objects defined by means of those events accumulate definite properties and the world around them becomes more focused. Whatever the merits of this picture as a theory of ultimate reality, it's surely a very natural way to couch an account of the unfolding of experienced reality in consciousness.

We've now discussed spacetime and quantum reality in terms of V-sets, far more briefly than they deserve but extensively enough to try your patience, I'm sure, so let's leave those topics there. Just one more deep idea remains to wrap up this approach to physics, namely that of symmetry and symmetry breaking.

Each world $V(n)$ can be followed by any of the possible worlds defined using the sets that exist in $V(n + 1)$. World $V(n)$ is *symmetrical* with respect to those successor worlds. That is, it can figure equally well in a consistent history of any of those successor worlds. When the universe evolves from state $V(n)$ to state $V(n + 1)$, that symmetry of the universe is broken. In this rendering of the saga of experience, each new state of consciousness is born by breaking a symmetry inherent in the previous state. Quite generally, symmetries are broken with each passing moment of time, indeed as they have been ever since the Big Bang.

Finally, note how we can gloss the breakdown of classical logic here. Each new world appears from a broken symmetry in an act of ontogenesis, and it was always claimed that ontology went beyond logic. Classical logic involves no existence assumptions, yet the invocation of new worlds cannot help but involve them, even when the new world is called into being by an event as tiny as a quantum jump. So our story respects that old claim.

Psychophysics

We've done the hard work on the logic and physics of subjective consciousness, or consciousness from the inside, and all that remains is to relate it to our best current view of consciousness from the outside, as seen by brain scientists. Again, to keep it short, I don't plan to review any details here. Plenty of other writers have covered this base, and anyone who can use a browser to search the Web can get a better update than I can provide using the glacially sedate medium of printed paper.

Consciousness in the human sense is clearly correlated with very specific states of the brain and body of a human being. Conscious subjects are awake and alert – or dreaming in REM sleep – and typically exhibit a certain focus in their attitude and behavior. Their brains are buzzing with neural activity at numerous levels, culminating in brain-wide decahertz (10–100 Hz) waves of electrical excitation as neuron populations fire rhythmically around thalamo-cortical loops.[11] These great decahertz excitations are nothing more or less than bunches of coherent photons that reflect the momentary states of mind of the subject, or reflect moments in the ongoing phenomenology that fills subjective consciousness.

Consciousness is evidently closely correlated with certain states of the electromagnetic field generated by neurons firing in the brain of the subject. Physically, these states are constituted by vast numbers of decahertz photons moving in unison, perhaps even in bosonic union, to form the coherent wavefronts that make up the gamma (35–45 Hz) waves that correlate best with conscious experience. Moreover, the coherence of these brainwaves appears to be crucial for their role in facilitating the neural organization that underlies structured perception.[12]

When photons form sufficiently coherent wavefronts for bosonic union, the right tool for studying them is quantum theory. When the photons involved are very tiny, as they are in decahertz waves, with energies in the femtoelectronvolt range, there are so many of them in structures as big as brainwaves that classical wave analysis can take us a long way, but strictly speaking we're dealing with a quantum reality here.

More to the point, the time uncertainties of these photons (via the Heisenberg uncertainty relation) are on the order of tens of milliseconds. By the sort of coincidence that screams for attention, the temporal granularity of human conscious experience is in this decahertz range. That is, the moments of specious present, the moments of *now* that create our sense of the flow of time, have durations of tens of milliseconds, which also coincides with the flicker fusion frequency, the frequency of physiological tremor, and the cycle time for neural firing around thalamo-cortical loops.

For me, the hypothesis suggests itself that our conscious minds are somehow embodied in the wavefronts as bosonic collective states of the photons. These collective states invite comparison with the coherent photonic states created in lasers. There are three obvious differences:

- Brainwave photons have much lower energies, on the order of 100 feV, so the time evolution of phenomena such as decoherence is trillions of times slower than that of visible-light laser beams.

- Brainwaves are not very sharply synchronized at all, so any quantum coherence they display must dissipate instantly, within the Heisenberg uncertainty time of the photons, which means in a few milliseconds.
- Brainwaves do not shoot off in any particular direction. They radiate in all directions and suffer instant attenuation in the brain and skull. So their physical effects can be expected to be very local indeed.

Let me call this my hypothesis: *consciousness is photonic*. Most neural activity is unconscious, but any such activity that grows strong enough to make waves in the electromagnetic field that flickers over the conscious brain become part of the conscious mind. The quantum behavior of this field gives rise to our experience of the temporal flow of a stream of phenomenal forms. Each new wavefront of photons reflects the conscious mind for a moment as it crests, pops a bubble of virtual photonic configurations, and beaches as a unique actual distribution of photons. The photonic hypothesis seems to account well for the following features of consciousness:

- We are conscious of a specious present with a duration of some tens of milliseconds. So far as I know, no classical account of consciousness can even begin to explain this basic fact. My quantum speculation may not be much better, but at least it offers hope.
- Our consciousness has limited scope. We are not conscious of most of what goes on in our brains, and we can only hold a few things in mind at once. We need something beyond neural activity for consciousness.
- The fringes of consciousness are very fuzzy and seem to shift or melt as we approach them. Core consciousness seems brighter than peripheral consciousness, and conscious states seem to shade off seamlessly into subconscious or unconscious states. Photonic waves with very large spatiotemporal uncertainties can explain this.
- The conscious state is fragile. A knock on the head or a reduction of blood pressure can interrupt it. Even a calm environment and reduced sensory input can cause it to fade away. Quantum coherence effects generally have this fragile quality.
- States of consciousness and their contents correlate very precisely with rhythmic neural firing, both over the entire brain and in smaller cortical regions. Generally, such precise correlations in science are good indicators of interrelated or shared causality.

All this moves me to vote for the cerebral decahertz electromagnetic (EM) field as the physical correlate of consciousness. But I part company with Johnjoe McFadden by arguing that a *quantum* view of the cerebral EM field is essential for understanding the temporal quality of subjective experience, and hence its phenomenal quality too. I predict that a classical view of the cerebral EM field will not solve the mystery of consciousness.[13]

The orthodox view, if one can call it that, is that the brain is so big and warm and sloppy that quantum physics can have no place in the story of consciousness and that an explanation in terms of classical physics must be enough. My reason for opposing this view is ultimately philosophical – the worldview of classical physics, temptingly sufficient as it is for everyday life, is just *wrong*. It's as wrong as the classical view in mathematics of an unchanging and eternal Platonic reality, temptingly sufficient as that view is for the arithmetic of everyday life. As I see it, consciousness is precisely the natural phenomenon that forces us to recognize as illusory the apparent stability of classical science, because classical science – as Thomas Nagel famously pointed out – is the *view from nowhere*. Classical science literally *erases the subject* in an attempt to achieve an objectivity that transcends intersubjective disagreement.

Now, in a post-almost-everything world of relativized objectivities and perspectival complementarities, we can afford to move on. Multiple worlds of experience, linked by chains of quantum jumps, are both natural forms for reproducing the logic of consciousness and apparently plausible candidates for reconstructing the quantum logic of temporal reality itself. The subject is not erased but identified with a series of worlds, like James' string of beads. Psychology and physics meet here.

The Aha Moment

There you have it – my epiphany as a philosopher, pinned down in words. The inner me is not just sitting in a theater watching the qualia, but wheeling and dealing, looping strangely in a recursively re-entrant world.[14] The loops close when the alpha and the omega of innermost subjective experience and ultimate objective reality meet in an advancing wavefront of decahertz photons that breaks successive symmetries to push my string of beads ever deeper into an ocean of quantum worlds that encode all possible futures.[15]

Real Time

My story of temporal experience is insufficient by itself as an account of the nature of physical time. But by a coincidence too happy to ignore, physicist Fay Dowker has recently helped develop a wonderfully compatible view in the austere domain of quantum gravity, no less:

> [I]n causal set theory, space-time can "grow" in such a way that time appears to flow rather than being a static dimension ... The impossibility of exceeding the speed of light provides an order to space-time because it prevents some points from being causally influenced by what happens at other points ... It turns out that if we started off not knowing the geometry of space-time, but instead knew this causal order of all the points within it, we could reconstruct almost everything about space-time ... Almost, because ... the physical "scale" is not given by the causal order. Causal set theory fills this gap ... [T]he Planck volume is 10^{-142} cubic centimetre seconds ... The set of these space-time elements is called the causal set, because the elements are ordered by causality ... [S]pace-time grows, element by element, starting with a single one. At each stage one new element is born, its existence caused by a set of ancestors chosen for it from amongst the already existing elements. The choice is made at random. Once the new element has had its ancestors assigned, it has become a part of the existing causal set and another element is ready to be born, and the process repeats. The growth appears as a real, inevitable physical process, and within it is the deep-held picture of a fixed past and a future that is open, with the ever-changing present as the boundary."[16]

In his 1989 book *The Emperor's New Mind*, Roger Penrose maintained that before we could understand consciousness, we would first need to develop a theory of quantum gravity. Well, maybe this is it.

Consciousness as a Physical Process

Consciousness is the crowning glory of *Homo sapiens*, the feature that still, in the third millennium, distinguishes us from machines. But we cannot yet explain consciousness. One of the most daunting scientific challenges of our times is to understand how our brains implement what we call conscious experience. Only when we have understood this can we hope to build human or superhuman levels of sentience into machines.

Consciousness is above all related to what we experience. As philosopher David Chalmers argues,[1] we each adopt a first-person perspective in consciousness that stands in contrast to the third-person perspective of sciences like psychology. There seems to be a gulf between the private contents of consciousness and the public contents of the world around us.

The most salient aspect of our experience is that all the phenomena we perceive form a unity in consciousness. In the terminology of Immanuel Kant,[2] a manifold of phenomena is categorized into a synthetic unity of apperception. This unity is a matter of perspective. Phenomena retain their variety but are bound together in various ways to build up a unified perspective in our minds. We each have a personal point of view to the extent that our conscious experience forms a unity.

The temporal flow of experience is the next salient feature of consciousness. The manifold of phenomena changes from moment to moment, and we track those changes in our subjective awareness. As subjects, we persist over time but change with each passing moment, as the present contents of consciousness become aspects of past moments, and new contents fill the present moment. As we change, traces of the previous contents of consciousness accumulate in memory to provide an ongoing personal history, or an autobiography.

A third salient feature of our conscious experience is its limited and fuzzy scope. We know we are not conscious of all that goes on either around us or within us, yet we are not aware of the boundaries to our awareness. Our experience fades seamlessly into oblivion in all directions, both spatially and temporally. For example, we are unaware of future events, but we cannot pin down exactly when the present moment gives way to the future. If we focus on a ticking clock, we seem to be locked in a loop with a cycle time of some fraction of a second. And if we dilate our awareness to contemplate history, we can seem to occupy a fuzzy duration of many years.

Other features of conscious experience deserve treatment in a more detailed science of consciousness, such as its qualitative feeling in various emotional or altered states, or its variable amplitude as we become sleepy or suffer injury, or its readiness to distinguish the self from the external world. But they can only be tackled once the three basics are clear.

Consciousness as Process

To a first approximation, conscious experience looks like a by-product of the operation of an information-processing system. That system is the brain, which is a network of neurons that can perform all the logical operations necessary to act like a digital computer.

The brain is a neuronet composed of some hundred billion neurons, each connected to thousands of neighbors. The neurons communicate with electrical pulses, each about 70 millivolts in amplitude and one millisecond in duration. Synchronized neural firing increases the strength of neural connections – cells that fire together wire together – so the network has a plasticity that is conditioned by its history of inputs and responses.

Philosophers have invented numerous metaphors to describe the phenomenon of consciousness. If the torrent of information that courses through the brain is like a waterfall, then consciousness is like the mist above the waterfall, a beautiful but incidental feature that plays no essential role in the process. This view of conscious experience as epiphenomenal is reinforced by the work over many years of neurophysiologist Benjamin Libet and his colleagues, which suggests that our conscious experience of making a decision lags behind its neural correlates by hundreds of milliseconds.[3] It is as if we only notice our decision after the event and then falsely predate it to preserve the illusion that we play a causal role in its production. The ensuing debate on this topic, including recent books by Daniel Dennett[4] and Daniel Wegner,[5] strongly suggests that the role of consciousness in decision making is not as it seems to casual introspection. We think we choose what we do, but it is more accurate to say that we merely endorse in thought the operations of a neurological process that has its own dynamics.

The problem with this view is that it fails to predict the appearance of consciousness in evolution. Our conscious experiences are very finely correlated with neurological processes, and those processes have an obvious functional role for survival. On the outside, we have physically definable external circumstances, and on the inside we have introspectively recognizable mental states. These external circumstances and inner states correspond so exactly to each other that we are all but forced to conclude that they are two sides or aspects of one and the same process.

The view that consciousness has a functional role for an organism requires more than these correspondences. It requires top-down causality, so that our conscious mental processes can influence our physical behavior. This need not occur in very fast causal loops, so we need not be disturbed by the Libet debate, but it does require that the neurological dynamics reflect mental states directly. At least on timescales longer than a second, our conscious manipulation of our own mental states must cause transformations of neurological states that can also be described in the language of physics.

This is a hard requirement to meet. The physics of electrical pulses in a neural network is based on classical electrodynamics of the sort that many engineers understand in detail, and leaves no room for conscious manipulation. Yet the evolutionary fine-tuning of conscious states to reflect our activities as organisms is inexplicable unless those states are coupled directly to neural dynamics. Either we fight centuries of cultural tradition and accept that our crowning glory as human beings is a functionally irrelevant epiphenomenon or we modify our understanding of the physics involved.

The Physics of Consciousness

No computer engineer has yet built a neuronet with anything like the complexity of a human brain. It is still an article of faith that an artificial neuronet (an ANN) can effectively emulate a cerebral neuronet (where an emulation is a perfect functional simulation).

To review the basics here, artificial neurons are threshold logic gates with a large number of inputs and one or more outputs. An artificial neuron adds the weighted sum of its input signals and fires if the sum exceeds a preset threshold. The weights may be large, small, or even negative (for inhibitory connections), and may change as a result of learning. In an ANN, large numbers of neurons are arranged in layers so that the output of one layer is the input for the next layer. The ANNs that can perform full truth-functional logic use a learning technique called backpropagation that resets weights to minimize the errors in output patterns compared with target patterns. But since the human brain contains some hundred billion neurons, each with thousands of connections to other neurons, and employs subtle and variable weighting and threshold functions, it will be a while yet before we can emulate it realistically in silicon hardware.

David Chalmers argues that such an emulation would work, essentially by pointing out that step-by-step replacement of neural groups by silicon chips, if done properly, must preserve conscious experience. The argument is plausible for limited replacements. But we know that when parts of the brain are injured and other parts take over their function, some aspects of behavior can be disturbed. Numerous authorities, such as Antonio Damasio, present cumulatively overwhelming evidence that damage to specific brain regions can irreparably harm mental abilities in ways that are often subtle and hard to identify at first.[6] Perhaps an ANN can approximately simulate cerebral function at the level of coordinating everyday behavior yet still lack our fine-tuned states of consciousness.

A *zombie* is a being of a kind that could in principle be conscious but in fact lacks consciousness. A philosophical zombie totally lacks consciousness, but a more realistic scenario admits zombie-like behavior at various levels. If consciousness can be more or less finely tuned, perhaps we are all zombie-like at some level. For example, an advanced extraterrestrial may consider all humans to be zombies, and many humans consider most animals to be zombies. In this sense, an ANN could simulate a good deal of human cerebral function yet remain largely zombie-like. As scientists standing outside such a neuronet, we may feel disinclined to call it conscious.

Perhaps ANNs are still missing something. In human brains, synchronous neural firing is known to play an essential role in perceptual binding. That is, our ability to perceive objects as having properties and stand in relations is a consequence of the relevant neurons having previously fired synchronously to fix certain patterns in the neuronet. These effects of synchrony are implemented only approximately in current ANNs.

However, work on ANNs is moving fast. In 2009, the Blue Brain project headed by Henry Markram and based in Lausanne, Switzerland, released its first results.[7] The project goal was to simulate a pyramidal column using a giant IBM supercomputer. Such a column is the repeating element making up the mammalian neocortex and contains some ten thousand neurons and many millions of synapses. The simulation was tested and tuned using detailed input from lab dissections of rat brains. The results were excellent: the simulation now behaves exactly like the biological original.

Even Blue Brain may not simulate all the features of natural neurons. For example, microbiologist Johnjoe McFadden argues that the electromagnetic field generated by large numbers of neurons firing synchronously can be strong and coherent enough to generate a resonant response in individual neurons.[8] That is, a feedback path may exist from the transcortical electromagnetic (TEM) field generated by the synchronous firing of many millions of neurons to the individual neurons, independently of how they are wired together.

This top-down feedback from the TEM field to individual neurons may be essential to the functional role of consciousness in modulating behavior. Since the dynamical behavior of the TEM field is complex and essentially unpredictable, this view may give some comfort to those who wish to see our conscious minds as sovereign in nature. It seems worth considering the hypothesis that the TEM field generated by neural firing is the primary substrate of consciousness.

The unity of consciousness is a natural consequence of the TEM hypothesis. The field unifies changing patterns of neural processing over the cortex and reflects them at a level that obscures the details. Introspection does not reveal mental activity that would directly reflect most of what goes on in the brain. Instead, our experience may correlate best with broad waves of activity entrained by a few neurons that fire strongly enough to get their neighbors to amplify the message.

The temporal pattern of consciousness is also an easy consequence of the hypothesis. When we are conscious, large populations of neurons fire synchronously with a frequency of about 40 hertz, which limits our conscious time resolution to about 25 milliseconds. If several cycles of field activity are required to define a state of consciousness, the duration of the specious present becomes some hundreds of milliseconds. This is consistent with the duration of experienced moments of *now*.

The hypothesis is also consistent with the limited and fuzzy scope of consciousness. Each field state is a distribution of electric potential that sums away or washes out any specific information about which neurons are firing. That is, the field states are macrostates with higher entropy than the exact microstates defined by the precise patterns of neural firing. The effect of the entropy of these macrostates on experience is to limit our ability to focus on specific neurons. And conscious states have fuzzy boundaries because the coherence of the field is not an all-or-nothing property.

All this lends credibility to the TEM field view of consciousness. But nature is full of electromagnetic fields. Are we committed to accepting that states analogous to consciousness are widespread in nature, even in such aggregates of inorganic matter as photospheric plasmas in stars? The risk of having to accept panpsychism on this scale is reason enough to look more closely at the logic and physics of consciousness.

The Logic of Consciousness

To a good approximation, the neuronets that sustain consciousness act as computers. Digitized input in the form of electrochemical pulses from the afferent nerves is processed in the brain to generate a stream of digitized output pulses that go to motor nerves. In principle, we could write a lookup table to relate possible inputs to corresponding outputs. This suggests the brain implements a Turing machine, the idealized computer that Alan Turing defined in 1936.[9] Three conditions must be met to implement a Turing machine:

- Digitized input and output. The machine processes a stream of input bits (such as pulses of high or low voltage representing 0 or 1) and generates a stream of output bits.
- Finite number of internal states. The total number of possible machine states, defined in terms of configurations of the logic elements inside it, is finite.
- Table relating inputs and outputs. For each combination of input bit and internal state, a lookup table specifies an output bit and the next internal state.

Turing imagined input and output digits written on an infinite tape, where at each step the machine can erase the current input digit and write the specified output digit in its place before moving on to the next input digit. One special internal state halts the machine. The set of digits on the tape when it halts is the output. In general, given a machine and its input, we cannot predict if or when the machine will halt.

Consciousness enters the picture when we consider the semantics behind the logic processing. The brain does not run precoded software and is hardwired with only limited functionality. The neuronet learns a lot of its ability to understand the world through a trial and error process based on regularities in sensory input, and this has the effect of optimizing its virtual code for survival. Its code is virtual in the sense that the syntax is not actually written anywhere. Like any logical syntax, it has semantics, and this somehow embodies the worlds that we experience in consciousness.

Logical worlds are virtual constructions that we experience either as imaginary or as real. Obvious examples arise from natural language, which we can regard as programming code optimized by human evolution to run in our brains. Novels and stories of all kinds conjure up fictional worlds in our imagination that can sometimes seem as real as the world we learn about in daily news bulletins. The brain spins these worlds from words in an apparently magical transformation of syntax into semantics that Daniel Dennett felicitously calls the operation of the Joycean virtual machine,[10] after the novelist James Joyce, whose depiction in soliloquy of the stream of consciousness was a high point of twentieth-century literature.

Evolution has coupled the logical worlds that we generate very tightly to our natural environment. The result is that the worlds we each experience at each moment and the worlds we respectively experience in our separate minds are very closely correlated, so much so that for many purposes we regard ourselves as living in a single world. This single world is the real world that serves as the point of reference for science and daily life. We can see the real world as a macrostate of reality that glosses over the differences between all the microstates that we inhabit from moment to moment.

All these logical worlds can be modeled in set theory. Harvard logician Willard Van Orman Quine was a leading practitioner of set theory.[11] In the mid-twentieth century, Quine continued the work of Gottlob Frege and Bertrand Russell in reducing mathematics to set theory and went on to pioneer a similar reduction of natural language to set theory. Essentially, the program he envisaged was to reduce any ontology to sets. Ontologies are familiar to computer programmers as the sets of entities that provide the semantics for their programming syntax. Quine argued that reducing our natural ontologies to sets would clarify our mental landscapes.

The basic ideas of set theory are simple. Sets are classes of elements, and almost all classes and elements are sets. In general, sets have two sides. From below or inside, they are classes, or concepts. From above or outside, they are elements, or objects. Anything we assert can be translated into a corresponding assertion about sets. For example, the sentence "HAL is a sentient being" says that the object with the name HAL is a member of the class of sentient beings.

In naïve set theory, sets have subsets and sets of sets have unions, intersections, and so on. But set theory became hard as a response to a series of paradoxes that mathematicians discovered in naïve set theory. For example, in 1901, Bertrand Russell discovered the paradox that the set of all sets that are not members of themselves is a member of itself if and only if it is not a member of itself.[12] The idea of the set of all sets is therefore problematic. Mathematicians responded by building up universes of sets carefully, layer by layer. In what are now regarded as standard approaches to axiomatic set theory, such as Zermelo–Fraenkel (ZF) set theory,[13] sets are ranked in a cumulative hierarchy that is absolutely infinite in the sense that every attempt to limit it by a defined class merely provides the basis for new sets that go beyond it.

The cumulative hierarchy can be ranked into quasi-universal sets called V-sets. John von Neumann defined these V-sets by means of a recursive ranking function:

- The V-set of rank zero is the empty set, 0.
- For each finite level n, the V-set of rank n is the power set of the previous V-sets (a power set of a set X is the set of all its subsets, including 0 and X itself).
- At transfinite limit levels, the new V-set is the union of all previous V-sets.

Set theory applies to the virtual worlds of consciousness because logical worlds can always be mapped into V-sets. Thus the cumulative hierarchy contains all possible worlds in a single mathematical structure that serves as the ultimate ontology.

Recall that each momentary state of mind brings a manifold of phenomena to a unity. We can represent a state of mind as a class of phenomenal elements. The cerebral neuronet assembles such classes of elements into more complex structures, but all these can still be modeled as sets. In general, set-theoretic structures can represent complex mental states. These structures constitute the ontologies for which neural configurations provide an implementation. We have a natural coupling of semantics with virtual coding here that in principle we can correlate as tightly as we like.

To summarize, we can represent global states of consciousness as V-sets and represent the passage of time as transitions between V-sets. In this way, set theory provides an abstract logical model for all three basic features of consciousness:

- Unity – each V-set is a single object, the set of all sets of lower rank.
- Time flow – comprehending successive ranks of sets is analogous to experiencing successive moments of time.
- Limited and fuzzy scope – each V-set is a limited and fuzzy reflection of the absolutely infinite universe of all sets.

A Quantum View of Consciousness

The logical view of consciousness implies that if states of electromagnetic fields can realize states of consciousness at all, those field states must embody very specific structures. Just as an arbitrary bit string is almost certainly not the code for a digitized Hollywood movie, so an arbitrary electromagnetic field state is not a state of consciousness. Panpsychism is therefore not a serious problem.

However, both the temporal transitions in conscious experience and its blurred limits are still puzzling. Why are we always located at a small and fuzzy moment in time and not in a more extended state? And why is the past so unlike the future? The equations of classical physics are reversible with respect to time. Even in thermodynamics, the accumulation of entropy is a statistical phenomenon that leaves microphysics reversible. In relativistic physics, time and space are interdefined as a single pre-existing four-dimensional continuum in which the fact that we occupy a steadily moving point on a worldline is simply taken as given.

In quantum physics, the obvious asymmetry of past and future has a deeper foundation. We represent the general state of a system as a superposition of pure states, where the pure states form the base dimensions of an abstract state space. A vector in the state space represents the state of the system, and the nonzero components of the vector in the base directions give the pure states in its superposition.

If we measure the state of the system, we always find it to be in a unique pure state. The probability of finding it to be in state S is proportional to the square of the length of the component of the state vector in the direction for state S in the state space. Two kinds of time evolution of such a system are possible:

- If the system is undisturbed from outside, its state vector changes smoothly in accordance with the Schrödinger equation. This kind of change is common among elementary particles.
- If the system is disturbed in some way, its state vector snaps into the direction of a unique pure state. This abrupt change in the state of the system has no classical analog.

How and why a system alternates between smooth and abrupt changes is not yet understood, although we have numerous hypotheses.

If we apply this picture to states of consciousness, we can imagine a slightly blurred state of consciousness represented by a superposition of sharp states that evolves for a while until something causes it to snap to a sharp state. This state then slowly blurs out until again it snaps to a sharp state, and so on. We can now ask if it is possible to match the frequency of this physical process to the rhythm of conscious experience. If it can, the discrete evolution of momentary states of consciousness may correspond to a physically fundamental process, and the flow of experience may reflect a changing reality.

The TEM field is in fact a quantum field even if a classical description suffices for most purposes. It consists of vast numbers of photons with frequencies in the decahertz range (that is, tens of cycles per second) and Heisenberg time uncertainties of tens of milliseconds, which is in the same ballpark as the duration of *now* and the rhythm of conscious experience. The quantum picture associates conscious states with field states that conform to the quantum statistics of random elementary processes.

There is a major problem of principle with the quantized view of time. Our best concept of time comes from relativity theory, and quantum theory and general relativity have not yet been satisfactorily united. Attempts to unite them in a theory of quantum gravity are ongoing. Sir Roger Penrose, who has made great contributions to developing such a theory, maintains that consciousness will remain unexplained until we have a satisfactory theory of quantum gravity.

Happily, new approaches to quantum gravity offer hope. As Lee Smolin reports in the January 2004 issue of *Scientific American*,[14] loop quantum gravity has developed well in recent years and looks like the natural way to unite quantum mechanics and general relativity. In this theory, spacetime is quantized at the Planck scale and time passes in discrete steps. The size of these steps is almost inconceivably tiny: the number of minimal voxels that add up to the volume of a single atom is on the order of 10^{75} and there are some 10^{43} minimal time steps in each second, so these steps have almost nothing in common physically with the perceived moments of *now*. All they share is the subtle logic of discrete, step-by-step realization of unique, actual, present states from superpositions of possible, virtual, future states, in a process that no-one quite understands.

The picture that emerges here is indeed subtle and surprising. Physical reality is not a fixed and final construction, waiting for us to discover it layer by layer as we advance in time. This was always an odd idea, for it left us with the intractable mystery of why we cannot find some means to rise out of our embeddedness in the present and travel in time, despite all the contradictions that embroil us when we try to spell out the idea of time travel.

Rather, physical reality itself is realized in time, and we surf along on the crest of that self-realization. The physical self-realization is granular on so fine a scale that we have no hope of approaching it in conscious experience, but the granularity of our own experience is nevertheless related. Just as the self-realization of spacetime quanta gives rise to the logic of temporal flow that governs physical processes and generates entropy, so the self-realization of decahertz photons in phenomenal consciousness gives rise to the temporal flow that we experience as epistemically unidirectional. The physical scales are very different, but the logic is the same.

The mathematical metaphor of unfolding set-theoretic universes can help us here. Recall that the cumulative hierarchy of sets is open-ended in the sense that we face paradoxes and contradictions if we suppose that it can be closed off in a definite V-set. The most natural picture to use is that we are surfing through the hierarchy layer by layer, where the layers are ranked in accordance with the V-function. Any theory we adopt corresponds to a layer in the sense that it has a natural model in some V-set, but any such theory immediately gives rise to a successor theory and thus takes us a step further through the hierarchy. In this way, our logical ascent through the hierarchy is a mathematical analog of our physical progress in time.

We can take the analogy further. In the physical universe, the sum total of everything that can have a causal effect on us is contained in our past light cone, which we experience as the cosmic sphere bounding the observable universe in every direction as we look out from the Earth with telescopes. According to relativity theory, nothing outside this sphere has had enough time since the Big Bang to have any effect on us. The surface of this sphere is an enormously magnified image of the primordial fireball that veiled the first few teraseconds in the life of the cosmos. The past light cone is a large but finite set of elements of quantized spacetime, and this set gets bigger with every passing moment. We can model each momentary set of elements in a V-set, and hence map each step in the temporal expansion of our past light cone to a step upward in the hierarchy from one V-set to the next. Thus the temporal realization of quanta corresponds to the logical realization of sets.

We can even relate cosmology to consciousness. The TEM field realizes itself in discrete steps with a decahertz rhythm. We experience these steps as the ongoing temporal realization of definite states of mind. Perhaps this process is as physically fundamental as the stepwise realization of elements of spacetime. If so, the phenomenal self-luminosity and partial translucency of our states of mind may be features of physical reality as a whole.

There are plenty of mysteries as well as loose ends in this whole story, quite enough to dispel any sense of familarity we may feel with the idea that the TEM field generated by synchronous neural firing in the cortical neuronet is the physical correlate of conscious experience. The TEM field has highly convoluted dynamics, which makes our own conscious future impossibly hard for us to predict. We have no reason to suppose that we can neglect the quantum behavior of the TEM field, and the challenge of building semantic theories for its representational states may lead us beyond the world of classical computing. There may be deep surprises in store as we learn more about the amazing fields we carry about in our heads.

Purpose in Life and Science

Problem

As I look at my face in the bathroom mirror, I see an uneven pulp of ageing flesh around two beady eyes. My stare becomes hypnotic and the flesh seems to melt. I see a spectral zombie face shimmering behind two black holes. The holes glaze over and I get dizzy. Who am I, where is this, why does it go on? My gaze shifts and the conventional answers swim back into focus.

When we contemplate the deeper questions of life, answers are hard to find. Philosophers have argued about them since time immemorial. Organized science weighs in with new answers, slicker and more complex than before but often unsatisfying. Science fiction author Douglas Adams imagined asking a giant computer the ultimate question of the meaning of life, the universe, and everything, and getting the answer forty-two.[1] Something is missing.

A life without purpose is no life at all. This mantra, addressed to the bathroom mirror, homes in on my unease. Science is pretty good at telling me who I am and where this is, and I have learned to accept its answers with good grace, but science is weak on meaning and purpose. Philosophers gloss this by stressing the contrast between facts and values. Yet a sense of purpose and the values that express it are essential to the life we contemplate in the mirror. The problem is that they must come from somewhere. I cannot just invent a purpose and expect it to work for me any more than I can invent facts and expect scientists to be grateful for them.

I plan in this essay to tackle the problem indirectly by looking at how science frames the ultimate question and its possible answers. Maybe forty-two is not so hopeless after all. But if finding the purpose of life is our goal here, we had better start with a preliminary definition of purpose in its most general form. To have a purpose is to be oriented toward a projected future state that one may desire or intend and that may cause one to act in order to realize that state. The definition presupposes a reality in which an active subject with some form of both imagination and free will experiences a series of states of reality that are ordered in time.

Time

The problem of purpose starts in logic itself. If events are ordered in time, any purposes attached to my actions here and now are explicable in full only by reference to future events. And this leads to a failure of epistemic closure, where in principle I can never know enough about things to make watertight plans. For example, if my purpose now is to slake my thirst, I cannot know everything in advance about the causal nexus that determines how, in a range of hypothetical circumstances, my thirst will respond to my drinking some liquid from the kitchen. So my action will be a shot in the dark, made on the basis of a presumptive model of how things will turn out. If my mental model is wrong and I drink the wrong liquid, the consequences may be dire. My model may be constructed in accordance with the best methodology and so on, but still turn out to be quite false, and only a confrontation with reality can help me improve the situation. In the longer term, we shape our purposes by trial and error. But however we do so, our purposes are abstractions, shaped now on the basis of idealized models of future states that ignore various complications and entanglements that may easily invalidate them.

The problem of timing here is inexorable. We live in the present and have knowledge of the past. We use that knowledge to build models of the future, and shape our purposes accordingly. But the models are hypothetical. If we build them using the right facts and a deep enough appreciation of the laws and regularities that bind those facts into an intelligible unity, we can plan and act with confidence. Even then, unforeseen circumstances can intervene. Given the epistemic asymmetry of past and future, and our location in a moving present with a limited view, all our plans, purposes, promises, and prophecies are hostages to fortune.

Randomness

There is an irreducible randomness about the future. Our concept of randomness turns out to be so central to the story we tell in physics and biology that it is worth spelling out first, before we dive deeper. Our paradigm of a random process is throwing dice, where each of the numbers one through six has an equal probability of appearing on the uppermost face of a die, and no available theory enables us to predict which of the six will show up in a given throw.

To analyze a dice throw, we sort all possible future states into six groups and say the probability for the future state realized by the throw to be in any one of these groups is the same as for the other five groups, and is therefore one sixth, given that the probabilities all add up to one. This is a symmetry argument. The probabilities are the same because the groups are equivalent in all but spot count on the uppermost die face. The throw breaks that symmetry. Now one face is uppermost and the spot count is fixed. This group of outcomes now has probability one, and the probability of all the other outcomes, given this fact, collapses to zero. To confirm randomness, we can throw the dice a few more times and check that all the numbers one through six come up with frequencies that become more equal the longer we keep throwing. If the individual results are unpredictable, the series is random.

Examples like this of apparently random processes suggest that the best definition of a random series is that no exact description of such a series can be given that is shorter than simply listing its successive terms. In this sense, the series is algorithmically incompressible. By contrast, the digits in the decimal expansion of pi, for example, can be given by various simple mathematical formulas, so that series is algorithmically compressible and not random.

This definition appeals to a presumed impossibility that we may not always find plausible. Depending on the example, we may suspect that algorithmic compression is possible in principle and merely difficult or tiresome in practice. So we may allow a process to be practically random even if a deeper analysis could conceivably unearth algorithmic simplicity.

Entropy

Physics abounds with random processes and erects huge theoretical edifices on them. Any typical physical system, such as a glass of water, involves vast numbers of tiny parts, such as water molecules, whose combination in physically interesting configurations generates spaces of possible system states with even vaster numbers of inhabitants.

The dynamical laws that govern these huge configurations of particles are either deterministic or probabilistic. If the laws that govern the evolution of a system from one state at an earlier time to another state at a later time are deterministic, then from an exact specification of the earlier state we can compute an exact specification of the later state, and if we are fast enough we can predict system states. If the laws that govern the evolution of a system are probabilistic, the best we can do is to predict probabilities for the various possible outcomes as a system evolves from an earlier to a later state.

Classical mechanics is deterministic in principle, though not always in practice, since inaccurate measurements in systems that admit chaotic behavior may limit predictions very severely, so that such systems show effectively random behavior. If I spill some water, the splash is random for all practical purposes.

Quantum mechanics is deterministic in principle, assuming that systems can be in superpositions of several states at once, though hardly ever deterministic in practice, since any measurements or interactions at all disturb a system and cause it to change its state randomly. If I measure the thermal motion of an atom in a water molecule, whether it jiggles this way or that is random. The difference between classical and quantum mechanics is that what seems like a mere practical constraint in classical systems is a constraint of principle, with no hint of a way out, in quantum systems.

The second law of thermodynamics says that as any closed system evolves in time, its entropy tends to increase. That is, if the overall configuration of the state of a system has a certain probability, relative to a set of states including both that state and any states into which it may evolve, then after a lapse of time, the later state of the system has an overall configuration with at least as high a probability. What this means is that a system tends to evolve along a path through a given state space in the direction of increasingly probable configurations. This law is well confirmed, fundamental, and universal. A dropped glass shatters, ice melts in warm water, and we all die in the end.

The law also works in reverse, for retrodiction as well as prediction. Given a state of a system at some later time, the temporal symmetry of the fundamental dynamical laws dictates that retrodicting an earlier state of the system in the state space should also find an increase in entropy. So given a partially melted ice cube in a drink, we can retrodict that it was even more melted a few minutes earlier. Failing additional assumptions about the earlier state of the drink, this is a valid retrodiction. In general, given only a first state and some dynamical laws, any second state is probably going to be at least as probable as the first. Temporal asymmetry appears only when we locate special events in the past, such as the big bang or putting ice in the glass.

Evolution

Entropy applies to closed systems, but living systems are open. A living system is a process that feeds on inputs with low entropy and produces outputs with high entropy. In more concrete terms, living processes convert things with rather special or improbable forms, such as foodstuffs, into a few things with even more improbable forms, such as fresh eggs, and a lot of things with rather ordinary forms, such as waste. The more ordinary or probable a thing, the more randomness is involved in the assembly of its ingredients.

Randomness is minimal in genetic material. Information is negentropy and genes are compressed packages of information. Genes are coded recipes for constructing convoluted protein molecules. These molecules work together as nanomachines and ultimately as organisms. So genes carry instructions for replicating organisms. But despite the most elaborate copying and quality control mechanisms, randomness infects genes too, to create mutations. Some mutations are preserved by natural selection and the result, over sufficiently many generations, is the evolution of new species. The evolution of species may be seen as the exploration of ever more complicated and indirect, yet effective, ways for genes to project copies of themselves into the future. In the process, information is concentrated and randomness is wrung out more and more thoroughly.

Humans have developed a new way to accelerate biological evolution by genetic engineering. The human genome is rather less than a gigabyte in size and replicates humans about once or twice per gigasecond. By contrast, file transfer over a broadband line can replicate gigabyte files instantly, and digital technology ensures arbitrarily high copying fidelity. Using such technologies, we are learning in this century to project organized information into the future with unprecedented speed, volume, and efficiency.

As to why this process of concentrating and replicating information should persist and intensify, we can see that the more efficient replicators crowd out the competition. Organisms are gene machines, and the genes replicate as freely as nature allows. By analogy, human brains are meme machines, where memes, roughly speaking, are ideas that prompt us to copy them. Memes replicate as freely as human nature allows. As Internet pioneers used to say, information wants to be free. This process goes on all the time, within us as well as around us. Purpose is still a puzzle.

Free Will

In the brain, the electrical firing of neurons conforms to physical laws. Changing concentrations of neuromodulator and neurotransmitter molecules cause neurons to send tiny electrical signals to each other. Over the cortex, billions of neurons create a vibrating field of electrical energy that carries the symphonic states we experience in consciousness. Cerebral neurodynamics are more complex than anything we can yet model accurately, but we have no reason to doubt that known physical laws can in principle explain everything of functional significance that goes on in our brains.

A cerebral neuronet is a physical structure that realizes a succession of states in time. In principle, we can use information about a particular state plus physical laws to predict its evolution in time. Mention of evolution here is quite fitting. Each state of the system propagates in a lawlike way to a successor state, with occasional random variations. And neural groups in the brain compete with each other for resources and for opportunities to fire and control their neighbors. Organized patterns of neural activity arise through a process of natural selection much like that governing simple organisms in a nutrient medium.

Seen from within, the activity in human brains may appear to be regulated and even dominated by plans and purposes, but from a laboratory perspective our thoughts form and reform like clouds in the sky to give at best a self-generated illusion of purpose. As neural groups in our brains interact and get organized, stable cognitive structures evolve that computer scientists call demons. A ceaseless pandemonium in our heads creates a flickering background of thoughts and images and ideas, from which we make up our own minds, get ourselves together, and exercise what we like to regard as free will, in an astonishingly complex process of self-organization. Almost all of this action in our brains is unconscious, and it is only from within that we can even begin to imagine that our conscious thoughts and choices somehow govern the rest. Scientists who have studied this agree that there is a good deal of illusion in our thoughts and opinions, both about the ongoing drama of our own selves and about our presence and influence in the external world, and they disagree only about the depth and incorrigibility of the illusion. So opinions differ on whether this author is free to go and fetch a glass of water.

All this seems to marginalize the concept of purpose. We can easily enough imagine a purpose behind the process of life in general, just as we can describe our own thoughts in terms of purpose. We can even enjoy a striking sense of explanatory power when we relate purposes to human passions and the tumult of our everyday lives. Nevertheless, the concept appears to be superfluous in science. We expect in principle to be able to translate without loss any references to purpose in our lives and thoughts into neutral scientific terms. These terms conform to the simple logic that past states plus universal laws are enough to predict in principle and thus far explain future states. The question is whether purpose is now redundant.

Purpose

If purpose in life or mind is no more real than cosmic purpose, then perhaps cosmic purpose is no less real than my purpose in fetching a glass of water. We can see the dynamic of reality as a whole as being to propagate ever more efficiently packaged and organized information into future states of reality. From the big bang to the present, the entire evolution of the universe has been in the direction of generating increasingly concentrated and convoluted packages of information that persist in what looks like an increasingly randomized environment. We can indeed imagine a purpose of sorts here, but it is abstract and empty, with no hint of a mechanism for foresight or control. It certainly seems a far cry from human purposes.

Consider how we use the concept of purpose in everyday life. I envisage a desired future state of myself and the world and I constrain my actions accordingly with the purpose of realizing that goal. This involves a series of functional mechanisms at the neural, organismic, and societal levels that are explicable within the frame we have reviewed so far. Such purposes find a place within the scientific vision of a strictly mathematical universe in which states unfold in time with an impersonal majesty that dwarfs our fleeting lives.

A problem with the majestic scientific vision is that we who conceived it are humans. People with pandemonium in their heads somehow tamed their demons sufficiently to develop mathematics and science far enough to enable them to see the vision. There is a bootstrap process here that demands a closer look. We need to understand how naturally evolved survival machines built up from protein macromolecules can grasp the fundamental principles that purportedly govern the entirety of natural creation.

The bootstrap process not only gave rise to science but is recapitulated in ontogeny. A baby has a brain that sees phenomenal surfaces vividly but understands very little. Soon mother and family emerge, and the story of purpose gathers momentum. As the child grows to adulthood, ever more of the world and its history makes sense in a cosmic drama with the self in the starring role. Then, with advancing age, the cold majesty of the big vision sinks in, and the passions of life, as well as its purpose, begin to seem as spectral as the zombie in the bathroom mirror. The sense of purpose first waxes, then wanes. As time goes by, state after state of reality unfolds, and each state replaces its predecessor as the objective setting for the ongoing realization of the unifying subject.

An anthropic principle holds sway here. On both the personal and societal levels, we say that creation unfolded as it did because we, here and now, are the ones who are looking back and reconstructing it. As a matter of logic, we need to explain our own existence. So purpose exists because we see it, and we are part of creation.

Solution

We have a story in which we are free to say that purpose permeates the whole of creation. But to stand at the summit of such a story, we need to be worthy of it. The idea is absurd that I, your humble author, about to go and fetch a glass of water, sit at the summit and pinnacle of cosmic destiny.

We can do better. Our civilization has begun to project a generic image of our collective self. The scientific consensus on our shared universe, our shared biological ancestry, our shared genome, our shared neurodynamics, our collective immersion in the same meme bath, and our common planetary destiny, adds up to a portrait of an envelope self. Each of us, until we die, pushes out the envelope in some tiny way and thus enriches this growing self. Everything in our universe leads up to this potentially infinite living being and finds there a vision of its ongoing purpose.

Long ago, the royal we was invoked to denote the universal ambition of the enlightened monarch. Now, in science, we can assert something similar. We are the subject of cosmic history, the purpose of creation. The innermost self of each human being is bathed in the light from the radiant sun of science. Purpose is a concept we must deploy to suit our passion, and if our passion is to explain the universe, then our purpose is realized when the universe makes sense. As our passion goes out to loved ones, they share our purpose in the epic of creation. Each of us has a cosmic soul. We glimpse this soul when we sense the sense of creation. Purpose is immanent in creation, and is realized when we find the harmony of all the states and parts that make it up.

If this sounds overblown, consider my purpose in fetching a drink. To realize that this is indeed my purpose, I need only consider the harmonious symphony of actions I succeed in undertaking to fetch a glass, pick up the pitcher, pour the water, and carry the glass to my desk. There, I did it! This miraculous interplay of neurons and sinews, not to mention the synchrony of expectation and reality as the glass and water behave as my mental model predicts, is as glorious as the entire cosmic drama, just smaller. Even that zombie in the mirror has a purpose, to boot the brain into action. As I see it, purpose is what makes life worth living.

Roads to Reality

Contenders

Sir Roger Penrose, recently retired Rouse Ball Professor of Mathematics at the University of Oxford and collaborator with Stephen Hawking on black hole theory, has written "a complete guide to the laws of the universe" called *The Road to Reality*.[1] His publisher calls it the most important and ambitious work of science for a generation.

Penrose caused quite a furore in the world of consciousness studies with his 1989 book *The Emperor's New Mind*, which boldly conjectured a new mechanism for consciousness, and two further books, *Shadows of the Mind* (1994) and *The Large, the Small, and the Human Mind* (1997).[2] Indeed his ideas still keep a faithful band of researchers busy with models based on microtubules and the like. Sadly, their excitement is fizzling out. The title of the 2002 Tucson "Toward a Science of Consciousness" conference poetry slam winner was: *Microtubules – my ass!*

Stephen Wolfram, by contrast, is a maverick loner. Educated at Eton, Oxford, and Caltech, active in particle physics, recipient of a MacArthur "genius" award, multimillionaire creator of *Mathematica* (which he says is "now the world's leading software system for technical computing and symbolic programming"), he is both author and publisher of the massive volume *A New Kind of Science*.[3] He regards it as the most important and ambitious work of science for three centuries. Yes, Wolfram wishes to be known as the next Newton.

Wolfram is not much impressed by consciousness as a defining feature of human beings. He sees human mental processes as embodied computations and hence as equivalent to many irreducible processes in nature, such as weather or the particle dance in rocks. In this computationalist view, it is not that we are trapped in the Matrix, we *are* the Matrix.

Whose book should you read?

Omnium

For Penrose, the road to reality cuts boldly through the twin cities of mathematics and physics. The white line on his road is what he calls the "magic" of complex numbers. The current orthodoxy in both relativistic and quantum physics is to presuppose a real spacetime continuum. Combinatorial constructions from such elementary items as particles or fields in this continuum form dizzyingly large worlds or sets of worlds. Penrose advocates a metaphysics comprising a complex continuum that is no less dizzying but slightly more mathemagical. To denote the resulting totality, he prefers the pleasantly neutral term *omnium* to such loaded terms as "multiverse".[4]

Classically, the omnium has four real dimensions. Classical reality is Einstein's cosmos, in which we occupy an expanding bubble of observable spacetime that we call our *celestial sphere*. Penrose offers an authoritative and informative guide to this reality, including a nice view of the celestial sphere in Minkowski spacetime. Our celestial sphere includes everything in the universe that we can interact with causally, which roughly means everything we can observe in the night sky. Penrose sees it as a *Riemann sphere*, which can be represented as a curved surface in Euclidean 3-dimensional space but is more exactly the manifold with a single complex dimension obtained when the complex plane is "compactified" by adding a single point representing infinity and projecting it onto a sphere, such that the axes become great circles through the poles zero and infinity and the unit circle becomes the equator.

But there is a big problem here. Einstein's beautiful theory of gravity, as the curvature of spacetime, needs a complete overhaul to accommodate quantum theory. Penrose argues forcefully against the claims of superstring theorists to have solved quantum gravity. He is sympathetic to the loop quantum gravity approach, but finally he favors his own *twistor theory* to tackle the problem.

Sets

Mathematics was so successfully formalized in the twentieth century that people like Penrose who believe in the reality of the classical continuum can make life easy for themselves. The foundations of mathematics in logic and set theory are simple, and going down to the foundations can clarify the issues. Powerful concepts, like powerful machines, enable us to do more by leveraging our previous powers.

The late Harvard logician and philosopher Willard Van Orman Quine did pioneering work on the foundations of mathematics. As a young man, he was an avid disciple of Bertrand Russell, whose own pioneering work in mathematics, especially on the authoritative trilogy *Principia Mathematica* together with his senior collaborator Alfred North Whitehead, derived in large part from the impressive work of German mathematician Gottlob Frege. In 1879, Frege published a short book on logic that introduced functional notation to represent the subject-predicate form of sentences and thus created the predicate calculus. He went on to create the first foundations for classical mathematics in set theory. His effort was flawed, as Russell pointed out, and Russell and Whitehead attempted to finish the job. But as Kurt Gödel said later, their work represented a step back in terms of rigor compared with Frege's achievement. Yet the project was launched, and the concerted efforts of a generation of gifted mathematicians created a family of axiomatic systems of set theory that, for all practical purposes, formed a logical foundation for all of classical mathematics.

Quine's role in this story was, first, to tidy up Russell and Whitehead's formalism with a couple of improved axiom sets of his own for set theory, second, to clarify and collate a series of additional refinements in the set-theoretic representation of mathematical notions, and third, to make plain the extent of the equivalence between many of the leading axiomatizations of set theory.[5] As an outcome of all this activity, he promoted the grand project of regarding set theory as the foundation not only of mathematics but also of the systematic sciences in general, and thus supported the general ambition of the logical positivists to see a logical structure behind reality as a whole. That ambition found one of its purest expressions in Wittgenstein's oracular *Tractatus Logico-Philosophicus*.[6]

That revolution in logic gave rise to computers. Alan Turing transmuted Gödel's incompleteness theorems for formal systems like that of *Principia Mathematica* to prove equally fundamental results for all possible classical digital computers. This paved the way for the entire computer revolution. Mathematicians still need their brains, but like Wolfram they now routinely use computers to help them prove new results.

Computers are digital machines that work with discrete logic. All the sets you need to do computer science are finite or countable. Computer scientists can be sceptical about the metaphysics of the classical continuum.

That metaphysics has wobbly foundations. In the nineteenth century, Georg Cantor created a new theory of transfinite numbers and sets. His "diagonal" proof that the cardinality of the continuum (the uncountable set of real numbers) is strictly greater than that of the infinite set of all finite numbers (the countable set of natural numbers) was a triumph of the human intellect that led directly to the theorems that made Gödel and Turing famous.[7]

Cantor said two infinite sets have the same cardinality (or are equinumerous) if and only if a one-to-one mapping can be defined between them. Using this criterion, the set of natural numbers is equinumerous with the set of rational numbers, and the real line has the same cardinality as any real or complex space with a finite or countable number of dimensions. But imagine an infinite list of real numbers, each written out as an infinite series of digits. You can now define a new real number that never appears in the list just by defining each n-th digit to be other than the n-th digit in the n-th number in the list. To learn to live in peace with this result, it may help to recall that the accepted way to model a real number is as an infinite series of rational numbers that border ever more closely on the real number and thus form the walls of an infinitely deep "cut" into the continuum. A typical real number is equivalent to an infinite set of rational numbers, so it should come as no surprise that there are "more" reals than rationals.

Cantor built a towering transfinite hierarchy of higher infinities on this foundation. For mathematicians of constructivist temper who sympathize with the intuitionist rejection of his infinitistic argument, the foundation is unacceptably wobbly. Cantor's paradise, as David Hilbert called it, has been a divisive issue for mathematicians ever since, with some seeing it as the ultimate refuge for pure Platonic thought in an otherwise utilitarian world and others seeing it as a fantasy with no relevance to the discrete world of practical science and technology.

Qubits

We live in a quantum world, where continuum limits may be meaningless and where reality may allow no more than countable sets of answers to questions that can always be reduced to binary questions, such that these *projection* sets, if they have models at all, have discrete models. In this approach, each consistent set of possible answers defines a possible world, and it makes no sense to ask more of a world than that it answers posed questions and thus instantiates a consistent history.[8] Penrose has only limited sympathy with such views for the reason that they are too close to the fuzzy mysticism of Niels Bohr's "Copenhagen interpretation" of quantum reality in terms of complementarity.

On the other hand, if talk of the continuum is accepted as meaningful, a quantum omnium may be much richer than a classical reality. Because of entanglement, the task of creating an exact simulation of a quantum system is too much for a classical computer, as Richard Feynman asserted and David Deutsch proved.[9] Quantum information is measured not in bits but in *qubits*, where each qubit has a wavefunction ψ that is a superposition of the classical bit states 0 and 1, which can be written in Dirac ket notation as

$$|\psi\rangle = \alpha|0\rangle + \beta|1\rangle,$$

where α and β are complex coefficients, and the set of possible superpositions of ψ has the cardinality of the continuum.[10] So the infinities of quantum theory are no less dizzying than those of Cantorian arithmetic.

Entropy

The temporal unfolding of phenomenal reality is not in fact predictable, and seems not even in principle to be deterministic. Multiple alternative possible future states of reality coexist until a unique such state emerges as the present reality, and quantum theory gives a puzzling account of how that evolution occurs. Sadly, the account makes no sense at all in an Einstein cosmos. Penrose is candid about his obsession with this issue and about our failure to date to solve the problem convincingly.

Be that as it may, classical or quantum reality as we now partially understand it has a feature that invites the deepest gloom, namely the inexorable rise of *entropy*. Various possible future states have various probabilities of becoming actual as present states and then formerly actual or factual as past states. These probabilities are such that the deeper into the future we try to peer, the more random or disordered the future states we can discern appear to be. Curiously, if we try to look back into the past, armed only with our knowledge of the present state of reality, the same thing happens, and the more remote past states look ever more random.[11] What saves the past and distinguishes it from the future is that it is full of *facts*, which are specific states that embody *information* or negentropy. The first fact, the Big Bang itself, has an astonishingly low entropy, with betting odds of one in ten raised to the power ten raised in turn to the power 123, in Penrose's off-the-cuff calculation.[12] The universe has been running downhill since then, entropy-wise, and is fated to get steadily worse. The best we can hope for is that a new theory of quantum information will improve the outlook.

Twistors

In quantum theory, one of the most paradoxical issues is the *entanglement* of multiple particles in superposed states, which Schrödinger illustrated with his cat and which Einstein considered a *reductio ad absurdum* of quantum mechanics.

Penrose calls quantum entanglement *quanglement*.[13] For example, a pair of photons emitted by the mutual annihilation of an electron and a positron is quangled because the photons have correlated spins. Whatever spin you measure on one of them, you know the other has precisely the opposite spin. The big problem with quanglement is that it may be pervasive. Almost every particle in the universe may be quangled with numerous others. In that case, most of the apparently random state reduction events – or *qwiff pops*, to use Fred Wolf's cute phrase [14] – that occur all the time, all around us, could be correlated with each other in innumerable ways. It may even be impossible to trace the extent of the quanglements. Only if they were so pervasive or so focused that they measurably distorted classical statistics would we be able to detect them. For example, Johnjoe McFadden has speculated that if we could not explain the evolution of certain genetically important sequences of base pairs in DNA molecules without exceeding the improbability bounds that statistical theory allowed, we could conjecture that evolution exploited the quanglement of electrons shared by the base pairs.[15]

Quanglement may even be so pervasive that it creates a classical surface for our phenomenal reality. Physical reality may be a multiversal omnium including infinities of counterfactual and possible worlds, as it is in the Everett scenario so beloved of philosophers,[16] but the plain fact remains that all we see is a unique classical world. That may be because we quangle with anything we touch and thus force it to join our world.[17]

Penrose is thoroughly unimpressed by the claims of superstring theorists to have essentially solved quantum gravity, and his arguments are powerful. His review of loop quantum gravity is agnostic and his presentation of more radical approaches is as brief as this quotation suggests:

> We have seen how the loop-variable approach to quantum gravity begins to take us away from the standard picture of a continuous and smoothly varying spacetime and towards something of a more discrete topological character. Yet, some physicists would strongly argue that a far more radical overhaul of the ideas of space and time is needed ... Various ideas have been proposed ... Ahmavaara ... suggested that the real-number system, fundamental to the mathematics of conventional physics, should be replaced by some finite field

> ...obtained by taking the system of integers modulo [some extremely large prime number] ... Considerably more physically plausible are schemes like Raphael Sorkin's causal-set geometry (or certain closely related earlier ideas) according to which spacetime is taken to consist of a discrete, possibly finite, set of points for which the notion of causal connection between points is taken to be the basic notion. In ordinary classical terms, this 'causal connection' refers to the possibility of sending a signal from one of the points to the other, so one of the points lies on or within the light cone of the other. The largely random nature of the causal connections in Sorkin's scheme enables something like the Lorentz invariance of special relativity to emerge ... Other ideas leading to exotic spacetime structures arise from the quantum set theory or quaternionic geometry of David Finkelstein ... etc.[18]

Twistor theory is the approach Penrose favors to tackle the problem, and his presentation of the theory, so far as it goes, is a delight to read. Let me try to present an outline summary.

> Twistor theory has some relations to spin-network theory ... but it does not directly lead to any notion of a 'discrete spacetime'. Instead, its departure from real-number continuity is in the opposite direction, for it calls upon the *magic of complex numbers* as a primary guiding principle for physics. According to twistor theory, there is a fundamental underlying role for complex numbers in defining spacetime structure, in addition to the well-established basic role of these same numbers in quantum mechanics.[19]

Penrose recalls that the quantum mechanics of spin states can be described in terms of the spatial geometry of the Riemann sphere, directly for spin ½ particles and via the Majorana representation for higher spin, and that the celestial sphere in special relativity can be "validly regarded" as a Riemann sphere. The latter idea is taken up directly in twistor theory.

> Another guiding principle behind twistor theory is quantum non-locality. ... The 'quantum information' that represents quanglement, can 'travel' one way or the other along a quanglement line, or spin-network line. There is no specification of a *time* in spin-network theory ... It is possible to regard twistor theory as a continuation of the spin-network programme to obtain a *relativistic* scheme, in which idealized light rays (or their generalizations, with spin) appear to be, in a sense, the carriers of quanglement. Ordinary spacetime notions are not initially among the ingredients of twistor theory but are to be *constructed* from them.[20]

Roads to Reality

Now for the role of Riemann spheres:

> As a first step towards the understanding of twistor ideas, we may think of a twistor as representing a *light ray* in ordinary (Minkowski) spacetime   . One can regard such a light ray as providing the primitive 'causal link' between a pair of *events* (i.e. of spacetime points). But events are themselves to be regarded as secondary constructs, these being obtained from their roles as intersections of light rays. In fact, we may characterize an event R (spacetime point R) by means of the family of light rays that pass through R ... whereas in the normal spacetime picture a light ray Z is a locus and an event R is a point, there is a striking reversal of this in twistor space, since now the light ray is described as a *point* **Z** and an event is described as a *locus* **R**.
>
> The *twistor space* ... whose individual points represent light rays in   , is denoted by   . ... Thus, the point **Z** in   corresponds to the locus Z (a light ray) inside   and the point R in   corresponds to the locus **R** (a Riemann sphere ...) inside   . ... We see that the relationship between   and   is indeed a non-local correspondence, rather than a point-to-point transformation. ... This locus **R** inside   , describes the 'celestial sphere' (total field of vision) of an observer at R, the celestial sphere of R being regarded as the family of light rays through R ... this sphere is naturally a *Riemann sphere* which is a *complex 1-dimensional space* ... Thus we think of spacetime points as *holomorphic objects* in the twistor space   , in accordance with the complex-number philosophy underlying twistor theory.[21]

Penrose shows that if we make the light rays in this picture more realistic by assigning them spin and energy, the result is a *six*-dimensional space   , which can be interpreted as a complex space of three complex dimensions. As to quantization in this approach, spacetime events become fuzzy but light rays are left intact. In the twistor view, the condition for the intersection of light rays is subject to quantum uncertainties, so the notion of a spacetime point becomes fuzzy.

The Penrose magic continues. We obtain *compactified Minkowski space* $^{\#}$ from ordinary Minkowski space   by adjoining an infinite element, which identifies its future and past null infinities and is itself a light cone at infinity. The compactified space $^{\#}$ has the 15-dimensional symmetry of the conformal group, whereas   has only the 10-dimensional symmetry of the Poincaré group.

There is a nice way to describe $^{\#}$. Consider the light cone κ of the origin O in a pseudo-Euclidean 6-space ^{2,4} such that κ is given by the equation

$$w^2 + t^2 - x^2 - y^2 - z^2 - v^2 = 0,$$

where the metric ds^2 of $\mathbb{R}^{2,4}$ is

$$ds^2 = dw^2 + dt^2 - dx^2 - dy^2 - dz^2 - dv^2.$$

Now consider the section of the 5-cone κ by the null 5-plane $w - v = 1$. This intersection is a 4-dimensional paraboloid with the same metric as ordinary flat Minkowski 4-space. So $\kappa^{\#}$ is the abstract space of complete generators of κ, which are straight lines through O that lie on κ. Thus $\kappa^{\#}$ is the *celestial sphere* for an observer situated at the origin in $\mathbb{R}^{2,4}$.

The pseudo-orthogonal group $O(2, 4)$ acting on $\mathbb{R}^{2,4}$ consists of rotations that preserve the metric ds^2. This sends generators of κ to other generators of κ, so it sends $\kappa^{\#}$ to itself. Moreover, it preserves the conformal structure of $\kappa^{\#}$. Two elements of $O(2, 4)$ act as the identity on $\mathbb{R}^{2,4}$, one reversing the direction of each generator. Apart from this, $O(2, 4)$ is the conformal group.

Penrose asks – and answers – the obvious question here:

> How do twistors fit in with all this? The shortest – but hardly the most transparent – way to describe a (Minkowski-space) twistor is to say that it is a *reduced spinor* (or half spinor) for $O(2, 4)$. … In the present case … we have a 4-dimensional space of reduced spinors, referred to as *twistor space*. … Since twistors refer to an active group of spacetime transformations (the conformal group) where spacetime points get sent to other spacetime points under the action of the group, twistors are seen to be entities that refer globally to the spacetime, rather than to individual points in the spacetime. … In twistor theory, the magic of complex numbers is exploited to the full. Not only does twistor space turn out to be a complex manifold, but this complex manifold has a direct physical interpretation.[22]

Penrose now considers the physical interpretation of a general twistor. Using standard Minkowski coordinates t, x, y, z for a point R of $\mathbb{M}$ and taking the speed of light as unity, the full twistor space $\mathbb{T}$ for $\mathbb{M}$ is a 4-dimensional complex vector space for which standard complex coordinates Z^0, Z^1, Z^2, Z^3 may be used. Now we can say that a twistor **Z** is *incident* with the spacetime point R if it satisfies the matrix relation

$$\begin{bmatrix} Z^0 \\ Z^1 \end{bmatrix} = \frac{i}{\sqrt{2}} \begin{bmatrix} t+z & x+iy \\ x-iy & t-z \end{bmatrix} \begin{bmatrix} Z^2 \\ Z^3 \end{bmatrix}.$$

Each twistor **Z** has a complex conjugate **Z***, which is a *dual* twistor in a dual twistor space $\mathbb{T}^*$. We find that a twistor **Z** can be incident with an event in real Minkowski space $\mathbb{M}$ only if its norm vanishes: **Z*** **Z** = 0. In this case, we say that twistor **Z** is *null*.

Next, the *projective* twistor space is the complex projective 3-space ($\mathbb{CP}^3$) constructed from the complex vector space . The *null* projective twistors constitute the space , which is the 5-dimensional subspace of the 6-real-dimensional space for which the twistor norm vanishes. It turns out that we can reinterpret Minkowski space as the space of complex lines in (minus the infinite point), taking as the primary structure and as secondary. This amounts to taking light rays as more primitive than the spacetime points themselves. *Intersection* of light rays Z and X is represented by the existence of a projective line in containing the corresponding points **Z** and **X** of . The condition that two spacetime points are *null-separated* is represented by the condition that the corresponding projective lines **P** and **R** in intersect.

> Thus we see that twistor space provides a completely different perspective, on physical geometry, from the normal spacetime picture. Ordinary spacetime points are represented as Riemann spheres in . Points of are represented as light rays in spacetime. Either way the correspondence is non-local. Yet, we can pass from one picture to the other by precise geometrical rules.[23]

So much for special relativity. For quantum theory the picture is less clear. In the twistor view, quantization blurs spacetime events but leaves light rays sharp. The spacetime representation of the wavefunction of a free massless particle of general spin translates the Schrödinger equation to something called the *massless free-field equation*. For spin 0, this is the 4-dimensional wave equation $\psi = 0$, where is the D'Alembertian operator. For spin ± ½, it is a pair of equations setting the gradient of the wavefunction to zero. For spin 1, these two equations become Maxwell's free-field equations in the anti-self-dual and self-dual cases. For spin 2, they become the weak-field Einstein equation, split into anti-self-dual and self-dual parts, where spacetime curvature is regarded as an infinitesimal perturbation of flat Minkowski spacetime. To cut a long story short, it turns out that "the massless field equations seem to evaporate away in the twistor formalism, being converted, in effect, to 'pure holomorphicity'."[24]

But the further development of these ideas to quantum field theory in curved spacetime is for the future. And Penrose admits that twistor theory is not so much a physical theory as a mathematical reformulation without any new physics. All in all, Penrose's book is magical, but he is candid that there is still no final theory in sight.

Let us define *miph* as mathematics, informatics, and physics, and define the *quagmire* as the acronymic conjunction of the following issues:

- The unsolved problem of quantum gravity [25]
- The fathomless ocean of obscurities in M-theory, which is the shadowy theory that Ed Witten proposes to unify the five or so previous variants of superstring theory [26]
- The subtly puzzling concept of quantum information [27]
- The baffling issue of quantum state vector reduction [28]

Penrose is a master of miph but, like all the rest of us, he is defeated by the quagmire.

Automata

For Wolfram, the road to reality cuts through the rapidly growing conurbation of computational sciences. In *A New Kind of Science*, he notes that for the last three centuries theoretical physicists have been using differential equations to model nature. Their models are based on the classical continuum. His proposed new kind of science involves developing discrete models based on computer simulations. The aim of such science is simply to model the variety of natural phenomena in machines. If discrete models suffice for all practical purposes, interest in continuum models will fade.

Pursuing his new miph, Wolfram explored a large number of simple cellular automata simply by running them and looking at the patterns they generate. Intriguingly, he found that automata based on very simple rules sometimes emulate computations of arbitrary complexity. Although all processes can be seen as computations, even if only trivial ones, he concluded that many natural or artificial processes can be seen as *universal* computations.

> [I]f a system is universal, then it must effectively be capable of emulating any other system, and as a result it must be able to produce behavior that is as complex as the behavior of any other system. ... [U]niversality ... occurs in a wide range of important systems that we see in nature.[29]

Recall that integer arithmetic is universal because you can do arbitrarily complex computations in it. If you can count, add and multiply, fast enough, you can do anything a supercomputer can do. Wolfram's new principle:

> There are various ways to state the Principle of Computational Equivalence, but probably the most general is just to say that almost all processes that are not

obviously simple can be viewed as computations of equivalent sophistication.[30]

A sophisticated computation is irreducible, or algorithmically incompressible, and its result is random in the Chaitin–Kolmogorov sense.[31] Wolfram's final words:

> Looking at the progress of science over the course of history one might assume that it would only be a matter of time before everything would somehow be predicted by science. But the Principle of Computational Equivalence – and the phenomenon of computational irreducibility – now shows that this will never happen. ... [T]he Principle ... implies that all the wonders of our universe can in effect be captured by simple rules, yet it shows that there can be no way to know all the consequences of these rules, except in effect just to watch and see how they unfold.[32]

As I see it, the principle says less. It merely suggests that much of the apparent randomness in our universe may be explicable by means of underlying rules. These rules may be universal, and hence equivalent to each other in principle, but it's a long way from apparent randomness to life and mind.

Consciousness

The nineteenth-century German philosopher Hegel has few admirers in the Anglo-American philosophical community, for reasons that include some good ones. Nevertheless, a big idea stands out in Hegel's work that deserves continuing discussion. This is the governing idea of an *absolute* state of knowledge, which embraces all knowledge so far and relative to which truth claims can be evaluated. For Hegel it was axiomatic that the only truth is the *whole* truth and that partial knowledge, knowledge of parts, can only be provisional.

What this suggests, I hope unsurprisingly, is that contradictions between such current partial theories in physics as general relativity and quantum field theory are sure signs that we are not yet in the clear. We need to find a way to iron out the contradictions. This need is clearest in mathematics, where contradiction is intolerable. For example, confused and contradictory ideas about infinitesimals were forced to give way in the nineteenth century to a clean theory of limits. Indeed, contradictions in science and mathematics are even worth celebrating as opportunities for growth. In each historical epoch, certain contradictions are real, which is to say not yet overcome, and the concepts people in that epoch use to comprehend their reality are limited by those contradictions. The history of our struggle with such contradictions is interesting and instructive. This is what I learn from Hegel's philosophical work. To reduce his philosophy to a slick pun, it puts an evolutionary spin on our absolutes, which can keep us rolling along the road to reality.

In the realm of consciousness studies, confused and often contradictory ideas about how the brain does this or that to integrate the self it creates into a cognitive world need to be replaced by a clean story. For me, and I think for Penrose too, that story should be based on the miph of how a spatiotemporally limited perspective can take root and unfold to reflect a wider cosmic order that in turn serves as a more convincingly absolute standpoint. Cognitively, this amounts to performing repeated Copernican shifts of the sort that so impressed Kant.[33] To caricature the sort of progress our story needs to model, individual consciousness is centered on our own bodies, human consciousness is centered on our communities or divine images, and scientific consciousness is centered first on the Earth, then on the Sun, then on the inertial frame defined by the fixed stars, then on the isotropic microwave background, and so on, in a series of widening circles of concern with ever more remote centers.

For me, such cognitive models can all be represented in set theory, in ever-higher levels of the cumulative hierarchy, indeed such that machines as we now understand them can support them in principle too. The key idea is to put an evolutionary spin on the modeling process, essentially by implementing ascent and descent from level to level in the hierarchy of sets used to represent all available models. The process of stepping up a level is analogous to the diagonalization step Cantor used to deny the countability of the real numbers. We represent each available model at a minimal level in the hierarchy and rank the model by the rank of the topmost sets at that level. At this level, these sets are seen as proper classes. Recall that each level is seen as the universe of *all* sets, so its proper classes should be comprehended as elements in the universe, too. We take the step simply by comprehending them as sets. Our universe expands and we occupy a higher level in the hierarchy. Properly exploited, this strategy gives a cognitive agent a dynamic worldview comprising a potential infinity of models. Each such ranked worldview corresponds to a state of consciousness for the agent using this strategy.

The concept of consciousness thus stepwise expanded has no more than a vestigial connection to the cerebral cortex where animal awareness began, and is better regarded as *supervenient* on cortical states.

Penrose has given up trying to link his theoretical views to consciousness because the biology of cortical states so obviously has very little to do with

Roads to Reality 237

the Emperor's cosmic mind. He has just a few pages on consciousness toward the end of his new book:

> I have deliberately refrained from addressing, at any great length, the question of conscious mentality in this book, despite the fact that this issue must ultimately be an important one in our quest for an understanding [of] physical reality. (I have discussed such matters at detail elsewhere, and I have no wish to get embroiled here in many of the contentious issues that arise.)[34]

It is easy to sympathize. We can regard the biological concept of consciousness as orthogonal to the impersonal concepts deployed in mathematics and physics. We can see the realm of conscious thought either as embracing miphic activity in its entirety or as irrelevant to the objects of miph, which remain unchanged whether or not we are conscious of them.

For this reason, I suggest we regard states of consciousness simply as reflecting or complementing worlds or worldviews, and then go on to define these objectively in logic and physics. We can give an objective definition of each such combined state of subject and object by stepping outside the world or worldview thus instantiated, which we can represent formally simply as an upward step in the hierarchy in the set-theoretic representation of the process. In this way, we treat the concept of consciousness as *holistic* – it applies to any worldview as a whole, and the puzzle of how cortical processes can instantiate such a reflection or complementation of subject and object is separated cleanly from the worldviews themselves. But for Penrose the issue is not so clear:

> There is [an] important role played by consciousness in many interpretations of the **R** [reduction] part of quantum mechanics ... As far as I can make out, the only interpretations that do *not* necessarily depend upon some notion of 'conscious observer' are ... most of those ... that require some fundamental change in the rules of quantum mechanics, according to which **U** [unitary evolution] and **R** are both taken to be approximations of some kind of objectively real physical evolution. ... I am an adherent of this last view, where it is with gravitational phenomena that an objective **R** (i.e. **OR**) takes over from **U**. ... I envisage that the phenomenon of consciousness – which I take to be a *real* physical process, arising 'out there' in the physical world – fundamentally makes use of the actual **OR** process.[35]

How cortical processes can relate to **OR** is obscure, but **OR** is a quagmire issue that nobody expects to solve in the near future.

It seems to me that the Emperor's new mind, regarded as the subjective entity that reflects or complements *reality as a whole*, at least as we currently understand it, deserves to instantiate its own named variant of consciousness. I suggest that we call this variant *supracortical* consciousness, to exapt a term I first met in the works of A. K. Mukhopadhyay, an Indian professor of medicine who is also an accomplished mystical philosopher.[36]

Supracortical consciousness may be described to a first approximation as a unified state of phenomenal reality that quangles with the omnium from moment to moment and thus enables us to regard ourselves as living in a superficially classical physical world.

Perhaps not surprisingly for a computationalist, Wolfram has nothing much to add to conventional wisdom on consciousness:

> I am quite certain that in the end there will turn out to be nothing particularly special about the basic processes that are involved in human thinking. And indeed, my strong suspicion is that despite the apparent sophistication of human thinking most of the important processes that underlie it are actually very simple.[37]

For him, we are embodied computers, equivalent in principle to decaying rocks or stars or any other embodied universal automaton, just part of the cosmic computation.

The view of the universe as a big computation is not new with Wolfram. Indeed, given that the concept of computation applies to any rule-bound step-by-step process and that the basic aim of the science of cosmology is to generate a set of rules to describe the evolution in time of the universe, it is hard to see how the idea could even be controversial. *Scientific American* recently introduced an article by Seth Lloyd and Jack Ng on the view of black holes as computers like this: "In keeping with the spirit of the age, researchers can think of the laws of physics as computer programs and the universe as a computer."[38] The article ended with the wonderful words:

> What is the universe computing? As far as we can tell, it is not producing a single answer to a single question … Instead the universe is computing itself. Powered by Standard Model software, the universe computes quantum fields, chemicals, bacteria, human beings, stars and galaxies. As it computes, it maps out its own spacetime geometry to the ultimate precision allowed by the laws of physics. Computation is existence. … Although physicists do not yet possess a full theory of quantum gravity, they know it is intimately connected with quantum information. It from qubit.[39]

John Wheeler coined the phrase "it from bit" to suggest the link between physics and what was then the new science of information. Now, another quantum revolution later, we prefer the slogan "it from qubit."[40]

There is no need to say more here. The respective views of Penrose and Wolfram can both be accommodated in the new perspective.

Verdict

The symbiosis of mathematics and physics is nowhere more brilliantly depicted than in Penrose's new book. The dialectic of mathematical logic and physical intuition is like the interhemispheric traffic in a brain of cosmic dimensions, perhaps in the brain of the Penrosian Emperor whose very thoughts crystalize reality in a process of quantum-gravitational **OR**. There is much food for psychological thought in the astonishing series of victories won by mathematicians and physicists in recent centuries, and Penrose has prepared a banquet for those with appetite.

But the book has its flaws. Published in evident haste, it sports numerous typos and minor errors, and the level of both technical and rhetorical finish is very uneven. Material that Penrose has pondered for years is presented with brilliant clarity and precision, but some other stuff, such as the chapter on superstrings, is unsatisfactory and ragged. More damagingly, most readers without degrees in mathematics or physics will find the book impossible.

Wolfram's book is quite different. It is accessible at several levels. The main text is smooth and easy reading, but comprises less than half the total word count. The 349 pages of fine-printed and often very technical notes are a treasure trove for specialists. But the figures and their legends are the real focus of the work. Beautifully printed and presented using brilliantly minimalist notational schemes, many of them reward deep contemplation. The computational effort required to generate them all was obviously colossal, and their cumulative effect is to boggle the mind. The book clearly deserves cult status.

But its science is disappointing. Most of the views expressed in the main text on major scientific questions are vague and subjective (he often says without further support "I strongly suspect that X or something similar will turn out to be true" for a favored scientific assertion X), and most of his painstakingly computed technical results have only minor significance. Wolfram largely ignores two major topics:

- Memory size and organization are central both to human mental life and to the realism of the Turing machine idealization of computation.

- Processing speeds range over very many orders of magnitude. Slow processes may not compute much before they are brought to a halt.

And his much-heralded Principle of Computational Equivalence is close to ideas that are already familiar to most computer scientists.

Neither book delivers as much as its publishing hype promises. Penrose gives an inconclusive recap of current thinking and Wolfram gives an inconclusive survey of new vistas. Let Penrose educate you or Wolfram enthrall you – the choice is yours.

About Time

Abstract

This essay is an exercise in scientific metaphysics. Its aim is to sketch a unified account of time that both works in modern physics and makes sense in psychology. The raw materials for the sketch come from elementary logic and set theory. The experience of time flow is seen as a direct manifestation of a fundamental physical process. The ontology and epistemology of this experience can provide a foundation for psychology. If the physical sciences in their present form depict "the view from nowhere" onto reality, the new foundation can depict the view from anywhere.

Introduction

> Suppose that there is indeed a 'now' front, on the one side of which there are past events, adding up as the 'now' progresses, while on its other side there are no events, and hence, according to Mach, not even spacetime. Spacetime thus 'grows' into the future as history unfolds … What role does the wave function play in this creation of new events? The dynamically evolving spacetime allows a radical possibility. Rather than conceiving of some empty spacetime within which the wave function evolves, the reverse may be the case: The wave function evolves beyond the 'now', i.e., outside of spacetime, and its 'collapse' due to the interaction with other wave functions creates not only the events, but also the spacetime within which they are located in relation to one another.[1]

Time is arguably the most basic dimension of experience. Human consciousness seems conceivable only as a manifestation of temporal experience. Temporality implies ordered change, and a history of such changes is the autobiography of a conscious subject.

From a philosophical standpoint, the most fundamental task of an experiencing subject is to bring the manifold of phenomenal experience to a synthetic unity, and to do that on an ongoing basis by unifying the changing contents of the phenomenal manifold within the growing history of a uniquely located subject. This is essentially a Kantian view of the matter, but it remains viable as a one-sentence formulation of the metaphysics of rational subjectivity (where "rational" here means constrained by logic). When psychology is founded upon this basis, it presupposes a concept of time along with certain basic ontological concepts.

Time is normally regarded as a physical concept, and the physical view of time boasts not only great theoretical sophistication but also direct practical applicability. Yet the weakness in the physical concept of time is too basic and central to admit easy remedy. Despite centuries of progress in physics, the elementary experience of time flow remains unexplained. Indeed often, like Einstein, physicists feel free to regard the experience of time passing as a kind of illusion.[2] On this classical and traditionally determinist view, physical reality is eternally as it is, and we experience change as a corollary of our limited perspective on that reality.

If we concede the primacy of physical time as it is conventionally understood even for the scientific explanation of changing experience, we admit the possibility in principle of detaching the subject from any anchor in a unique history. This follows from the basic philosophical perspective of the conventional physical sciences that they depict "the view from nowhere," which is to say they describe arbitrary domains of objects but not the subjects that reflect or comprehend them.[3] Given a defined physical reality, the subject is inserted by hand in an *ad hoc* manner. So a free-floating subject seems able in principle to roam around at will in the spacetime continuum, and this raises deep philosophical problems, for example about time travel. But most such ideas are based on naïve psychology.

Experienced time

The experience of time flow is basic to any phenomenology.[4] A subject has a past and a present, and faces a future. The unifying activity of the subject brings successive constellations of the phenomenal manifold to conceptual order as a series of momentary perspectives with timestamps that constitute a layered history of the subject. These successive phenomenal configurations undergo transition from the present to the past.

The subject confronts the future as a domain of possible forms of the phenomenal environment. In human beings, environmental configurations typically appear with affective coloration that disposes an individual to act so as to realize a specific form of the world within that domain of possible forms. An ongoing human world is thus made progressively more specific as a personal history accumulates.[5]

Ontologically, the subject is embodied as a structure with a history. That history is a series of nested structures, each one of which represents the embodiment of the subject at an earlier time. Considered in terms of set theory, if each such structure is a set, with its own internal structure, then a history is an ordered series of sets, each one of which incorporates in some manner all of its predecessors in the series. Thus the history of a subject is the growth of such a series in time. New terms are added to the series as the subject brings successive initially future configurations of the phenomenal manifold to a synthetic unity.

Epistemologically, the subject recognizes ranges of phenomenal configurations as possible states of the world and selects specific states for realization in the present. The subject adds these states as new layers to an accumulating history. The process of bringing successive such selected configurations to a synthetic unity is epistemic, since it represents manipulations of concepts either within or beneath consciousness that have the effect of creating states of knowledge, and the study of that process is epistemological.

The temporal experience of a rational subject is thus reflected in an ongoing process with ontological and epistemological aspects. The process develops in time, and the subject grows a history. If we accept that the historical series of past states is part of the evolving subject whereas the domain of future possibilities is not, the experience of time is essentially asymmetric.

The problem for physicists who seek to understand temporal experience in terms of a physical concept of time is that time as a physical dimension seems to be symmetric between past and future.[6] Arguably, all attempts to date to explain the asymmetry of time in terms of concepts like entropy have been inconclusive.[7] Yet the asymmetry is obvious to anyone who watches a movie run backwards, and given the persistence of memory is obvious to anyone who simply thinks rationally for a few seconds. This aspect of the dynamics of everyday phenomena and their binding in rational apperception is still a puzzle in contemporary physics. There seems to be a mismatch between the physical and the psychological concepts of time.

One response to this mismatch is to distinguish two concepts of time. Physical time remains symmetric and may be treated by strict analogy with a spatial dimension, as in relativity theory, where the transformation between time and the spatial dimensions is scaled by a physical constant known as the speed of light. Psychological time, by contrast, is asymmetric, with a fixed past and an open future. This asymmetry may be seen as a consequence of the ontological nature of the psychological subject, who acts in time to realize a growing and evolving self.

A fundamental question arises from the distinction between psychological and physical time. The two concepts must be deeply related. Psychological subjects inhabit a physical universe, so psychological time should be derivative in some way from an ontologically more basic physical time. Yet physicists are psychological subjects, and hence any conception they have of physical time is as a matter of biographical fact derived somehow from their experience of time. At the very least, we must require that physics and psychology, as scientific disciplines, together form a self-consistent account of the reality in which we find ourselves. So the two accounts of time must dovetail neatly together.

Physical time

In most of physics, time is regarded as a free parameter and is represented by a variable that may take arbitrary numerical values. For physics as conventionally understood on the basis of Einstein's work, time and space together form a four-dimensional continuum in which point-like events have coordinates consisting of ordered sets of four real numbers.[8] Simultaneity is defined operationally in terms of the exchange of light signals, with the corollary that the prerelativistic concept of a single universal time coordinate for now, the present moment, becomes untenable.

Relativistically, events define four-dimensional light cones. Each event has a past light cone containing all other events that can possibly have had a causal influence, in principle via light signals, on the event. This past light cone contains small three-dimensional spatial volumes for the recent past and increasingly large volumes for increasingly remote times. And each event has a future light cone containing all possible future events that can be causally influenced by the event at its apex. The apical event is a sink for photons radiated from events in the past light cone and a source for photons radiating to events in the future light cone.

Curiously, light cones are bounded by "null infinities" for which time is unchanging. That is, the notional light rays that define the surface of a light cone form the locus of points that have zero temporal displacement from the apical event. The transformation equations for relativity imply that the proper time of an object, which is to say the time registered by a local clock for that object, dilates as the speed of that objects approaches light speed, as measured from an outside point. At light speed, the dilation becomes infinite and the local clock stops. Light rays are the traces of photons, and what this curiosity means is that time is nonexistent for a photon. If a photon were sentient, it would experience no passage of time at all between emission from a given material object, such as a star, and absorption in a faraway object, such as a human retina.

However, we cannot maintain that the spherical boundaries of the concentric spatial bubbles around an event in spacetime that touch the past and future light cones for that event define a set of events forming a relativistic analog of *now* for that event. That definition would extend the duration of now to infinity. Consider this example. At time zero, measured on a local clock, a photon is emitted toward to a remote mirror, where it is reflected back toward its source. Two years later, measured on the local clock, the photon is absorbed in an event with the same spatial coordinates as the emission event. The local time interval between the two events is thus two years, yet they are in the same *now* by the definition in terms of past and future light cones. This *reductio ad absurdum* applies to any events in the light cones. We need a better definition.

First, we define world lines. Events within the past and future light cones of an event are said to be separated by a timelike interval from that event. A pair of events with a timelike interval between them can be in causal interaction such that the earlier event may have a causal influence on the later event. By contrast, events outside the light cones are separated by a spacelike interval from the apical event, and are causally independent of that event. A world line is a set of events, each with a different time coordinate, such that all the intervals between the events are timelike and such that together they form either a continuous set (in the classical case) or a maximally dense set (in the case of discrete spacetime). That is, a world line is the possible history of a material particle.

Each event on a world line defines its own local *now*. And each event on a world line is related via possible or virtual photons with every other event on the world line. So *now* cannot be defined symmetrically in terms of photon exchange. But it can be defined asymmetrically. If each photon carries the timestamp of its source but not of its sink, then photons with timestamps in the past of a *now* event that are absorbed at that *now* event do not brand it with their old timestamp. And new photons emitted from the *now* event carry the *now* timestamp but do not stamp their absorption events with it. Their absorption events are in the future (even though the photons take no proper time to get there and hence still "think" the time is *now* when they get there). This definition implements a constructive metaphor according to which each momentary *now* is defined in terms of its past but not of its future, which has yet to be realized. Thus a world line is unidirectional, from past to future. Each event is defined by means of its past light cone, independently of its future light cone.

A neologism suggests itself here: a *world* is an event together with its past light cone. Thus a world line is either a continuous or a maximally dense series of worlds whose originating events form a timelike progression. Each world has a definite past but a wide range of possible or virtual futures. In this view, it makes no physical sense to say the future of a world is eternally there, just waiting to be discovered.

A world thus defined has a center, namely the event at the apex of its past light cone, and it has a definite *now*, namely the time coordinate of its apical event. A world thus defined is a relativistic invariant, since the causal history of an event (that is, the set of events that may in principle be in the causal ancestry of that event, namely the set of events in its past light cone) is the same to any observer of that event, in any state of (subluminal) motion relative to it. In everyday language, a world is a momentary "take" on the universe, centered at a specific spatiotemporal location.

The classical presumption that spacetime forms a continuum is thrown into question by quantum mechanics. The Heisenberg uncertainty relations between spatial location and momentum and between temporal location and energy limit the precision of possible measurements of the related items. Perfect precision in measurement of the spatiotemporal location of a particle would imply complete uncertainty in the momentum-energy measurement and vice versa. The minimum uncertainty in the product of the measurements is equal to the quantum of action known as Planck's constant, where an action is a spatiotemporally more or less localized quantity of what we can call "momenergy" (following Wheeler).[9]

The great discovery upon which quantum mechanics is based is that action is quantized. Relativistically, momentum and energy transform together like space and time, and energy is equivalent to mass, so what this means is that the smallest lumps of mass are spread out over a finite volume of spacetime. If the discrete elements of spacetime are sufficiently small to account for the facts, then it makes no empirical sense to insist that spacetime is continuous rather than discrete. Further, unless we can explain the infinities that would arise at singularities such as point masses or charges, it would make no theoretical sense to do so, either.

The quantum of action sets a specific scale to the granularity of spacetime. A photon has an energy proportional to the frequency of its corresponding electromagnetic wave. If there is a smallest physically possible increment of time, then there is a highest possible frequency, which specifies the largest possible quantum of energy. Similarly, a minimal spatial length corresponds to a maximal momentum in a given direction. Energy is equivalent to mass, and all mass exerts a mutual gravitational attraction. In general relativity, gravitation is a manifestation of the curvature of spacetime, as specified by Einstein's field equations, with a strength characterized by Newton's gravitational constant.[10] If we can mix quantum theory and general relativity in this way, a full circle of definitions and laws relates spacetime and mass using just three physical constants (for action, light speed, and gravitation). The measured values of the constants suggest that the ultimate granularity of spacetime is some twenty orders of magnitude below the diameter of a proton and some forty orders of magnitude briefer than a millisecond.

Accepting the discrete nature of spacetime seems to imply comprehending a finite number of worlds, where each world is a now event plus all the events in the past light cone of that event. Given the apparent fact that the universe has a finite age and the metaphysical claim that future events are possible but not (yet) actual, we can conjecture there are only finitely many actual worlds.

Quantum mechanics is centrally concerned with the collective behavior of events. Events are not spacetime points but nodes in a partial ordering, namely the causal or temporal ordering, which leaves some indeterminacy in the location of any entities they collectively realize. Collectively, events form structured setups or configurations called systems that instantiate states. A system can be something as simple as an elementary particle flying on some path from a source to a detector, and its state may be the specific path it takes, or its spin, or some other property. Predicting which states any given system will exhibit upon measurement is the main business of quantum mechanics.[11]

If past events are actualized whereas future events are no more than possible, any future discretely measurable state of a given system remains merely possible until such time as it either becomes or does not become actualized in the present as a result of performing a measurement. There is scope here for defining a special logic with a temporal modality, so that inferences to the past are classical but inferences to the future are probabilistic, but first we need to be clear on the physics.

Physical possibility is measured in terms of probability, and in quantum theory the mathematical tool for calculating probabilities is a complex function called the wave function. For a given system, the wave function specifies the evolution of the state of the system over time by encoding the respective probabilities of all its possible future states. There are two ways to calculate the probabilities of the future states of two or more systems, depending on whether the systems interact like particles or like waves. If the systems behave like particles and maintain their separate identities, their individual wave functions specify their respective probabilities to realize certain future states. But if the systems show wavelike behavior and interfere with each other, we need to add their wave functions before calculating the probabilities of the future states of the composite system.

Quantum theory raises puzzling questions about events. First, a quantum system can be in a superposition of multiple states. For example, a photon on its way from a source to a detector can be in a superposition of taking the left or the right path through a setup of mirrors, which is to say its behavior is wavelike despite its being an indivisible particle. This suggests that the events realizing the photon states do not yet suffice to determine a unique location for the photon. Second, there may be spatiotemporally extended entanglements between the parts of a quantum system. For example, a source may create two photons that fly off in opposite directions but remain entangled with each other so that any measurement of a property of one photon immediately determines the corresponding property of the other. This suggests that the events realizing the photon states do not yet suffice to determine separate locations for the two particles. Quantum superposition and entanglement are nonclassical notions.

Superposition of states suggests the coexistence of multiple realities, as possible or virtual states of a system, at least until the occurrence of an event that actualizes a unique state. A simple system (such as a single photon) may be in a mixed state with a nonzero probability to be in each of a number of unique states (such as photon spin states). A complex system (such as a number of photons) may be in a coherent state such that all its parts (such as photons) are in the same state. When a system in a coherent state interacts with another system, it may decohere into a mixture of different states. A complex system is generally in such a mixture of states, and the mixture evolves in time to blur into superposition any unique state that may arise. Given this idea, the most natural conception of the future is that it is a virtual (and not yet real) superposition of all possible outcomes.

Entanglement is a nonlocal phenomenon. The parts of a system in a coherent state are entangled with each other, and any interaction that changes the state of the system causes the entire system to change at once. The relative probabilities of states before and after such changes, both those predicted by quantum theory and those observed in experiments, are inconsistent with the view that they are caused by mechanisms operating subluminally.[12] Correlations exist between events with spacelike intervals between them, where we cannot invoke a classical, "local" mechanism to explain them. At the moment when two or more parts of a system become disentangled, the correlations between their states appear from a classical perspective to be sheer coincidences, even though quantum theory predicts them correctly. Typically, a new entanglement accompanies each disentanglement. For example, an entangled pair of photons from a distant star disentangles when one of them forms a new entanglement with particles in the eye of a human observer.

It seems to be an anthropic fact that we see unique states and not superpositions of multiple states. If a system is in a mixed state prior to measurement and we then measure it, it is a fact about humans that we now see only a single state. We occupy a single state, and we entangle with the set of possible future states and thus change their probabilities relative to our own state, until the probability of one possible state becomes unity and the state is actualized for us. It is a corollary of our rational grasp of reality that we occupy a single extended state. At the quantum level, reality may dissolve into a foam of entanglements and mixed states, but as quasi-classical observers we do not experience the foam directly. Instead, we surf over it in a series of logical jumps until we have brought it to the synthetic unity of apperception. But this answer raises problems of its own. For example, do the apparently future states have any spatiotemporal location at all prior to our locating them in the *now* zone? Is everything beyond the *now* world merely virtual?

However, we may see unique states simply because they are unique. The wave function may undergo what Penrose calls objective reduction at a scale determined by quantum gravity.[13] His idea is that since superposed states coexist in a shared spacetime, any states that differ by an energy big enough to produce a quantum change in spacetime may trigger reduction of the wave function to realize a unique state. This proposal suggests that the transition from the quantum to the classical regime occurs at a scale characterized by the Planck energy (which is about twenty micrograms). The proposal is consistent with experiments conducted so far and is amenable to testing.

To predict the evolution of a physical world from now into the future, quantum theory suggests we should use the "sum over histories" approach pioneered by Feynman.[14] We look at all the possible ways the world can evolve into the future, which is to say all the ways with nonzero probability, and add them up, or superpose them. The result is that a lot of states interfere destructively with each other, and thus cancel, and a lot of other states interfere constructively with each other and create extended entanglements. The path the world actually takes when it evolves from the *now* state into its next state is the path that minimizes the amount of action required to get there, in accordance with a quantum principle of least action. Naturally, this story glosses over a host of tricky technical details.

Mathematical time

Traditionally, mathematics is the study of eternal objects. Working mathematicians are often Platonists in the sense that they consider the realm of mathematical objects to be eternal and independent of human beliefs and choices.[15] This traditional view is hard to maintain in an evolutionary epistemology. The fact that no reference is made to time in the specification of mathematical objects and the systems they form does not suffice to make them eternal. Yet the status of mathematical objects is quite different from that of physical objects. And one corollary of the traditional view is surely right: given certain axioms and rules, consistency requires that only certain theorems may be derived from them. Yet the choice of axioms and rules is in part arbitrary.

Following Frege's work on the foundations of mathematics, it has become increasingly clear that mathematics is logic plus certain ontological assumptions, which are typically expressed as axioms and rules in a more or less formalized syntax. Given an initial ontology, the practice of mathematics is then in large part a formalistic game in which truths relative to that ontology are made explicit through a process of computation, which is not a very creative process. The creative aspect of mathematics is to comprehend ontologies that turn out to be fruitful in practice.

The concept of time has a logic that requires a certain amount of ontological baggage, which at its minimum is already instantiated in a simple line of numbers. The elementary act of counting natural numbers is a good formal prototype for a temporal process. In this simplest logical model for time, there is a first moment (represented by the number zero or one) and time is discrete, but already there is scope for an infinite future and for a flow from future to past via the present moment (represented by the number currently in the counter). A first model of infinite divisibility is represented by the rational number line, and a model permitting arbitrary specification of time points is available with the real number line.

The process of doing mathematics may be seen as a psychological process. A subject manipulates tokens in time. The tokens represent elements of an ontology that appears to be eternal. From an evolutionary perspective, the ontology is the outcome of a temporal process with a quite different timescale from that of the manipulations of any given human subject. The stability of the various kinds of numbers seems to transcend that of the physical universe, yet because we denote mathematical objects with syntactic tokens that have contingent limitations, we cannot guarantee absolute stability. For example, the limitations of our syntax for natural numbers (say via binary sums of ascending powers of two) and the mechanisms we have at our disposal to manipulate that syntax (such as logic gates in electronic computers) set a probabilistic upper bound to the numbers we can reliably specify. Somewhere beyond the numbers we use, the landscape of numbers fades off into an indefinite blur.

This is relevant to the concept of time. The future is not necessary sharp as far out as we care to imagine. Indeed there is no reason at all why it should not become a blur surprisingly soon after the present moment. For example, just as predicting the exact future evolution of a microphysical system can become impossible beyond a small fraction of a second, so the future in general may simply be undefined until it becomes actualized in the present. Thus we may see our successive acts as creating not only forms in time but also the moments of time itself.

A mathematical metaphor exists to make this intuition more precise. The metaphor uses a mathematical tool that is about a century old and may soon rival in fruitfulness the number systems that have supported the growth of science since the time of Galileo. This tool is set theory, which as a formal axiomatic theory sits in a toolkit alongside more specialized tools such as topos theory and category theory. In brief, the metaphorical power of set theory is to replace "the view from nowhere" with the view from anywhere, in the following sense. We can use sets to articulate a new concept of time, to recast physics in a way that accommodates time flow, and to model the evolution of a rational subject.

Axiomatic set theory grew as a response to the paradoxes of naïve set theory. Naïve set theory was pioneered by Boole and Frege, and is based on the idea that any grouping of given elements, however specified, defines a set. Sets can be members of sets, and structures of sets can be arbitrarily complicated. Russell discovered the paradox that the set of all sets that are not members of themselves is a member of itself if and only if it is not a member of itself, and soon the whole of set theory was revised thoroughly to give it more rigorous foundations. The result, a century later, is a more or less widely accepted set of axioms, formulated in first-order logic, whose natural or intended model is a cumulative hierarchy based upon the null or empty set.[16] This hierarchy suffices as a formal ontology for practically all of mathematics.

The cumulative hierarchy is ontology at its most abstract. All its elements are ranked, starting with the null set at rank zero, continuing with its unit set at rank one, then with two sets at rank two, namely, first, the unit set of the unit set of the null set and, second, the pair set of the null set and its unit set, and so on to infinity. Each indexed level of the hierarchy accumulates all ranks up to and equal to the index of that level. At each level, the universal set for that level (which following von Neumann may be called the V-set for that level) is the set of all sets of lesser rank, and has as its subsets all sets of lesser or equal rank.

The key construction that generates the cumulative hierarchy is the power set construction. The power set of a given set is the set of all its subsets, including the null set and the given set itself. If all the sets so far are finite, the result is a potentially infinite cumulative hierarchy of hereditarily finite sets that suffices for a large body of practical mathematics, including that required to pursue the computational physics of a universe of finite worlds defined over a discrete spacetime.

Mathematics is sometimes defined as the science of the infinite. When sets become infinite, the going gets tougher. Cantor's great contribution was to see that if two infinite sets have the same cardinality when they can be mapped one-to-one to each other, then the cardinality of the power set of a given infinite set is strictly greater than the cardinality of the given set. Thus the cardinality of a countable set like the set of natural numbers is less than the cardinality of its power set, and so on. Hence there are infinitely many different infinite cardinalities and the cumulative hierarchy is a transfinite structure.

With this step, set theory became mathematically challenging, and no-one knows how far into the realm of transfinite sets it can be built up consistently. For example, we do not know whether or not the cardinality of the power set of a countable set is the next transfinite cardinality above the cardinality of a countable set. The assertion that it is the next is called the continuum hypothesis. What we do know is that if the hierarchy is built up in a constructive fashion, which is to say by building always from given elements, always making minimal existence assumptions, the result is Gödel's constructive hierarchy in which the continuum hypothesis holds.[17] We also know that the universe can be "forced" to disobey the continuum hypothesis.[18] Numerous axiom systems exist, many of them agnostic on the continuum hypothesis, and the current favorite, ZF (Zermelo–Fraenkel) set theory, is just one among many options.[19]

Physicists who accept a discrete spacetime and regard information (and logic too) as related to physics are likely to question the need for transfinite set theory. But the concept of a limit, whereby an infinite continuation of a discrete process is taken as a conceptually completed construction, leads immediately to closed infinite sets and hence to the diagonal construction that generates Cantor's transfinite paradise. The concept of a limit is central to the infinitesimal calculus, and hence to complex analysis, which is still the main mathematical tool and foundation of theoretical physics. So ZF set theory is worth taking seriously.

In this picture, there is no ceiling at all to the cardinality of the universe of sets. Indeed the idea that there is a fixed universe of sets is paradoxical, since the universe would itself be a set, namely the set of all sets, and standard axiom systems such as ZF forbid any set from being a member of itself. In such systems, any attempt to define a universe of sets defines a V-set that is comprehended as an element in a more powerful theory, albeit a logically more perilous one.

It was a central plank of Quine's philosophy that any ontology may be mapped into an ontology of sets. The entities comprehended in any physical theory, or any scientific theory at all, if they are seen sufficiently abstractly, and if the theory is well defined and consistent, may be regarded as formally equivalent to the sets in some initial segment of the cumulative hierarchy.[20] The principle used here is that set theories with models in proper initial segments of the cumulative hierarchy are consistent. The difficulty is that proving their consistency requires the additional resources of set theories that can only be modeled in larger initial segments of the hierarchy. For theories whose smallest models are transfinite, proving their consistency requires theories whose own consistency is less assured than that of the theories for which they provide the putative proof.

This has consequences for a general theory of cognitive subjects in a physical universe. Any such subject can be represented logically by a suitable initial segment of the cumulative hierarchy. This may seem bizarre, but the idea is simple enough. A rational subject brings a cognitive landscape to a synthetic unity. If all the elements of that landscape are formally mapped to sets that have ranks below a certain level and hence are members of the V-set for that level, the subject may be mapped to that V-set. The growth of the subject into the future is then analogous to realization of successive V-sets, and the corresponding moves in time are analogous to counting through the indexes for the levels of the cumulative hierarchy.

The argument here works generally, both for the transfinite V-sets that believers in continuous spacetime need for their mathematical foundations and for the hereditarily finite V-sets that suffice for computational physics in discrete spacetime. But finite sets are much easier mathematically. Anyone impressed by Wolfram's advocacy of computational modeling as "a new kind of science" to replace the sciences based on the infinitesimal calculus and the metaphysics of the classical continuum will be happy to forget transfinite sets and work with finite worlds in the countable universe of discrete mathematics.[21]

Epistemological time

From an epistemological perspective, time is the dimension along which the knowledge of a rational subject evolves and in general grows. And as Popper pointed out, modern epistemology is the philosophy of science. Scientific knowledge does not simply accumulate but takes on new shapes that embrace what came before in new and often surprising ways. A temporal asymmetry is always evident. We can know past events but we cannot know future events. A structure of scientific knowledge is a logical structure (constrained to maximize consistency) in which knowledge of past events is put into some kind of order. If it is well adapted, such a structure need not be fundamentally revised every time new events are added to the growing past. The creative aspect of doing science is to adapt the structure of scientific theories in such a manner as to achieve precisely this stability in face of new facts.

The appearance of illusion in the passage of time that so impressed Einstein arises in part from the extent to which scientists have succeeded in achieving this stability in face of new facts. It appears as if the theorizing is already done and all that remains is to add details within the existing frame. But any major revolution in the history of science provides evidence that epistemology is not so simple. New vistas open out, and in the process old facts often gain new significance. Old facts can also fade into insignificance and even get lost, as a body of knowledge develops an independent life that survives robust encounters with awkward details.

This illustrates a feature of the temporal evolution of knowledge that merits careful attention. To model an evolving cognitive subject simply as a growing pile of V-sets is to ignore the revisionist and revolutionary aspects of new knowledge. A more indirect model is required. More carefully considered, a subject may be represented by a potentially arbitrary construction using the resources available within a V-set. Such a construction may represent the subject ignoring or forgetting aspects of previous experience, or reprocessing certain elements of experience so as to refashion the epistemic landscape. The formal resources of set theory allow any amount of such indirection. The temporal accretion of elements representing experience onto the growing pile of sets representing a developing history is analogous to the ongoing flow of input data to a computer. The computer may process that data in arbitrarily complicated ways to generate output that looks new and surprising.

Essential to the model of the temporal subject presented here is that a subject is defined by reference to the past and not the future. On the basis of a given past, the cognitive subject moves into the future and realizes new forms of subjectivity. This epistemic process is analogous to a physical process of growth or change, and we can describe it in terms of the fundamental process of symmetry breaking. Each momentary form of a subject remains embedded as a historical part of all possible futures of that subject. Logically, a future timeline includes possible future states of that subject if and only if it has an initial segment representing that history. The evolving subject represented by that initial segment has a symmetry with regard to those futures, which is broken when the subject evolves into a later form with a longer history, relative to which only a subset of those formerly possible futures remain possible. As time passes, the set of possible futures must be consistent with an ever longer and therefore more restrictive history.

To illustrate this point about symmetry by analogy, an object is more symmetrical when it looks the same from a wider range of perspectives, and an object can lose symmetry when it changes. For example, the symmetry of a ball is such that it looks the same from all angles, but it loses that symmetry when we paint a blob on it, since it now looks different from some angles. Similarly, a subject with a given history is consistent with a certain range of possible futures, but it loses consistency with part of that range when it evolves into a state with longer and more specific history. The additional historical facts are like the blob on the ball.

This issue is closely related to probability and entropy. A history may be encoded as information, and in general a longer history requires more information to encode it. Information is negentropy, so if more information is required to specify the state of a system then the entropy of that state is lower. If the different states of a system that are each specified by the same amount of information have equal probabilities to be realized, it follows that states with higher entropy have higher probabilities to be realized. Thus the epistemic state of a cognitive subject with a longer history, encoded as more information, has a lower entropy and hence a lower probability.

There is an apparent paradox here. As time passes, a system grows a longer history and hence become more improbable and loses entropy. Yet it is a central truth of thermodynamics that entropy tends to increase with time. To resolve the issue, we need to distinguish generic states from specific states, or in the terminology of thermodynamics, macrostates from microstates. Given a fully determined system, a generic state or macrostate of that system specified by less information is more probable than a less generic state specified by more information, because it is consistent with a larger number of fully specific states or microstates. If the system itself starts out in a relatively generic initial state with a short history and goes on to accumulate more "intrinsic" determinacy as it evolves in time toward a final specific state with a full history, then the later states of that system are more improbable. The earlier states of the system may be seen as more generic because they are consistent with a wider range of more specific future states, and the states of the system become less generic as time passes since more information is required to specify them. This is quite unlike the usual thermodynamic scenario, where an initial highly specified state evolves into a more random state that can be described approximately as a more generic state. So in fact there is no conflict with thermodynamics.[22]

Cosmological time

The account of time developed here is applicable quite generally, to cosmology no less than to the experience of a humble cognitive subject. The accounts of symmetry breaking and entropy apply unchanged on a universal scale, and carry the intriguing suggestion that the initial state of the universe, far from being maximally improbable as in the conventional modern story, was minimally informed and therefore maximally symmetric and maximally probable, but other aspects of the story invite further elucidation.

Any physical theory presupposes a background mathematical theory of some sort. Most physical theories are based on a fairly large body of mathematics, including number theory, complex analysis, and so on. Any such body of mathematics can be founded upon set theory, and more particularly upon the theory of some initial segment of the cumulative hierarchy such as the segment that serves as the natural model for ZF set theory. This is quite a lot to take on trust, and a philosophically well motivated cosmology would do well to start with less.

A logical cosmology can start with time and almost nothing else. As initial ontology it can take a single set, the universe, at level zero. This initial set is the null set, which falls into the first moment of time and thus becomes distinct from the universe, which is now determined as the level-one V-set whose only member is the null set. Given any existing levels filled with sets of given ranks, the universe is the superset of all the sets that can be built up from any of those ranked sets. Thus, by recursion, transfinite or otherwise, we build up a formal universe with a rich time dimension. This growing formal structure can be instantiated as a series of evolving physical entities in accordance with a standard big-bang story. In a story where spacetime is discrete and the total number of actualized worlds is always finite, the universe is always represented by a hereditarily finite V-set.

The special merit of this logical cosmology is that the mathematical entities do not exist in a shadow realm decoupled from physics, but arise with the physical universe in a cosmic bootstrap process. The bootstrap here is logical, and is required for a sequential account of cosmology that starts from a null description, independently of nature of the primordial state itself. The guiding idea here is that logic can only apply after the primal chaos reveals a first binary contrast. If spacetime is discrete, the total amount of information in any world with a finite history is always finite. It may be the case that logic cannot generate arbitrary levels of complexity in such worlds, but only complexity limited by the available information.

Essential to this story is that it is open-ended toward the future. Such a universe does not exist as a fixed formal structure, as in the "block" universe of classical relativity. It cannot exist as a closed structure, on pain of the sort of paradoxes that plagued naïve set theory a century ago. Models of time in an open-ended universe may represent closed futures with arbitrary levels of plausibility, but plausibility is not truth, and the only decisive test of any theory about a future state of affairs is to wait and see if that state of affairs is in fact realized. Scientists who favor a block universe are favoring a model that is ineluctably hypothetical.

Nevertheless, the open view of time is open to debate. Given the extremely exact and consistent corroboration of physical accounts of time in all areas of physics, we are strongly tempted to accept the conventional physical definition of time as absolute and abandon any remaining reservations as philosophical confusions. Time is what clocks measure and clocks are physical mechanisms, we are tempted to say, so belief in an open future and radical doubts about physical models are examples of prescientific thinking that merely betray lack of trust in physics.

Yet logic and mathematics tell a deeper story. Physics ignores the subject, and physical science articulates a view from nowhere. Logically, an appealing account of subjectivity is that subject and object are equal and opposite. Spelled out more fully, the rational subject of Kantian metaphysics is the reflective counterpart of the act of apperception that brings the manifold of phenomena to a synthetic unity. Each new realm of phenomenal content transforms the subject in a cognitive interaction that shapes both seen and seer. An ongoing subject is reflected in a series of momentary worlds that accumulate to build up a history. The transformations of this raw content in consciousness may be dramatic, so that the subjectively experienced result may bear little evident relation to any underlying physical process, but in principle the link remains as a tight coupling at some level. Views of the subject that lack such tight coupling run the risk of postulating a metaphysical ghost that drifts free of any plausible physical embodiment.

The mathematics of set theory can be deployed to back up this view of the subject. Any consistent universe of sets tops out in a V-set that reflects the universe so far. Yet we can count beyond any such V-set. In terms of time, any consistent view of the physical universe represents it at some time, as some specific world centered on a specific event, but time goes on and leaves that event behind. Any consistent view of the subject must be amenable to a similar logical argument.

In set theory, the topmost V-set as well as any sets with the same rank as that V-set are what set theorists call proper classes.[23] Any set has two sides: seen from below it is a class and seen from above it is an element. Every set is the class of its members, and its members are elements. On this view, proper classes are just those sets that are not yet recognized as elements. Conversely, a proper element does not have a class side. In pure set theory there is only one proper element, the empty set. This complementarity of classes and elements in set theory is strictly analogous to that of subject and object in ontology.

The complementarity is reflected directly in natural language. A typical informative sentence has a subject–predicate form. And an easy way to motivate naïve set theory is to say that a set is the extension of a predicate, which is to say a set is the class of all elements that satisfy the predicate or for which the predicate is true. Thus a standard way to go about generating semantics for natural language in set theory is to map a sentence in subject–predicate form to a formal statement asserting that the element or elements denoted by the subject of the sentence is a member or are members of the class representing the extension of the predicate.

We may readily go a step further and map the epistemic advance expressed by an informative sentence to a formal advance in the cumulative hierarchy from an initial level locating the element or elements denoted by the subject of the sentence to a final level locating the class denoted by the predicate. That is, the initial epistemic state required to provide a denotation for the subject of the sentence is still fuzzy in at least one regard, namely the regard specified in the predicate of the sentence, and the quantum of "defuzzification" provided by the sentence is precisely the difference between the initial and final epistemic states. In this story, both members of the pair of epistemic states are required to give a full semantic account of the informativeness of the sentence.

In physics, the open-ended cosmology suggested by set theory is currently under active technical investigation in connection with the quest for a consistent quantum theory of gravity. Conventional quantum theory presupposes a fixed background spacetime. Quantum field theory admits the equivalence of inertial frames defined by the Lorentz transformations and hence incorporates special relativity, but it still requires that distinct possible future distributions of mass-energy be regarded as superposing and interfering with each other in a single background spacetime. By contrast, general relativity requires that each distinct distribution of mass-energy corresponds to its own differently curved spacetime. In the classical picture of continuous spacetime, it is hard to see what criterion could be used to determine when spacetime branches into distinct configurations.

The causal set theory pursued by Sorkin and others represents a new approach to building a quantum theory of spacetime.[24] According to the causal set hypothesis, time is a process of becoming that corresponds to the continual birth of new elements of spacetime. In this approach, a discrete manifold embodies the metric relationships of spacetime and the structure of the manifold determines the temporal ordering of spacetime events.

A causal set (causet) is a discrete set of elementary events. A partial order is defined over the elements of a causet, where physically this ordering corresponds to the relation of *before* and *after* in time. In terms of causality, a given event is before another event if and only if the first event can in principle exert a causal influence on the second event.[25] A discrete world defined by a *now* event and its past light cone is an example of a causet.

This structure suffices to define a good approximation to the geometry of spacetime.[26] In general relativity, the local geometry of spacetime can be defined by ten numbers specified at each spacetime point. Nine of these numbers are determined by the light cone for each event. Knowing which events come before which others, as defined by the partial ordering, is equivalent to knowing the light cones. Thus if we know the causal ordering among events, we know nine of the ten numbers. The tenth number specifies spacetime volume. For causets, the spacetime volume of a region is simply the number of causet elements comprising that region.

The partial ordering that defines a causet is a pattern of ancestral relationships such that a given element is an ancestor of another element if and only if the first element temporally precedes the second. The development of a causet is a growth process in which elements are born one at a time. The growth starts from nothing, and each element that comes into being is born with a definite set of immediate ancestors. An element cannot be born before any of its ancestors, but otherwise the birth order is arbitrary, so different possible growth sequences are equivalent. In continuous spacetime, this equivalence corresponds to general covariance (which forbids a priori individuation of the points of a spacetime manifold as spatiotemporal events). For causets, it leads to a family of dynamics called classical sequential growth models. Work is ongoing to produce a quantum version of these models.

A successful prediction based on the causet view is that the finite stretch of time from the big bang to now corresponds to an energy uncertainty that is similar in size to recent empirical estimates of "dark energy" based on the accelerating expansion of the universe. This prediction suggests that the search for new sources of "dark energy" will fail to find any.

The puzzling issue of entanglement gets a new look in an open-ended cosmology. Spacetime grows discretely as new facts pop into existence. Measurements create new facts. Measurements that reveal nonclassical correlations between objects at separate locations can be interpreted as creating the separation. That is, the facts of such correlations first become local when measurements locate them. Two particles with a common origin retain a shared quantum state that causes a measurement of one of them to reveal a fact also about the other. The new interaction breaks the shared state and entangles the interacting particle with the measuring system – and also establishes a new spatiotemporal location for the interacting particle. The new location both breaks the correlation and creates the separation, and the apparent nonlocality of the correlation gets a natural explanation. This new look to an old and hard problem is encouraging for the causal set view of spacetime.

The general idea behind this new view of spacetime is that the *now* we experience as conscious subjects defines a wavefront in the growing cosmic network. The universe is only visible as a momentary world, with its own definition of *now*, and as the universe evolves around us we see a succession of worlds and a changing *now*. Metaphorically, our conscious lives surf on an advancing cosmic wavefront of crystalization marking the ongoing transition of possibilities to actualities.

Psychological time

The abstract and formalized rendition presented here of the subject is proposed as the central concept of a scientific psychology. To generalize Wittgenstein's assertion that "I am my world," the world is a world for a subject, and the idea of a world without a subject makes no sense.[27] The first subject is the knowing self, and that self is primordially coterminous with its world. Only later, with growing psychological sophistication, does a self learn that the world extends far beyond consciousness and includes other selves.

Correspondingly, in physics, only with the twentieth-century revolutions that superseded the solipsistic world view of Newtonian mechanics (with its absolute space and time implicitly reflecting a Kantian transcendental subject) has it become accepted that there is a plurality of worlds and that the time line is not a single rigid ruler for all purposes. The quantum revolution forced acceptance of possible future worlds, on a virtual par with each other, whose ongoing interaction generates a series of unique actual worlds.

Yet talk of worlds must be disciplined if the parallel and possible worlds of quantum theory are to be reconciled with the worlds of consciousness in Jamesian psychology.[28] The dated physical world defined by a causal nexus of events filling a past light cone represents a drastic transmutation and conceptual reduction compared with the worlds of human consciousness. In a fuller account, we need to recognize worlds at different levels. The set of photons that has impinged upon a given human being up to a given point in time is unique to that person, and this fact already ensures that the worlds of consciousness that collectively define a person are also unique to that person, but at a more macroscopic or generic level all humans share the same series of dated worlds. And given the highly adapted structures of our means for accommodating changes in time without having to rethink everything, at a yet more macroscopic or generic level we all inhabit a single shared world, or rather what we regard as a unique universe. Fine distinctions between microlevels and rough, pragmatic aggregations into macrolevels are among the everyday tools we deploy to bring different kinds and levels of unity to our variegated experiences. The stability of the background logic and physics for this picture offers no reason to deny its dizzying polymorphism at the psychological level.

Each world is centered on an event. The instantiation of the world as a state of affairs is a fact, and given that fact, the local state at the apical event has probability one. The fixed event states in the past light cone for that event also have probability one, and the causal nexus they form may be seen at the appropriate macrolevel as entangling all those events into a single massive fact, which is equivalent to the conjunction of a vast number of atomic facts. As subjects centered on the apical event for a world, we entangle with its quantum spectrum of possible futures and realize a definite state, defined *post facto* as having probability one, which becomes the new world of our next incarnation. Thus we incarnate ourselves in a succession of momentary factual states, ordered along an epistemo-ontic dimension that we experience as time.

As human subjects, we do not experience the physically fundamental quanta of time directly. Our windows of specious present define a psychological *now* with a fuzzy duration of somewhere between many milliseconds and many seconds, depending on the granularity of *now* that best makes sense of our experience. This granularity is related to the size of the cycles of action and reaction that characterize our dealings as human agents, and is certainly remote by many orders of magnitude from the underlying quantum physics.

More generally, the specious present of human consciousness is the basis for all subjective apprehension of physical time spans. Crudely, any time span entertained in any way by a person corresponds via some symbolic mapping to a span of *now* in consciousness, and as a matter of logical principle any symbolic mapping is as good as any other for assigning a specific duration to *now*. For example, a person gazing into a starlit sky and reflecting on the cosmos may regard *now* as an era spanning billions of years. It is not obvious that this is any less realistic than measuring *now* in milliseconds, or in Planck intervals. In any case, the logic is the same. A landscape realizing some ontology is regarded as present, and is preceded by a past landscape. Ahead, possible future landscapes represent changes relative to the present. The envisaged sequence of landscapes is always a series of symbolic constructions.

Relatively recent research reveals that this series of symbolic constructions is realized or implemented in neurophysical processes with millisecond timescales of their own. Libet's discovery that those processes may begin hundreds of milliseconds before the conscious deliberations they implement suggests that the levels of symbolic coding between the first neural operations and the introspected results are built sequentially in a substantial computation that remains largely below the threshold of consciousness.[29] This in turn suggests that the symbolic unification achieved in the synthetic unity of conscious apperception is merely the tip of a computational iceberg.

To generalize the picture yet further, humans recognize levels of subjectivity. The shared subjectivity of human societies finds various representations in science and culture, for example as popular creation stories for the universe or as economic or religious models of how a society should be organized, but this level of subjectivity is generally widely separated from that of individual human beings living their everyday lives, who may have very personal perspectives and beliefs. A first recognition of this separation is deeply entrenched in the view of the self prevalent in societies where a universal deity represents an ultimate level of shared subjectivity. In such societies, it is by no means obvious how the personal self relates to the universal deity. Certainly, no simple mapping in set theory suggests itself. In general, then, hierarchies of subjects may be as complex as hierarchies of objects, and human subjects may be embedded deeply within such hierarchies.

Multiple levels of subjectivity are also deeply internalized within individual humans. Each of us is capable of adopting different perspectives to suit our circumstances, and in the process sliding up and down between levels from generic or cosmic to specific or personal, but each of us also holds at least two contrasting perspectives permanently in mind. Roughly, we each realize our own lived world from below or within and our own living self from above or outside.

We experience our own reality from within, cognitively or introspectively, when we internalize a model of an entire world, or in philosophical terms an intentional representation of the external world, as our apprehension of how things are or how reality seems to us.[30] This apprehension surfaces in consciousness but is partly unconscious. We project this model world onto the external world of our sensorimotor interaction without bearing constantly in mind that what seems to surround us is essentially a model that we have adapted over a lifetime of mostly unconscious fine-tuning to fit the ongoing stream of now mostly corroborative input from the senses.

We enact ourselves as if from the outside, like a puppet, within that model world. The puppet or analog self within that world is the projected self of our deliberations and rationalizations. If the inside view is analogous to an image of an external reality on a computer screen, the puppet self is like the blinking cursor on the screen, which is to say the focal point for willed action and change. The puppet self is the locus of feelings and emotions and the agent of actions and processes that are attributed to the self. The puppet self appears in consciousness as the introspected self of self-consciousness.

These two apparently opposite views are in fact views of one and the same person, as closely matched as hand and glove. The view from within defines a standpoint or station and the view from outside defines the occupant of that station. There is an obvious set-theoretic analogy to a class and an element within that class. Indeed the adaptive fitting of self and world is precisely the iterative process of accommodation that generates an epistemo-ontic series of materialized V-sets.

To review the argument, time is the logical shadow of an epistemo-ontic process. Whether this shadow maps uniquely to the physical time of conventional theory is a secondary matter, which we may even regard as a criterion for evaluating the explanatory success of the underlying physics. The epistemo-ontic process in turn is the formal outline of a psychological process, which in humans may best be regarded as taking the contingent form of ongoing evolutionary reprogramming within a cerebral neuronet that is coupled via sensorimotor interaction to a natural environment.

A world of consciousness is a cognitive structure implemented in a cerebral neuronet. It takes the form of an information structure that we can call a virtual reality reflecting more or less imperfectly via some more or less indirect symbolic mapping the facts surrounding that cognitive agent. This virtual reality evolves more or less in lockstep with the external environment via the sensorimotor interaction that constitutes the life of the cognitive agent. The evolution is reflected as a series of momentary worlds, where each builds on its predecessors. This building process may be arbitrarily complicated and involve arbitrarily indirect relationships between layers, but all this is in principle capable of being modeled in a computer and therefore in discrete set theory. Each momentary form of the virtual reality is reflected in some V-set, where in general later forms will often be more complex and hence require larger V-sets. The picture that emerges would seem to invite implementation in robotic systems.

Recall that an axiom for this conception of consciousness is that at some level subject and object are equal and opposite. Ontologically, the most natural level for this complementarity is at rock bottom. In a discrete perspective based on quantum information theory, rock bottom may be the minimal qubits defining the elementary events that constitute reality. On this view, any sufficiently complex and dynamically interactive construction of qubits would instantiate subjectivity on a formal par with human subjectivity, and any particular state of human subjectivity would admit reduction without residue to a suitable constellation of qubits. This would imply that any finite subject may in principle be teleported as a stream of qubits, and thus travel to any future world containing a suitable resurrection machine. Conceptually, this is not so much time travel as suspended animation.

Returning to cosmology, the view that time is realized in the past and still virtual in the future concedes great ontological importance to the present. Physically, it accords a unique status to the apical event that defines a momentary world. Psychologically, given the primarily epistemo-ontic status of experienced time, it leaves open the possibility of radical novelty in the emergence of new worlds. If the cosmos is so far only determined up to *now* and the cloud of future possibilities must entangle with *now* to become bound into a definite past, then creation is ongoing and the cosmos is never complete.

Conclusion

Two concepts of time have been distinguished. Physical time is epistemologically flat in that it presupposes some more or less definite body of background physical theory, which may include special or general relativity, quantum decoherence and entanglement, and so on. Given such a background, time is defined independently of the experiences of cognitive agents. In effect, the experiencing subject of physical time is the correlate of a series of light-cone worlds. Psychological time records an epistemo-ontic process in which a self reflects a world in a succession of momentary configurations with an arbitrarily complicated logic. Psychologists may remain fairly agnostic on how that process is represented in physics. Current research indicates that in humans the process is embodied as an ongoing sensorimotor coupling with a virtual reality implemented in the cerebral neuronet.

The relation between these two views of time is obvious. Each presupposes the other. The present event of the light-cone view would make no sense if there were not some locally embodied observer at the now point to entangle with the possibilities and realize a definite factual landscape. And the explanation of human mental life in terms of brain states would make no sense without some detailed and specific background physics.

The metaphysical union of these two views may be called psychophysical. In principle, the phenomenology of time precedes its reduction to psychophysical science. In fact, phenomena seem to settle down by themselves into a specific spatiotemporal order and to bind of their own accord into the stable patterns that define us as psychic subjects interacting with physical objects. Defining time as a psychophysical category is thus rather natural.

Blinded by the Light

Christian de Quincey[1] sees light as a metaphor for consciousness. He posits a scale of consciousness running from total darkness to cosmic enlightenment. As he sees it, philosophers seem to be stuck on the binary distinction between darkness and light, psychologists focus on various levels between dim and bright in ordinary human consciousness, and people with a spiritual bent tend to yearn for a consciousness so brilliant that all fine distinctions are lost in the glare.

This is fair enough until we meet the bootstrap problem. We need consciousness to study consciousness. An inexorable recursion starts with some elementary act of consciousness such as the assertion "I think therefore I am" and rolls on to nirvana. Our logical faculties are powerless to stop the juggernaut. To revert to a liquid metaphor, we are immersed in consciousness. Dan Dennett has coined a nice pair of words for our predicament. Left alone, each of us drowns in the autophenomenology of our own consciousness, and only a heterophenomenologist can save us by mapping the horizons of our subjective worlds from outside. This rescues enough logic to give science a foothold and explain what can be explained.

The explanation leaves the big vision of the light metaphor untouched. For a transcendentalist whose enlightenment admits no externality, the entirety of creation, the whole shebang, is a single brilliant nexus of hyperconsciousness in which our everyday personal lights are mere shadows, just waiting for the day they dissolve in the radiance. Anyone who has been ravished by such a revelation will find it hard to take the scientific explanation of this or that feature of everyday consciousness very seriously. It will seem like mere stamp collecting.

Hard as it is, the interpersonal science of personal worlds is easy enough in principle. We can study with arbitrary exactitude the logic, physics, chemistry and biology of cerebral neuronets and predict the topology of subjective worlds with all the precision we have come to expect from modern big-budget science. We shall doubtless learn to map forms of consciousness and treat aberrations of awareness so reliably that our former methods of thought control will seem like shamanistic medicine by comparison. Yet a hard problem will remain.

Each one of us performs acts of consciousness every day. Anything and everything we do willfully or deliberately may be seen as an act of consciousness. Each such act is accompanied by an acting self that forms an inner horizon to the subjective world in which the act is located and has meaning. To a heterophenomenologist, the acting self may be regarded as a logical dangler to the act. If consciousness is a process that takes actors from state to state via their acts, the sheer existence of actors with autophenomenologies is a hard problem. The hard problem for the transcendentalist with a revelation of cosmic hyperconsciousness is one blindingly obvious loose end. But meaning is not the problem, contra de Quincey.

Will Robots See Humans as Dinosaurs?

Prehistory

The JCS report on the ASSC10 conference at St Anne's College, Oxford, in June 2006, by Claude Pasquini,[1] was delightfully evocative of a delightful conference. But I was startled to read this dramatic paragraph:

> 'Just like these guys' – Andrew Ross pointed to the giant skeletons of the dinosaurs – 'are now the remnants of our distant past, we humans will be the remnants of the distant past of robots which will replace us humans. From the point of view of those future machines the world as we know it will be their primeval soup and humans will have been some biological dirt one could dispense with.' [2]

These are not my exact words, of course, but Pasquini has captured the general sense (or nonsense) of my proclamation quite nicely. The question is whether we should take this sort of utterance seriously. Is there any good reason for believing such ideas? I think there is, and with your indulgence I shall now try to explain.

Robots

The future is hard to predict, but the robots we now build will almost certainly soon be seen as primitive machines. Consider how we now see museum specimens of the machines built only a few decades ago, which our grandparents regarded as the first forerunners of spaceships that would colonize the solar system and so on. Every generation has its utopian visions, it seems, and ours is no exception. Our collective vision, suggested by numerous science-fiction movies as well as by technology futurologist Ray Kurzweil,[3] is apparently that robots in some form will overshadow us not only in high-tech factories but also more generally.

The basis for this idea is a generalization of Moore's law that has some initial plausibility. Moore's law, to remind you, is the claim that the electronics industry will continue to double the speed and component count per chip of integrated circuits every eighteen months or so for many years. Formulated by Gordon Moore,[4] this "law" still reflects the facts quite well, and is expected to do so for another few doublings at least. This kind of exponential progress is visible in the initial histories of many new technical developments, such as in the performance of cars or aircraft, although the doubling time of the microelectronics graph is shorter than that of any previous such development. Kurzweil expects similarly fast exponential growth to be evident soon in three new fields: nanotechnology, genetic engineering, and robotics.

The basis for the growth of robotics is the increasing power of the microprocessors that serve as the 'brains' of robots. As progress in nanotechnology allows continuing miniaturization of the components on those chips, robot designers will be able to build more and more intelligence into their products. Human brains have some hundred billion neurons in them, and within a decade our biggest computers will have some hundred billion logic gates in them, so in principle we shall be able to simulate, understand, and implement in hardware the higher cognitive functions of human beings.

Lest this be seen as trivializing the task of understanding our higher cognitive functions, consider how parallel developments elsewhere may converge to accelerate progress. The Blue Brain project led by Henry Markram at the Brain Mind Institute in Lausanne[5] is using an IBM Blue Gene supercomputer to create the most detailed and accurate simulation to date of neural processes in the mammalian neocortex. The neocortex is a folded layer of brain tissue that consists essentially of a large number of pyramidal columns that each contain some ten thousand neurons. The rat cortex contains a few thousand of these columns and the human cortex contains a few million of them. The project is simulating one such column. If we understand in detail how the columns work, we shall have understood in principle how the cortex as a whole works. The IBM Blue Gene contains over eight thousand processors, so the Blue Brain simulation devotes the processing power of a few hundred million transistors to the simulation of each neuron in a column. The simulation is being tuned to reflect exact results obtained from ongoing laboratory work on rat brains.

One can argue that the Blue Brain project is a 'brute force' approach to understanding the brain, but it is not the only approach currently under way. To cite just one example among many, studies involving functional magnetic resonance imaging can realistically hope to achieve in the near future a spatial resolution on the order of a single cortical column and a temporal resolution on the order of an action potential or at least a post synaptic potential.[6] These and other studies should increase our understanding of the brain in the next few years by at least as much as the work done in the last decade of the twentieth century, the 'Decade of the Brain', which advanced our understanding by orders of magnitude.

With such understanding and with nanotech supercomputers the size of a grapefruit not too far away, we can expect to be able to build robots that equal us in terms of raw intellect in the foreseeable future. The hardest question here is how to program such brutes to work intelligently and safely with people. The art of computer programming as it now exists offers little comfort. But new ideas from evolutionary programming based on genetic algorithms and approaches based in outline on how humans learn such skills as how to walk and talk and how to understand what they see and hear show more promise. We can hope that such ideas will enable us to build robots that coexist harmoniously and productively alongside humans.

The other side of the story is motivation, and there the message is clear. Numerous well funded groups worldwide are building robotic systems for a wide variety of purposes, from domestic tasks such as vacuum cleaning through routine tasks such as driving vehicles over natural terrain to more telegenic tasks such as playing football at tournament level. Purely military applications bring more funding to the table. Pentagon projects for unmanned combat air vehicles involve massive robotics investment and bring readily defensible benefits in terms of delivering ordnance precisely on target without risking pilots. More benignly, medical robots slaved to a surgeon working through a remote interface can already perform operations beyond the ability of unaided humans. In all these ways, we are welcoming robots into our lives as fast as we can.

Humans

For all its faults, this is a golden age in the history of *Homo sapiens*. We have achieved unprecedented knowledge of ourselves and our past, as well as our natural environment in the physical universe, and realized just how insignificant we are in the cosmic perspective. Yet despite this humbling knowledge, we are still able to see ourselves as lords of creation, in the sense that we are not yet aware of any creatures anywhere whose powers essentially exceed our own.

There are two main ways in which this could change. Either we could discover extraterrestrial planets hosting advanced civilizations that make their presence known to us in ways we cannot or dare not imagine. Or we could build robots that build more robots and so on to build beings whose powers transcend our own.

Given the astronomical distances between earthlike planets and the discouraging effect of that distance on any communication between them, as well as the fact of our cosmic isolation to date, it seems quite likely that our demise as lords of creation will be our own doing. We can either endure an ignominious demise, as we blow each other up or drown in our own toxic waste and get replaced by a master race of cockroaches, or we can enjoy a more decorous demise, like that of parents who give up all they have to their children. More likely, some of us, those who build and control the robots, will retire decorously to pampered communities that will be in effect human zoos, while all the less privileged will ultimately be forced to go down fighting. But now, before that parting of the ways, each of us individually has the choice of either resisting every incursion of the machines or relaxing and learning to see them as our collective progeny.

Apart from all that, there is a different and more likely way in which humans as we now know them will probably soon cease to be the lords of creation, namely that we shall learn to rebuild and improve ourselves. This is the promise of genetic engineering. Our enhanced successors may call themselves *Homo superior* and look back on us as simian old saps who were lucky to have survived as long as we did. Their superior enhancements may take them a lot further than the present state of genetic engineering would suggest. Genetic engineering is still in what we might call the tinkering phase, where methods are inefficient and our detailed understanding of gene functions and interactions is limited, but this is changing fast. In parallel with advances in nanotechnology and robotics, and building on many of the same enabling developments in science and society, progress in genetic engineering, or rather synthetic biology, will accelerate exponentially, too, until we can essentially rebuild our genomes to realize any traits we can competently design.

The key to understanding the opportunities that await us here is to remember that DNA molecules together with RNA and ribosomes function as nanoscale Turing machines and can be reprogrammed as freely as any computer.[7] All we need is a suitable set of nanomanipulation tools and some reasonable idea of what we want to do. Soon we shall be building synthetic organisms to do such things as recycle waste materials or environmental toxins. Soon after, we shall build organisms to seek and destroy tumors or rejuvenate telomeres. But these are the baby steps.

Imagine what this capability could do for people who want to "improve" themselves. Long legs, superenhanced immune systems, arbitrarily extended lifetimes, genius intellects, cosmic consciousness, pimple-free faces, and so on will be just the beginning. Whatever turns someone on will be available at a price, whether others like it or not. People will inject themselves with nanobots that seek out and upgrade their DNA to keep up with the latest fashions. In more organized societies, mass production of superman clones will be sure to follow. Soon after that, disenchanted by the random variety of species that nature has evolved, our superior cousins will doubtless embark upon some serious extermination programs.

However, the greatest benefit of all this genetic reprogramming will be that *Homo superior* will achieve convergence with machines. Instead of staring at images on screens, we shall be able to shoot the bit streams that made up the images directly to visual cortex via carbon nanotube electrodes plugged into individual neurons. Then we shall refashion the bit streams to reduce the computational load on those superior brains and thus enhance their capacity to cerebrate on the refashioned contents. And instead of controlling machines via levers and buttons, we shall rely on the nanotube electrodes to relay our thoughts to the machines. We shall drive rovers on Mars or flap our own robot wings as easily as we focus our thoughts.

The same technology will enable enhanced people to commune with each other directly, brain to brain, and, if it turns them on, to enjoy about the same transmission bandwidth between their brains as we have between our cerebral hemispheres via the corpus callosum, and thus effectively remove interpersonal barriers between each other. If used widely for daily intercourse, this will achieve for the superior beings a kind of collective consciousness. When globally networked machines become integrated as intimately as this with enhanced humans, the entire regimented and engineered ecosystem of life on Earth will become for all practical purposes a single global organism.

This is still science fiction. But the elements are compelling, for me at least, and the juggernaut of science and technology, as well as the global economic machine that supports it, is clearly moving in this direction.

Dinosaurs

The convergence of humans with machines is likely to happen both incrementally, with no sudden discontinuity, and faster than we might now expect. By analogy, consider how far we have come already, and how fast. Ten thousand years ago, people considered things like rainproof houses or warm clothing to be luxuries. One thousand years ago, false teeth and eyeglasses were still rarities. A hundred years ago, people still walked a lot and died of things like the common cold. Ten years ago, people still communicated everyday information on paper. Now most of us in the Western world can hardly imagine life without air conditioning, cars, televisions, drugs for all our ailments, schools that teach evolution and big bang cosmology, online living via email and the web, and so on.

Everything in recent history suggests that even with the crises and catastrophes that will doubtless plague us in future, the exponentially accelerating intimacy of our embrace of the products of our own technology will continue. Our successors in the not-so-distant future will probably find the prospect of life without those products simply unthinkable. Indeed if they mess up their natural environment fast enough, the sort of unaugmented lifestyles that some of us can still enjoy will become simply impossible.

We look back a hundred million years to see the dinosaurs. Given the exponential increases in the rates of evolution of new forms, either of biological species or of technological products, in the terrestrial exosphere, we need only look forward a few centuries to imagine how humans as we know them now may seem to our superior successors to be more like dinosaurs than fellow beings.

Let us imagine, then, that the enhanced humans who live in symbiosis with the machines a few centuries hence are genetically augmented to resist engineered viruses pumped into air and water to keep down the feral humans who still lurk in desert caves and jungles. These genetically enhanced symbionts communicate wirelessly via nanotech implants in their skulls, like the Borg drones in the inspired *Star Trek* stories, and do so in a global web with enough bandwidth to sustain a collective consciousness. This is worth elaborating more carefully for my more discerning readers.

Consciousness has two sides. We are conscious of an external world and we are conscious of ourselves. Nowadays, with the help of science and modern media, we know fairly well how most of our fellows see and understand the external world, and our remaining scruples about their inscruta-bility tend to fall back on such things as the ineffability of the color red or the difficulty of sharing the feelings of people from radically different cultures. As for our selves, we know that they are in part constructions of limited validity, made and remade to suit our social purposes, and based on feelings arising from a body that has its own unique constitution and history but is similar in all essentials to every other human body. If we could know each other's thoughts as easily as our own left and right hemispheres know each other's thoughts, which I believe will soon be within the bounds of technical possibility, then nothing would prevent us from claiming quite reasonably to share a collective consciousness. Nothing in our present understanding of consciousness prevents such sharing in principle, and plenty in the transpersonal tradition suggests that sharing in this way could be both benign and enlightening.

To be more specific about this enlightened community of symbionts, imagine that they live in intelligent pods that are connected into a body I shall tendentiously call the Global Online Dominion, which executes governance functions for the entire integrated and online global economic machine. Whenever the symbionts emerge from their pods, they do so in robotic exoskeletons that they plug into via nanotube implants to allow direct neural control. Further, these robotic suits interface seamlessly in turn with cars and aircraft and so on, to provide what they regard as the normal implementation of physical empowerment, as opposed to the virtual empowerment they enjoy as online agents when they are physically in their pods.

These posthuman organisms regard their robot suits as parts of themselves. We can well imagine they love their robosuits and obsess about the latest accessories for them. They think of their shrunken and repurposed biological bodies as mere cores. They see their own DNA coding rather as we see Windows, as mere functional code that is subject to overnight automatic update from a genome bank in the Global Online Dominion. For practical purposes these posthumans are inseparable from their pods and their suits. We need not pursue the fantasy further, since such ideas have been well mined by science fiction authors.

The point of this extended fantasy is that such enhanced and superior members of a global collective organism, inseparable as they are from their pods and their robosuits, will no longer think of themselves as human at all. They are more likely to see themselves as robots with soul. Their posthuman cores will serve as mere gateways to the online collective consciousness veiling what for them is the mystic union of their souls. In fact they may see themselves as angelic beings who each day become temporarily incarnate as robotic cyborgs to maintain their physical world.

Now to the crunch. These angels will sometimes contemplate the prehistory of the global organism they naturally call GOD. Perhaps they will visit museums and view dioramas representing the earlier subspecies of humans, accurately depicted in representative scenes, for example on a campsite by a beach, surrounded by old cars, messy dogs, filthy toilets, flyblown garbage, smoky barbecues, melting ice cream, and so on. They will look at the people and see flabby bellies, blotchy skins, brutish hair, clawlike nails, rotten teeth, and the like. Perhaps they will imagine the contents of those primitive minds, filled with images of hard-core sex and junk food, football and fast cars, scanty clothes and celebrity gossip, and think ... *dinosaurs!*

Hitting On Consciousness

Honderich Versus McGinn

Ted Honderich, 74, formerly Grote Professor of the Philosophy of Mind and Logic at the University of London, recently published a short book on consciousness (Honderich, 2004).[1] Colin McGinn, 57, his former colleague at University College London and now a professor of philosophy at the University of Miami, Florida, reviewed it (McGinn, 2007a).[2] The review is quite long and detailed, but the first sentences set the tone. McGinn on Honderich:

> This book runs the full gamut from the mediocre to the ludicrous to the merely bad. It is painful to read, poorly thought out, and uninformed. It is also radically inconsistent.

The review elicited a long and pained reply from Honderich, who posted his review of the review on his website.[3] Honderich on McGinn on Honderich:

> If I were to join McGinn in his habits, the word 'shoddy' would come to mind about this performance. … McGinn does not make me dream of changing a comma.

Other philosophers joined in a chattering chorus of responses, some on either side and much of it recorded in a thread on Brian Leiter's celebrated philosophy blog.[4] All this prompted McGinn to rally to his own defense.[5] McGinn on Honderich on McGinn on Honderich:

> To repeat, I found Honderich's book to be quite the worst thing I've ever read – an insult to the reader, no less – so I was duty-bound to pan it. And I did give my reasons.

Girlfriends and Nausea

The story goes deeper. In the December 21 issue of *The Guardian*, Stuart Jeffries reports that he called Honderich and McGinn to get their latest thoughts on the controversy.[6] To quote his report of what they said, Honderich described the review as "a cold, calculated attempt to murder a philosopher's reputation." But McGinn was unrepentant:

> It's not like you're hitting someone over the head with a hammer. Ted is not very good at philosophy. That's the problem. ... I know Ted and know I don't think much of him as a philosopher. But if you ask did that affect the way I wrote the review, absolutely not. ... Ted deserved it. It had to be done.

Prompted by Jeffries, Honderich ventured an opinion as to how all this may have started:

> Nobody on Earth believes that his review is not motivated by animus. To suggest the tone wasn't dictated by any history of hostility between us is crazy. ... At UCL we had a jokey locker-room relationship. But then I made a misstep. I suggested to him that his new girlfriend was not as plain as the old one, and I could see the blood drain out of his face. That was possibly the start of our frostiness.

Can we make anything of this? Well, I was acquainted with Colin's first wife Marie back in the Seventies. She and I went to the same graduate seminars on truth and meaning, where John McDowell and Gareth Evans were the stars. Marie was slim and well groomed, and I imagine she distracted the stars regularly as she sat in the front row in her miniskirt. She once told me plainly that she would rather die than give up philosophy. Perhaps Colin went downhill after that.

Be that as it may, McGinn later wrote a review of a posthumous collection of papers by A.J. Ayer, edited and introduced by Honderich.[7] Ayer was Honderich's predecessor as Grote professor at UCL. In his review, McGinn called the introduction, which was a reprint of Honderich's funeral eulogy for Ayer, "ill-written, plodding and faintly nauseating in places." And Honderich remembered those words in his autobiography:

> My old colleague McGinn ... put me in mind of someone's earlier observation that he distinguished himself not only as the Wilde Reader in Oxford but also as the Wilde Writer. Conceivably out of justified spite about a line of mine, he had earlier said in a review of Freddie's posthumous collection of essays that my memorial-meeting speech for him, reprinted as the introduction, was ill-written,

plodding and faintly nauseating in places. Was it for this reason that I was disinclined to his stuff about giving up in the philosophy of mind? [8]

For readers unacquainted with Alfred J. Ayer, a former student of his said he "was like an eighteenth-century rationalist voluptuary." Ayer lived in a world of wealth and privilege and mixed in fashionable circles. In his biography of Ayer,[9] Ben Rogers describes him as precocious and narcissistic as well as "remote from some of the more ordinary human emotions." To back this up, Rogers names dozens of Ayer's mistresses. Ayer's first book, *Language, Truth and Logic*, was published when he was 25, and achieved cult status on the strength of his militant and iconoclastic empiricism. In all his books he was merciless at finding nonsense where others saw truth, and he gained a reputation for mercurial brilliance.

At any rate, Honderich, himself no slouch in the womanizing arts, admired Ayer greatly:

> As executor with Dee of the literary estate of Freddie Ayer, it is good that the biography of him by Ben Rogers is so fine. Still the mighty little McGinn in reviewing it could write that Freddie not only never had an original idea in his life, but also never had a good idea, his own or anyone else's. I thought he had one or two. [10]

(To clarify Ted's words, he and Ayer's last wife Dee Wells were the executors.) In fact, Honderich is unusually impressed by Ayer as a philosopher, to the point that he not only dismisses Bertrand Russell's mathematical talent and ignores Ayer's own admiration for Russell's work but even inverts the usual ranking of British philosophers by setting Ayer above Russell in his personal pantheon. And recalling McGinn's nauseous reaction to the eulogy years later still drives Honderich to fury: "It's as though it was a piece of shit by some adolescent muckraker. But anyway, with that he was the first to insult me in print."

Hatchet Jobs and Terrorism

Before we descend any further, you may wonder why the *JCS* is reporting all this. As it happens, both Ted Honderich and Colin McGinn published their philosophical autobiographies just a few years ago,[11] and since I knew them both personally I wrote an extended *JCS* review of their words on themselves and on consciousness.[12] There is a lively history here that sheds light on the more serious issue of how far either of the protagonists succeeds in advancing our understanding of consciousness.

More light dawns when we recall a rhetorical shot at the younger McGinn with which Honderich spiced up his autobiography. Honderich on McGinn:

> To confine myself to standard eccentrics, ... The envy of my small colleague Colin McGinn, also vegetarian, extended even to wanting to be Martin Amis.[13]

This is a thrown gauntlet. It is also much more. Your humble reporter was once well enough acquainted with Martin Amis to know what lies behind this throwaway line. In fact, the reference to Martin is the key to understanding Colin's recent outburst of curmudgeonliness. For Martin is the English-speaking world's most terrifyingly dangerous book reviewer. With a few witty words, Martin can drive the shaft so deep that an author's reputation will never recover. You don't need to read many of his reviews to see how this works. From his assault on Norman Mailer:

> On every page Mailer will come up with a formulation both grandiose and crass. This is expected of him. It is also expected of the reviewer to introduce a lingering 'yet' or 'however' at some point, and say that 'somehow' Mailer's 'fearless honesty' redeems his notorious excesses. He isn't frightened of sounding outrageous; he isn't frightened of making a fool of himself, and, above all, he isn't frightened of being boring. Well, fear has its uses. ... Mailer thinks on his feet and writes off the top of his head. ... 'One kissed the devil indeed', says Mailer. What is he writing about? Prize-fighting? Crossing the road? 'Brutal-coarse, intimate, snide, grasping, groping, slavering ...' It turns out that Mailer is writing about book-reviewing. But then he does tend to take things personally.[14]

Maybe Colin took this to heart. For Colin, book reviewing is evidently a serious business. Unfortunately, his go at Ted doesn't look a bit like artful work with the blade. It looks like a hatchet job. Blood and guts everywhere, the would-be assassin as messed up as the target.

The first step in the task of clearing up the mess here is to identify the respective philosophical perspectives of the protagonists. Once we know where they are coming from, we can begin to evaluate their arguments in more detail.

Intellectually, Honderich and McGinn hold very different positions on consciousness. Honderich calls himself a radical externalist on consciousness. In short, as he told Jeffries, radical externalism is the view that "my perceptual consciousness now consists in the existence of a world."

McGinn thinks this is no good. As he explained to Jeffries, "Ted's saying that one's perceptual content just is that thing, a table for example. But if you close your eyes, does the table stop existing? On Ted's account it seems to, which is just wild."

By contrast, McGinn is well known as a leading proponent of the 'new mysterianism' whereby the problem of consciousness is insoluble. To quote the Wikipedia entry for "New Mysterianism", it is "a philosophy proposing that certain problems will never be explained or at the least cannot be explained by the human mind at its current evolutionary stage. The problem most often referred to is the hard problem of consciousness."

I shall not repeat what I said about McGinn's mysterianism in my earlier review of his words on consciousness, which he presents in his excellent and readable introductory monograph *The Mysterious Flame*.[15] Let me just say that one can only pity a man whose defining intellectual insight, which on his own account he experienced as if it were a spiritual epiphany,[16] was that we shall never understand the human mind.

Honderich derides mysterianism. To Jeffries, he described it as a "form of intellectual wimpishness." However, in defense of radical externalism he added, "how dare McGinn rubbish my position." Attaboy, Ted!

Mercifully perhaps, as well as continuing to advocate his "position", Honderich devotes some of his energies to cultivating the themes of political radicalism and violence that occupied him in earlier years. His post-9/11 book *After the Terror*[17] managed to earn him the simultaneous hostility of Palestinians and Jews. Astonishingly, British leftist Tariq Ali said of the book, "reading the words of Ted Honderich is a rare delight." And notoriously, in the book Honderich asserted the moral right of Palestinians to resist "ethnic cleansing" by the Israelis with terrorism, for which a Jewish leader in Germany attacked him bitterly in the media.

"To call me an antisemite was just a lie," said Honderich to Jeffries. "My first wife was Jewish, I have Jewish children and grandchildren, and I have always gone on record as a supporter of the right of the state of Israel to exist. That's why the Palestinians are opposed to me. What I don't support is Israel's expansionism after the 1967 war." He later successfully sued a student magazine that accused him of anti-semitism.

The real argument is about Honderich's radical externalism (RE). Rather than either repeat his words on RE here or struggle to write my own, both of which would be redundant in view of the fact that the entire July–August 2006 issue of *JCS* was devoted to RE, I have selected and edited seven helpful texts (A1–A7 below) that not only bring the outlines of RE freshly to mind but also present a sufficiently decisive criticism of the position to dispel most doubts. As a bonus, they convey the drama of the struggle with McGinn so well that further commentary on my part would be superfluous.

As outcome of the drama, all the evidence available to me suggests that Honderich the person will easily shrug off McGinn's assault. The more pertinent question is how well the philosophy community can accommodate such discord.

My Contribution to RE

Before we rush to judgement on all this, I have a confession to make. I may have encouraged Honderich to develop the detested doctrine of radical externalism. Whether my contribution to his work made any real difference is not for me to judge, and I would certainly not wish to claim any credit for the form in which Honderich, without help from me, finally cast his ideas, but the fact that I added some input should be on record.

It happened in Sweden, at a conference in Skövde in August 2001. I gave a talk illustrated with a colorful slide set that went down well with Ted.[18] We talked afterwards and I mailed him the slides. Later he mailed me the hastily written manuscript for his terrorist manifesto,[19] and I conveyed my forthright detestation of its propositions. In May 2002, he mailed me a draft for what became the second half of his book on consciousness and I made a few token criticisms. In July 2002, the *JCS* published my review of his autobiography.

My own view of consciousness developed over the years from 1997 to 2004, and I published the papers marking my progress in an online book.[20] In short, my view was that consciousness is the phenomenal inner transparency of a world. A world is a re-entrant logical structure that can be modeled in set theory. As inspiration for my whole approach, I found a wonderful quotation from William James:

> The axis of reality runs solely through the egotistic places – they are strung upon it like so many beads ... The world of our present consciousness is only one out of many worlds of consciousness that exist.[21]

I was also inspired by Wittgenstein, who said:

> 5.63 I am my world. (The microcosm.)
> 5.631 There is no such thing as the subject that thinks or entertains ideas. ...
> 5.632 The subject does not belong to the world: rather, it is a limit of the world.
> ...[22]

In my understanding, a world of objects appears to itself through a re-entrant logical loop, which defines a subject as a perspectival limit to that world.

Honderich avoids trying to explain mental events in terms of two components, subject and content, and says that what it is for you to be aware of a room is for there to be a certain phenomenal world out there. This seems to depart from my view that we live in an evolving virtual reality that makes intentional contact with the physical world out there. Here I believe that I am following the views of Metzinger.[23] But I suspect that Honderich did not study my approach in detail, and McGinn certainly didn't.

Seven Helpful Texts

To spare you the work of hunting for background material either online or in your local philosophy library, I present below seven texts. I have radically abbreviated the pieces and smoothed the prose as best I can. Of course, if you wish to find out what the authors really said you should consult their original texts.

The first text is my cut of a review of Ted's book by Barbara Hannan published in *Mind* in 2005, which shows that a professional philosopher can be civil about Honderich's book. The second text is my cut of a critical essay on Honderich's radical externalism by Paul Snowdon, which similarly demonstrates that one can take Honderich's position apart without resort to rhetoric. The third text is taken from McGinn's now famous review, in case you have not read it and wish to sample its contents. The fourth is a short summary based on the latest Honderichian material of the position, radical externalism, that so incensed McGinn. The fifth is the gist of Honderich's attempt to rebut McGinn's criticism blow by blow, more to give a sense of both sides than to address the issues themselves. The sixth is a part of McGinn's response to the controversy so far. The seventh and final text is a series of edited quotations from the Leiter blog in which various philosophers react to the controversy. I trust that with these seven texts you will be well equipped to draw your own conclusions about the whole saga.

A1 Hannan on Honderich

Barbara Hannan published a review of Honderich's book in *Mind*.[24] My drastically shortened and slightly tidied-up version presents some background and introduces consciousness as existence, which Honderich now calls radical externalism.

—

In *On Consciousness*, Honderich returns to various papers he wrote over the past twenty years or so and revises them to present the progression of his thought on the mind-body problem. He conceives of the mind-body problem as that of explaining the relation of mental events to simultaneous neural events. From dissatisfaction with property dualism, Honderich moved to his own union theory and then to a newer theory, which he calls consciousness as existence of a world.

Honderich concludes that Davidsonian anomalous monism accords too little causal relevance to mental properties. Neural properties do all the causal work, and mental content just hangs around doing nothing. So anomalous monism is unsatisfactory. Honderich denies that mental properties are anomalous and insist that mental properties are in a lawlike relationship with underlying neural properties. He calls this view mind-brain correlation with non-mental causation. But this seems not to solve the epiphenomenalism problem.

Honderich intended his union theory to be an improved variety of physicalism. The union theory says that both mental and neural events are physical in the sense that they are both spatiotemporal and in causal relations with perceived events. The theory unites simultaneous mental and neural events but does not explain the nature of mental events or of consciousness.

Honderich's new theory, consciousness as existence, avoids trying to explain mental events in terms of two components, subject and content. Thus he seeks to overcome cranialism, the attempt to locate mental content inside the head. Consciousness as existence is primarily a theory of perceptual consciousness. Something going on in your cranium is necessary to your being conscious, but the cranial events are not your awareness of the room you are in. What it is for you to be aware of the room is for there to be a certain state of affairs outside your head. This state of affairs, outside your head, is your phenomenal world, your mental world.

Honderich's book does not solve the mind-body problem, but it has the merit of raising central problems in a bold and provocative way.

A2 Snowdon on Honderich

In my biased opinion, Paul Snowdon's article "Honderich's radical externalisms" [25] is the best critique of RE that I have found. Paul Snowdon is the Grote Professor of the Philosophy of Mind and Logic at the University of London and the direct successor to Ted Honderich in that chair. The article was his response to Honderich's target article in the summer 2006 issue of *JCS*, where Honderich replied: "Paul Snowdon's paper is as formidable as any in this collection."

The following shortened and smoothed essay presents what I trust is the heart of Snowdon's critique of RE. I should disclose that Snowdon was my undergraduate tutor some 35 years ago for the philosophy of Kant and the philosophy of mind. It is thanks in part to his efforts that these are both fields that continue to flourish in my mental life. I have taken pains with my editing to preserve the quality of the piece in order to reassure you that all hope is not lost of achieving clarity on the important issues at stake here. For the rest of this section, "I" refers to Snowdon.

―

I want to concentrate on two questions. First, what exactly is the thesis about consciousness that Professor Honderich is proposing? Second, what are his main reasons for his proposal and are they persuasive?

Honderich says "perceptual consciousness consists in an external state of affairs." Let us read him as proposing that S's seeing the page is identical with the page's being there, where the claim that something is there is simply that it exists at the place we mean by "there". Let us assume that in the theory talk of something's being there is to be interpreted in this completely normal way. I call this thesis Radical Externalism 1 (RE1).

RE1 cannot be true. The page's being there, understood as indicated, does not contain enough to amount to the fact that S is seeing the page. The page can be there without S existing at all, or if we assume that S exists, without S's being conscious. Presumably, it should also be said that S's hearing X is X's being there, and that S's feeling X is X's being there. In these equivalences there is nothing which says what seeing X as opposed to feeling X or hearing X is.

Another problem is this. S sees the page and the page is there. But also between S and the page is a collection of oxygen molecules and so on, and where the page is there is also a large number of atoms and so on. These are all there, but are not seen. The identity theory fails to explain why amongst those things it is the page and not the rest that is seen.

RE1 also fails to explain the way the seen object is seen. Suppose S sees some water and a straight stick next to it. The stick looks straight. Next, suppose that S sees a straight stick in water. The stick looks bent. There is a difference in the perceptual situation, but in both scenes what is there is a straight stick. Thinking solely in terms of what is there does not explain the difference.

These examples locate aspects of the phenomenon of perception. We distinguish within the class of what is there between the visible and the invisible, within the class of the visible between what we do and do not actually see, and between the ways seen things look. The phenomenon is complex, and cannot be reduced simply to the being there of what is there.

So Honderich's radical externalism had better not be RE1. Honderich says, "the page's being there, and more generally your world of perceptual consciousness is things being in space and time, with such further properties as colour, and being dependent on a scientific or noumenal world underneath and also dependent on you neurally." A consistent reading would be that the state of affairs of your being perceptually conscious of some object involves both the object's being there and how you are neurally.

Let us call this thesis RE2. It leaves out the claim that neurons or neuronal events are not components in consciousness. It says of nothing else whether it is involved. It therefore fails to say something that Honderich wants to say, but perhaps it says only things that he does want to say.

RE2 seems to fit two other claims that Honderich wants to make. He insists that radical externalism does not reduce to the claim that what is there is what we perceive. And he opposes the idea that the occurrence of perceptual consciousness has a sufficient condition in the subject's brain. RE2 claims that the conscious occurrence involves external objects.

RE2 needs to be distinguished from the indisputable claim that if a subject S is genuinely perceptually aware of a G then there is a G. For example, if I actually see an ape in front of me then there is an ape in front of me. But RE2 is not a thesis about what has to be there for seeing an object to count as occurring. It is, rather, a thesis about what the conscious occurrence, the experience considered in itself, involves or consists in. RE2 claims that the experience considered in itself cannot be separated from the perceived object. Disjunctivists seem to claim this about perceptual experience. I am sympathetic to this idea.

Honderich relies on a principle that "with consciousness, what there seems to be is what there is." I call this the Positive Seems Principle (PSP). He then claims that when you see a page it seems that your consciousness consists in the page being there. Given PSP, it follows that what it does consist in is the page's being there.

It seems to me that both premises in this argument are questionable. Whether the second premise is true is a rather delicate issue. Consider how a subject might react to two questions. Suppose we ask S: what seems to you to be there in front of you? S says: it seems to me there is a page. But suppose we ask instead: what does it seem to you that your consciousness consists of? I suggest that S would in all likelihood be puzzled. I think the difficulty is that in undergoing the perceptual experience of seeing the page there is no such item as the subject's consciousness which seems some way to the subject.

The case against PSP is much stronger. Consider the example of a perfect hallucination of a gigantic pink rat. Clearly this is an episode of consciousness in which it seems to the subject that there is a pink rat ahead, but where there actually is no such pink rat. We cannot rely on PSP to support a theory of perceptual consciousness.

Honderich: "With consciousness, what there seems to be is what there is. What there seems to be is all there is." The further principle seems to be that an episode of consciousness only has a property P if it seems in undergoing it to be P. So if it is not the case that the episode seems to be P then the episode is not P. I call this the Negative Seems Principle (NSP).

A proponent of NSP must claim that each episode of consciousness seems to fulfil NSP. I suggest that this is obviously false. When I have a pain it does not seem to me that the episode has no other properties beyond those it seems to have. My pain can be improved by taking paracetamol. It does not seem so. Also, Honderich seems to think that perceptual consciousness depends on how the subject is neurally. But does it seem so?

We should not rely on PSP or NSP in developing a theory of consciousness.

I want now to engage with the idea that consciousness should be conceived of as not having any "neurons in it'" and as not having "your visual cortex in it". I want to argue both that no good reasons are presented for refusing to speak as the materialists do, and that anyway the conclusion is relatively unimportant to the metaphysics of consciousness.

If we say that your visual cortex is a part of seeing the page then it follows that there is more to seeing the page then your consciousness of it. Honderich seems to think that the problem with this consequence is that our ordinary assumption is that your visual cortex is no part of your being conscious. The materialist claims that the neural event is part of the sighting. This is like saying that part of my apple is a certain pip, which implies that there is more to know about my apple than simply that it is an apple.

Honderich adds that since dualists deny that consciousness involves brain events and we can understand their claim then "talk of your consciousness has to be understood as not itself talk of your brain." However, the materialist claim is that the referent of "my sighting" is a conglomeration of neural events, not that the meaning of "my sighting" is to be given in neural terms.

RE2 is not alien to materialism. There is no conflict. But is Honderich's radical externalism actually RE2? I suspect it is not. Honderich describes his theory as conceptual revolution. But RE2 can be seen as a form of naive realism! What then is the conceptual revolution? I have to end with an expression of bafflement.

A3 McGinn on Honderich

This is not the offending review but my shortened and smoothed version, in case you want to get some idea of what all the fuss is about but have no desire to reach beyond this journal.

—

This book runs the full gamut from the mediocre to the ludicrous to the merely bad. It is painful to read, poorly thought out, and uninformed. It is also radically inconsistent.

The structure of the book consists of a series of previously published papers, somewhat modified, with short introductory sections, going back to 1981. The first half criticizes Davidson's anomalous monism, Putnam and Burge on anti-individualism about meaning, the identity theory, and functionalism. The second half tries to develop a new theory of consciousness, according to which the positive theses of the first half of the book are all wrong. Throughout, the book is woefully uninformed about the work of others and at best amateurish. Honderich's understanding of positions he criticizes is often weak to nonexistent, though not lacking in chutzpah. And the view he ends up defending is preposterous in the extreme and easily refuted.

Honderich begins by saying it is difficult to see how the mental *qua* mental can have causal efficacy since the mental properties appear to dangle. He quickly establishes a "union theory" by asserting that anything causal must be spatial, so that mental events are also in the head next to their neural correlates. Why this is not just intracranial token dualism is not explained.

Honderich's final view is that consciousness is the world we are aware of – it is what we would normally say that our perceptual consciousness reveals. Your consciousness is actually identical to a state of affairs outside your head in the perceived environment! He assures us that he is not defending the innocuous view that perceptual awareness is intentional directedness to the environment. His view is that consciousness is the state of affairs around you. Consciousness is not the awareness of the room, it simply is the room.

He appears to be a direct realist about perception, supposing that we see objects that exist independently of us. These objects cannot be regarded as mental products of some kind. They are not supervenient on what is in the head. Yet they are what consciousness is. But if consciousness is a state of affairs existing in the perceived environment, doesn't it follow that hallucination is impossible? His answer is that there simply cannot be perceptual hallucinations.

With perceptual consciousness thus taken care of, Honderich tries to extend the theory to thinking. Here, to sum up, his theory is that thinking is the perceiving of external representations like pictures and words, plus some inner representations. But wait: you can think about something and perceive no external representation of it. And those inner representations undermine the entire picture, since he is now invoking a relation between subject and object, not just the object considered in itself.

The short reply to Honderich's existence theory is that he is confusing vehicle and content, act and object. My experience of a room is the vehicle of a certain content, rather as a word is a vehicle of meaning. Seeing is a relation to an object, rather as referring is. If Honderich has simply decided to call a state of affairs in the environment "consciousness" then the obvious reply is that this is not what we call consciousness, and we'd like a theory of that.

A4 Honderich on Radical Externalism

The following text is my unauthorized summary of Honderich's latest short account of radical externalism. He presented this account in response to McGinn's criticism, so we may take it as superseding the criticized account. Honderich already published a longer account of RE as the target article in the July–August 2006 issue of *JCS*,[26] where it appeared together with a series of critical responses. So the account in the pilloried book is now doubly obsolete. I have taken the opportunity to tidy up Honderich's prose.

—

Perceptual, reflective and affective consciousness are different. They are also of the same general kind, to give the general question of what it is for something to be conscious. Questions about the three kinds of consciousness are about your having something, or its being given to you, or presented to you.

Contemporary philosophy of mind is centrally about the general question of the nature of consciousness. There have been two kinds of answers to the question. Physicalists say that your being conscious consists in physical facts. Physicalists include naturalists, identity theorists, reductionists, monists, eliminative materialists, functionalists, and so on. Dualism makes a fundamental distinction between conscious things and things not conscious. It also comes in several forms.

There are many criteria for judging physicalism and dualism. One problem with dualism seems to be that it cannot deal with the fact of causal interaction between consciousness and physical events. One problem with physicalism seems to be that it cannot account for the primary and subjective nature of consciousness.

More particularly, what is had, given or presented when we are conscious is not in general neural activity. If we keep our minds on the analysis of what it is for something to be had, given or presented, it is inconceivable that the general answer is neural activity.

Spiritualism is quite as impossible. It is not possible to contemplate that what is had, given or presented, in general, is spirituality, mentality, or subjectivity in an elusive sense having to do with a subject or self.

My book defends a theory different from both physicalism and spiritualism, although it is near physicalism. Its first proposition is that what it is for you to be conscious of the place you are in, say the room, is for a room to exist in a defined sense, outside your head.

You and I each have something when we are both aware of the room we are in. As we ordinarily say, there is the room as you see it and there is the room as I see it. However these two things are to be understood, they are different. Your or my world of perceptual consciousness has a dependency on you or me neurally and also on external physical facts.

Take the physical world as having two parts or levels, the things in space with perceived properties not dependent on any particular person, and the things in space in lawlike connection with the first things. So the physical world is chairs and the like and atoms and the like.

Evidently your world of perceptual consciousness, like mine, is akin to the physical world in its perceived part or level. Your world of perceptual consciousness is real despite not being objective in several senses.

What is had, given or presented is a world of perceptual consciousness. Our saying this puts no self, no relation of intentionality or directedness, no sense data, no vehicle of content, and so on, into our consciousness. The theory says that what it is for a world to be had, given or presented is for it to exist. Out of the metaphors comes a reductive theory.

This theory goes further than other externalisms in the recent philosophy of mind. To the account of perceptual consciousness are added related accounts of reflective and affective consciousness. These demand different treatments. Seeing is not believing or desiring.

Radical externalism gives a conceivable answer to the general question of what it is for a person or whatever to be conscious, what it is for something to be had, given or presented. It puts no real difficulty in the way of psychophysical relations. Worlds of perceptual consciousness are as spatial as the physical world.

A5 Honderich on McGinn on Honderich

Honderich's online reply to McGinn's offensive review is quite long, quite hard work to read, and full of close references to McGinn's words. I present a drastically shortened and smoothed version here. For the rest of this section, the first person is Honderich.

—

McGinn says the book is radically inconsistent. "The second half tries to develop a new theory of consciousness, according to which the positive theses of the first half of the book are all wrong."

My aim was to republish some papers and to show some progress in thinking about consciousness. My aim was to argue for RE by showing inadequacies of alternatives, including my own earlier ones. Six papers present the alternatives:

Paper 1 rejects Donald Davidson's anomalous monism.

Paper 2 rejects a theory I call mind-brain correlation with non-mental causation.

Paper 3 rejects functionalism and advocates the union theory.

Paper 4 criticises the work of Hilary Putnam and Tyler Burge and further promotes the union theory.

Paper 5 argues against John Searle and admits that the union theory is pretty outrageous.

Paper 6 struggles to make sense of perceptual consciousness and ends with an admission of failure.

The papers make up a line of argument. The book proceeds from these unsatisfactory theories to RE, which is advocated at length in place of all of them. To believe that such a book is inconsistent would be juvenile.

McGinn says the book is woefully uninformed about the work of others and at best amateurish. "Honderich's understanding of positions he criticizes is often weak to nonexistent, though not lacking in chutzpah."

The book divides previous views on consciousness into physicalism and dualism. The fact that there is a lot of material in contemporary physicalism and naturalism does not touch the fact that there are the two traditions. Effective generalization is part of inquiry. If anyone's concern is with a general characteristic of a collection of things, it is both unnecessary and irrelevant to spend time on particulars that distinguish them. And two people can differ reasonably about what is most relevant to a question, what is of most value in answering it, even about what it is more or less essential to consider.

McGinn says that something called the union theory "attempts to paste the mental and physical together inside the brain, with mental events declared spatial and physical (though not neural)". He reports that the union theory "is quickly established by asserting that anything causal must be spatial, so that mental events – which are held to be distinct from neural events – are also in the head next to their neural correlates, as well as being physical (because spatial)" and complains that it is not explained "why this is not just intracranial token dualism (with the usual epiphenomenalist consequences)".

I object to his saying the theory of lawlike or nomic correlation between mental and neural properties is not a theory, as if a theory were something better than a lawlike explanation. He does not dispute lawlike connection between mental and neural events, or the shortcomings of alternative views.

In the union theory, mental events are spatial and of course physical, so this cannot be dualism. There is nothing in the union theory that leads to epiphenomenalism. Psychoneural pairs or unions are specified as causal with respect to later such things. There is no dualism to make it epiphenomenal.

McGinn says my view in RE is that "consciousness is the state of affairs around you ... Consciousness is not the awareness of the room (Honderich can make no sense of such 'ofness'); it simply is the room ... He also appears to be a direct realist about perception, supposing that we see objects that exist independently of us; again, how this is consistent with those peculiar neuron-dependent objects is not explained."

This report of RE is ambiguous. What RE says your perceptual consciousness consists of is sometimes the physical world, nothing else, and sometimes more or less what RE calls a world of perceptual consciousness. At the start of his review, McGinn informs his readers that RE is preposterous. But this depends on the ambiguity. One of the two propositions in question is indeed the preposterous one that your being perceptually conscious consists in the existence of the physical world. The other is not preposterous at all. The other is more or less RE, the theory in question.

McGinn objects that the mistake in RE about perception is the direct realism, the idea that perceptual consciousness is not about things intermediate between external things and something else. But RE is fundamentally different from direct realism in excluding a subject from what is given. What it is for a world of perceptual consciousness to be given is only for it to exist in the defined way.

McGinn asks: "if consciousness is a state of affairs existing in the perceived environment, doesn't it follow that hallucination is impossible? Honderich finally gets round to considering this critical question ... His answer is that his theory refutes any such possibility – there simply cannot be perceptual hallucinations."

I concede that my treatment of the argument from hallucination was not good enough. A better approach is disjunctivism, developed by Paul Snowdon and others: in taking ourselves to see things, we are either doing so or thinking we are doing so. This can be understood in terms of perceptual or reflective consciousness. Hallucination is reflective consciousness. Indeed RE leaves it open whether what we take to be our perceptual consciousness is always reflective consciousness. So RE does not vanquish scepticism or pretend to.

My book distinguishes between perceptual, reflective and affective consciousness. An adequate account of consciousness will have to give different accounts of the three things.

The account of perceptual consciousness is that what it is for you to be perceptually conscious is for what makes up a world of perceptual consciousness to be had, given or presented. When you are aware of the room, what is had or the like is not a self or sense data or some relation of intentionality, but a room.

According to RE, reflective consciousness consists in the existence of representations, these being things both outside and inside of heads that share some of the effects of what they represent. This account of reflective consciousness can thus be said to give a place to intentionality.

McGinn says: "Honderich assures us that he is not defending the innocuous view that perceptual awareness is intentional directedness to the environment … he totally rejects the whole notion of intentionality."

McGinn continues: "Honderich tries to extend the theory to thinking. Here, to sum up, his theory is that thinking is the perceiving of external representations like pictures and words, plus some inner representations. Two problems: first, you can think about something and perceive no external representation of it … second, those latter inner representations, introduced by Honderich in a sudden moment of sanity, undermine the entire picture he is promoting. He has thereby acknowledged the importance of intentionality …"

This is a shambles. The first speech is ambiguous and thus wholly misleading. The second speech is inane in the vagueness of the declaration that with reflective consciousness I am letting in intentionality. The RE picture has parts because consciousness is not simple.

McGinn says perceptual consciousness "is surely the presentation of a world (or at least a bit of one) to a conscious subject; but no such obvious thought is what Honderich is advocating. He thinks such an account would be 'circular' since it is tantamount to saying that perceptual consciousness is the awareness of a world, and we were trying to say what awareness is."

McGinn again: "The short reply to Honderich's existence theory is of course that he is confusing vehicle and content, act and object. My experience of a room is the vehicle of a certain content, rather as a word is a vehicle of meaning. My seeing the room is not the room I see but the means by which I see it; the seeing is not its own object."

These items are as close as McGinn gets to stating an alternative theory of consciousness. I say an analysis of consciousness containing unexplained occurrences of "consciousness" or the like is no great achievement.

McGinn: "Are we to assume ... that he has simply decided to call a state of affairs in the environment 'consciousness'? In which case, the obvious reply is that this is not what we call consciousness, and we'd like a theory of that."

My book proceeds in terms of criteria for an adequate theory of consciousness. We have to keep clearly in mind the primary nature of consciousness, the fact of causal relations between consciousness and physical events, considerations of subjectivity, and so on. The book seeks a conception of consciousness that satisfies the criteria.

A6 McGinn on Honderich on McGinn on Honderich

Again, I have shortened McGinn's text. For the rest of this section, the first person is Colin.

—

Honderich's reply to my review speculates about the source of my harsh judgment. He suggests that it comes from my annoyance at his remarks about me in his autobiography. I had skimmed that work, and did indeed find his comments about me (and others) myopic, tendentious and foolish. But my review was dictated by my actual critical response to the text of *On Consciousness* and not by any supposed past slights.

For those not inclined to take my word for this, supposing that really my negativity arose from personal considerations, Honderich notes, correctly, that I had much earlier (1990) in the *London Review of Books* described his preface to a collection of A.J. Ayer's writings as "ill-written, plodding, and faintly nauseating in places".[27]

The constant factor here is obviously Honderich's writing itself, not any supposed resentment on my part to his unflattering comments about me in his later memoir. I just think he writes bad philosophy badly, that's all. Indeed, the wild speculation suggests itself that Ted's remarks about me in that book may have been influenced by my earlier nasty comment about his Ayer preface.

To repeat, I found Honderich's book to be quite the worst thing I've ever read – an insult to the reader, no less – so I was duty-bound to pan it. And I did give my reasons.

A7 The Leiter Blog

Brian Leiter hosts a well known philosophy blog where on October 31, 2007, he started a thread on the already notorious McGinn review.[28] He kicked off the debate with a few words:

> Disputes about 'tone' almost always mask, of course, disputes about 'substance,' which is probably why McGinn was disinclined to 'soften the tone' since he presumably thought it properly matched to the substance. Assuming the substance of the criticisms are sound, what do readers think about the 'tone' of the review? Are the two separable? It seems to me that there are too few honest book reviews out there, and too many puff pieces. But even if one agrees with me about that one might still think McGinn's approach to this is wrong. I find McGinn's approach refreshing, but I wonder what others think?

Comments were quick to accumulate. Here are just a few edited quotations to suggest the general drift:

> I am left with the impression that the reviewer has a personal vendetta against the author of the work reviewed, which in turn leads me to become suspicious of the substantive criticisms offered in the review. (R. Vangala, October 31)

> Reviews should, in my view, serve to introduce readers to books the reviewers think are worth taking seriously, for all their flaws. (Mark Sacks, October 31)

> This sort of tone is appropriate, I think, when dealing with unserious mediocrities who are mysteriously accorded stature well beyond what they deserve in the profession. (David J. Watkins, October 31)

> McGinn is perhaps righteously angry about incompetence or time wasted, but I'm inclined to suppose it's what he regards as a frustrating fact of publication of a sub-standard work of scholarship. (Dean C. Rowan, October 31)

> McGinn's choice of words goes far beyond the informative. You can say a book has no value and should be avoided without a mocking or abusive tone. (Tony, November 1)

Public discussion of a work is probably more likely to achieve its goals if conducted on the basis, mutually understood, that errors, confusions, trivialities may be pointed out publicly but not condemned or ridiculed. (Sharif, November 1)

McGinn's tone is right on the money for reasons having to do with how contemporary analytic philosophy is perceived in the wider culture. (Paul Raymont, November 1)

If the goal is to promote higher esteem for analytic philosophy, then best avoid saying things like this when interviewed by The Times: '[Philosophers] look terrible to start with. I don't like people looking terrible. Their clothes are terrible. They will be intolerant of people whom they don't think of as at their intellectual level. People who are very nice, interesting people, they're just not interested in them.' [said McGinn] (John Turri, November 2)

I can't help feeling, having been tutored by both Honderich and McGinn at UCL and having read each of their autobiographies, that there was never any chance Colin McGinn would write an impartial assessment of Honderich's book. I suspect he knew before he picked the book up that his review would be scathing. I don't find it hard to believe that the substantive criticisms are on the mark, but I do find it hard to take McGinn's review as evidence for that fact. In fact, I've never read a McGinn review in any context without getting the sense that it's all about self-promotion. (Andrew Black, November 3)

Book reviews in our profession tend to be unreliable, erring almost always on the side of being far too generous to work that is indeed culpably deficient. (Brian, November 5)

If we don't strongly discourage negative rhetoric, we're more likely to see reviews where the focus is on rhetoric and not content. (Kris, November 5)

Fortunately, with the ease of publishing reviews on the Internet, the trend to only positive reviews may be short-lived. (Christian Perring, November 6)

The problem to me seems to be when brutal reviews are written in such a way as to raise more questions than they answer, even if the forcefulness of the critique is warranted by the quality of the book. (Simon Cabulea May, November 6)

It's appropriate for a reviewer not only to say when a book is bad, but also not to understate just how bad it is. (Keith DeRose, November 7)

The Bigger Picture

There is much to be learned about the current state of academic philosophy of mind in this unseemly tale. For me, the main lesson is that professional philosophers have no monopoly of wisdom in consciousness studies, either in writing books about consciousness or in reviewing the efforts of their peers. The *JCS* illustrates with its judicious balance of peer-reviewed articles and other texts (such as the present metareview) that consciousness studies can be enriched by reaching beyond conventional academic work.

Spare a final moment to consider the longer implications of the catfight you have just witnessed. Googling "Honderich" or "McGinn" will regularly find the two names paired with each other for the rest of digital eternity. Whether they like it or not, the two prickly protagonists are now sparring partners in cyberspace, bound in a fellowship of reciprocal contempt and vituperation. Perhaps future generations of philosophers will amuse themselves with animatronic replays of the Ted and Colin show, where photorealistic avatars trade vile words with heated fluency in comic clips.

In any case, the philosophical soil in which this debate is rooted will soon be ploughed over. I suspect that neither radical externalism nor the new mysterianism will attract much attention once we witness the arrival of the first conscious robots.[29]

Chapter Notes

Portrait of a Philosopher

1. The *Lord of the Rings* trilogy had just been released in one paperback volume (Tolkien 1968) and was already a cult classic. Other authors and themes I liked around then included Martin Gardner on recreational mathematics, Arthur Koestler and Hans Eysenck on psychology, Einstein and others on relativity, and Heisenberg and others on quantum physics.
2. Imre Lakatos submitted a Platonic dialog on the philosophy of mathematics (later published as Lakatos 1976) as his doctoral thesis when he emigrated to Britain following the Hungarian uprising in 1956. His Popperian views are spelled out more fully in (Lakatos & Musgrave 1979) and are comparable to those of (Kuhn 1971), although Kuhn's terminology is smoother.
3. The work of Chomsky and Kripke, especially (Chomsky 1965) and the lectures later published as (Kripke 1980), shaped a decade of work in philosophy, not only in America but also in Oxford and London.
4. The novel *Ulysses* is now available with a corrected text as (Joyce 1986), although the text I read was the much older Penguin edition. For me, the sheer idea of writing a long book about a single day was psychedelic.
5. My 1975 manuscript *Dialectical Logic* is now lost to me. I believe that Daniel Isaacson in Oxford still has a copy, and another copy may still exist in the philosophy department at Yale.
6. The philosophy books I reviewed were *The Central Questions of Philosophy* by Alfred Ayer (1976) and *Unended Quest* by Karl Popper (1976). My copies of the reviews have long since vanished.
7. The books were *History of Western Philosophy* (Russell 1961), *Hegel* (Taylor 1975), *History of the World* (Roberts 1976), *Wittgenstein on the Foundations of Mathematics* (Wright 1980), Karl Marx's early writings and Nietzsche's *Also sprach Zarathustra* (Penguin translations), together with the New Testament and the Koran (Penguin translations).

8. I read several serious Japanese novels (in translation), not only by Yukio Mishima but others too, as well as *The Tale of Genji* itself. And I read books on *samurai* and the Edo period, politics and economics, the language and people – most notably that fine general introduction, *The Japanese* (Reischauer 1977). And I vividly remembered my 1975 reading of Pirsig's insightful novel *Zen and the Art of Motorcycle Maintenance* (1974).
9. Anyone who wishes to read the book can find the full text on my website. Applications are welcome for the right to publish a paper edition.
10. Alwyn Scott's book *Stairway to the Mind* (1995) was edited in the Springer New York office under the Copernicus imprint, not by me, but I was galvanized when I saw it and read it. Due to illness, he was unable to attend the Elsinore meeting, but he had worked hard to organize it.
11. The T2K conference, during the climactic tumescence of the dotcom bubble, may have been the best in the series. The events in alternate years outside Arizona are smaller, and the 2002 meeting was overshadowed by 9/11.
12. The Skövde meeting in August 2001 was a good opportunity for serious work. To be isolated for a week on a rain-lashed hill in southern Sweden with only philosophers of consciousness for company – it put me in mind of Thomas Mann's novel *Der Zauberberg* [The Magic Mountain], which is set in a mountain sanatorium just before the First World War.
13. The review is reprinted in chapter 6.
14. The report is reprinted in chapter 7.
15. The essay on business at the speed of evolution appeared in the first edition of *Mindworlds* but it has nothing in particular to do with consciousness.
16. This essay is reprinted in chapter 11.
17. Penrose's *Roads to Reality* (2004) is much meatier and more interesting than his books on consciousness (1989, 1994, 1997).
18. For the record, the four omitted essays are as follows. The first was a 1985 attempt to persuade a group of Mormons that the concept of the soul could be reimagined as a software construct, and hence a Platonic universal. Another was a sketch for a book about software "angels" that owed too much to my novel *Lifeball*. Another was the one-page essay on the evolution of business software that I wrote in 2003. And the last was the edited transcript of e-mail exchanges with two medical practititioners who specialize in consciousness.
19. Ross (2009a) – my SAP book has no interest for students of consciousness.
20. Ross (2009b) – the style of *Godblogs* is conversational and the salad is well garnished with what are supposed to be amusing rhetorical flourishes.

Fundamentals of Consciousness

1. David Chalmers is the protagonist of the "hard problem" of consciousness. For the full story, see his big book (1996).
2. Daniel Dennett (1991) is the source of a lot of anti-qualia rhetoric, as well as the terms "autophenomenology" and "heterophenomenology". See chapter 6.
3. Readers acquainted with Wittgenstein's *Tractatus* (1922/61) will recognize this as proposition 5.63. See also slide 8 in chapter 5.
4. Wittgenstein's *Tractatus*, proposition 1.1, with the initial "the" replaced by "my" in accordance with proposition 5.62, sentence 3.
5. The multiple drafts model is prominent in Dennett's 1991 book and the general evolutionary idea in his 1995 book.
6. Dirk Van Dalen presents intuitionist ideas on the foundations of mathematics in his chapter in (Fraenkel *et al.* 1958/73).
7. The more recent application of constructive ideas in computer science is nicely outlined in (Gries & Schneider 1993).
8. My defining acquaintance with Gödel's incompleteness theorems came through Elliott Mendelson's textbook (1964/79). But the wider issues raised by the theorems get their ultimate airing, so far as I am concerned, in Douglas Hofstadter's astonishing fugue (1979).
9. Saul Kripke's formal semantics for intuitionist logic (1965) were decisive in persuading me to take the logic seriously. On his formal semantics for modal logic more generally, see (Popkorn 1994).
10. Paul Davies has written a lot on this general theme. His 1986 essay on time asymmetry and quantum mechanics is a more specific source for these ideas.
11. Richard Feynman argued for the importance of this contrast in the probabilistic treatment of quantum systems – see (Feynman *et al.* 1965).
12. Again, no-one has done more to promote the QED treatment of light than Richard Feynman – see his book *QED* (1985).
13. Schematic attempts at quantum accounts of consciousness are common enough. The two that got me started were (Zohar 1990) and (Stapp 1993).
14. Roger Penrose developed this idea in collaboration with Stuart Hameroff and presented it in his 1994 book. Subsequent work on microtubules by Jack Tuszynski – which does nothing to corroborate the Penrose–Hameroff hypothesis – is reported in (Satinover 2001).
15. In *The Emperor's New Mind* (1989), Penrose worked hard to argue that a quantum theory of consciousness is required to overcome the problem he sees in any computational theory of mind along classical lines.
16. The quotation is from (Penrose 1987), p. 118.

17. John Searle has written a lot on this topic, but a good presentation is (Searle 1981). You don't have to agree with him to admire his style.
18. Gerald Edelman won a Nobel Prize for work on this theme. His book *Bright Air, Brilliant Fire* (1992) popularizes his ideas on the evolution of neural groups in the individual brain.
19. Julian Jaynes created a cult classic with his 1976 book on the historical origin of consciousness. His model is now unconvincing, but as an account of the origin of *personal* consciousness, it still bears reading.
20. Willard Van Orman Quine gave Otto Neurath's metaphor a prominent place in his classic *Word and Object* (1960).
21. Famously, or perhaps notoriously, Stephen Hawking ends *A Brief History of Time* with this hope (1988, p. 175).

Consciousness: A Logical Model

1. Chalmers expressed this view in (Chalmers 1999).
2. Chalmers has made the hard problem famous. He developed it at length in his big book (Chalmers 1996) and discussed it with numerous critics in the anthology (Shear 1997). The problem has a long history in philosophy.
3. Psychology and the brain sciences enjoyed a big boost in the 1990s and now face newcomers with a daunting mountain of required reading. For example, (Churchland 1986) is a modern classic, (Clark 1997, Cotterill 1998) emphasize cognitive science, (Crick 1994) is by the DNA Nobelist, (Damasio 1999, Ramachandran 1998) emphasize clinical aspects, (Edelman 1992) is by the neuroscience Nobelist, (Gazzaniga 1998) is a handsome course text, (Greenfield 1995, Scott 1995) are elegant monographs, (Metzinger 1995, Rose 1998) are good anthologies, and (Pinker 1997) is a long but light overview.
4. Wittgenstein expounded his earlier philosophy in (Wittgenstein 1922/61), a brief and difficult text based on the logical philosophy of Frege and Russell. Later philosophers substantially enriched that foundation using semantic ideas due to Alfred Tarski and others.
5. Cantor's diagonal argument to prove that the infinity of reals has a higher cardinality than the infinity of rationals is the basis for transfinite set theory. For a readable introduction to the higher infinities, see (Rucker 1982).
6. Wittgenstein expounded his later philosophy most clearly in (Wittgenstein 1953/58). His anthropological view of meaning radically transformed his earlier views and cleared the way for modern linguistics (Pinker 1994).
7. Karl Popper stressed the importance of repeated cycles of corroboration and falsification in an evolutionary epistemology that he refined over several

decades (Popper 1972). His views were defended and developed by the contributors to (Lakatos 1979) in response to Thomas Kuhn's sociological view of normal science and paradigm shifts (Kuhn 1971).

8. Daniel Dennett "explains" consciousness with a *pandemonium* model of the mind in which our conscious states result from political upheavals within a society of cognitive demons that compete for key roles in the ongoing drama of our lives (Dennett 1991).

9. Saul Kripke reinvigorated the discussion of names and definite descriptions with his lectures (Kripke 1980), where he first described names as rigid designators. Bertrand Russell analyzed definite descriptions in 1905 thus: "The big bag is full" means "There is an x such that x is a big bag, and for all y such that y is a big bag, $y = x$ and y is full." For a fuller discussion of this and related issues, see (Dummett 1973).

10. In any active field of science, scientists freely go different ways without sacrificing the denotation of their terms. For example, in modern cosmology, Alan Guth proposes that the early universe went through a brief period of exponential inflation powered by vacuum decay and repulsive gravity (Guth 1997), Lee Smolin that our universe was borne from a black hole and is tuned to reproduce them (Smolin 1997), and Brian Greene that our universe may have 11 dimensions in a randomly fluctuating topology at the Planck scale (Greene 1999). It seems unlikely that all three stories are true (although it is conceivable), yet they all clearly denote the same universe.

11. At least, we need QC to formalize mathematics. But formal methods are necessary in such exotic fields as transfinite set theory. Even in discrete math (where uncountable infinities are banished and constructive methods prevail), formal methods track levels of constructivity and allow automated proofs (Gries 1993).

12. Frege tried to prove that arithmetic was pure logic. Today, we see arithmetic as logic plus the assumption that an infinity of natural numbers exist that satisfy something like the Peano axioms (Mendelson 1964/79).

13. Gödel's incompleteness theorem is presented fully in numerous texts, such as (Mendelson 1964/79). Douglas Hofstadter discusses it in the context of a meditation on art, music, brains, and computers in (Hofstadter 1979).

14. Gödel's second theorem is also presented in (Mendelson 1964/79). Gregory Chaitin takes the theme of undecidability in arithmetic further in the context of his algorithmic information theory: by his definition of randomness, some truths in arithmetic are random (Chaitin 1998).

15. Willard Van Orman Quine built a general philosophy (Quine 1960) on the idea that with sufficient prestidigitation we can reduce any ontology to sets. The idea works well in mathematics, at least (Quine 1963/69).
16. Zermelo–Fraenkel set theory is presented more fully in numerous texts, such as (Jech 1971/97, Mendelson 1964/79, Quine 1963/69).
17. The philosophy of set theory, its history, and its mathematical motivations are discussed in (Benacerraf 1964, Fraenkel *et al*.1958/73, Quine 1963/69).
18. The notion of comprehending all subsets of given sets is not as innocent as it seems. For all infinite sets x, there are uncountably many subsets of x. More generally, the power set of any set x has higher cardinality than x. Cantor's continuum hypothesis is that for countable x (with cardinality $\aleph_0$), the power set of x has the first uncountable cardinality ($\aleph_1$).
19. Gödel constructed his constructible universe L as a "minimal" model of the ZF axioms in order to prove the consistency of the axiom of choice and the continuum hypothesis with those axioms. Much later, Paul Cohen invented a new method of "forcing" to prove the independence of the axiom of choice and the continuum hypothesis from the axioms of ZF (Cohen 1966).
20. The von Neumann–Bernays–Gödel axiomatization of set theory is described in (Bernays 1968, Mendelson 1964/79, Quine 1963/69).
21. Hofstadter made great play in (Hofstadter 1979) with loops and self-reference, so he might like my ∞ loop. For more reflections on self-loops, including some nice ones by Raymond Smullyan, see also (Hofstadter & Dennett 1981). Gödel's time-loop solution to Einstein's equations is discussed in (Hájek 1996) and (Yourgrau 1999, 2005).
22. Immanuel Kant contrasted the transcendental and phenomenal worlds in his classic *Kritik der reinen Vernunft* (first published 1781). In that massively influential work, Kant confronts the reader with an unsparingly rigorous post-metaphysical analysis of the *a priori* architecture supporting the phenomenology of consciousness.
23. Kripke's work is the inspiration behind the recent resurgence in modal logic. He proved the completeness of various axiomatizations of modal logic using what are now known as Kripke structures, which are sets of possible worlds plus accessibility relations defined over them. For an introduction to the field, see (Popkorn 1994).
24. Evolutionary epistemology is a Darwinian competition in which candidate theories proliferate and suffer attrition under testing. See (Dennett 1995). Such evolution can even work in computers (Michalewicz 1992/96).
25. Before we identify the dimension of epistemological evolution with time, we should check the physics of time, in particular its unidirectionality (entropy), its

relativistic absorption in spacetime, and its quantum properties. For example, see (Deutsch 1997, Flood 1986, Penrose 1989).
26. The actual world of contemporary science is a multiauthorial palimpsest, a moving target rather than a defined entity. For me, it is the world described by the last few hundred issues of *Scientific American*.
27. The subject of the universe can be represented by its reflection in the more or less unified core of ideas in cosmology. This core has only settled down recently, if at all, with the long-awaited marriage of general relativity and quantum field theory in some variant of superstring theory, or rather in a generalization of superstring theory called M theory (by Edward Witten). See (Greene 1999, Smolin 2006).
28. David Deutsch has made a highly original analysis of VR worlds based on computability theory (Deutsch 1997). See also (Heim 1993, Metzinger 2009).
29. Symmetry and symmetry breaking are technical concepts in physics. If the universe at time t is described by a theory in which changing parameter p leaves the physics unchanged, then the universe at time t is symmetrical with respect to p. See the last lecture in (Feynman *et al.* 1963).
30. The coexistence of superposed states in quantum mechanics has led to a long and so far inconclusive debate. Abner Shimony gives a good brief review of the whole field in (Davies 1989). Short introductions include (Feynman 1985, Rae 1986). Original ideas appear in (Deutsch 1997, Lockwood 1991).
31. It may seem that collapse times for coherent states in quantum systems must be too short to explain any empirically reasonable rhythm of conscious states. But recall that by the Heisenberg uncertainty principle, the collapse time T for a superposition of states of a photon with energy E is such that the product $ET \approx h$ (the Planck constant). And photon energy $E = hf$, where f is the frequency of the photon. So, for $f = 40$ Hz, the collapse time is O(25 ms), in rough agreement with the flicker fusion rate.
32. The question of whether quantum phenomena play an important role in brain function has an unedifying history. Speculation abounds on the role of 40 Hz resonances, the properties of Bose–Einstein condensates, quantum gravity, laser action in microtubules, and more. For example, see (Penrose 1989, 1994, Stapp 1993, Wolf 1981, Zohar 1990). Scepticism is still appropriate.
33. The standard interpretations of quantum mechanics feature a more or less central observer. Of those that do not, Everett's "many worlds" interpretation seems popular: see (Chalmers 1996, Deutsch 1997, Lockwood 1991).
34. The *Weltgeist* ("world spirit") seems to be the main subject in large parts of Hegel's *Phänomenologie des Geistes* (first published 1807). This obscure and difficult classic tells an extraordinary story of the evolution of consciousness.

Strongly influenced by Kant, Hegel built a dialectical idealism that used contradictions as stepping stone to the truth. See (Taylor 1975).
35. Martin Buber's *Ich und Du* is a philosophical classic (Buber 1923/70). His analysis of "I" leads on to some theological thoughts.
36. The mathematician Hardy once said that all mathematicians are isomorphic. He meant they all think the same way. I would go further and say that mathematicians deal not only with mental constructs but also with the same (platonic) realm, so they are of *one mind*.
37. That we face complications when we try to define how humans instantiate consciousness will come as no surprise to readers of (Damasio 1994, 1999, Ramachandran 1998, Weiskrantz 1997).
38. For a technical introduction to artificial neural networks, see (Rojas 1996).
39. I sensed this excitement at the second ASSC conference "Neural Correlates of Consciousness: Empirical and Conceptual Questions" held in Bremen in 1998.
40. Wolf Singer reports this work in (Singer 1998, 2000, 2002).
41. In the past, consciousness was often seen as a special attribute of human beings. Julian Jaynes even argued in (Jaynes 1976) that humans first became conscious in biblical times, but I think his argument is best seen as showing that humans first developed modern *personal* consciousness then. The Bible and other early documents can plausibly be read as recording the slow emergence of the concept of a person.
42. It is not merely my own view that we are beginning to develop the infrastructure for a global consciousness. See (Russell 1991, Stock 1993).

Mindworlds

1. The quotation is from William James (1902) and became an inspiration for my whole mindworlds construction.
2. This is proposition 5.63 in Wittgenstein's *Tractatus* (1922/61). Recall its centrality (as axiom 1) in chapter 3.
3. On transformational grammar, see (Chomsky 1965). The idea that a single formalism can express the deep structure of any language is central to the whole logical approach pursuded here.
4. This follows from Quine's thesis of indeterminacy of translation, aired in his book *Word and Object* (1960).
5. I hope I need no citations to attribute the view that numbers are abstractions of arbitrary physical things to John Stuart Mill or Edmund Husserl, since the view was common at the time. Similarly, the idea that numbering reflects the pure

intuition of time is well known from Immanuel Kant's *Kritik der reinen Vernunft* or L.E.J. Brouwer's writings on intuitionism.

6. The respective ideas that number theory is a prototype for any first order theory, any computable theory, any algorithmic theory, or any virtual reality must also be familiar enough to any student of the works of Kurt Gödel, Alan Turing, Gregory Chaitin, and David Deutsch.
7. The formal theory of arithmetic is presented in (Mendelson 1964/79). The same theory is presented in the same fashion in (Hamilton 1978).
8. Gödel's incompleteness theorem is proved in (Mendelson 1964/79). For a full and entertaining discussion, see (Hofstadter 1979).
9. See (Penrose 1989, 1994, 1997). But Penrose seems to have backed off from defending this view more recently (see Penrose 2004).
10. A good source text on artificial neuronets is (Rojas 1996). A declaration of interest: the author thanks me in the preface.
11. The definition of numbers in terms of sets is the second of Frege's great contributions to logic (his first was quantification). The definition of natural numbers as sets of their predecessors is due to John von Neumann. Other definitions, especially those due to Frege and Zermelo, can serve equally well, on all of which see (Quine 1963/69).
12. The breakhrough in the foundations of mathematics that followed Frege's work had the result that set theory is now the foundation of our entire miph. Quine's ambitious program of ontological slum clearance (see Quine 1960) would leave us ultimately with nothing but sets, anywhere.
13. For definitive discussion of ZF, see (Fraenkel *et al.* 1958/73). Fraenkel was the author of the replacement schema that distinguishes ZF from Zermelo's earlier theory and gives ZF the power to model all of classical mathematics. For a more mathematical discussion of axiomatizations (albeit in a curiously unorthodox notation), see (Quine 1963/69).
14. The status of the continuum hypothesis relative to ZF remained an active question for most of the twentieth century. Gödel used his constructive universe L to prove its consistency with ZF, and Paul Cohen used his new method of forcing to prove its independence from ZF; see (Cohen 1966).
15. From Wittgenstein's *Tractatus* (1922/61), proposition 1.1.
16. Categories are definitively presented in (Mac Lane 1998). For a few introductory words on them, see (Baez & Dolan 2001).
17. The concept of strangeness here is from (Hofstadter 1979).
18. The best discussion I know of the logical theory of virtual reality is by David Deutsch (1997).

19. Much of this modal logic, and in particular the formal semantics, is due to Saul Kripke. For a recent introduction, see (Popkorn 1994).
20. Deterministic chaos occurs when tiny variations in the accuracy with which initial conditions are measured give rise to huge differences in predicted behavior. Edward Lorenz investigated this effect for weather forecasting and the field boomed; see (Gleick 1987, Peitgen *et al.* 1992).
21. Quantum electrodynamics is widely admired as the most precisely confirmed and successful physical theory ever made. Paul Dirac created its first form (Dirac 1930/58), and Richard Feynman tamed it sufficiently to make it work right (Feynman *et al.* 1965, Feynman 1985). At about the same time as Feynman, Sin-Itiro Tomonaga and Julian Schwinger independently tamed QED, and all three shared the Nobel Prize for their efforts. At risk of adding to a personality cult, a good biography of Feynman is (Gleick 1992).
22. According to Richard Feynman, these two experiments and calculations encapsulate the whole mystery of quantum mechanics; see lecture 1 in (Feynman *et al.* 1965).
23. Heisenberg uncertainty is introduced in all elementary quantum mechanics texts. Quantum field theory is hard to introduce. The short book (Teller 1995) is a brave try, but still hard going. But a full presentation, such as (Weinberg 1995) is much harder – the annotated sentence is from that book.
24. On the block universe, see (Barbour 1999). For a more technical treatment, see (Hawking & Penrose 1996).
25. The consistent histories approach to quantum mechanics is most prominently associated with Roland Omnès (1999a, 1999b). It is ably popularized in (Lindley 1996).
26. On quantum foam, see (Wheeler 1998). For a much fuller treatment, see (Misner *et al.* 1973) and (Callender and Huggett, eds., 2001).
27. Kant published his *Kritik der reinen Vernunft* in 1781. For a very short introduction to his philosophy, see (Scruton 2001).
28. Hegel published his *Phänomenologie des Geistes* in 1807. For an introduction to his philosophy, see (Taylor 1975). See also the biography (Pinkard 2000).
29. Gödel's time-loop solution of Einstein's cosmological equations forms the central focus of the works of Palle Yourgrau (Yourgrau 1999, 2005).
30. The contrasting first-person and third-person perspectives on the conscious mind/brain form the central theme of the modern classic (Chalmers 1996).
31. All this quantum logic is from (Nielsen & Chang 2000), pp. 13–21.
32. This statement is from Rolf Landauer (Nielsen & Chang 2000), p. 1.
33. This statement is from (Llinás 2001), p. 120. See also chapter 13.

308   Mindworlds

34. I heard Wolf Singer report his work on the role in perceptual binding of coherent gamma waves at the ASSC conference held in Bremen in June 1998. He also presents it readably in (Singer 1998, 2000, 2002).
35. Llinás explains what he means by isochronous states in (Llinás 2001). Sacks refers to the idea in (Sacks 2004).
36. The idea that time stands still for a photon is due to Einstein. It follows immediately from his special theory of relativity (Einstein 1922).
37. Biophotons were investigated by F.-A. Popp in the 1980s and G. Albrecht-Bühler in the 1990s; for a brief report, see (Daviss 2002).
38. The Penrose–Hameroff Orch OR model is presented in (Penrose 1994). The biophysics of microtubules has been researched in detail by Jack Tuszynski and his team; see (Satinover 2001, Appendix B).
39. The testability criterion is due to Karl Popper; see (Popper 1972).
40. The "paradigm" paradigm is due to Thomas Kuhn; see (Kuhn 1971).
41. Michael Faraday said this when asked about the utility of his researches into electricity and magnetism.
42. Further suggestions for investigating QTC are offered in chapter 8.
43. From the early pages of (Ramachandran 1998).
44. Kuhn (2000), p. 49. The quotation is from a televised debate between "Dave" and other experts. The book presents a series of debates on various topics.
45. Kuhn (2000), p, 49. From the same debate.

First-Person Consciousness

1. The two autobiographies are (Honderich 2001) and (McGinn 2002).
2. Honderich (2001), pp. 16–17.
3. Honderich (2001), p. 7.
4. Honderich (2001), pp. 9–10.
5. Honderich (2001), p. 20.
6. Honderich (2001), p. 8.
7. Honderich (2001), p. 14.
8. Honderich (2001), pp. 157–158.
9. Honderich (2001), p. 173.
10. The "dry tome" is (Honderich 1988) and the introduction is (Honderich 1992).
11. Honderich (2001), pp. 301–314.
12. The Oxford Companion was published as (Honderich 1995).
13. Honderich (2001), pp. 27–28.
14. The two books on Wittgenstein are (McGinn 1984) and (Kripke 1982).
15. McGinn (2002), p. 157.

16. Honderich (2001), p. 222.
17. The autobiography is (Amis 2000).
18. McGinn (2002), p. 182.
19. The paper is reprinted in McGinn (1991). The *Scientific American* article is in an issue I have been unable to trace.
20. Honderich (2001), p. 365.
21. Published as (Honderich 1973).
22. Honderich (2001), pp. 182–183.
23. Published as (Honderich & Burnyeat 1979). The essay by Donald Davidson is also reprinted in (Chalmers 2002).
24. Honderich (2001), p. 227.
25. Honderich (2001), pp. 244–246.
26. Honderich (2001), p. 261.
27. Popper & Eccles (1977).
28. Honderich (2001), pp. 271–272.
29. Libet *et al.* (1979), p. 222.
30. Popper & Eccles (1977), p. 364.
31. Penrose (1989), p. 570.
32. Dennett (1991), p. 162.
33. Heil & Mele (1993).
34. Searle (1992).
35. Honderich (2001), pp. 355–356.
36. Honderich (2001), p. 364.
37. Honderich (2001), p. 371.
38. McGinn (1999). A front-cover sticker quotes *The New York Times*: "There is [no] better introduction to the philosophy of consciousness than this."
39. McGinn (1999), pp. 4–5.
40. Honderich (2001), p. 161.
41. McGinn (1999), p. 9.
42. McGinn (1999), p. 11.
43. McGinn (1999), p. 17.
44. McGinn (1999), p. 18.
45. McGinn (1999), pp. 23–24.
46. McGinn (1999), pp. 25–27.
47. McGinn (1999), p. 36.
48. Pinker (1997).
49. McGinn (1999), pp. 40–42.
50. McGinn (1999), pp. 56–58.
51. McGinn (1999), p. 62.

52. McGinn (1999), p. 66.
53. McFadden (2002) – a seminal paper.
54. McGinn (1999), pp. 83–84.
55. McGinn (1999), p. 87.
56. McGinn (1999), pp. 91–92.
57. McGinn (1999), p. 95.
58. McGinn (1999), pp. 98–99.
59. McGinn (1999), p. 104
60. McGinn (1999), pp. 111–114
61. McGinn (1999), p. 140.
62. McGinn (1999), pp. 156–162.
63. McGinn (1999), pp. 182–183.
64. McGinn (1999), p. 185.
65. McGinn (1999), p. 197.
66. McGinn (1999), p. 214.
67. McGinn (1999), p. 230.
68. Wittgenstein's *Tractatus* (1922, current English translation 1961) and Ayer's *Language, Truth and Logic* (1936, second edition 1946) are the classics of logical positivism.
69. Quine (1960) argues for the indeterminacy of translation.
70. Hofstadter's big book on Gödel (1979) is a milestone in philosophy, or at least a milestone in the philosophy of Artificial Intelligence.
71. The German tradition in post-Kantian philosophy from Hegel through Husserl to Heidegger does not survive well in translation. Sartre captured its spirit (in French) in *L'Etre et le Néant* but like many of his German contemporaries let his later views drift toward a fashionable Leftism.
72. Metzinger (1995), p. 4.
73. Honderich (2001), p. 3.
74. The creation and development of quantum theory is undoubtedly the biggest story in the history of ideas in the twentieth century. For a scholarly history, see (Pais 1986) and for a more popular account see (Crease & Mann 1986).
75. Aczel (2001) gives a nice popular account of post-Bell developments.
76. On consistent histories, see (Omnès 1999a,b) and (Lindley 1996).
77. Chalmers (1996), pp. xii–xiii.
78. Chalmers (1996), p. 4.
79. Dennett (1991) makes a strong case against entertaining qualia.
80. Chalmers (1996), p. 33.
81. Chalmers (1996), p. 87.
82. Chalmers (1996), p. 106.

83. Chalmers (1996), p. 123.
84. Chalmers (1996), p. 126.
85. Chalmers (1996), p. 379.
86. Chalmers (1996), p. 173.
87. Dennett (1991) not only explains consciousness but explains it away, as John Searle said in his review of the book in *The New York Times*.
88. Chalmers (1996), p. 218.
89. Chalmers (1996), p. 284.
90. Chalmers (1996), p. 292.
91. Chalmers (1996), pp. 302–303.
92. Deutsch (1997) presents a wide view of the physical roots of quantum information theory and (Nielsen 2000) shows how fast the field of quantum computation is developing.
93. Chalmers (1996), p. 314.
94. Chalmers (1996), p. 334.
95. A lot has been written on the Everett interpretation. For good discussions, see (Lockwood 1989) and (Deutsch 1997).
96. Chalmers (1996), p. 347.
97. For me, Schrödinger's cat is best discussed in (Lindley 1996).
98. Dennett (1991), p. 29.
99. Dennett (1991), pp. 172–173.
100. Blackmore (1999) gives a fine introduction to memes.
101. Dennett (1991), p. 210.
102. Dennett (1991), p. 228.
103. Dennett (1991), pp. 253–254.
104. Dennett (1991), p. 281.
105. Dennett (1991), p. 416.
106. McGinn (1991), pp. 103–104.
107. Dennett (1991), p. 434.
108. Llinás (2001), p. 120.
109. Honderich (2001), p. 389.

The Self: From Soul to Brain

1. LeDoux (2002), p. ix.
2. LeDoux (1993), p. 149.
3. LeDoux (1996).
4. Churchland (2002a).
5. Schacter (1996, 2001).

6. Hauser (2000).
7. Lewis (1992).
8. Wegner (1989).
9. Wegner (2002).
10. Wegner (2002), p. ix.
11. Damasio (1994, 1999).
12. Damasio (2003).
13. The mindness state is introduced in (Llinás 2001).
14. The syndromes are described in (Feinberg 2001).
15. Dennett (1991, 1995).
16. The anthology is (Hofstadter & Dennett 1981).
17. Wright (2000), chapter 21, footnote 14.
18. Ainslie (2001).
19. Dennett (1991), p. 164.
20. The quotation is from (Ramachandran & Blakeslee 1998).
21. Dennett (1984). I don't have a page reference.
22. The new book is (Dennett 2003).
23. LeDoux (2002), p. 1.
24. McFadden (2002a,b).
25. Ledoux *et al.* (eds. 2003).

A Photonic Theory of Consciousness

1. Feynman (1985), pp. 7–8. The exact quotation is of no particular importance, since the claim it expresses suffuses Feynman's whole outlook.
2. Chalmers (1996) and Velmans (2000) both endorse the *personal* nature of the contrast between the views from inside outward and from outside inward.
3. McGinn (1999). For a critique, see chapter 6.
4. Dennett (1991) introduced these wonderful words – see chapter 6.
5. Chalmers (1996), p. 22. In the next sentence he refers to Gilbert Ryle (1949), who said there are no "neat" sensation words.
6. The private language argument appears in (Wittgenstein 1953/58) and is discussed in (Kripke 1982) – tendentiously, says McGinn (1984).
7. Quine discusses ontological relativity in *Word and Object* (1960) and of course in the title essay of (Quine 1969).
8. Popper presents his story of conjecture and refutation in a mature form in *Objective Knowledge* (1972), though with more engaging passion in his earlier collection *Conjectures and Refutations* (1963). Lakatos applied the story to mathematics in his *Proofs and Refutations* (1976).

9. For a proof of the theorem, see (Mendelson 1964/79). For a commentary, see (Hofstadter 1979).
10. For example, see the discussion of nonmonotonic inference in (Charniak & McDermott 1985) and the criticism of that approach in (Abdallah 1995).
11. The completeness proofs for the more standard variants of modal logic are due to Saul Kripke, who later gave some brilliant lectures on the philosophy of modality (1980). For a modern technical introduction, see (Popkorn 1994).
12. Omnès (1999a,b); see also (Lindley 1996).
13. The many authors include those of the magisterial texts (Mendelson 1964/79) and (Quine 1963/69) from my student days.
14. The natural authority on ZF set theory is Fraenkel himself, author of its characteristic replacement schema; see (Fraenkel et al. 1973).
15. All the essentials of the theory presented were settled in the early twentieth century, albeit in various conceptual and notational forms. Here I outline the ideas in what I hope is a safely consensus fashion. For a typical example of how they are presented to students, see chapter 11 of (Atkins 2002).
16. On Bell's theorem, see (Bell 1987). The rather subtle logic involved is discussed in a vast secondary literature. The predicted nonclassical statistics have been confirmed in numerous experiments. See (Aczel 2001).
17. So far as I know, Wheeler introduced the term in the monumental tome (Misner et al. 1973). Nonspecialists should see his math-lite introduction to general relativity (Wheeler 1998).
18. The Schiller poem is quoted at the end of (Hegel 1807). A good modern translation of Hegel's tome is (Hegel 1977).
19. Folse (1985) includes a good discussion of complementarity.
20. See (Tegmark 2003).
21. On the block universe, see (Barbour 1999).
22. On the hope that gravity may be quantized, see for example (Hawking & Penrose 1996) and (Smolin 2000).
23. On Gödel's almost mystical view of time, see (Yourgrau 1999, 2005).
24. Famously, or notoriously, this is historic claim in (Dawkins 1982).
25. An excellent survey of experimental results on cerebral EM waves is (McFadden 2002a). For a follow-up discussion, see (McFadden 2002b).
26. On Singer's work, see (Singer 1998, 2000, 2002).
27. Gerald Edelman won a Nobel Prize for this work; see (Edelman 1992, 2000).
28. Penrose presents the Orch OR theory in (Penrose 1994).
29. The conference was held in New York in September 2002. See chapter 7.
30. See (Llinás 2001).
31. You may recognize this quotation from (James 1902).

Toward a Theory of Consciousness

1. McFadden (2002a,b).
2. Blackmore (2003). Susan's textbook is written for psychology students who want to explore the frontiers, but it also provides a readable review for any consciousness buff who wants to keep in touch with conventional wisdom.
3. See Quine's famous classic *Word and Object* (1960) for the argument and his lesser-known masterpiece *Set Theory and Its Logic* (1963/69) for the machinery.
4. For example, the rank function is defined in (Mendelson 1964/79), p. 214.
5. Quine (1963/69) explains the distinction between sets and classes using his own notation and his theories NF and ML, and Fraenkel *et al.* (1958/73) do so by reference to the von Neumann–Bernays–Gödel (NBG) variant of the Zermelo–Fraenkel (ZF) axiomatization of set theory.
6. Wittgenstein (1922/61), proposition 5.63.
7. The argument is prominent in Stephen Wolfram's big book (2002).
8. For more about photons fanning out, see (Feynman 1985).
9. For more about entanglement, see (Aczel 2001).
10. For more about quantum computation, see (Johnson 2003).
11. Llinás (2001). See also chapter 8.
12. Singer (2000).
13. For example, as described by (McGinn 1999).
14. Douglas Hofstadter (1979) described that world brilliantly – for me at least.
15. Cosmologist Max Tegmark presented a nice survey of the quantum ocean in *Scientific American* (2003).
16. Fay Dowker (2003). The causal set theory approach was first proposed in 1987 by Rafael Sorkin. Subsequent developments embrace general covariance, accelerated cosmological expansion, and black hole entropy.

Consciousness as a Physical Process

1. Chalmers (1999) and elsewhere.
2. Immanuel Kant's classic *Kritik der reinen Vernunft* (1781) is available in several modern translations, but a good modern analytical commentary or gloss on the work, such as (Scruton 2001), is much easier to take in.
3. Libet (2003) and references therein.
4. Dennett (2003).
5. Wegner (2002).
6. See all the listed works by Antonio Damasio.

7. I have written this paragraph anew for the print edition of this book. In my view, the Blue Brain project (Markram 2009) is currently the most promising approach to simulating the brain. It will need to be scaled up a millionfold to do justice to a human brain, and will need a body, but these are early days.
8. McFadden (2002a,b).
9. For a good technical account of Turing machines, see (Mendelson 1964/79).
10. Dennett (1991). See also chapter 6.
11. Quine (1940/51) continues Russell's work, but the system he builds there is not much pursued nowadays, and is anyway more perspicuously introduced in his later survey *Set Theory and Its Logic* (Quine 1963/69).
12. Bertrand Russell discovered his paradox in 1901 and told Gottlob Frege immediately. Frege was rather disconcerted, as it wrecked his life's work, but he recovered well. Russell was so excited by it that he devoted the best years of his mathematical life to an energetic but ultimately rather unsatisfactory attempt to sort out the mess, which resulted in his long collaboration with Alfred North Whitehead on the celebrated trilogy *Principia Mathematica*. Gödel called the work a step backward in terms of rigor compared to Frege.
13. On Zermelo–Fraenkel and similar set theories, see all the usual references, especially (Quine 1963/69) and (Fraenkel *et al.* 1958/73).
14. Smolin (2004).

Purpose in Modern Science

1. Adams (1986).

Roads to Reality

1. Penrose (2004).
2. Penrose (1989, 1994, 1997). The first of these works really excited me, but I confess that I did not finished reading the other two.
3. Wolfram (2002).
4. Penrose (2004), p. 784.
5. The best single source for this work is (Quine 1963/69).
6. Wittgenstein (1922/61).
7. For a modern and readable account, see (Rucker 1982).
8. Omnès (1999a).
9. Deutsch (1997).
10. For example, see (Nielsen and Chuang 2000), pp. 13–15.

11. See chapter 6 of (Greene 2004). Greene seems to have learned a lot about entropy from conversations with David Albert – see (Albert 2000).
12. Penrose (2004), p. 730. See also (Penrose 1989), p. 445. Equivalently, 10^{123} is the (maximum) number of bits in our universe (Lloyd & Ng 2004, p. 39).
13. Penrose (2004), p. 407.
14. Wolf (1981). A *qwiff* is a quantum wave function, and it *pops* when its unitary evolution as a widening superposition collapses in a state reduction. Wolf appeared as a quantum guru in the movie *What the Bleep Do We Know!?* (Arntz et al. 2005).
15. McFadden entertains this idea in his popular but in part speculative book *Quantum Evolution* (2000).
16. For example, David Chalmers (1996), David Deutsch (1997), and Michael Lockwood (1989) all cast their votes for the Everett scenario.
17. On the question of how pervasive entanglement may be, see (Aczel 2001) and (Lindley 1996).
18. Penrose (2004), pp. 958–959. On Sorkin's causal set ideas, see (Dowker 2003) and the last section of chapter 9 in this book. Penrose acknowledges Fay Dowker on p. xxiii of *The Road to Reality*.
19. Penrose (2004), p. 962.
20. Penrose (2004), p. 963.
21. Penrose (2004), pp. 964–965.
22. Penrose (2004), pp. 972–974.
23. Penrose (2004), p. 978.
24. Penrose (2004), p. 986.
25. On quantum gravity, see (Smolin 2000, 2004) and (Greene 2004).
26. On M-theory, see (Penrose 2004), pp. 914–915, and (Greene 1999, 2004).
27. On the concept of information, see (von Baeyer 2003). On quantum information, see (Nielsen & Chuang 2000) and David Deutsch's contribution "It from Qubit" in (Barrow et al. 2004).
28. The literature on quantum state reduction is overwhelming. I like to recall Richard Feynman's opinion that no-one understands it.
29. Wolfram (2002), pp. 643–644.
30. Wolfram (2002), pp. 716–717.
31. Chaitin (1990), p. 15.
32. Wolfram (2002), p. 846.
33. It is well known that Kant was strongly impressed by the Copernican shift and hoped his *Kritik der reinen Vernunft* would achieve a comparable effect on the way people thought.
34. Penrose (2004), p. 1030.

35. Penrose (2004), pp. 1031–1032.
36. Mukhopadhyay (2000). This may be politely described as an inspirational book. It does not meet normal academic standards of intellectual sobriety. Mukhopadhyay first used the term "supracortical consciousness" in 1985.
37. Wolfram (2002), p. 631.
38. Lloyd and Ng (2004), p. 31.
39. Lloyd and Ng (2004), p. 39.
40. The phrase is due to Paolo Zizzi. David Deutsch uses it for the title of his chapter in the Wheeler *Festschrift* (Barrow *et al.* 2004).

About Time

1. Elitzur *et al.* (2005), p. 346.
2. Barbour (1999) agues that time is an illusion and advocates a phase-space generalization of the classical block universe (see slide 95 in chapter 5, above).
3. Nagel (1986) seems to have coined the phrase "the view from nowhere."
4. Atmanspacher (1997).
5. Velmans (2000).
6. See, e.g., (Flood 1986, Price 1996, Lockwood 2005).
7. Greene (2004).
8. Einstein (1922/69) is worth recalling directly here.
9. I don't know where or when Wheeler coined the word "momenergy" but he uses it in (Wheeler 1990/99).
10. Wheeler (1990/99).
11. See, e.g., (Feynman 1965, Shimony 1989, Lindsey 1996, Omnès 1999).
12. Bell (1987).
13. See, e.g., (Callender 2001, Penrose 2004).
14. Feynman (1942/2005).
15. See especially the articles by Gödel reprinted in (Benacerraf 1964).
16. See, e.g., (Mendelson 1964/79).
17. See, e.g., (Jech 1971/97).
18. Cohen (1966).
19. The options are well surveyed in (Fraenkel *et al.* 1958/73, Quine 1963/69).
20. Quine (1960).
21. Wolfram (2002).
22. Albert (2000); see also (Zeh 1989/92).
23. Bernays (1958).
24. Dowker (2003). See also (Sorkin 2005).
25. Sorkin (1991).

26. Reid (1999). For a similar approach, see (Ambjørn *et al.* 2006, 2008).
27. Wittgenstein (1922/61). See also chapter 5, slide 8.
28. James (1902). See also chapter 5, slide 5 and others.
29. Libet (2004).
30. Metzinger (2003, 2009) offers deep insight into this mechanism.

Blinded by the Light

1. De Quincey (2006).

Will Robots See Humans as Dinosaurs?

1. Pasquini (2006).
2. Pasquini (2006), p. 86.
3. Kurzweil (2005). In 2009, Kurweil and others, with backing from Google and NASA, founded the Singularity University in California.
4. Moore (1965).
5. Markram (2009). The results from the Blue Brain project, as of 2009, are encouraging. The tuned simulation has begun to behave like the real rat pyramidal columns that are used to provide tuning input, which suggests convergence to a correct model.
6. Bandettini *et al.* (2005).
7. Shapiro and Benenson (2006).

Hitting on Consciousness

1. Honderich (2004).
2. McGinn (2007a).
3. Honderich (2007).
4. Leiter (2007).
5. McGinn (2007b).
6. Jeffries (2007).
7. Ayer (1990).
8. Honderich (2001), p. 365.
9. Rogers (1999).
10. Honderich (2001), p. 387.
11. Honderich (2001) and (McGinn 2002).
12. Reprinted here as chapter 6.
13. Honderich (2001), p. 222.

14. Amis (2001), pp. 267–268.
15. McGinn (1999).
16. McGinn (2002).
17. Honderich (2002).
18. The slides became input for chapter 5.
19. Honderich (2002).
20. The book was the first edition of this volume.
21. James (1902). See also slide 5 in chapter 5.
22. Wittgenstein (1922/61).
23. Metzinger (2003). More accessible is (Metzinger 2009).
24. Hannan (2005).
25. Snowdon (2006).
26. Honderich (2006).
27. McGinn (1990).
28. Leiter (2007).
29. See chapter 15.

References

Abdallah, Areski Nait (1995). *The Logic of Partial Information*. Berlin: Springer.

Aczel, Amir D. (2001). *Entanglement: The Greatest Mystery in Physics*. New York: Four Walls Eight Windows.

Adams, Douglas (1986). *The Hitch-Hiker's Guide to the Galaxy*. A Trilogy in Four Parts. London: Heinemann.

Ainslie, George (2001). *Breakdown of Will*. Cambridge: Cambridge University Press.

Albert, David Z. (1992). *Quantum Mechanics and Experience*. Cambridge, MA: Harvard University Press.

Albert, David Z. (2000). *Time and Chance*. Cambridge, MA: Harvard University Press.

Ambjørn, J., J. Jurkiewicz, R. Loll (2006). The universe from scratch. arXiv:hep-th/0509010v3

Ambjørn, J., J. Jurkiewicz, R. Loll (2008). The self-organized de Sitter universe. arXiv:0806.0397v1

Amis, Martin (1995). *The Information*. New York: Harmony Books.

Amis, Martin (2000). *Experience*. London: Jonathan Cape.

Amis, Martin (2001). *The War Against Cliché*: Essays and Reviews 1971–2000. London: Jonathan Cape.

Arntz, William, Betsy Chasse, and Mark Vicente (2005). *What the Bleep Do We Know!?* Discovering the endless possibilities for altering your everyday reality. Deerfield Beach, Florida: Health Communications.

Atkins, Peter and Julio de Paula (7th edn. 2002). *Physical Chemistry*. Oxford: Oxford University Press.

Atmanspacher, Harald, and Eva Ruhnau (eds. 1997). *Time, Temporality, Now*. Experiencing time and concepts of time in an interdisciplinary perspective. Berlin: Springer.

Ayer, Alfred J. (1936, 2nd edn. 1946). *Language, Truth and Logic*. London: Gollancz.

Ayer, Alfred J. (1976). *The Central Questions of Philosophy*. London: Penguin.

Ayer, Alfred J. (1990). *The Meaning of Life*. New York: Scribner.

Baeyer, Hans Christian von (2003). *Information: The New Language of Science.* London: Weidenfeld & Nicolson.

Baez, John C. and James Dolan (2001). From finite sets to Feynman diagrams. In Björn Engquist and Wilfried Schmid (eds.), *Mathematics Unlimited – 2001 and Beyond.* Berlin: Springer.

Bandettini, P. A., N. Petridou, and J. Bodurka (2005). Direct detection of neuronal activity with MRI: fantasy, possibility, or reality? *Applied Magnetic Resonance,* 29(1). http://fim.nimh.nih.gov/people/pab/P48

Barbour, Julian (1999). *The End of Time: The Next Revolution in Our Understanding of the Universe.* London: Weidenfeld & Nicolson.

Barrow, John D. and Frank J. Tipler (1986). *The Anthropic Cosmological Principle.* Oxford: Oxford University Press.

Barrow, John D., Paul C. W. Davies, and Charles L. Harper, Jr. (eds. 2004). *Science and Ultimate Reality: Quantum Theory, Cosmology and Complexity.* Cambridge: Cambridge University Press.

Bauer, Friedrich L. (1997, 3rd edn. 2002). *Decrypted Secrets: Methods and Maxims of Cryptology.* Berlin: Springer.

Bell, John S. (1987). *Speakable and Unspeakable in Quantum Mechanics: Collected Papers on Quantum Philosophy.* Cambridge: Cambridge University Press.

Benacerraf, Paul, and Hilary Putnam (eds. 1964). *Philosophy of Mathematics.* Reading, MA: Prentice-Hall.

Bernays, Paul (1968). *Axiomatic Set Theory.* Amsterdam: North-Holland.

Blackmore, Susan (1999). *The Meme Machine.* Oxford: Oxford University Press.

Blackmore, Susan (2003). *Consciousness: An Introduction.* London: Hodder & Stoughton.

Bloom, Harold (1992). *The American Religion: The Emergence of the Post-Christian Nation.* New York: Simon & Schuster.

Bloom, Howard (2000). *Global Brain: The Evolution of Mass Mind from the Big Bang to the 21st Century.* New York: Wiley & Sons.

Bolc, Leonard and Piotr Borowik (1992). *Many-Valued Logics I: Theoretical Foundations.* Berlin: Springer.

Boorstin, Daniel J. (1983). *The Discoverers: A History of Man's Search to Know His World and Himself.* New York: Random House.

Boyer, Pascal (2001). *Religion Explained: The Human Instincts that Fashion Gods, Spirits and Ancestors.* London: Heinemann.

Brody, Thomas (1993). *The Philosophy Behind Physics.* Berlin: Springer.

Buber, Martin (1923, translated by Walter Kaufmann 1970). *I and Thou.* Scribner.

Callender, Craig, and Nick Huggett (eds. 2001). *Physics Meets Philosophy at the Planck Scale.* Contemporary theories in quantum gravity. Cambridge: Cambridge University Press.

Chaitin, Gregory J. (1987, 2nd edn.1990). *Information, Randomness and Incompleteness: Papers on Algorithmic Information Theory.* Singapore: World Scientific.

Chaitin, Gregory J. (1998). *The Limits of Mathematics: A Course on Information Theory and The Limits of Formal Reasoning.* Berlin: Springer.

Chalmers, David J. (1996). *The Conscious Mind – In Search of a Fundamental Theory.* New York: Oxford University Press. See also www.u.arizona.edu/~chalmers.

Chalmers, David J. (1999). First-person methods in the science of consciousness. *Consciousness Bulletin*, The University of Arizona.

Chalmers, David J. (ed. 2002). *Philosophy of Mind: Classical and Contemporary Readings.* New York: Oxford University Press.

Charniak, Eugene and Drew McDermott (1985). *Introduction to Artificial Intelligence.* Reading, MA: Addison-Wesley.

Chomsky, Noam (1965). *Aspects of the Theory of Syntax.* Cambridge, MA: MIT Press.

Chopra, Deepak (2000). *How to Know God: The Soul's Journey into the Mystery of Mysteries.* New York: Harmony Books.

Churchland, Patricia Smith (1986). *Neurophilosophy: Toward a Unified Science of the Mind/Brain.* Cambridge, MA: MIT Press.

Churchland, Patricia Smith (2002a). Self-Representation in Nervous Systems. *Science*, 296: 308–310.

Churchland, Patricia Smith (2002b). *Brain-Wise.* Studies in Neurophilosophy. Cambridge, MA: MIT Press.

Churchland, Patricia Smith and Paul M.Churchland (1990). Could a machine think? *Scientific American* (January).

Clark, Andy (1997). *Being There: Putting Brain, Body, and World Together Again.* Cambridge, MA: MIT Press.

Cohen, Paul J. (1966). *Set Theory and the Continuum Hypothesis.* New York: Benjamin.

Cotterill, Rodney (1998). *Enchanted Looms: Conscious Networks in Brains and Computers.* Cambridge: Cambridge University Press.

Crease, Robert P. and Charles C. Mann (1986). *The Second Creation: Makers of the Revolution in 20th Century Physics.* New York: Macmillan.

Crick, Francis (1994). *The Astonishing Hypothesis: The Scientific Search for the Soul.* New York: Simon & Schuster.

Crinella, Francis M., and Jen Yu (eds. 1993). *Brain Mechanisms. Papers in Memory of Robert Thompson*. Annals of the New York Academy of Sciences, 702.

Damasio, Antonio R. (1994). *Descartes' Error: Emotion, Reason, and the Human Brain*. New York: Grosset/Putnam.

Damasio, Antonio R. (1999). *The Feeling of What Happens: Body and Emotion in the Making of Consciousness*. New York: Harcourt Brace & Co.

Damasio, Antonio R. (2003). *Looking for Spinoza: Joy, Sorrow, and the Feeling Brain*. Orlando, FL: Harcourt.

Davies, Paul C. W. (1986). Time asymmetry and quantum mechanics. In R. Flood and M. Lockwood (eds.) *The Nature of Time* (pp. 99–124). Oxford: Basil Blackwell.

Davies, Paul C. W. (ed. 1989). *The New Physics*. Cambridge: Cambridge University Press.

Daviss, Bennett (2002). *Body Talk*. New Scientist, 173 (2331), pp. 30–33.

Dawkins, Richard (1982). *The Extended Phenotype*. San Francisco: W. H. Freeman.

De Quincey, Christian (2006). Switched-on consciousness: clarifying what it means. *Journal of Consciousness Studies*, 13(4), pp. 7–12.

De Quincey, Christian (2008). Reality bubbles: can we know anything about the physical world? *Journal of Consciousness Studies*, 15(8), pp. 94–101.

Dennett, Daniel C. (1978). *Brainstorms: Philosophical Essays on Mind and Psychology*. Montgomery, VT: Bradford Books.

Dennett, Daniel C. (1984). *Elbow Room: The Varieties of Free Will Worth Wanting*. Cambridge, MA: MIT Press.

Dennett, Daniel C. (1991). *Consciousness Explained*. New York: Little, Brown & Co.

Dennett, Daniel C. (1995). *Darwin's Dangerous Idea: Evolution and the Meanings of Life*. New York: Simon and Schuster.

Dennett, Daniel C. (1996). *Kinds of Minds: Towards an Understanding of Consciousness*. New York: Basic Books.

Dennett, Daniel C. (1998). *Brainchildren: Essays on Designing Minds*. Cambridge, MA: MIT Press.

Deutsch, David (1997). *The Fabric of Reality*. London: Allen Lane.

Diamond, Jared (1998). *Guns, Germs and Steel. A Short History of Everybody for the Last 13,000 Years*. New York: Random House.

Dirac, P. A. M. (1930, 4th edn. 1958). *The Principles of Quantum Mechanics*. Oxford: Oxford University Press.

Dowker, Fay (2003). Real time. *New Scientist*, 180 (2415), pp. 36–39 (4 October).

Dummett, Michael A. E. (1973). *Frege: Philosophy of Language*. London: Duckworth.

Edelman, Gerald M. (1992). *Bright Air, Brilliant Fire: On the Matter of the Mind.* New York: Basic Books.

Edelman, Gerald M. and Giulio Tononi (2000). *A Universe of Consciousness: How Matter Becomes Imagination.* New York: Basic Books.

Edelman, Gerald M. (2004). *Wider Than the Sky: The Phenomenal Gift of Consciousness.* New Haven, CT: Yale University Press.

Einstein, Albert (1922, 5th edn. 1969). *Grundzüge der Relativitätstheorie.* Braunschweig: Vieweg.

Elitzur, Avshalom C., Shahar Dolev, Nancy Kolenda (eds. 2005). *Quo Vadis Quantum Mechanics?* Berlin: Springer.

Feinberg, Todd E. (2001). *Altered Egos: How the Brain Creates the Self.* New York: Oxford University Press.

Feynman, Richard P. (1942/2005). *Feynman's Thesis.* A new aproach to quantum theory. New Jersey: World Scientific.

Feynman, Richard P. (1985). *QED: The Strange Theory of Light and Matter.* Princeton: Princeton University Press.

Feynman, Richard P., Robert B. Leighton, and Matthew Sands (1963). *The Feynman Lectures on Physics.* Volume I. Mainly Mechanics, Radiation, and Heat. Reading, MA: Addison-Wesley.

Feynman, Richard P., Robert B. Leighton, and Matthew Sands (1964). *The Feynman Lectures on Physics.* Volume II. Mainly Electromagnetism and Matter. Reading, MA: Addison-Wesley.

Feynman, Richard P., Robert B. Leighton, and Matthew Sands (1965). *The Feynman Lectures on Physics.* Volume III. Quantum Mechanics. Reading, MA: Addison-Wesley.

Flood, Raymond, and Michael Lockwood (eds. 1986). *The Nature of Time.* Oxford: Blackwell.

Floyd, Christiane, Heinz Züllighoven, Reinhard Budde, and Reinhard Keil-Slawik (ed. 1992). *Software Development and Reality Construction.* Berlin: Springer.

Folse, Henry J. (1985). *The Philosophy of Niels Bohr: The Framework of Complementarity.* Amsterdam: North-Holland.

Fraenkel, Abraham A., Yehoshua Bar-Hillel, and Azriel Lévy (1958, 2nd edn. 1973). *Foundations of Set Theory.* Amsterdam: North-Holland.

Freeman, Walter J. (1999). *How Brains Make Up Their Minds.* London: Weidenfeld & Nicolson.

Gazzaniga, Michael S., Richard B. Ivry, and George R. Mangun (1998). *Cognitive Neuroscience: The Biology of the Mind.* New York: W. W. Norton.

Gleick, James (1987). *Chaos: Making a New Science.* New York: Viking Penguin.

Gleick, James (1992). *Genius: Richard Feynman and Modern Physics*. New York: Random House.
Goldberger, Ary L., David R. Rigney, and Bruce J. West (1990). Chaos and fractals in human physiology. *Scientific American* (February).
Greene, Brian (1999). *The Elegant Universe: Superstrings, Hidden Dimensions, and the Quest for the Ultimate Theory*. New York: W. W. Norton.
Greene, Brian (2004). *The Fabric of the Cosmos: Space. Time, and the Texture of Reality*. New York: Alfred A. Knopf.
Greenfield, Susan A. (1995). *Journey to the Centers of the Mind: Toward a Science of Consciousness*. San Francisco: W. H. Freeman & Co.
Gries, David, and Fred B. Schneider (1993). *A Logical Approach to Discrete Math*. Berlin: Springer.
Guth, Alan H. (1997). *The Inflationary Universe: The Quest for a New Theory of Cosmic Origins*. London: Jonathan Cape.
Hájek, Petr (ed. 1996). *Gödel '96: Logical Foundations of Mathematics, Computer Science and Physics – Kurt Gödel's Legacy*. Berlin: Springer.
Hamilton, A. G. (1978). *Logic for Mathematicians*. Cambridge: Cambridge University Press.
Hannan, Barbara (2005). Review: On Consciousness. *Mind*, 114, pp. 743–747.
Hauser, Marc D. (2000). *Wild Minds: What Animals Really Think*. London: Allen Lane.
Hawking, Stephen W. (1988). *A Brief History of Time: From the Big Bang to Black Holes*. London: Bantam.
Hawking, Stephen W. (2001). *The Universe in a Nutshell*. London: Bantam.
Hawking, Stephen and Roger Penrose (1996). *The Nature of Space and Time* Princeton: Princeton University Press.
Heil, John, and Alfred Mele (eds. 1993). *Mental Causation*. Oxford: Oxford University Press.
Hegel, Georg Wilhelm Friedrich (1807, paperback edn. 1988). *Phänomenologie des Geistes*. Hamburg: Felix Meiner Verlag.
Hegel, Georg Wilhelm Friedrich (1977, translated by A.V. Miller). *Phenomenology of Spirit*. Oxford: Oxford University Press.
Heim, Michael (1993). *The Metaphysics of Virtual Reality*. Oxford: Oxford University Press.
Hofstadter, Douglas R. (1979). *Gödel, Escher, Bach: An Eternal Golden Braid*. A metaphorical fugue on minds and machines in the spirit of Lewis Carroll. New York: Basic Books.
Hofstadter, Douglas R. and Daniel C. Dennett (eds. 1981). *The Mind's I: Fantasies and Reflections on Self and the Soul*. New York: Basic Books.

Hofstadter, Douglas R. and the Fluid Analogies Research Group (1995). *Fluid Concepts and Creative Analogies: Computer Models of the Fundamental Mechanisms of Thought*. New York: Basic Books.

Honderich, Ted (ed. 1973). *Essays on Freedom of Action*. London: Routledge & Kegan Paul.

Honderich, Ted (1988). *A Theory of Determinism – The Mind, Neuroscience, and Life-Hopes*. Oxford: Oxford University Press.

Honderich, Ted (1993). *How Free Are You? The Determinism Problem*. Oxford: Oxford University Press.

Honderich, Ted (ed. 1995). *The Oxford Companion to Philosophy*. Oxford: Oxford University Press.

Honderich, Ted (2001). *Philosopher – A Kind of Life*. London: Routledge.

Honderich, Ted (2002). *After the Terror*. Edinburgh: Edinburgh University Press.

Honderich, Ted (2004). *On Consciousness*. Edinburgh: Edinburgh University Press.

Honderich, Ted (2006). Radical externalism. *Journal of Consciousness Studies*, 13(7–8), pp. 3–13.

Honderich, Ted (2007). Honderich on McGinn on Honderich on consciousness. http://www.homepages.ucl.ac.uk/~uctytho/HonderichOnMcGinnOnHonderich.html.

Honderich, Ted, and Myles Burnyeat (ed. 1979). *Philosophy As It Is*. London: Allen Lane.

James, William (1902). *The Varieties of Religious Experience*. New York: Longman.

Jaynes, Julian (1976). *The Origin of Consciousness in the Breakdown of the Bicameral Mind*. Boston, MA: Houghton Mifflin.

Jech, Thomas (1971, 2nd edn. 1997). *Set Theory*. New York: Springer.

Jeffries, Stuart (2007). Enemies of thought. *The Guardian*, December 21. http://books.guardian.co.uk/departments/politicsphilosophyandsociety/story/0,,2230971,00.html.

Johnson, George (2003). *A Shortcut Through Time: The Path to the Quantum Computer*. London: Jonathan Cape.

Joyce, James (1986). *Ulysses*. New York: Random House.

Koch, Christof (2004). *The Quest for Consciousness: A Neurobiological Approach*. Englewood, CO: Roberts & Co.

Kripke, Saul A. (1965). Semantical analysis of intuitionistic logic. In J.N. Crossley & M.A.E. Dummett (eds.), *Formal Systems and Recursive Functions* (pp. 92–130). Amsterdam: North-Holland.

Kripke, Saul A. (1980). *Naming and Necessity*. Oxford: Blackwell.

Kripke, Saul A. (1982). *Wittgenstein on Rules and Private Language: An Elementary Exposition*. Oxford: Blackwell.

Kuhn, Thomas (2nd edn. 1971). *The Structure of Scientific Revolutions.* Chicago:University of Chicago Press.

Kuhn, Robert Lawrence (ed. 2000). *Closer to Truth: Challenging Current Belief.* New York: McGraw-Hill.

Kurzweil, Ray (2005). *The Singularity is Near: When humans transcend biology.* London: Duckworth.

Lakatos, Imre (1976). *Proofs and Refutations.* New York: Cambridge University Press.

Lakatos, Imre, and Alan Musgrave (eds. 1979). *Criticism and the Growth of Knowledge.* Cambridge: Cambridge University Press.

LeDoux, Joseph E. (1993). Emotional memory: in search of systems and synapses. In Crinella (1993), pp. 149–157.

LeDoux, Joseph E. (1996). *The Emotional Brain: The Mysterious Underpinnings of Emotional Life.* New York: Simon & Schuster.

LeDoux, Joseph E. (2002). *Synaptic Self: How Our Brains Become Who We Are.* New York: Viking Penguin.

LeDoux, Joseph E., Jacek Debiec, and Henry Moss (eds. 2003). *The Self: From Soul to Brain.* Annals of the New York Academy of Sciences, 1001.

Leiter, Brian (2007), Leiter Reports: A Philosophy Blog (http://leiterreports.typepad.com/blog/).

Lewis, Michael (1992). *Shame: The Exposed Self.* Free Press.

Libet, Benjamin, E.W. Wright, B. Feinstein, and D.K. Pearl (1979). Subjective referral of the timing for a conscious sensory experience. *Brain*, 102, 193–224

Libet, Benjamin (2003). Can Conscious Experience Affect Brain Activity? *Journal of Consciousness Studies*, 10 (12), pp. 24–28.

Libet, Benjamin (2004). *Mind Time: The Temporal Factor in Consciousness.* Cambridge, MA: Harvard University Press.

Lindley, David (1996). *Where Does the Wierdness Go? Why Quantum Mechanics Is Strange, But Not as Strange as You Think.* New York, Basic Books.

Llinás, Rodolfo R. (2001). *I of the Vortex – From Neurons to Self.* Cambridge, MA: MIT Press.

Lloyd, Seth, and Y. Jack Ng (2004). Black hole computers. *Scientific American*, 291 (5), pp. 30–39.

Lockwood, Michael (1989). *Mind, Brain and the Quantum – The Compound 'I'.* Oxford: Blackwell.

Lovelock, James (1982). *Gaia: A New Look at Life on Earth.* Oxford: Oxford University Press.

Lovelock, James (1988). *The Ages of Gaia: A Biography of Our Living Earth.* Oxford: Oxford University Press.

Mac Lane, Saunders (1998). *Categories for the Working Mathematician*. Berlin: Springer.

Markram, Henry (2009). http://bluebrainproject.epfl.ch

McFadden, Johnjoe (2000). *Quantum Evolution: Life in the Multiverse*. London: HarperCollins.

McFadden, Johnjoe (2002a). Synchronous firing and its influence on the brain's electromagnetic field: evidence for an electromagnetic field theory of consciousness. *Journal of Consciousness Studies*, 9 (4), 23–50.

McFadden, Johnjoe (2002b). The conscious electromagnetic information (cemi) field theory: the hard problem made easy? *Journal of Consciousness Studies*, 9 (8), 45–60.

McGinn, Colin (1984). *Wittgenstein on Meaning – An Interpretation and Evaluation*. Oxford: Blackwell.

McGinn, Colin (1990). The Meaning of Life by A.J. Ayer. *London Review of Books*.

McGinn, Colin (1991). *The Problem of Consciousness – Essays Towards a Resolution*. Oxford: Blackwell.

McGinn, Colin (1999). *The Mysterious Flame – Conscious Minds in a Material World*. New York: Basic Books.

McGinn, Colin (2002). *The Making of a Philosopher – My Journey Through Twentieth-Century Philosophy*. New York: HarperCollins.

McGinn, Colin (2007a). McGinn on Honderich. http://www.homepages.ucl.ac.uk/~uctytho/McGinnReview.html

McGinn, Colin (2007b). McGinn's rejoinder to Honderich's reply to his review. http://www.homepages.ucl.ac.uk/~uctytho/McGinnRejoinder.html

Mendelson, Elliott (1964, 2nd edn.1979). *Introduction to Mathematical Logic*. New York: D. Van Nostrand Co.

Metzinger, Thomas (ed. 1995). *Conscious Experience*. Paderborn: Schöningh / Exeter: Imprint Academic.

Metzinger, Thomas (2003). *Being No-One: The Self-Model Theory of Subjectivity*. Cambridge, MA: MIT Press.

Metzinger, Thomas (2009). *The Ego Tunnel: The Science of the Mind and the Myth of the Self*. New York: Basic Books

Michalewicz, Zbigniew (1992, 3rd edn. 1996) *Genetic Algorithms + Data Structures = Evolution Programs*. Berlin: Springer.

Misner, Charles W., Kip S. Thorne, and John A. Wheeler (1973). *Gravitation*. San Francisco: W. H. Freeman.

Moore, Gordon (1965). http://www.intel.com/technology/silicon/mooreslaw/

Mukhopadhyay, A.K. (2000). *The Millennium Bridge*. New Delhi: Conscious Publications.

Nagel, Thomas (1986). *The View from Nowhere*. Oxford: Oxford University Press.
Nielsen, Michael A., and Isaac L. Chuang (2000). *Quantum Computation and Quantum Information*. Cambridge: Cambridge University Press.
Omnès, Roland (1999a). *Understanding Quantum Mechanics*. Princeton: Princeton University Press.
Omnès, Roland (1999b). *Quantum Philosophy: Understanding and Interpreting Contemporary Science*. Princeton: Princeton University Press.
Pais, Abraham (1986). *Inward Bound: Of Matter and Forces in the Physical World*. New York: Oxford University Press.
Pasquini, Claude (2006). A (mostly) sunny and sober anniversary. *Journal of Consciousness Studies*, 13(6), pp. 79–100.
Peitgen, Heinz-Otto, Hartmut Jürgens, and Dietmar Saupe (1992). *Chaos and Fractals: New Frontiers of Science*. New York: Springer.
Penrose, Roger (1987). Quantum physics and conscious thought. In B.J. Hiley and F.D. Peat (eds.), *Quantum Implications* (pp. 105–120). London: Routledge & Kegan Paul.
Penrose, Roger (1989). *The Emperor's New Mind: Concerning Computers, Minds, and the Laws of Physics*. Oxford: Oxford University Press.
Penrose, Roger (1994). *Shadows of the Mind: A Search for the Missing Science of Consciousness*. Oxford: Oxford University Press.
Penrose, Roger (1997). *The Large, the Small, and the Human Mind*. Cambridge: Cambridge University Press.
Penrose, Roger (2004). *The Road to Reality: A Complete Guide to the Laws of the Universe*. London: Jonathan Cape.
Pinkard, Terry (2000). *Hegel: A Biography*. Cambridge: Cambridge University Press.
Pinker, Steven (1994). *The Language Instinct: The New Science of Language and Mind*. London: Allen Lane.
Pinker, Steven (1997). *How the Mind Works*. London: Allen Lane.
Pirsig, Robert M. (1974). *Zen and the Art of Motorcycle Maintenance*. New York: Bantam.
Popkorn, Sally (1994). *First Steps in Modal Logic*. Cambridge: Cambridge University Press.
Popper, Karl R. (1963). *Conjectures and Refutations*. London: Routledge & Kegan Paul.
Popper, Karl R. (1972). *Objective Knowledge: An Evolutionary Approach*. Oxford: Oxford University Press.
Popper, Karl R. (1976). *Unended Quest*. London: Fontana.
Popper, Karl R., and John C. Eccles (1977). *The Self and Its Brain*. New York: Springer.

Price, Huw (1996). *Time's Arrow and Archimedes' Point: New Directions for the Physics of Time.* Oxford: Oxford University Press.

Prigogine, Ilya and Isabelle Stengers (1984). *Order Out of Chaos: Man's New Dialogue with Nature.* New York: Bantam.

Quartz, Steven R. and Terrence J. Sejnowski (2002). *Liars, Lovers, and Heroes: What the New Brain Science Reveals About Who We Are.* New York: HarperCollins

Quine, Willard Van Orman (1940). *Mathematical Logic.* Cambridge, MA: Harvard University Press.

Quine, Willard Van Orman (1960). *Word and Object.* Cambridge, MA: MIT Press.

Quine, Willard Van Orman (1963, 2nd edn. 1969). *Set Theory and Its Logic.* Cambridge, MA: Harvard University Press.

Quine, Willard Van Orman (1969). *Ontological Relativity and Other Essays.* New York: Columbia University Press.

Rae, Alastair I. M. (1986). *Quantum Physics: Illusion or Reality?* Cambridge: Cambridge University Press.

Ramachandran, V.S., and Sandra Blakeslee (1998). *Phantoms in the Brain: Human Nature and the Architecture of the Mind.* London: Fourth Estate.

Reid, David D. (1999). Introduction to causal sets: an alternate view of spacetime structure. http://arxiv.org/abs/gr-qc/9909075

Reischauer, Edwin O. (1977). *The Japanese.* Cambridge, MA: Harvard University Press.

Roberts, J. M. (1976). *The Hutchinson History of the World.* London: Hutchinson.

Rogers, Ben (1999). *A.J. Ayer: A Life.* New York: Grove Press.

Rojas, Raul (1996). *Neural Networks: A Systematic Introduction.* Berlin: Springer.

Rose, Steven (ed. 1998). *From Brains to Consciousness?* Essays on the new sciences of the mind. London: Allen Lane.

Ross, J. Andrew (1991). The Globall Hyperatlas: a development proposal. *The Visual Computer*, 8, pp. 1–7.

Ross, J. Andrew (1996). *Lifeball – Birth of a New God.* www.andyross.net/lifeball.pdf

Ross, J. Andrew (2001). The Miph of Consciousness: The Mathematics, Informatics and Physics of Consciousness and Its Place in Nature. www.andyross.net/miph.pdf

Ross, J. Andrew (2002). First-person consciousness: Honderich and McGinn reviewed. *Journal of Consciousness Studies*, 9 (7), pp. 55–82.

Ross, J. Andrew (2003a). The Self: From Soul to Brain. *Journal of Consciousness Studies*, 10 (2), pp. 67–85.

Ross, J. Andrew (2003b). A Photonic Theory of Consciousness. www.andyross.net/prague.pdf

Ross, J. Andrew (2003c). Business at the Speed of Evolution. *Internal Auditing and Business Risk*, 27(12), p. 12.

Ross, J. Andrew (2004). *Mindworlds* – Consciousness and Related Studies. First edition of this book. www.andyross.net/mindcars.pdf

Ross, J. Andrew (2005). Roads to reality: Penrose and Wolfram compared. *Journal of Consciousness Studies*, 12 (2), pp. 78–83.

Ross, J. Andrew (2006). Blinded by the light. *Journal of Consciousness Studies*, 13(4), pp. 32–33.

Ross, J. Andrew (2006). Will robots see humans as dinosaurs? *Journal of Consciousness Studies*, 13(12), pp. 97–104.

Ross, J. Andrew (2008). Hitting on consciousness. *Journal of Consciousness Studies*, 15(1), pp. 109–128.

Ross, J. Andrew (2009). *SAP NetWeaver BI Accelerator*. SAP Press Essentials 42. Boston, MA: SAP Press.

Roth, Gerhard (2001). *Das Gehirn und seine Wirklichkeit*. Frankfurt: Suhrkamp Verlag.

Rucker, Rudy (1982). *Infinity and the Mind: The Science and Philosophy of the Infinite*. Brighton: Harvester Press.

Russell, Bertrand A.W. (2nd edn. 1961). *History of Western Philosophy*. London: George Allen & Unwin.

Russell, Peter (1982, rev. edn. 1991). *The Awakening Earth: The Global Brain*. London: Arkana.

Ryle, Gilbert (1949). *The Concept of Mind*. London: Hutchinson.

Sacks, Oliver (2004). In the River of Consciousness. *The New York Review of Books*, LI (1), pp. 41–44.

Satinover, Jeffrey (2001). *The Quantum Brain: The Search for Freedom and the Next Generation of Man*. New York: Wiley.

Schacter, Daniel L. (1996). *Searching for Memory: The Brain, the Mind, and the Past*. New York: Basic Books.

Schacter, Daniel L. (2001). *The Seven Sins of Memory: How the Brain Forgets and Remembers*. Boston, MA: Houghton Mifflin.

Scott, Alwyn (1995). *Stairway to the Mind: The Controversial New Science of Consciousness*. New York: Copernicus.

Scruton, Roger (2001). *Kant: A Very Short Introduction*. Oxford: Oxford University Press.

Searle, John R. (1981). Minds, brains, and programs. In D.R. Hofstadter & D.C. Dennett (eds.), *The Mind's I* (pp. 353–373). New York: Basic Books.

Searle, John R. (1990). Is the brain's mind a computer program? *Scientific American* (January).
Searle, John R. (1992). *The Rediscovery of the Mind*. Cambridge, MA: MIT Press.
Shapiro, Ehud, and Yaakov Benenson (2006). Bringing DNA computers to life. *Scientific American*, 294(5), 32–39. http://www.sciam.com
Shear, Jonathan (ed. 1997). *Explaining Consciousness – The 'Hard Problem'*. Boston, MA: MIT Press.
Shimony, Abner (1989). Conceptual foundations of quantum mechanics. In: Paul Davies (ed.). *The New Physics*. Cambridge: Cambridge University Press.
Singer, Wolf (1998). Consciousness from a neurobiological perspective. In Steven Rose (ed.), *From Brains to Consciousness?* London: Allen Lane.
Singer, Wolf (2000). Phenomenal awareness and consciousness from a neurobiological perspective. In T. Metzinger (ed.), *Neural Correlates of Consciousness*. Cambridge, MA: MIT Press.
Singer, Wolf (2002). *Der Beobachter im Gehirn*. Frankfurt: Suhrkamp Verlag.
Smolin, Lee (1997). *The Life of the Cosmos*. New York: Oxford University Press.
Smolin, Lee (2000). *Three Roads to Quantum Gravity*. London: Weidenfeld & Nicolson.
Smolin, Lee (2004). Atoms of Space and Time. *Scientific American*, 290 (1), pp. 56–65.
Snowdon, Paul (2006). Honderich's radical externalisms. *Journal of Consciousness Studies*, 13(7–8), pp. 187–212.
Sorkin, Rafael D. (2005). Geometry from order. www.einstein-online.info/en/spotlights/causal_sets
Sorkin, Rafael D. (1991). First steps with causal sets. In: R. Cianci, R. de Ritis, M. Francaviglia, G. Marmo, C. Rubano, P. Scudellaro, (eds.). *General Relativity and Gravitational Physics*. Proceedings. Singapore: World Scientific.
Stapp, Henry P. (1993). *Mind, Matter, and Quantum Mechanics*. Berlin: Springer.
Star, Jonathan (trans. 1997). *Rumi – In the Arms of the Beloved*. New York: Tarcher/Putnam.
Stock, Gregory (1993). *Metaman: Humans, Machines, and the Birth of a Global Super-Organism*. New York: Bantam.
Taylor, Charles (1975). *Hegel*. Cambridge: Cambridge University Press.
Tegmark, Max (2003). Parallel Universes. *Scientific American*, 288 (5), pp. 30–41.
Teller, Paul (1995). *An Interpretive Introduction to Quantum Field Theory*. Princeton: Princeton University Press.
Tolkien, J. R. R. (1968). *The Lord of the Rings*. London: George Allen & Unwin.
Velmans, Max (2000). *Understanding Consciousness*. London: Routledge.

Velmans, Max (2002). How Could Conscious Experience Affect Brains? *Journal of Consciousness Studies*, 9 (11), pp. 3–29.
Wegner, Daniel M. (1989, new edn. 1994). *The White Bear and Other Unwanted Thoughts: Suppression, Obsession, and the Psychology of Mental Control.* New York: Viking / Guilford Press (new edn).
Wegner, Daniel M. (2002). *The Illusion of Conscious Will.* Cambridge, MA: MIT Press.
Weinberg, Steven (1995). *The Quantum Theory of Fields.* Volume I. Foundations. Cambridge: Cambridge University Press.
Weiskrantz, Lawrence (1997). *Consciousness Lost and Found: A Neuropsychological Exploration.* Oxford: Oxford University Press.
Wheeler, John Archibald (1990, 2nd edn. 1999). *A Journey into Gravity and Spacetime.* New York: Scientific American Library.
Wheeler, John Archibald with Ford, Kenneth (1998). *Geons, Black Holes, and Quantum Foam: A Life in Physics.* New York: W. W. Norton.
Will, Clifford M. (1986). *Was Einstein Right? Putting General Relativity to the Test.* New York: Basic Books.
Wittgenstein, Ludwig (1922, translated by D.F. Pears and B.F. McGuinness 1961). *Tractatus Logico-Philosophicus.* London: Routledge and Kegan Paul.
Wittgenstein, Ludwig (1953, translated by G.E.M. Anscombe 1958). *Philosophical Investigations.* Oxford: Basil Blackwell.
Wolf, Fred Alan (1981). *Taking the Quantum Leap: The New Physics for Nonscientists.* San Francisco: Harper & Row.
Wolfram, Stephen (2002). *A New Kind of Science.* Champaign, IL: Wolfram Media.
Wright, Robert (2000). *Nonzero: The Logic of Human Destiny.* New York: Pantheon.
Wright, Crispin (1980). *Wittgenstein on the Foundations of Mathematics.* Cambridge, MA: Harvard University Press.
Yourgrau, Palle (1999). *Gödel Meets Einstein: Time Travel in the Gödel Universe.* Chicago: Open Court.
Yourgrau, Palle (2005). *A World Without Time: The Forgotten Legacy of Gödel and Einstein.* London: Allen Lane.
Zeh, H.-Dieter (1989, 2nd edn. 1992). *The Physical Basis of the Direction of Time.* Berlin: Springer.
Zohar, Danah (1990). *The Quantum Self.* London: Bloomsbury.
Zuse, Konrad (1993). *The Computer – My Life.* Berlin: Springer.

Index

Achilles, 76
Adams, Douglas, 215
Ahmavaara, Yrjö, 229
Ainslie, George, 160
Ali, Tariq, 281
All Souls College Oxford, 18
Althusser, Louis, 18
Amelia Jackson Studentship, 18
Amis, Martin, 15, 25, 115, 280
amygdala, 142, 158
analog self, 57, 264
anomalous monism, 284
Anthony Freeman, VIII
anthropic principle, 222
Apple Macintosh, 24
Aquinas, Thomas, 145
Armstrong, Neil, 15
arrow of time, 185
artificial consciousness, 105
artificial neural networks, 59
artificial neuronet, 72, 205
Asimov, Isaac, 14
Aspect, Alain, 130
Association for the Scientific Study of Consciousness, VIII, 9, 25, 269
Atlanta, Georgia, 28
Augustine, St., 145
Austin B. Fletcher Professor, 159
autism, 154
autistic perspective, 164
autobiography, 108, 203, 241, 282
autophenomenology, 32, 135, 139, 164, 184, 267
Ayer, Alfred J., 18, 109, 114, 129, 278, 294
Baars, Bernard, 133
Baker, Gordon, 16
Banaji, Mahzarin Rustum, 153
Bauer, Friedrich L., 24, 25
Beatles, 15, 16
Beethoven, Ludwig van, 17
Bell, John (logician), 19
Bell, John (physicist), 98, 130, 177
Berners-Lee, Tim, 27
binding problem, 60
bioethics, 145
Black, Andrew, 296
Blackmore, Susan, VIII, 136, 190
Blue Brain project, 206, 270
Bohr, Niels, 85, 130, 178, 227
Boltzmann's constant, 85
Boole, George, 252
Boolean algebra, 165
Bose–Einstein condensate, 38
Bose–Einstein state, 100
Bose–Einstein statistics, 86
Bowie, David, 17
Brain Mind Institute, Lausanne, 270

Index 335

Bremen, Germany, 25
Brouwer, L.E.J., 34, 69
Buber, Martin, 57
Buddha, 63
Burge, Tyler, 119, 288, 291
Burnyeat, Myles, 117
Bush, George W., 148, 151
California Institute of Technology, 146
Cantor, Georg, 76, 80, 172, 226, 252
Cantor's paradise, 162, 253
Capgras syndrome, 157
Cartesian dualism, 137
Cartesian theater, 60, 158, 159, 190
causal set theory, 259
cellular automata, 234
cerebellum, 158
Chaitin, Gregory J., 69
Chaitin–Kolmogorov randomness, 235
Chalmers, David, VII, 2, 4, 25, 26, 32, 43, 107, 109, 128, 130, 164, 203, 206
Chichele Professor, 113
child development, 149
Chomsky, Noam, 17
Churchland, Patricia Smith, 142
City University of New York, 112, 116
Clarke, Arthur C., 14
classical logic, 66
cogito ergo sum, 92, 95, 127
Cohen, Jerry, 113
Cohen, Paul, 78, 80
Columbia University, 158
conjoint self, 151
Conrad, Joseph, 16
consciousness is photonic, 186, 200
consciousness transforms, 37

Conservative Party, 113
constructive logic, 65, 68, 194
Copenhagen interpretation, 227
Copernican shift, 236
corpus callosum, 30, 156
cosmic soul, 222
Craig, Edward, 20
cumulative hierarchy, 78, 171, 172, 185, 192, 194, 198, 210, 213, 236, 252
Damasio, Antonio, 154, 206
Dartmouth College, 150
Data Processing (magazine), 20
Davidson, Donald, 68, 117, 129, 291
Davis, Laing and Dick Tutorial College, London, 20
Dawkins, Richard, 136
Daytime Emmy Awards, 28
Decade of the Brain', 271
decahertz EM waves, 96, 100, 104, 182, 186, 189, 199
decahertz photon field, 102
decahertz photonics, 188
delayed gratification, 148
Dennett, Daniel, VII, 4, 28, 29, 32, 47, 109, 117, 119, 133, 135, 142, 159, 164, 204, 209, 267
DeRose, Keith, 297
Descartes, René, 9, 92, 95, 127, 145
determinism, 84, 110, 112
Deutsch, David, 69, 81, 134, 228
dialectic, 34, 47, 79, 167, 239
Dirac ket notation, 228
Dirac, P.A.M., 130
disjoint self, 151
disquotation, 68
DNA molecules, 272
Donnellan, Keith, 114
Doors (rock band), 16

Dostoyevsky, Fyodor, 16
Dowker, Fay, 202
Duke University, 149
Dummett, Michael, 18
Dylan, Bob, 16
Eccles, John, 118
Edelman, David, 28
Edelman, Gerald, 7
Einstein, Albert, 41, 91, 128, 130, 179, 242
Einstein's cosmological equations, 52, 94
Einstein's field equations, 247
Einstein's special theory of relativity, 129
Einstein's theory of gravity, 225
Electron (magazine), 20
Elsinore, Denmark, VII, 2, 25
entanglement, 170, 176, 177, 187, 229, 248
entropy, 54, 85, 97, 169, 181, 207, 217, 228, 243, 256
epiphenomenal dangler, 183
Escher, M.C., 152
Evans, Gareth, 115, 278
Everett scenario, 229
Everett, Keith, 130, 134
evolutionary epistemology, 168
Exeter College Oxford, 15, 18
extended phenotype, 183
Farleigh, Peter, 26
Feinberg, Todd, 158
Fermi–Dirac statistics, 86
Feyerabend, Paul, 16
Feynman Lectures on Physics, 15, 22
Feynman, Richard, 164, 228, 250
finististic set theory, 51
Finkelstein, David, 230
Firestone, Shulamith, 18

first-order logic, 66, 165, 171
flicker fusion rate, 100
Fodor, Jerry, 160
formal arithmetic, 48, 70
fountain of phenomenology, 181
Fraenkel, Abraham, 75
Frankfurt, Harry, 8
Frege, Gottlob, 42, 50, 74, 111, 129, 165, 171, 209, 226, 250, 252
Freudian orthodoxy, 138
Frith, Uta, 154
Fuller Theological Seminary, 144
functional magnetic resonance imaging, 271
functionalism, 127
Galileo, Galilei, 69, 251
Gandy, Robin, 18
Gazzaniga, Michael, 150, 156
genetic engineering, 219, 270
genomic metaphysics, 146
genomic self, 162
Global Online Dominion, 275
Globall Hyperatlas, 24
Gödel, Kurt, 42, 49, 68, 69, 72, 179, 226
Gödel's constructible universe, 51, 78
Gödel's incompleteness theorem, 18, 49, 70, 129, 167, 226
Golden Brain Award, 154
Green English Conversation School, 21
Greenfield, Susan, 26
Greer, Germaine, 18
Grote Professor, 108, 110, 277, 278, 284
Guardian (newspaper), 278
Hacker, Peter, 16
Hadamard transform, 96
Hagan, Scott, 26

Index

Hameroff, Stuart, 26, 96, 184
Hamilton, W. D., 160
Hannan, Barbara, 283
Hannay, Alastair, 118
Hants and Dorset Omnibus Company, 15
Happé, Francesca, 154
Hardy, G. H., 41
Harris, Sam, 29
Hartnackschule, Berlin, 17
Harvard University, 143, 148, 153
Hauser, Marc, 148
Hawking, Stephen, 7, 41, 132, 224
Hegel, G.W.F., 17, 42, 92, 129, 177, 235
Hegelian Weltgeist, 57
Heidegger, Martin, 129, 145
Heidelberg, Germany, 23
Heil, John, 119
Heisenberg uncertainty, 101, 175, 196, 199, 246
Heisenberg, Werner, 87, 130
Hemingway, Ernest, 109
hemispatial neglect, 157
Henry and Lucy Moses Professor, 141
Heraclitus, 63
Hesse, Hermann, 16
heterophenomenology, 32, 135, 139, 160, 164, 267
hierarchy of Buddhas, 162
Hilbert, David, 227
Hiley, Basil, 26
hippocampus, 142, 158
Hofstadter, Douglas, 21, 52, 95, 129, 134, 159
Homo superior, 272, 273
Honderich, Ted, VII, VIII, 3, 4, 9, 17, 26, 108, 277
Howard Hughes Medical Institute, 146, 158
Huddersfield, Yorkshire, 13
Hume, David, 152
Humpty-Dumpty problem, 146
Hussein, Saddam, 22
Husserl, Edmund, 69, 129, 155
hylomorphism, 146
IBM supercomputer, 206, 270
indeterminacy of translation, 129
Institute of Administrative Accounting and Data Processing, 20
intentionality, 191, 293
International Publishing Corporation, 20
intuitionism, 67
intuitionist logic, 34, 194
Inwood, Michael, 20
Isaacson, Daniel, 19
Ishiguro, Hidé, 21
Isis (magazine), 18
James, William, 63, 144, 155, 187, 190, 261, 282
Jaynes, Julian, 40
Jefferson Airplane, 16
Jeffries, Stuart, 278
John Locke prize, 114
Johns, Captain W. E., 13
Johns, Gordon, 153
Joyce, James, 209
Joycean stream of consciousness, 137
Joycean virtual machine, 209
Kandel, Eric, 158
Kant, Immanuel, 9, 16, 42, 54, 69, 74, 92, 145, 203, 236, 285
Kaplan, David, 114
Kennedy, John F., 14
Kenny, Anthony, 117
King's College London, 154

Kinnock, Neil, 113
Koch, Christof, 7
Koran, 20
Kripke, Saul, 17, 35, 42, 83, 111, 114
Kronecker, Leopold, 34
Kuhn, Thomas, 16
Kuratowski, Kazimierz, 75
Kurzweil, Ray, 9, 269
Labour Party, 113
Lahee, Angela, VIII, 8
Laing, Ronald, 18
Lakatos, Imre, 16
Lansdowne Tutors, London, 22
Lausanne, Switzerland, 206
Leary, Timothy, 18
LeDoux, Joseph, VII, 141
Lego brick model of mind, 123
Leiter, Brian, 277, 295
Lenin, V. I., 18
Leverhulme Studentship, 16
Lewis, Michael, 150
Libet, Benjamin, 7, 118, 160, 204, 263
light cones, 244
Llinás, Rodolfo, 100, 139, 155, 162, 184
Lloyd, Seth, 238
logical positivism, 129
London School of Economics and Political Science (LSE), 16
Louisiana State University, 142
Luton, Bedfordshire, 13
Mac Lane, Saunders, 80
MacArthur award, 224
Mach, Ernst, 129
magic of complex numbers, 225
Mailer, Norman, 16, 280
Major, John, 113
Mallaber, Judy, 16

Mao Zedong, 18
Marcuse, Herbert, 18
marine snail, 158
Markram, Henry, 206, 270
Markus, Hazel Rose, 150
Marx, Karl, 20
Mathematica, 224
Matisse, Henri, 159
Matrix, 224
Mauron, Alexandre, 145
Maxi Jazz, 159
Maxwell's equations, 233
Maxwell–Boltzmann statistics, 86
May, Simon Cabulea, 296
McDowell, John, 278
McFadden, Johnjoe, VIII, 27, 124, 162, 189, 201, 207, 229
McGinn, Colin, VII, VIII, 4, 9, 27, 108, 164, 277
McGinn, Marie, 278
McLuhan, Marshall, 18
medial frontal cortex, 154
Mele, Alfred, 119
meme machines, 219
Merleau-Ponty, Maurice, 155
methodological autism, 186
Metzinger, Thomas, 7, 129, 283
Microsoft Windows, 275
Microsoft Word, 24
microtubules, 96, 101, 102
Mill, John Stuart, 69
Miller, Arthur, 109
Mind (journal), 283
Ministry of Defence, London, 19
Minkowski spacetime, 225, 233
miph, 3, 234
Mishima, Yukio, 21
modal logic, 35, 53, 80, 168, 194
molecular mechanisms of memory,

158
Monk, Ray, 113
Moore, Gordon, 270
Moore, Patrick, 13
Moore's law, 270
Morpeth, Northumberland, 13
Moses, 162
Mount Sinai School of Medicine, New York, 4, 27, 141
Mukhopadhyay, A.K., 238
multiple drafts model, 136
Murdoch, Iris, 19
Murphy, Nancey, 144
mysterianism, 109, 132, 281
Nagel, Thomas, 26, 120, 131, 138, 201
nanotechnology, 270
National Academy of Sciences, 155
NATO ASI Series F, 24
NATO Headquarters, Brussels, 19
NATO Special Programme on Advanced Educational Technology, 24
naturalistic dualism, 132
Neumann, John von, 51, 74, 77, 172, 192, 197, 210, 252
Neumann–Bernays–Gödel set theory, 52
neural correlates of consciousness, 59
Neurath, Otto, 41
neurological self, 162
New Testament, 20
New York Academy of Sciences, VII, 4, 27
New York Times, 144
New York University, 141
New York University School of Medicine, 155
Newsweek, 29

Newton, Isaac, 224
Newton's gravitational constant, 247
Ng, Jack, 238
Nietzsche, Friedrich, 20, 145, 155
North East London Polytechnic, 17
NP problems, 73
Omnès, Roland, 130, 170
omnium, 225, 238
ontogenesis, 77, 191, 198
Orch OR, 101, 184, 237
Oxford Intensive School of English, 20
panpsychism, 125, 208, 211
Pasadena, California, 144
Pasquini, Claude, VIII, 9, 28, 269
Peacocke, Christopher, 115
Penguin (publisher), 113
Penrose, Roger, VIII, 7, 28, 38, 69, 72, 96, 184, 202, 212, 224, 249
Penrose–Hameroff microwave reduction, 101
perceptual binding, 183
Perring, Christian, 296
phenomenal world, 36, 180
phenomenological tradition, 129
Philosophy, Politics and Economics (PPE), 16
photonic self, 162
physical time, 244, 265
Pinker, Steven, 122
Piper, Arthur, 27
Pirsig, Robert, 21
Pitt Rivers Museum, 9, 28
Planck scale, 84, 90, 101, 102, 177, 212
Planck, Max, 85
Planck's constant, 85, 175, 246
Playfair, Giles, 121
Poole Grammar School, 13

Poole, Dorset, 13
Popper, Karl, 16, 18, 118, 167, 254
Power of Purpose Awards, VIII, 7
Prague, Czech Republic, VII, 5, 27, 62, 189
Princeton University, 146
Principia Mathematica, 226
principle of computational equivalence, 234, 240
probability, 17, 54, 248, 256
propositional calculus, 45
protophenomenology, 181
psychological time, 244, 265
psychoneural intimacy, 109
psychophysics, 182
Putnam, Hilary, 119, 288, 291
quagmire, 234
qualia, 32, 44, 54, 104, 137, 190
quanglement, 229, 238
quantificational calculus, 48
quantum correlates of consciousness, 100, 104
quantum electrodynamics, 85, 164
quantum gravity, 202, 212, 225, 229, 259
quantum logic, 170
qubits, 96, 135, 197, 228
Quincey, Christian de, VIII, 8, 267
Quine, W.V.O., 16, 42, 68, 74, 111, 129, 191, 209, 226, 253
Quinn, Naomi, 149
Radcliffe, 153
radical externalism, 281, 290
Ramachandran, Vilayanur, 107, 159, 160
randomness, 216
Rawls, John, 113
Raymont, Paul, 296
reflection principles, 172

Reich, Wilhelm, 18
relativistic cosmology, 91
relativistic spacetime, 178
Riemann sphere, 225, 230
Robert Wood Johnson Medical School, 150
Roberts, J. M., 20
robotics, 270
Rogers, Ben, 279
Rolling Stones, 16
Rosenthal, David, 28
Roth, Philip, 16
Rothko, Ed, 159
Rouse Ball Professor, 224
Routledge (publisher), 112
Rowan, Dean C., 295
Royal Institute of Philosophy, 120
Russell, Bertrand, 16, 20, 42, 50, 111, 129, 171, 209, 226, 252, 279
Russell's paradox, 74
Rutgers University, 108, 116, 150
Sacks, Mark, 295
Sacks, Oliver, 7
Salk Institute, 146, 154
SAP AG, Walldorf, Germany, 25
SAP NetWeaver Business Intelligence Accelerator, 28
SAP Press, 29
Sartre, Jean-Paul, 16, 129
Schacter, Daniel, 143
Schiller, Friedrich, 177
Schrödinger equation, 175, 233
Schrödinger, Erwin, 130, 229
Schrödinger's cat, 56, 135
Science Museum, London, 13
Scientific American, VIII, 6, 179, 212, 238
Scott, Alwyn, 25
Scruton, Roger, 113

Searle, John, 38, 107, 119, 127, 134, 160, 291
Seattle, Washington, 27
Sejnowski, Terrence, 146
Shankar, Ravi, 15
Sheffield University, 118
Sheffield, England, 28
Sheldonian Theatre, Oxford, 21
Sherrington, Charles, 155
Shizuoka City, Japan, 21
Singer, Wolf, 60, 124, 147, 183
Skinner, B.F., 129
Skövde, Sweden, VII, 3, 26, 62, 109, 282
Sloterdijk, Peter, 145
Smarties task, 154
Smith, Peter, 118
Smolin, Lee, 212
Snowdon, Paul, 16, 283, 284
Sokal, Alan, 8
solipsism, 39
Sorkin, Rafael, 230, 259
specious present, 200
Sperry, Roger, 156
Spinoza, Baruch, 41, 155
split-brain research, 156
Springer (publisher), 8, 23
St. Anne's College Oxford, VIII, 19, 28, 269
Stanford University, VII, 2, 23, 150
Stapledon Exhibition, 15
Star Trek, 30, 151, 274
Stewart, Al, 16
Strawson, Peter, 126
stream of consciousness, 190
superposition, 56, 169, 176, 177, 197, 211, 228, 248
supervenience, 131, 237
supracortical consciousness, 238

Sutherland, Keith, 4
symmetry breaking, 55, 84, 185, 198, 255
synthetic biology, 272
synthetic unity of apperception, 33, 92, 180, 203, 249
Tarski, Alfred, 68
Taylor, Charles, 20
Tegmark, Max, 179
Templeton Foundation, VIII, 7, 27
temporal flow of experience, 203
temporal granularity, 184
thalamo-cortical loops, 100, 147, 156, 184, 186, 199
The New York Review of Books, 7
The Visual Computer, 24
Thompson, Hunter, 18
Thompson, Robert, 142
time as a psychophysical category, 266
time flow, 241, 242
Tolkien, J.R.R., 15
Tolstoy, Leo, 16
transcendental ego, 33, 35
transformational grammar, 67
Trotsky, Leon, 18
truth outruns provability, 49
Tucson, Arizona, VII, 3, 26, 62
Tufts University, 159
Turing machine, 70, 208, 240, 272
Turing test, 105
Turing, Alan, 18, 68, 69, 72, 208, 226
Turner Tomorrow Award, 24
Turri, John, 296
twistor theory, 225, 230
Ulysses, 17, 137
UNESCO Albert Einstein Gold Medal Award in Science, 155
United Nations Association, 15

unity of consciousness, 60
University College London, 17, 108, 110, 114, 277
University of California, Los Angeles, 114
University of California, San Diego, 142, 146
University of Geneva, 145
University of Iowa, 154
University of London, 17, 277, 285
University of Manchester, 114
University of Miami, Florida, 277
University of Oxford, 15, 18, 224
University of Southern California, 114
University of Sussex, 110
Vangala, R., 295
Vatican Observatory, 144
Velmans, Max, 164
Velvet Underground, 15
Vienna Circle, 129
view from nowhere, 241, 251, 258
Vinge, Vernor, 9
virtual reality, 55
von Neumann architecture, 136
Wall, Josephine, 3
Washingon Post, 29
Watkins, David J., 295

Watson, J.B., 129
Wegner, Daniel, 151, 160, 204
Weinberg, Steven, 132
Wells, Dee, 279
Wheeler, John A., 133, 177, 239, 246
white bear, 151
Whitehead, Alfred North, 9, 226
Who (rock band), 16
Wiggins, David, 117
Wikipedia, 281
Wilde Reader in Mental Philosophy, 115, 278
Witten, Edward, 234
Wittgenstein, Ludwig, 16, 20, 32, 42, 46, 79, 127, 129, 135, 166, 192, 226, 261, 282
Wolf, Fred Alan, 229
Wolfram, Stephen, VIII, 7, 195, 224, 254
worlds are centered, 54, 174
Wössner, Hans, 24
Wright, Crispin, 18, 20
Wright, Robert, 160
Zermelo, Ernst, 50, 171
Zermelo–Fraenkel set theory, 50, 75, 172, 210, 253
zombie, 40, 206, 222
Zuse, Konrad, 24